THE INDIGENOUS WORLD 2008

Copenhagen 2008

THE INDIGENOUS WORLD 2008

Compilation and editing: Kathrin Wessendorf
Regional editors:
   The Circumpolar North & North America: Kathrin Wessendorf
   Central and South America: Alejandro Parellada
   Australia and the Pacific: Kathrin Wessendorf
   Asia: Christian Erni and Mille Lund
   Africa: Marianne Wiben Jensen
   International Processes: Lola García-Alix
Cover and typesetting: Jorge Monrás
Maps: Berit Lund and Jorge Monrás
English translation and proof reading: Elaine Bolton
Prepress and Print: Eks-Skolens Trykkeri, Copenhagen, Denmark

HURRIDOCS CIP DATA

Title: The Indigenous World 2008
Edited by: Kathrin Wessendorf
Pages: 578
ISSN: 1024-0217
ISBN: 9788791563447
Language: English
Index: 1. Indigenous Peoples – 2. Yearbook – 3. International Processes
Geografical area: World
Publication date: April 2008

The Indigenous World is published annually in English and Spanish.

Director: Lola García-Alix
Administrator: Anni Hammerlund

Distribution in North America:
Transaction Publishers
300 McGaw Drive
Edison, NJ 08837
www.transactionpub.com

This book has been produced with financial support from the Danish Ministry of Foreign Affairs, NORAD, Sida and the Ministry for Foreign Affairs of Finland.

INTERNATIONAL WORK GROUP FOR INDIGENOUS AFFAIRS
Classensgade 11 E, DK 2100 - Copenhagen, Denmark
Tel: (45) 35 27 05 00 - Fax: (45) 35 27 05 07
E-mail: iwgia@iwgia.org - Web: www.iwgia.org

IWGIA

CONTENTS

PART II - INTERNATIONAL PROCESSES

PART III - General Information

Cover: The background text is the UN Declaration on the Rights of Indigenous Peoples in Nenets, an indigenous language spoken in northern Russia. Source: Yasavey Manzara.

EDITORIAL

EDITORIAL

With the adoption of the United Nations Declaration on the Rights of Indigenous Peoples on 13 September, 2007 has become a milestone in the history of indigenous peoples' struggles for their rights and recognition at international level. The Declaration had been discussed for more than 20 years in the former Commission on Human Rights and, later, in the General Assembly, and was passed with 144 votes in favor, 11 abstentions and 4 votes against. The text recognises a wide range of basic human rights and fundamental freedoms to indigenous peoples. Among these are the right to self-determination, an inalienable collective right to the ownership, use and control of lands, territories and other natural resources, rights in terms of maintaining and developing their own political, religious, cultural and educational institutions, and protection of their cultural and intellectual property. The Declaration highlights the requirement for prior and informed consultation, participation and consent in activities of any kind that impact on indigenous peoples, their property or territories. It also establishes the requirement for fair and adequate compensation for violation of the rights recognised in the Declaration and establishes measures to prevent ethnocide and genocide.

Indigenous peoples celebrated the adoption of the Declaration and used this historic moment to draw attention to their situation and raise awareness within their home countries. Many of the articles in this Yearbook thus reflect the national and local importance of the Declaration. It remains to be seen how governments and international institutions will follow-up on adoption of the Declaration and whether others will follow the example of Bolivia and transpose the declaration into national law. Unfortunately, some governments that voted in favor of the Declaration, such as Thailand for example, have already announced that the Declaration will only be implemented if subordinate to the laws and constitution of the country. The major challenge will be to put the Declaration into practice, to gain respect for and implement indigenous peoples' rights in all aspects of society and life.

In Latin America, and particularly in Ecuador and Bolivia, a tendency to include indigenous peoples' concerns in constitutional revisions can be observed. In Bolivia, the indigenous movement played an important role and contributed significantly to the constitutional process throughout 2007 and the ratification and transposition of the UN Declaration on the Rights of Indigenous Peoples into national law allowed the strengthening of indigenous issues in the Constitution (see this volume). In Nepal (this volume), a country that ratified ILO Convention 169 in 2007, indigenous peoples tried to become involved in the constitutional developments throughout 2007. Unfortunately, an Interim Constitution signed in November did not adequately reflect indigenous peoples' rights and this led to protests by the indigenous movement. It is to be hoped, however, that the Declaration will play a role in future constitutional and legal developments and will thereby have a concrete impact on indigenous rights at national level.

One of the important principles of the UN Declaration on the Rights of Indigenous Peoples, and one that is mentioned in many of the articles in this volume, is free, prior and informed consent. Many country reports demonstrate that this principle is central to indigenous peoples' rights and well-being. It is therefore crucial that it should be actively implemented and included not only in the policies of states but also in those of industry and of financial institutions such as the World Bank. Furthermore, and above all, any projects that have an impact on indigenous peoples' lands need to take indigenous peoples' collective rights to their lands and resources into consideration. And yet numerous examples show that states and industries do not prioritise this principle and, indeed, proceed with development projects on indigenous lands without consulting the people living on and from the land that they will affect. Natural resource use is expanding and indigenous peoples the world over live on lands rich in minerals, oil and gas and/ or covered with forests. Many indigenous peoples are therefore affected by mining, hydroelectric dams, fossil fuel development, logging and agro-plantations, as well as tourism. The impact of natural resource development on indigenous peoples' lands, lives and well-being is illustrated in every article of this book.

At its 6th session in May 2007, the UN Permanent Forum on Indigenous Issues urged states to take measures to halt land alienation on indigenous territories through, for example, a moratorium on the sale and registration of land - including the granting of land and other concessions - in areas occupied by indigenous peoples. It also reaffirmed indigenous peoples' central role in decision-making with regard to their lands and resources (UN Permanent Forum on Indigenous Issues, this volume).

At the same time, indigenous peoples are increasingly affected by a worldwide trend towards protecting the environment. The creation of national parks, conservation areas, wildlife protection and other measures can have a significant impact on indigenous peoples living on that land. The case of the violent eviction of pastoralists from their traditional lands in the Usangu plains in Tanzania due to the creation of a national park to protect a water catchment area, which is providing water for a hydropower plant, illustrates just such a case and is well described in this volume. This example also shows that environmental measures are often directly related to development or industrial projects. Other cases of displacement due to hydroelectric dams are described in the articles on Panama and Russia. Article 10 of the Declaration on the Rights of Indigenous Peoples states that "no relocation shall take place without the free, prior and informed consent of the indigenous peoples concerned...." Unfortunately, as readers of *The Indigenous World 2008* will learn, relocation, resettlement and expulsion from their lands is a very common and widespread reality for indigenous peoples. Without their prior and informed consent, and without the real participation of indigenous peoples, who are the traditional owners of these lands, these people will also face further impoverishment, loss of culture and a decrease in their living standards in the future.

Indigenous peoples' traditional knowledge and their participation in policy development and their consent to any development taking place on their lands is of increasing importance in the current discussions on climate change. Indigenous peoples have shown remarkable capacity to adapt to a changing environment. Indigenous peoples interpret and respond to climate change in creative ways, drawing on their traditional knowledge of the natural resource base and other technologies to find solutions.

International and national climate change research and mitigation strategies, however, most often do not take indigenous interests into consideration and overlook their rights to their lands, thereby directly posing a threat to indigenous peoples' territories. Hydro-electric developments may form part of a government's mitigation strategy whilst at the same time leading to displacement, as the Tanzania case illustrates. Mono-crop plantations for bio-fuels affect the ecosystem, the water supply and the whole anatomy of the landscape on which indigenous peoples depend and this will be one of the biggest threats to indigenous peoples' livelihoods in the future. As the article on Indonesia shows, the various mitigation schemes appear to be a bigger threat to indigenous communities than climate change itself.

To indigenous peoples, climate change is not simply a matter of physical changes to the environments in which they live. It also brings additional vulnerabilities and adds to existing challenges, including political and economic marginalization, land and resource encroachment, human rights violations and discrimination. The potential threat of climate change to their very existence, combined with various legal and institutional barriers that affect their ability to cope with and adapt to climate change, makes climate change an issue of human rights and inequality to indigenous peoples.

Unfortunately, having made considerable progress within the human rights bodies, the international arena lags behind in including indigenous voices in the discussions on climate change. This became clear during the 13th Conference of the Parties of the United Nations Framework Convention on Climate Change (COP 13) in Bali, where indigenous peoples' representatives were not allowed to present their statement at the opening ceremony. Hopefully, the thematic focus on climate change of the UN Permanent Forum on Indigenous Issues in 2008 will provide support to indigenous peoples' voices, at least at UN level.

The climate change issue, as a human rights issue, may also be a topic to be considered by a new human rights mechanism within the UN. The UN Human Rights Council decided in December 2007 to establish an "Expert Mechanism on the Rights of Indigenous Peoples". The new mechanism will consist of five independent experts on indigenous peoples' rights and will report directly to the Human Rights

Council. This Council will be a forum in which indigenous peoples will have the possibility of reporting on their experiences of the severe marginalisation, discrimination and human rights abuses they still suffer and to which this volume also bears witness.

About this book

IWGIA would like first and foremost to thank all the contributors to this volume for their commitment and their collaboration. Without them, IWGIA would never be able to publish such a comprehensive overview of the past year's developments and events in the indigenous world. The authors of this volume are indigenous and non-indigenous activists and scholars who have worked with the indigenous movement for many years and are part of IWGIA's network. They are identified by IWGIA's regional coordinators on the basis of their knowledge and network in the regions. All the contributions are offered on a voluntary basis and IWGIA does not pay for the articles to be written. This volume includes 60 country reports and 5 reports on international processes. This year, around 60% of the articles were reviewed by external reviewers. The articles in the book do, however, express the views and visions of the authors and IWGIA cannot be held responsible for the opinions thus stated. We therefore encourage those who are interested in obtaining more information about a specific country to contact the authors directly. It is nonetheless our policy to allow those authors who wish to remain anonymous to do so, due to the sensitivity of some of the issues raised in their articles. On the other hand, and based on the wishes of some authors, we have this year decided to include the authors' biographies after each article instead of in a list of contributors at the beginning. We would like once again to take this opportunity to mention that we have in the past received comments from readers who find our geographical organization of the book's contents inappropriate. The aim of the book is to offer a space to indigenous writers and advocates to present developments and important events in 2007 as seen from an indigenous angle. A number of country reports presented here therefore take their point of departure as ethnographic regions rather than following strict state boundaries.

This is in accordance with indigenous peoples' world-view and cultural identification which, in many cases, cuts across state borders.

The Indigenous World should be seen as a reference book and we hope that you will be able to use it as a basis for further information on indigenous issues worldwide.

Kathrin Wessendorf, Editor and Lola García-Alix, Director
April 2008

IN MEMORY OF GEORG HENRIKSEN

It was with deep regret and sorrow that IWGIA received the news that Georg Henriksen had died in Bergen on 23 May 2007, only 67 years old. This sad news was not altogether unexpected. Georg had received a cancer diagnosis a few years ago and was not given long to live although his physical and mental strength remained stronger than the cancer for some time. Georg was determined to stay alive with his family, he was determined to continue his work with indigenous peoples, and he insisted on finishing his monograph "'I Dreamed the Animals'. Kaneuketat: The Life of an Innu Hunter". He managed – against all odds – to finish it and, just a few weeks before his death, he received the good news that Berghahn Books in Oxford had accepted it for publication. At the same time, Berghahn has taken over the rights to his classic book "Hunters in the Barrens", and intends to re-publish this alongside the new monograph.

Georg decided to pursue a career in social anthropology and was a Research Fellow at the Institute of Social and Economic Research (IS-ER), Memorial University of Newfoundland, Canada from 1966-68 and 1969-70. Between 1966 and 1968, he was also a research assistant at the Institute for Social Anthropology at the University of Bergen, Norway where he later became an assistant professor and a fully-fledged professor in 1991. Georg served on numerous boards and commissions at the University of Bergen (including as Dean of the Faculty of Social Sciences) and at the Norwegian Research Council.

From his first stay in Canada, he was constantly carrying out fieldwork among different indigenous peoples, the Naskapi Indians (now Mushuau Innu) in Labrador, Canada, the Cree Indians of James Bay and Hudson Bay, the Mic Mac Indians of Nova Scotia and Prince Edward Island, the Turkana pastoral nomads of Kenya and the Sámi pastoralists in Norway.

In 1968, Georg was one of the founding fathers of IWGIA. He was a Board member from 1981 to 2005 and Chair of the Board for 15 years. Under Georg's wise leadership the organisation developed from being a small NGO run by volunteers and a couple of staff members into being a professional organisation with some 15 em-  ployees, a substantial publications programme and work supporting a large number of indigenous projects in all corners of the world. Georg's personal integrity and his insistence on combining anthropological knowledge, political advocacy and solidarity with indigenous peoples has been a guide to everyone in the organisation.

We in IWGIA will miss Georg, as a person and as a colleague. He understood the importance of loyalty and friendship among IWGIA members but he also demonstrated that, without friendship and solidarity with our indigenous partners, our work becomes hollow.

We will always remember his intense commitment to world politics and the plight of indigenous peoples, his commitment to his friends, colleagues and students, with whom he freely shared his insights, and his keen sense of humour! Last November, he said he was proud to be considered as having engaged in a form of humanistic anthropology - and a true humanist he was!

Georg leaves behind a wife Berit, two daughters and a grandson.

PART I

COUNTRY REPORTS

THE CIRCUMPOLAR NORTH

GREENLAND

The population inhabiting the vast east and west coast of the island of Greenland numbers 57,000, 88% of whom are ethnic Greenlanders (Inuit). Greenland is a self-governing region within the Danish realm. The first Danish colonial settlement was established in 1721 close to the current capital, Nuuk, on the west coast. In 1953, Greenland became an integral part of Denmark by law and, in 1979, Home Rule was established following negotiations between Greenland and Denmark. Since then, Greenland has had its own parliament and government responsible for most internal matters. Since 2004, the Danish and Greenland governments have negotiated further self-government for Greenland.

Standstill in self-government negotiations

In 2004, a Danish-Greenlandic Self-government Commission was established with the aim of negotiating an agreement to replace the 1979 Home Rule arrangement. Both parties had hoped that an agreement would be reached in 2007 but extensive and long discussions over the disposition of revenues from future oil, gas and mineral resources led to delays. When the Danish Prime Minister suddenly called a general election in November, all negotiations in the Self-government Commission were put on hold. It therefore came as a great surprise to many when, in his New Year speech, the Greenland Premier, Hans Enoksen, announced a referendum on self-government for Greenland to be held on November 25, 2008. It is, however, expected that the Commission will be able to finalise its work in 2008.

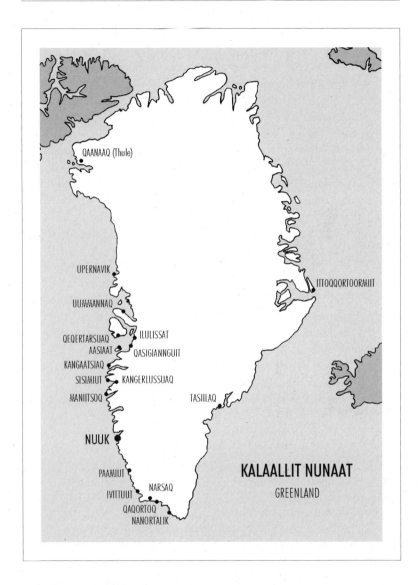

Election and political turbulence

Greenland elects two members to the Danish Parliament. For many years, the two seats were divided between the social-democratic Siumut and the conservative Atassut but, since 2001, the socialist Inuit Ataqatigiit has taken one of the two seats. Most spectacular in the November election was the fact that a young woman from Inuit Ataqatigiit, Juliane Henningsen, toppled the party's lead candidate, Josef Motzfeldt ("Tuusi"). Josef Motzfeldt was chair of Inuit Ataqatigiit and a powerful Home Rule Minister of Finances and Foreign Affairs until the Northern Lights Coalition between Siumut, Inuit Ataqatigiit and Atassut broke down in the spring. The election also revealed that Inuit Ataqatigiit was, for the first time, the largest of the four political parties (Inuit Ataqatigiit, Siumut, Atassut and the Democrats) and it was also the first time that the number of votes cast for female candidates equalled that of men. This development may reflect the focus of the campaign, which was on social malaise in general and the conditions of children in particular.

When the Northern Lights Coalition collapsed, Siumut appointed Member of the Danish Parliament and former Premier Lars Emil Johansen to replace Josef Motzfeldt as Minister of Finances and Foreign Affairs but the supervisory commission of the Greenland Parliament rejected his candidacy because he was also a member of the Danish Parliament, and he therefore had to step down as minister. He preferred to remain a member of the Danish Parliament in order to finish his work within the Self-government Commission, and he was re-elected in the November election. He was replaced by Ms Aleqa Hammond (Siumut) as Minister of Finances and Foreign Affairs.

In 2007, the Siumut party was able to celebrate its 30-year anniversary. Siumut emerged as the first political group in modern Greenland in 1975 and was established as a party two years later. Siumut was the father of Home Rule and has ruled Greenland (most often with one or other party) since Home Rule was introduced. This demonstrates the stability and unequivocal political success of Home Rule. Nevertheless, the public are often confronted with reports of social malaise and ill feeling between Danes and Greenlanders. In 2007, the media in both Denmark and Greenland focused intensely on the critical social condition of many children, which triggered strong criticism from both the media and politicians. When Premier Hans Enoksen declared the adoption of a new Greenlandisation policy in which all heads of Home Rule departments would be Greenlanders speaking Greenlandic, he was widely criticized. Such events indicate that there are social and educational problems that are being cloaked with ethnic labels. While most developed countries try to attract foreign specialists and experts, Greenland thus seems for some time to have been moving in the opposite direction.

When Home Rule was established, Greenland inherited a colonial municipal structure that had, in general terms, existed for more than 200 years. The country was divided into 18 municipalities, each with a varying number of settlements. The political system, the legal system, the health system, the educational system, etc. were formed of a structure that had originally been established with the aim of being supplied from Copenhagen. The structure never matched the Home Rule system but, once established with 18 councils, 18 salaried mayors, 18 chief administrators, etc, etc, it was politically difficult to make changes. It has taken years of discussions for a new system to be adopted, with four major regions to be established when the first elections have taken place in 2008.

Economy

Greenland has a technologically advanced fishing sector and also an important subsistence-based hunting and small-scale fishing economy. This has always been the mainstay of the economy. To this must be added annual block grants from Denmark, covering a substantial part of public expenditure. Today, however, it is generally recognised that mineral, oil and gas exploitation is the only way to make Greenland a sustainable self-governing country. Great expectations are also being placed on the use of hydro-electric power for aluminium smelting, and exploration for oil and gas has intensified. But, for the time being, there are only two small-scale mining ventures.   ❏

Jens Dahl is an anthropologist, adjunct professor at the Department of Cross-Cultural and Regional Studies, University of Copenhagen and former director of IWGIA.

SÁPMI – NORWAY

The Saami are the indigenous people of Norway. There is no available information on how many the Saami people are. A 1999 linguistic survey found that 23,000 people speak the Saami language but the actual number of Saami is estimated to be many times higher than this.[1] Their status as a people is recognized by constitutional amendment 110a to the Norwegian constitution (*Grunnloven*).

The Saami people's traditional territories cover large parts of the Norwegian mainland. Their lands and territories, traditionally used for reindeer herding, fishing, hunting and gathering, are under constant pressure from international and national mining corporations, state energy enterprises, the Norwegian Armed Forces, and others.

The *Sámediggi* (the Saami Parliament) is the democratically elected political body of the Saami people; its representatives are elected by and amongst the Sámi themselves. The *Sámediggi* regulates its business within the framework laid down by an Act concerning the *Sámediggi* and other Saami legal matters (the Sámi Act).

Norway has ratified all relevant international human rights instruments, including both 1966 Human Rights Covenants and ILO Convention 169.

Guidelines for the Finnmark Act

The Finnmark Act and the Board of the Finnmark Estate (see also *The Indigenous World 2007*) have been in force since January 2006. In June 2007, the Norwegian Ministry of Labour and Social Inclusion approved the Saami Parliament's guidelines for assessing Saami con-

cerns regarding changes in the use of uncultivated land in Finnmark (*Sametingets retningslinjer for vurderingen av samiske hensyn ved endret bruk av meahcci/utmark i Finnmark*).[2] The Saami Parliament developed these guidelines in accordance with Paragraph 4 of the Finnmark Act. Changes in the use of uncultivated land can involve activities such as mining, windmills, infrastructure etc. The Saami Parliament based the development of the guidelines on principles now recognised in the UN Declaration on the Rights of Indigenous Peoples, namely free, prior and informed consent and consultations.

The Saami Rights Committee's report

In 2001, a renewed Saami Rights Committee was appointed to report in general on questions relating to the Saami population's legal position as regards the right to, and disposition and use of, land and water in traditional Saami areas from county Troms southwards to areas within the county of Hedmark. The Committee's mandate was partly to give an account of historic relationships and of the current law as regards the use of land and water in these areas and partly to give a reasoned assessment of the desired changes to the prevailing law. Its final report was presented in December 2007.[3]

In this report, the Committee acknowledges the need to map rights to land and resources and proposes drafting an act to identify and recognise existing rights in the traditional Saami areas from and including Troms county southwards. A commission corresponding to the Finnmark Commission is suggested for a thorough mapping of these rights issues.

The Committee further proposes two solutions for managing the remaining state land within the area in question. For the counties of Troms and Nordland, where 44 % of the land area is considered state land, the proposal is to replace the current Norwegian State Forest and Land Corporation (*Statskog*) regime with Hålogaland common land (*Hålogaland-allmenning*) and local land-management boards for the day-to-day management of the common land. This would transfer management from the state to local and regional ownership. This solution is considered to give Saami people a weaker position than the Finnmark Act did.

For the South Saami region, the county of Nord-Trøndelag, parts of the Fosen peninsula and the inner areas along the Swedish border in Sør-Trøndelag county, the North-Eastern parts of Hedmark County and some areas in Trollheimen and its environs, the proposal is to revise the existing Uplands Act - in Norwegian known as *Fjellova* - for reindeer herding areas, in order to ensure Saami participation in the management of land areas and natural resources, following obligations under international law.

Consultations and laws

In 2005, the Saami Parliament and the Norwegian Government signed a consultation agreement. This has enabled the Saami Parliament to take a clear position in relation to state authorities on laws and administrative initiatives concerning Saami society. There were several ongoing consultation processes throughout 2007, for example on the new minerals act, marine resources act, biological diversity act, etc. Experiences of the consultations, their procedures and outcomes, have been both good and bad. The ministries are often left with limited room in which to find solutions with the Saami Parliament due to the lack of a clear mandate from the government; when in consultation the Minister cannot really negotiate but needs to get back to the government on all issues. There has also been a lack of information and documents on the various processes from the ministries, and questions concerning indigenous rights are saved for later or parallel processes, and are thus not treated or assessed in a holistic manner. With regard to the Planning and Building Act, however, the Saami Parliament has achieved the right to raise objections to planning processes that considerably disturb the Saami resource base.

Saami Peoples' Fund – justice for Saami elders

The Norwegian Government established a Saami Peoples' Fund in 2000. However, the Saami Parliament would not accept the fund until certain requirements were fulfilled: that a consultation agreement between the Saami Parliament and the Norwegian Government be established, along with a proper system of compensation for those generations that were not offered adequate primary education due to the Norwegianization process and Second World War.

With the consultation agreement that was signed in 2005 and the resolution of the first compensation issues with Saami elders, the Saami Parliament considered these obligations fulfilled and was thus able to accept the fund. In November 2007, the first set of priorities for the use of the fund was thus approved and the very first pot of money set aside in the budget for 2008. Three areas were identified as a priority in order to strengthen and revitalise the Saami language and culture: 1) projects and programs for revitalization of the Saami language among children and parents, 2) documentation and protection of traditional knowledge and 3) publishing of Saami literature.

Change in power at the Saami Parliament

2007 was quite a turbulent year for the Saami Parliament, led by its president Aili Keskitalo. Due to a break in the Parliamentary Council coalition, Keskitalo's Council decided to step down. As a result, Egil Olli and the Labour Party, which was the biggest opposition party, formed a Parliamentary Council in September with a Labour party minority.

This is the first time that the NSR has not held power since the inauguration of the first Saami Parliament in 1989. It is also the first time a sitting Parliamentary Council has stepped down, and the first time a minority Parliamentary Council has been formed.   ❑

Notes

1   Maps and more information about the Sámi in Norway can be found on the Sámi
    Parliament Norway website: www.samediggi.no
2   Saami Parliament's guidelines for assessing Saami concerns regarding changes in
    the use of uncultivated land in Finnmark can be found here in Norwegian and
    Saami:
    http://www.lovdata.no/cgi-wift/ldles?doc=/sf/sf/sf-20070611-0738.html
3   Summary of the Sami Rights Committee's report in English: http://www.regjer-
    ingen.no/nb/dep/jd/dok/NOUer/2007/NOU-2007-13.html?id=491883

Gunn-Britt Retter is a Saami from the Varangerfjord in northeast Norway and chair of the local Saami Association, Unjárgga Sámi Searvi. She is a member of the Saami Parliament in Norway and head of the Arctic and Environmental Unit in the Saami Council.

SÁPMI - SWEDEN

The Sámi people are the indigenous people of the northern part of the Scandinavian Peninsula and large parts of the Kola Peninsula. The Sámi people therefore live in the four countries of Sweden, Norway, Finland and Russia.

Politically, the Sámi people are represented by three Sámi Parliaments, one in Sweden, one in Norway and one in Finland, whereas on the Russian side they are organised into NGOs. In 2000, the three Sámi Parliaments established a council of representatives between them, called the Sami Parliamentary Council.

There is no reliable information as to how many Sámi people there are; it is, however, estimated that they number between 50,000 – 100,000 in total. Around 20,000 live in Sweden, which is approximately 0.22 % of Sweden's total population of 9 million.

The north-west part of the Swedish territory is based on the Sámi people's traditional territory. These lands are traditionally used by the Sámi for reindeer herding, small farming, hunting, fishing and gathering. There are three specific laws governing Sámi rights in Sweden, namely the Sámi Parliament Act, the Sámi Language Act and the Reindeer Herding Act.

The Sámi Parliament

The Sámi Parliament in Sweden is elected by and represents the Sámi people in Sweden. It is also a governmental authority that has to carry out the policies and decisions of the Swedish Parliament and Swedish government. Since its establishment in 1993, the Sámi Parliament's main tasks have been defined by Swedish law. These are:

to decide on the distribution of state subsidies to Sámi culture, to lead work on the Sámi language, to take part in social planning to ensure that Sámi needs are considered, and to provide public information on all aspects of Sámi life.[1]

In January 2007, the Sámi Parliament received the additional responsibility of managing some issues that had previously been under the responsibility of either the Swedish Board of Agriculture or the northernmost County Administrative Boards. These issues relate mainly to aspects of reindeer husbandry, such as the registration of *Sameby* (Sámi villages), the determination of Sameby grazing areas, appeals against Sameby decisions regarding membership, appeals against Sameby decisions on other issues, the branding of reindeer and holding of a register of these brands. Issues regarding the administration of land and supervision of reindeer herding were not transferred from the County Administrative Boards to the Sámi Parliament at this time.[2] It can therefore be said that the Sámi Parliament received administrative duties but no fundamental powers. On receiving these new but limited administrative tasks, the Sámi Parliament defined it as "structural discrimination" and criticised the fact that they did not receive more authority or resources for practising self determination.

Reindeer grazing

Due to periods of abnormally warm weather in an otherwise normally cold 2006/2007 winter, large parts of the reindeer pasturelands became covered in ice and the reindeer could not graze. In order to prevent disaster, the reindeer herders had to either buy fodder to feed the reindeer or move them to places with no ice on the ground. This put a real strain on the reindeer herding communities. After an investigation, the Sámi Parliament applied for disaster funding from the Swedish government to cover some of the reindeer herders' extra costs. The Swedish government granted subsidies and helped to avoid disaster.

In 2005, three Sámi villages in the county of Västerbotten were sued by non-Sámi landowners who claimed that the Sámi had no right to let their reindeer graze on their private property in the municipality of Nordmaling, by the coast of Bottenviken. In similar earlier court

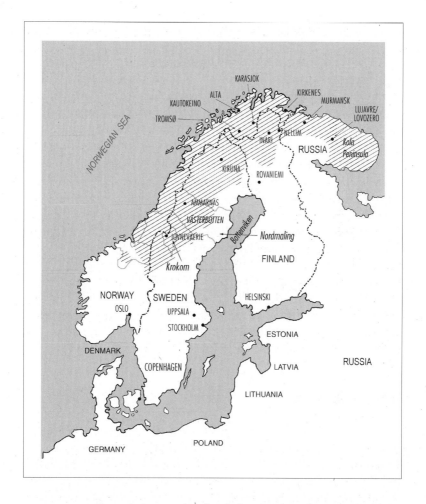

cases concerning winter grazing lands in more southern parts of the traditional Sámi area in Sweden, some other Sámi villages had lost the right to graze their reindeer. In these previous rulings, the courts considered that the Sámi parties had not provided burden of proof. The Nordmaling case is therefore set to be decisive for the future of reindeer grazing in these geographical areas. The Sámi villages in question won this case in the district court and, in September 2007, the Court of Appeal upheld the verdict.[3] The landowners have now lodged an appeal with the Supreme Court, which has yet to decide if it will try the case.

There was conflict during 2007 regarding reindeer grazing areas in Troms county (*fylke*), which is on the Norwegian side of the border. A reindeer grazing convention between Norway and Sweden has since 1919 prevented Sámi people with Swedish citizenship from using areas on the Norwegian side of the border, and in some cases vice-versa, that form large parts of their traditional grazing areas. Instead, the Norwegian government has given these grazing areas to other Sámi with Norwegian citizenship. Today, the Sámi people who initially used these areas believe that some lost grazing areas will be returned to them, whereas the Sámi people who received these areas from the Norwegian government have now established themselves and do not want to be forced to quit their tradition. An agreement between the affected parties has thus far been difficult to reach. This situation is a result of earlier policies of the relevant states and it seems to be difficult for today's governments to address them properly. It has put a strain on the parties in question and has led to some tensions within the Sámi community. The Swedish and Norwegian governments have been working on a draft of a new reindeer herding convention throughout 2007 but no results have been made public.

Implementing international law

The question of whether Sweden will ratify ILO Convention No. 169 was not settled during 2007. The government is considering the issue and how to proceed but nothing has yet been proposed or decided.

In October 2005, an expert working group presented the Draft Nordic Sámi Convention. This draft convention is considered to be a consolidation of applicable international law, consolidating the rights of the Sámi people and obligations of the states. The question of ratification has been discussed by the governments of Sweden, Norway and Finland but with no results so far.

Non-discrimination

During 2007 and 2008, the Ombudsman against Ethnic Discrimination, or DO (*Diskrimineringsombudsmannen*) is continuing to run a general campaign focusing on discrimination in order to make the rights of minorities and indigenous peoples more visible. In one specific case, the DO demanded that the municipality of Krokom pay damages for discrimination of the Sámi people. Despite clarifying rulings from the Supreme Administrative Court (*Regeringsrätten*), the municipality has ignored what the Jovnevaerie Sámi village (*Sameby*) has to say in at least 15 building permit matters. The municipality believes that it can by itself assess whether a building permit may harm reindeer grazing or not, and that the consultations should be kept to a reasonable level. The DO says that it cannot accept that a group is denied its rights just because an authority thinks it is easier that way.[4]   ❑

Notes

1   Sametingslag 1992:1433 (Translated into English: The Sámi Parliament Act SFS No. 1992:1433)
2   Prop. 2005/06:86 Ett ökat samiskt inflytande (Translated into English: The governments proposition regarding increased Sámi influence)
3   Hovrätten för Övre Norrland dom 2007-09-19, mål nr T 155-05, angående renskötselrätt vintertid inom Nordmalings kommun.
4   www.do.se

Johan Strömgren is a Sámi lawyer who grew up in Ammarnäs on the Swedish side of Sápmi. He works as a researcher at the Nordic Sámi Institute in Guovdageaidnu, and is a Ph.D. candidate at the Faculty of Law at Uppsala University in Sweden.

SÁPMI - FINLAND

Finland still treats its approximately 7,000 Saami as a national linguistic minority rather than an indigenous people. The Finnish state refuses to acknowledge that indigenous people require culturally appropriate legislation for their rights to be secured. This problem is highlighted by disputes over Saami reindeer-herding territories in Finnish Sápmi. Finnish Sápmi is unique in that reindeer herding is not an exclusive right of Saami, as it is in Sweden and Norway. The same legislation governs both Saami and Finnish reindeer-herding practices. For the Finnish state, equal citizenship means the *same* treatment for everyone.

As reported in *The Indigenous World 2006*, the Nellim case has been of major significance for Finnish Sápmi in recent years. In November 2005, the UN Human Rights Council called on Finland to halt logging in Nellim, the traditional reindeer-grazing areas of the Padaar brothers. During 2007, this remained a key issue for the Finnish state and Saami society as the conflicts escalated once again. The Nellim case is not simply a local conflict. Rather, it highlights several serious challenges posed to the Finnish state and Saami society.

Internal tensions

The first challenge concerns the issue of internal divisions within Saami communities in Finnish Sápmi. The Nellim case illustrates this challenge well. The Padaar brothers belong to the Nellim Herding Group, which is a Saami sub-group within the Ivalo Reindeer Herding Co-operative (RHC). The Padaar brothers are the original traditional owners of the territory that the Ivalo RHC now claims as its own. Many of the other members of the Ivalo RHC are Saami from southern areas of Sápmi, who were themselves forced to move to the Nellim area after their own reindeer pastures were flooded as a result of extensive hydro-power developments. Forced relocation was common in Saami areas throughout the early 20th century as the state expanded its industrial developments. This historical industrial colonisation of Saami lands have led to internal conflicts between some Saami groups, including those groups within Ivalo RHC. There have long been disagreements within the RHC over a number of issues, including the current conflicts over forestry activities being carried out by the state logging enterprise Metsähallitus. These internal conflicts reached a peak in late 2007 when the Board of the Ivalo RHC attempted to forcefully slaughter the entire reindeer herd belonging to the Nellim herders.

The majority of the Ivalo RHC has accepted the logging and Metsähallitus often refers to the Ivalo RHC as a model example of coexistence between forestry and reindeer herding. The Nellim Herding Group, however, has been opposed to logging and has tried to break away from the RHC and form its own reindeer-herding group (more in line with a traditional Saami *siida*[1]). They have not succeeded in this effort. The Finnish government, Metsähallitus and the Finnish forestry industry are also aware of the problems within Ivalo RHC. Indeed, Stora Enso, the largest historical purchaser of wood from Metsähallitus in these areas, consistently refers to internal Saami disputes as the *problem* per se.[2] However, in light of the appropriation of Saami lands by the forestry industry, and the devastating impacts of forestry and other related industrial activities on Saami culture, internal disputes within RHCs and Saami society should be viewed as a *consequence* of this colonial and industrial history.

Need for transparent and fair negotiations

The second challenge concerns the urgent need to establish a transparent and fair process for Saami involvement in developing new legislation on the question of land ownership, land use and reindeer herding in traditional Saami areas of Finnish Sápmi. For example, while the Finnish Ministry of Justice and Finnish Ministry of Agriculture are currently negotiating *between* their Ministries on the question of new legislation for reindeer herding and a new land-use model for Saami areas, there is no formal process of negotiation between the Finnish state and Saami organisations or Saami communities on these issues. The only communication that has taken place is between the Finnish Saami Parliament and the Ministries, and this communication has neither been transparent nor has it been clear what mandate the Finnish Saami Parliament has to negotiate on behalf of those Saami reindeer herders most immediately affected by the conflicts. There is currently no representative organisation for Saami reindeer herders in Finnish Sápmi with the resources or capacity to represent the concerns of Saami reindeer herders. Nor does the Finnish state have any intention of empowering or giving resources for such an organisation to emerge. Currently at stake in Finland is the development of new laws and governance structures for Saami areas without any consultation with Saami reindeer herders. Moreover, the Finnish government refuses to address the question of Saami land rights. This is ironic given that land rights are *least* disputable in those areas where traditional reindeer herding is still being practised. Or perhaps Saami reindeer herders are being excluded from current negotiations because, if they were included in the process, their claims would be the most difficult to ignore.

Equality or sameness?

The third and perhaps most complicated challenge concerns the classic view held by the majority Finnish society that states that equal rights mean the *same* treatment of all citizens. This limits the ability of Saami to enjoy their right to self-determination, as demonstrated in the conflicts over reindeer herding in Finnish Sápmi. While both Saami and ethnic Finns are involved in reindeer husbandry, ethnic Finns generally practise a form of reindeer *farming*, as opposed to reindeer herding. Reindeer farming is an industrialised form of reindeer herding (with a dependence on pellet feeding and smaller grazing areas), as opposed to traditional Saami reindeer herding, which is based on free-grazing and natural pastures. Due to increased industrial developments in Saami areas (logging, mining, road infrastructure etc), and the effects of Finnish assimilationist practices, some Saami reindeer herders have been more or less forced to combine these methods, and some have completely adopted an industrialised form of reindeer herding. Despite the differences between these forms of reindeer herding, the current Reindeer Herding Act makes no distinction between the two. Indeed, the Act makes it possible to discriminate against those Saami practising traditional forms of free reindeer grazing. The attempted forced slaughter of the Nellim herders' reindeer by the Ivalo RHC Board was in fact completely within the law. Yet, as outlined in international human rights law and other instruments, equality and the recognition of indigenous rights is achieved through *recognising difference* not ignoring it.

Moreover, the Finnish political approach to the current conflicts is not only blind to difference but is also blind to *history*. Current "negotiations" over new proposals for land-use legislation in Saami areas give no recognition to the fact that conflicts are related to past injustices and a state-sanctioned industrial colonisation of Saami lands. Instead, the Finnish state sees itself as a neutral actor, without any vested interests in Saami territories.

The Nordic Saami Convention

Looking ahead, we have reason to be seriously concerned. Not only is the Finnish state slow to negotiate national legislation with Saami organisations and communities, it is also lagging on the international front. A draft Nordic Sámi Convention was presented in 2005 to the governments of Finland, Norway and Sweden, and all three Saami Parliaments have endorsed the draft. Talks between the relevant Ministries responsible for Sami policy in Finland, Norway and Sweden have been underway ever since. The latest information is that discussions will be conducted during 2008 with regard to the proposal. So far, the schedule of discussions has already been delayed, not least due to Finland's failure to establish its negotiating position within the set timeframe. Let us hope that the international spotlight will encourage Finland to live up to its international reputation as a defender of human rights and address its colonial legacies in Saami areas.   ❏

Notes

1   A *siida* is a traditional Saami unit that can consist of a village, family, clan, fishing group or reindeer-herding group etc. It is a traditional form of alliance, recognised by others, and forms the basis of current legislation in Sweden and Norway in which membership of such groups is required in order to practise pastoralist rights. A *siida* usually has rights over a certain territory/ area, which is agreed with other *siidas*. A *siida* can refer to the group's territory as well as the inhabitants of that territory. It thus has a meaning of alliance between a territory and its inhabitants. Nowadays, a *siida* often refers to a "reindeer pastoralistic district," which is a Saami reindeer foraging area, a group of reindeer herders and a corporation working for the economic benefit of its members.

2   See **Lawrence, R., 2007:** *Corporate Social Responsibility, Supply-chains and Saami claims: Tracing the Political in the Finnish Forestry Industry.* Geographical Research, 45:2, 167-176; and **Lawrence, R. & Raitio, K., 2006:** *Forestry conflicts in Finnish Sápmi: Local, National and Global Links*, Indigenous Affairs (4), IWGIA, Copenhagen.

Pauliina Feodoroff comes from a reindeer herding family on the Finnish side of Sápmi. She has been a member of the Saami Council since 2004 and its President since March 2007.

Rebecca Lawrence comes from a coal-mining family in Newcastle, Australia. She is working on a PhD at the Department of Sociology, Stockholm University, Sweden and the Department of Human Geography, Macquarie University, Australia. Her research has focussed on the impacts of logging on Saami rights in Finland. Rebecca also acts as advisor to the Saami Council and to Saami communities throughout Sápmi in their negotiations with the proponents of resource developments.

RUSSIA

In the Russian Federation, the only officially recognised indigenous peoples are the "numerically small indigenous peoples of the North, Siberia and the Far East". These peoples all number less than 50,000 individuals. To date, 44 numerically small peoples have been recognized.[1] In total, they number around 250,000 individuals. The largest groups, the Evenk and Nenets, number 35-45,000 individuals and the smallest groups, such as the Enets and Orok, number only a few dozen or a few hundred.

The historical settlement territories of these indigenous peoples cover 64% of the area of the Russian Federation. These are the territories from which the bulk of Russia's wealth in natural resources is being extracted. The numerically small indigenous peoples are protected by Article 69 of the Russian Constitution and three federal framework laws,[2] which establish the cultural, territorial and political rights of indigenous peoples and their communities. In addition, the indigenous peoples are governed by a number of administrative rules and legislative texts, depending on the province in which they live. Even though the federal legal framework has been in place since 2001, many of its provisions remain theoretical. This is true first and foremost for land rights, which continue to be denied, while skyrocketing oil prices have increased the pressure on indigenous territories.

New law to protect indigenous peoples' lands

As long ago as 2001, the Russian Federation adopted a framework law aimed at establishing a permanent legal status for the territories traditionally used and inhabited by indigenous communities. According to this law, indigenous peoples have the right to establish so-called Territories of Traditional Nature Use, or TTP as they are known in Russia. Even though these territories would remain state property, they would be controlled by the indigenous peoples and, to a certain extent, be protected from extractive industries. Due to its general and declarative content, however, the law depends on the adoption of by-laws governing the specifics of the territories' establishment and management. Despite the indigenous organisations' best efforts, these by-laws have never been adopted and, consequently, not a single TTP has been created in the whole of Russia.

The battle for indigenous peoples' land rights continued in 2007. During their protests against the oil industry in 2005, the indigenous peoples of Sakhalin demanded the implementation of a so-called "ethnological impact assessment" in addition to the environmental impact assessment. The term "ethnological impact assessment" was defined by the federal law "On guarantees of the rights of indigenous minority peoples of the Russian Federation" as a way of evaluating the impact of any activities on lands traditionally used by indigenous peoples for their traditional way of life and culture. Despite numerous proposals and demands from RAIPON to legislatively determine a process for conducting ethnological impact assessments, the authorities have accomplished nothing since the law's initial passage eight years ago.

In 2007, the Committee of Nationalities Affairs of the Russian State Duma undertook intensive work to develop a draft federal law "On the protection of the environment, traditional way of life, and traditional natural resource use of numerically small indigenous peoples in the Russian Federation", which would have made ethnological impact assessments a reality and would have secured lands of traditional tenancy and traditional natural resource use for indigenous peoples' communal enterprises (*obshchinas*).

However, the Russian federal government rejected the first draft of the law. In its opinion, indigenous issues were already exhaustively regulated by Russian federal legislation and the approval of the proposed law was not necessary. In contrast, regional governmental agencies stressed the need for such a federal law.

On 24 October, public hearings on the subject of "Ensuring the rights of indigenous peoples of the North, Siberia, and the Far East of

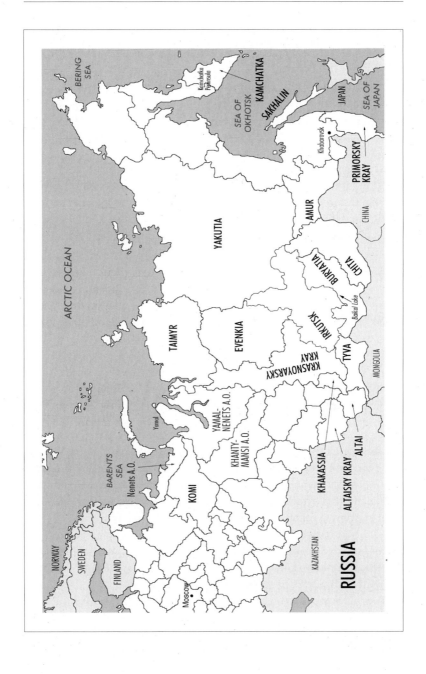

the Russian Federation" took place at the initiative of the Russian Association of Indigenous Peoples of the North, Siberia, and the Far East
(RAIPON), the national indigenous umbrella organization, together
with the Public Chamber (a consultative body to the Russian president, consisting of civil society representatives), with the goal of supporting indigenous needs. On October 25, 2007, parliamentary hearings were organized in both houses of parliament, at the initiative of
RAIPON and the Committee for Northern Affairs.

The State Duma Council has now approved the draft federal law
"On the protection of the environment, traditional way of life, and traditional natural resource use of numerically small indigenous peoples
in the Russian Federation", which indicates the State Duma's acceptance of the draft's general concept. In order for the draft to become
law, however, the government's negative opinion must be changed at
least to one of neutrality.

Proposed amendments to the Land Code

One of the major legal obstacles to the realization of indigenous land
rights in Russia is the land code (*zemelny kodex*) which, in 2001, was
revised in a spirit of economic liberalization and privatization. While it
paves they way for land to be bought and sold, it largely ignores indigenous peoples' traditional land use and management. Most crucially, it
does not ensure that indigenous peoples have the right to freely use
the territories they require to sustain themselves without having to
pay. Since the land code recognizes only private property and rent as
valid forms of ownership, it effectively prevents indigenous land titles
such as the TTPs from becoming a reality. It thus effectively annuls the
legal guarantee enshrined in the framework laws on indigenous rights,
namely, that indigenous peoples have the right to freely use all categories of land necessary for conducting their traditional way of life. It has
therefore been one of RAIPON's main goals to bring the land code into
line with indigenous peoples' needs and traditions.

A draft law proposing amendments to the Land Code of the Russian Federation was prepared and introduced to the State Duma with
the assistance of the Committee for Northern Affairs. This bill is the

latest attempt to re-establish indigenous rights to freely use the lands they traditionally inhabited. Surprisingly, the draft law received a neutral opinion from the government, but was not accepted in 2007.

This was due to the government's concurrent resurrection of the bill "On changes to legislative acts of the Russian Federation" designed to bring them into line with the Russian Federal Land Code. This bill was approved at its first reading in 2004 and would have resulted in changes to a multitude of federal laws touching on issues of land use. The Russian regional parliaments gave a negative assessment of the new law, however, and the bill was reviewed by the State Duma in 2007. It was nonetheless voted into law on May 25.

The consequences for laws protecting indigenous peoples' rights are the following:

- A regulation in the law "On territories of traditional natural resources use…" has been eliminated. This provided that indigenous communities had the right to use land free of charge within the boundaries of territories of traditional resources use. However, a similar paragraph in the law "On the guarantees of indigenous peoples' rights…" was not affected.
- It has also eliminated the authority that determines the borders of lands used for traditional natural resource use by numerically small indigenous peoples as well as the system providing relevant peoples with the use of federally-owned lands (Point 1, Article 38).
- The Russian administrative regions' governmental authority that determines systems for allocating, using and protecting land owned by the Russian regions and used for traditional natural resource use by numerically small indigenous peoples has also been eliminated (Point 2, Article 38).

As of a result of this law's passage, the process for creating territories of traditional natural resource use has been completely paralyzed, and the status of lands already acquired by indigenous peoples' communities (*obshchinas*) has become unclear. Indigenous organizations are now reporting that, in some Russian regions, *obshchinas* are required to re-register lands for rental and rental payments (Krasnoyarsk Krai, Republic of Altai, Kamchatka Krai) while others permit indigenous peoples to use the lands free of charge (Nenets, Yamal-Nenets, Khanty-Mansi Autonomous Okrugs).

The inconsistency of the Russian federal government's policies in relation to indigenous land rights was reflected in several documents accepted in 2007, for example, the *Comprehensive Plan for the Preparation and Execution of the Second International Decade of Indigenous Peoples of the World in the Russian Federation* as well as the *Federal Program for Socio-Economic Development of the Northern Regions by 2015*. Both documents identify the need to develop legislation for the free use of lands for traditional natural resource use and for processes regulating the creation and function of territories of traditional natural resource use, along with methodologies for evaluating damage inflicted by industrial projects in areas traditionally occupied and used by indigenous peoples. The government has invited RAIPON to work with it to create such documents. RAIPON experts are formulating and arguing their proposals.

In practice, however, the government is delaying implementation of these programs. It is simple to explain the inconsistency of the Russian federal government's position when it comes to legally protecting indigenous peoples' rights to lands and evaluating the impacts of industrial development.

Industrial projects

The Russian government plans large-scale projects to extract and transport fossil fuels abroad. These activities include the construction of pipelines from Nenets Autonomous and Yamal-Nenets Autonomous Okrugs to the West, from Western Siberia to China in the South Siberia by way of Altai, from Eastern Siberia to the Pacific Ocean, and increased oil and gas extraction on the Sea of Okhotsk shelf. Moreover, energy projects are also backed by the Kremlin. These include for example the proposed Evenkiiskaya (formerly Turukhanskaya) hydroelectric dam in Eastern Siberia, which will create the world's largest artificial lake, flooding huge areas in the former region of Evenkiya, plus a cascade of hydroelectric stations along the Aldan River in southern Yakutiya. All of these projects would be implemented on lands traditionally occupied by indigenous peoples. Judging from the legislative and consultation processes, the government seems to believe that articulate and consistent legislation for indigenous land rights and damage assessment for harm done to lands by industrial projects would greatly complicate and raise the costs of implementing the aforementioned projects.

In the author's opinion, this is a terrible error. Addressing the ecological, economic and social harms that these projects cause when they are implemented without consultation with indigenous peoples and local residents may be much more costly for our country than incorporating prevention or mitigation efforts into the project planning stages.

The indigenous peoples of the North, Siberia and the Far East are experiencing a very complex and critical period in the Russian Federation's contemporary economic development.

While large-scale industrial projects are aimed at strengthening the economic power of the country and its energy potential, there is an unprecedented and tremendous appropriation of and reduction in the territories of traditional husbandry, sacred sites, grazing lands, hunting and fishing grounds of indigenous peoples of the North, Siberia and the Far East on the part of industrial development projects or companies, and this is bound to have a negative impact on the economic, cultural and spiritual life of the peoples. Some especially small peoples are facing a real threat to their ethnic survival.

The well-being and future of these peoples directly depends on a comprehensive state policy and practical measures to support indigenous peoples in terms of the level of integration and support of their traditional livelihoods under market conditions, the state of the environment and the legal resolution of disputes with subsoil users.

The key issue is: to what extent do the current agreements with industrial companies meet the interests of indigenous peoples of the North, Siberia and the Far East?

Trends in recent years show a growing momentum in the negotiating process and the conclusion of agreements between indigenous peoples and industrial companies. There are several reasons for this:

Increasing pressure from companies on the traditional territories of husbandry is creating a growing - sometimes spontaneous but far more organized - movement of indigenous peoples for the protection of their rights, which potentially could stop project implementation by means of mass protest actions and court proceedings. For example, the Komi Izhems peoples in the Komi Republic reached an agreement with SU-AL, the biggest Russian aluminium company, which is constructing a factory on their traditional lands, following conflict regarding the impact on and degradation of pastures and river contamination. The Evenk peoples in Evenkia have been fighting RAO EES ROSSIA, the biggest energy company, by means of letter campaigns, consultations and through the mass media. This company plans to construct a hydroelectric dam on their traditional land that will lead to their forced reallocation and will have an impact on their traditional livelihood.[3]

Investments made by the Western financial institutions, such as the International Finance Corporation and others, as well as the growing interest of international corporations in Russia, must comply with international standards on indigenous rights. The Sakhalin II case is an illustration of this, where protests started with roads blocks and civil actions and ended with an agreement between Sakhalin Energy and the indigenous peoples on a Development Plan.[4] Often, Western companies and their affiliates are put under pressure from investors (such as international banks) to follow international standards, and this makes it possible to avoid the application of "double standards", i.e. using different standards according to national laws and practice, and to use best international practices and encourage regional administrations and the federal government to develop a clear and explicit procedure for taking the interests of indigenous peoples into consideration.

The national and international role and influence of the Association of Indigenous Peoples of the North, Siberia and the Far East of the Russian Federation (RAIPON) is crucial, as it conducts targeted monitoring of large-scale industrial projects on the territories of indigenous peoples and provides for regular exchange of information with regional organizations, in order for them to respond promptly to new challenges. It should be stressed that the higher the level of negotiations with the company and the better the coordination between indigenous organizations on all levels (community – regional association – national association), the better the chances of a fair conclusion of the agreement and its legal, organizational and financial support.

Nevertheless, the most difficult and tense situation can be seen in the work of indigenous organizations with state-owned companies. Gazpom, for example, the state-owned gas monopoly, is planning to construct a pipeline from Altay to China through an indigenous sacred site. Other projects include those of RAO UES and Hydro OGK in Krasnoyarsk Kray and Yakutia, Transneft in Yakutia and the Amur region and Rosneft in Sakhalin and Kamchatka. The list is growing and, as we have seen above, the Russian Federation has yet to develop legislation to resolve this complex issue in the sphere of land and natural resource rights.

The most important thing for the indigenous peoples of the North are not programs, nor the invention of redundant structures to address specific problems (alcoholism, health, education etc.), nor simply obtaining land rights and self-government. Changes are made not by structures but by people, who give credit to the fact that justice and partnership are not just idle words, that they live in a society of equal people, that their future lies in their own hands. And this belief, as a vision of a better future, occurs not on the basis of promises and paternalism but through the state's recognition of the injustices of the past, along with a fair division of economic and political power between indigenous peoples and the dominant society. Appropriate changes become realistic only as a result of combined, interactive (mutually supportive) activities. At this point, the key issue is to restore indigenous peoples as nations – substantial groups of people with a shared sense of national identity who make up the dominant part of the population of a certain area or several areas, obtaining a land and resource base for economic development and their own government institutions, and forming the national-territorial level of management, along with the federal and regional levels.

Capacity building and awareness raising efforts of RAIPON

Russian indigenous peoples have become significantly better informed of their rights in recent years. A broad information network exists across the regions. RAIPON's Moscow office distributes literature on the rights of indigenous peoples, conducts seminars to educate indigenous leaders on legal and information issues, and gathers information on current events from the regions by way of regional associations and information centers. In 2007, RAIPON conducted eleven seminars in particular hotspots where assistance was requested. Regional associations' suggestions for seminar topics usually include legal assistance in filing for land rights (TTP) and assistance in assessing opportunities to conduct ethnological impact assessments (*etnologicheskie ekspertizy*) of industrial projects planned for lands traditionally occupied by indigenous peoples.

At the end of 2007, RAIPON began questioning regional associations with regard to the outcomes of regional projects to establish territories of traditional natural resource use (TTPs), with the aim of assisting *obshchinas* to assess the lawfulness of rejected applications to create TTPs and analyzing the general situation surrounding the contradictory land rights of indigenous peoples in Russia. Indigenous peoples also need consultation and practical support to organize ethnological impact assessments in hotspots where industrial projects have already begun or are planned. Broadening and strengthening the network of regional information centers and attracting indigenous youth must play a central role in RAIPON's work to implement these plans.   ❑

Notes

1   The indigenous peoples are: the Aleut, Alutor, Veps, Dolgan, Itelmen, Kamchadal, Kereki, Kety, Koryak, Kumandin, Mansi, Nanaitsy, Nganasan, Negidaltsy, Nenets, Nivkhi, Orok, Orochi, Saami, Selkup, Soioty, Tazy, Telengit, Teleut, Tofolar, Tubalar, Tuvin-Todjin, Udege, Ulchi, Khanty, Chelkantsy, Chuvantsy, Chukchi, Chulymtsy, Shor, Evenk, Even, Enets, Eskimosy, Yukagir and Izhma-Komi. The Izhma Komi or Izvatas have been accepted by RAIPON but are still seeking recognition by the state.
2   1) On Guarantees of the Rights of the Numerically Small Indigenous Peoples of the Russian Federation 2) on General Principles of the Organization of Communities [obshinas] of the Numerically Small Indigenous Peoples of the North, Siberia and the Far East of Russian Federation 3) On Territories of Traditional Nature Use of the Numerically Small Indigenous Peoples of the North, Siberia and the Far East of the Russian Federation.

3 Other examples can be found in Primorsky krai, Nenets Autonomous Okrug, Yamal Nenets Autonomous Okrug, Khanty Mansisk Autonomous Okrug, Komi Republic, Evenkia and the Amur region.

4 Other examples can be found in Yamal Nenents Autonomous Okrug, Nenets Autonomous Okrug, Chukotka, Magadan and Irkutsk.

Olga Murashko is an anthropologist and co-founder of the IWGIA local group in Moscow. She works for RAIPON as an expert on indigenous peoples' legal rights in Russia.

Rodion Sulyandziga is an Udege from Krasny Yar, Primorsky Kray and director of the Center for Support of Indigenous Peoples of the North (CSIPN). He has a PhD in sociology.

ARCTIC CANADA
THE NORTHWEST TERRITORIES AND NUNAVUT

Canada's Northwest Territories (NWT) has a total population of some 42,000. Aboriginal people – mainly Inuvialuit, Dene and Métis - comprise approximately half of this figure. The territory of Nunavut was carved out of the NWT in 1999, following a land claim in the early 1990s. Inuit there comprise 82% of the population of 27,000. Over the last 25 years, land claims and self-government negotiations have meant the recognition of Aboriginal rights. In the NWT, the Inuvialuit achieved a land claim in 1984, the Gwich'in in 1992 and the Sahtu Dene in 1994. Negotiations for land, resource and self-government rights continue with the Deh Cho First Nations, while negotiations for self-government are in progress with the Inuvialuit, Gwich'in and the Sahtu Dene community of Deline. Although traditional hunting, trapping and fishing practices remain vital social, cultural and economic pursuits, important for the daily lives of Aboriginal people in the Northwest Territories and Nunavut, commercial fishing and extractive industries increasingly provide opportunities for employment. The recognition of indigenous peoples' rights has meant that many Aboriginal communities have entered into resource development projects through joint ventures with industry and government, impact benefit agreements and environmental monitoring projects.

The Northwest Territories and the Mackenzie Gas Project

The Canadian North as a whole is on the verge of major developments in the oil and gas industries. In the Northwest Territories

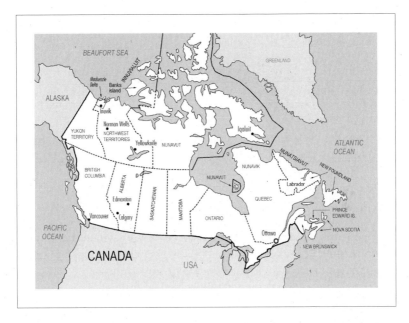

(NWT), many issues were overshadowed in 2007 by the continuation and eventual completion of the regulatory process and public hearings for the environmental and technical assessment of the Mackenzie Gas Project, a Can$16.2 billion (US$ 16.0 billion) project proposed by Shell Canada Limited, Conoco Phillips Canada (North) Limited, ExxonMobil, Imperial Oil Resources Ventures Limited and the Aboriginal Pipeline Group (collectively referred to as the Proponents). The Proponents intend this energy mega-project to develop natural gas from three anchor fields in the Mackenzie Delta area for delivery to markets in Canada and the United States, as well as to power further development in Alberta's rapidly growing oilsands industry. The oilsands of northern Alberta contain enormous deposits of bitumen – an estimated 1.7 to 2.5 trillion barrels of oil trapped in a viscous mixture of sand, water and clay that require heated water and hydrocarbons to extract them.

The total length of the pipeline would be about 1,300 kilometres but major construction would also take place in the Mackenzie Delta on the anchor fields and a gathering system of pipelines near Inuvik. Despite support for the project by many Aboriginal leaders, the hearings revealed that opinion in Aboriginal communities (and even within families and households) is divided on its impacts and benefits. Many people are concerned about irreversible negative social, economic and environmental impacts, including a loss of traditional hunting, trapping and fishing territory, while others see it as a critically important way to provide employment and prosperity to Northern communities.

Public hearings began in Inuvik in January 2006, comprising both technical hearings by Canada's National Energy Board (NEB) along with parallel hearings on environmental, social and economic issues conducted by the federal government-appointed Joint Review Panel (JRP). The hearings were carried out in 26 communities in the Northwest Territories, along with communities in Alberta (including the provincial capital Edmonton). The National Energy Board hearings were concluded in December 2006, although the JRP continued its hearings until November 2007. A major review of evidence and testimony is being undertaken by the NEB, which will recommend a decision on the project to the Canadian federal government.

Negotiations concerning the unresolved land claim of the Deh Cho First Nations in the central Mackenzie Valley continued throughout 2007. The Deh Cho issue also remains problematic for the Proponents of the Mackenzie Gas Project. The proposed pipeline route is approximately 40% in Deh Cho traditional territory. Although not opposed to the project, nor to membership of the Aboriginal Pipeline Group, the Deh Cho maintain that a land claim settlement is a precondition before discussions can begin on their involvement. The Deh Cho First Nations claim entitlement to revenue from the Mackenzie gas pipeline paid to them directly as a separate level of government. The Deh Cho emphasize that they have never surrendered title to their lands and territories and that treaties made with the Crown confirm they are the governing authorities on their lands. On 23 May 2001, the Deh Cho First Nations signed two agreements with the governments of Canada and the NWT: 1) A Framework Agreement which sets out the objectives, agenda of topics and negotiating principles of the treaty-making process and 2) An Interim Measures Agreement which establishes land-use principles and procedures that are to be observed during the several years it will take to negotiate and ratify a Final Agreement. These two agreements are the first steps towards a comprehensive agreement on outstanding land and self-government issues which, in effect, will be a modern treaty between the Deh Cho and Canada.

Inuit, Polar Bears and Caribou: arguments over endangered species

At the beginning of 2007, the United States Department of the Interior began a 12-month review to assess whether the polar bear should be listed as threatened throughout its range under the U.S. Endangered Species Act, following a proposal put forward by the U.S. Fish and Wildlife Service in January 2007. The petitioners to this proposed ruling include the Center for Biological Diversity, Greenpeace and the Natural Resources Defense Council. Canadian Inuit responded to the proposed rule by requesting that the polar bear should not be listed. In a jointly signed letter to the Marine Mammals Management Office of the U.S. Fish and Wildlife Service, the leaders of Inuit Tapiriit Kanatami (ITK), the national Inuit organization, and the Inuit Circumpolar Council (ICC - Canada) both argued that any proposal to restrict the hunting and use of polar bears, either within or outside of Canada, would affect the rights and interests of Inuit in Canada directly and substantively. Both ITK and ICC advance claims that Inuit in Canada have conserved polar bear populations at healthy levels through proper and responsible wildlife management, research and monitoring, and sustainable harvesting practices. Canadian Inuit argued that listing polar bears as threatened will impose scientifically unfounded penalties and hardships on communities, undermining Inuit conservation strategies in Nunavut and the Northwest Territories for the sustainable harvest of polar bears.

In Nunavut, the co-management of polar bears (as for the co-management of all wildlife) is legislated through the Nunavut Wildlife Management Board (NWMB), an institution of public government under the Nunavut Land Claims Agreement. It cooperates closely with Inuit hunters' and trappers' organizations. The incorporation of Inuit traditional knowledge into its research operations and management principles is particularly strong, allowing Inuit to practice a traditional, and sustainable, subsistence harvest.

To support the listing proposal, the U.S. Secretary of the Interior instructed the U.S. Geological Survey (USGS) to carry out research on polar bears and their sea ice habitats. The findings were released in nine administrative reports on 7 September 2007, with an overall conclusion that projected changes in future sea ice conditions would result in the loss of approximately two-thirds of the world's current polar bear population by the mid-21st century. The USGC warned, however, that the observed trajectory of Arctic sea decline may be underestimated, making its assessment a conservative one. The NWMB response to the nine reports was unequivocal. The board argued that it had failed to find evidence that would provide the basis for range-wide up-listing of polar bears.

In June 2007, Canadian Inuit hunters and Nunavut wildlife management organizations were further angered by a Canadian federal government proposal to add the Peary caribou to its list of species on the brink of extinction. Again, based on scientific advice that climate change is altering the habitat of Peary caribou with disastrous effects, and in light of a huge decline in the population from 50,000 to 8,000 in recent years, Canadian Environment Minister John Baird advised wildlife officials in Nunavut of his intention to apply the new Species at Risk Act to Peary caribou and Barren-ground caribou (which would be listed as a species of special concern). The NWMB disputes federal estimates of the size and health of the Peary caribou population. In 2005, the first attempt to list the Peary caribou failed following threats from the Inuit to sue the federal government for failing to adequately consult them about the population's status. Like the polar bear, arguments over the future of Peary caribou pit the expert scientific knowledge against the claims for recognition of the knowledge of Inuit who live, travel and hunt on the land.   ❑

Mark Nuttall is a social anthropologist and has worked extensively in Greenland, Canada, Alaska, Finland and Scotland. His current work looks at indigenous peoples and climate change in the Arctic, the social and cultural dimensions of Arctic oil and gas development, and the political ecology of human-animal relations in Canada and Finland. He holds the Henry Marshall Tory Chair in the Department of Anthropology, University of Alberta, Canada, and is also Academy of Finland Distinguished Professor at the University of Oulu, Finland.

NORTH AMERICA

CANADA

The indigenous peoples of Canada are collectively referred to as "Aboriginal people". The *Constitution Act, 1982* of Canada recognizes three groups of Aboriginal peoples: Indians, Inuit and Métis.

First Nations (referred to as "Indians" in the Constitution and generally registered under Canada's Indian Act[1]) are a diverse group of 698,025 people, representing more than 52 nations and more than 60 languages. 55% (383,914) live on-reserve and 45% (314,111) reside off-reserve in urban, rural, special access and remote areas.[2]

The Inuit number 50,480 people, living in 53 Arctic communities in four Land Claims regions: Nunatsiavut (Labrador); Nunavik (Quebec); Nunavut; and the Inuvialuit Settlement Region of the Northwest Territories. The Inuit Land Claims regions span across four provinces and territories, the Northwest Territories, Nunavut, Quebec, and Newfoundland and Labrador. The Métis constitute a distinct Aboriginal nation, numbering 389,780 in 2006, many of whom live in urban centres, mostly in western Canada.

The Métis constitute a distinct Aboriginal nation, numbering 389,780 in 2006, many of whom live in urban centres, mostly in western Canada. "The Métis people emerged out of the relations of Indian women and European men prior to Canada's crystallization as a nation."[3]

The policies of Canada's Conservative government continue to be an area of frustration for Aboriginal peoples in Canada, particularly with regard to self-determination and recognition of rights. While the adoption of the UN Declaration on the Rights of Indigenous Peoples ("the Declaration") was heralded as a victory for indigenous peo-

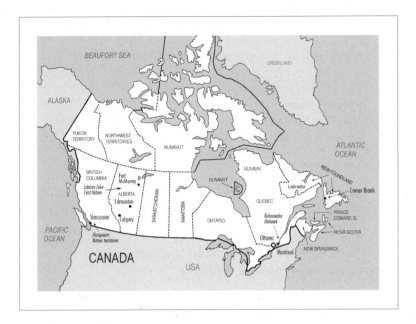

ples around the world, it was a bittersweet moment for Aboriginal peoples in Canada. Canada's vote against the Declaration in the General Assembly marred the country's reputation as an international leader in human rights.[4] Since the election of the Conservative government, much of Canada's engagement in international processes has taken a 180-degree turn in relation to indigenous peoples. It is now with watchful eyes that Aboriginal Peoples monitor Canada's participation in the Organization of American States and the associated drafting of the American Declaration on the Rights of Indigenous Peoples.[5]

Canada and the Draft American Declaration on the Rights of Indigenous Peoples

Drafting continues on the American Declaration and there is currently no projected time frame for its completion. This may have both positive and negative consequences. On the positive side, with speculation of a winter 2008 election in Canada, a new federal government may bring with it a renewed and more supportive Canadian government to the negotiation table. Over the past year, Canada and Columbia have maintained particularly strong positions with regard to indigenous rights in their territories and this has created roadblocks for indigenous groups involved in the drafting. The issue of a timeframe for completion has divided indigenous groups; on the one hand they could move forward with a potentially weaker American Declaration, while on the other continued negotiation and a new government could mean Canadian support for the American Declaration.[6] Aboriginal Peoples in Canada must watch this process closely given Canada's vote against the UN Declaration on the Rights of Indigenous Peoples.

Mission to Canada by the United Nations Special Rapporteur on Adequate Housing

In 2007, the United Nations Special Rapporteur on Housing, Miloon Kothari, conducted a mission to Canada, the general objectives of which were to examine and report on the status of realization of the right to adequate housing in Canada.[7] The Rapporteur visited the Kahnawake Mohawk and Musqueam Nation territories, and a number of major cities where he met with Aboriginal representative organizations. Rapporteur Kothari brought to light the deplorable state of Aboriginal housing in Canada and admonished Canada for the state of housing and the ever weakening role of the Canada Mortgage and Housing Corporation in Aboriginal housing, stating that its focus was increasingly only on Aboriginal housing research rather than increasing access to safe and adequate housing. He further stated that Canada was not meeting its obligations under international laws. Prior to his departure, the Rapporteur held a press conference where he identified some preliminary recommendations. With regard to indigenous peoples, he called on the federal government to take action in the following areas:

The federal government needs to commit funding and resources for a targeted national Aboriginal housing strategy – both on and off-reserve – that ensures that Aboriginal housing and services are under Aboriginal control.

Place a moratorium on all oil and extractive activities in the Lubicon region until a settlement is reached with Lubicon Lake First Nation. The federal government should resume negotiations with the Lubicon consistent with human rights law instruments, including the Declaration on the Rights of Indigenous Peoples.

Struggle of the Lubicon Nation

The Lubicon Nation of north central Alberta continue their struggle for recognition of rights to their traditional lands. In 2007, discussions to resolve the dispute were non-existent with the federal and provincial governments.[8] The situation of the Lubicon has been further complicated by increased global demand for hydrocarbon fuels. With world demand intensifying so have extraction activities, and plans have been established to build a pipeline that would pass through lands that have not been ceded by the Lubicon to the hub centre of the industry in Fort McMurray. The company in question, TransCanada, presented the Lubicon with a Memorandum of Understanding in 2007 acknowledging potential surface rights to the lands but ignored calls for it to acknowledge that the lands had never been ceded by the Lubicon. While resolution at a domestic level has been unsuccessful, the Lubicon have made gains within the United Nations system and the UN has repeatedly called on Canada to resolve the dispute, most recently with the mission to Canada by the UN Rapporteur on Housing, Miloon Kothari, who urged Canada to resume negotiations with the Lubicon.

Aboriginal women's issues

In 2005, the Native Women's Association of Canada (NWAC) launched its "Sisters in Spirit" initiative to raise awareness about violence against Aboriginal women. The 2007 trial of Robert William Pickton, who was convicted of the murder of six women and will be tried on a further 20 counts, focused the attention of the country and the world yet more on the plight of women in the downtown east side of Vancouver, British Columbia, as a large majority of the victims were Aboriginal women. According to NWAC:

> *There have been literally hundreds of missing and murdered Aboriginal women across Canada over the last few decades. The high profile nature of this case has drawn significant public spotlight on this tragic reality and helped to raise awareness of the violence targeting Aboriginal women and to support and protect one another.*[9]

NWAC also held national and international Sisters in Spirit vigils to denounce violence, and released a Violence Prevention Tool Kit.

National Aboriginal Women's Summit

In June 2007, the first ever National Aboriginal Women's Summit was held in Corner Brook, Newfoundland and Labrador. It was the culmination of joint planning led by the Native Women's Association of Canada and the Province of Newfoundland and Labrador and involved a number of national and sub-national Aboriginal women's groups as well as national representative Aboriginal organizations.[10] Planning began in 2006 and, as a result of intensive and collaborative efforts by Aboriginal women and provincial, territorial, and federal agencies, Aboriginal women sat in a forum with the Premiers of Canada's provinces and territories as well as several federal-level Ministers. Under the overarching theme of "Strong Women, Strong Communities", Aboriginal women discussed issues such as violence against Aboriginal women, equality and empowerment of Aboriginal women, child welfare and poverty, as well as health and well-being.[11] Aboriginal women developed recommendations for change and government support for transformative action was evident – at the end of the first event the then-Premier of the Northwest Territories, Joe Handley, committed to hosting the second National Aboriginal Women's Summit, which would focus on progress made on the recommendations of Aboriginal women, as well as mechanisms to further advance longer term recommendations made at the first summit.[12]

Fifth Continental Meeting of Indigenous Women of the Americas
This international event was held in the traditional Mohawk territory in Kahnawake, Quebec in July 2007 and was hosted by the Quebec Native Women Inc. The theme of the conference was "Restoring Our Balance", and involved indigenous women from 17 countries across North, Central and South America. Indigenous women discussed issues of shared importance such as the promotion of non-violence, intellectual property and the international recognition of indigenous peoples' rights. Indigenous women were encouraged to share their spiritual wisdom and teachings with the aim of strengthening cultural identity and language.[13] Important exchanges also took place with regard to capacity building, indigenous women's health, research, entrepreneurship and economic development. An additional message that surfaced at the event was a resounding call from the indigenous women of the Americas urging the Canadian government to recognize and accept the United Nations Declaration on the Rights of Indigenous Peoples.

Matrimonial Real Property

In the Canadian legal system, matrimonial property is generally defined as property owned by one or both spouses and used for a family purpose. Matrimonial real property (MRP) includes the land and anything permanently attached to the land, such as the family home. Provinces have jurisdiction over property and civil rights and have enacted laws protecting spousal interests in matrimonial property. However, because reserve lands fall under federal jurisdiction, case law has established that provincial legislation cannot apply to alter individual interests in MRP located on reserve lands.[14] Further, there are provisions in the Indian Act and the Canadian constitution that protect reserve lands from alienation and ensure that they are preserved for the use and benefit of band members. What this means is that in the event of a marriage breakdown, spouses on- reserve find themselves without legal protection or remedy to address the issue of the matrimonial home in the same way that Canadians can ask the courts to order a division of assets, or award the home to one of the parties.[15]

Starting in 2006, the Assembly of First Nations (AFN), NWAC and the Department of Indian and Northern Affairs Canada (INAC) entered into a dialogue with First Nations across the country to develop solutions to the issue of Matrimonial Real Property. The *Indian Act* does not contain provisions addressing Matrimonial Real Property - there is currently no legal provision for equitable division of matrimonial real property for First Nations on reserve.[16] This legislative void has had devastating affects on families and individuals. This dialogue was initially received as a very positive movement towards creating substantive solutions by the AFN and NWAC.

To further facilitate this dialogue, the Conservative government appointed a Ministerial Representative, Wendy Grant-John, who was given responsibility for reporting to the Minister of INAC on the results of the initiative. Following numerous meetings, workshops and interviews with First Nation Peoples across the country aimed at developing solutions, NWAC, the AFN and the Ministerial Representative met to begin jointly developing recommendations based on consensus. The resulting recommendations were compiled in a report and submitted to the Minister of INAC.[17]

In a press release issued by the Assembly of First Nations in April 2007, the following report recommendations were highlighted:

The federal government should make funding available to First Nations communities to establish dispute resolution bodies and provide legal aid funding to First Nations families to address access to justice issues

The federal government should introduce interim federal rules that would allow courts to make orders regarding the possession of homes on reserve.

While the report was recognized as an important step forward, the AFN indicated concern that the interim rules should not "…affect the constitutionally protected Aboriginal title and Treaty rights of First Nations". In other words, the interim rules should not affect the protection of reserve lands and other treaty and Aboriginal rights.

In June 2007, NWAC indicated that, following the submission of the report, they - along with the AFN - were being increasingly excluded from the process by the federal government, which failed to share documentation or information about their activities. This has effectively brought the consensus-building exercise to a standstill.

Redefining Success in Aboriginal Learning

First Nations, Inuit and Métis recognize the importance of education in contributing to overall community well-being. At the same time, indigenous peoples in Canada have long advocated the recognition of indigenous ways of knowing and the value and importance of experiential and cultural ways of understanding – forms of learning that do not necessarily occur within a Western model of understanding. 2007 saw significant developments in this area. The Canadian Council on Learning, an independent not-for-profit corporation whose mandate is to promote and support evidence-based recommendations for learning throughout all stages of life, facilitated sessions with First Nations, Inuit and Métis that led to the creation of a Life Long Learning Model for all three groups.[18] The Life Long Learning Models recognize that there are two ways of learning or understanding for indigenous people in Canada, one within a formal classroom setting (a Western framework) and one through the cultural or community experience. The models recognize that incorporating both forms of "knowing" will foster the necessary conditions for nurturing healthy sustainable communities. ❑

Notes and References

1 The *Indian Act* remains the principal vehicle for the exercise of federal jurisdiction over "status Indians", and governs most aspects of their lives. It defines who is an Indian and regulates band membership and government, taxation, lands and resources, money management, wills and estates, and education. **Hurley, Mary C., 1999:** *The Indian Act.* http://dsp-psd.pwgsc.gc.ca/Collection-R/LoPBdP/EB/prb9923-e.htm

2 These numbers have been established by Statistics Canada and are not considered reliable, as many First Nations citizens do not participate in the Census process. **Statistics Canada, 2008**: *Aboriginal Identity Population, 2006 Counts, for Canada, Provinces and Territories - 20% Sample Data.* http://www12.statcan.ca/english/census06/data/highlights/Aboriginal/pages/Page.cfm?Lang=E&Ge

o=PR&Code=01&Table=1&Data=Count&Sex=1&Age=1&StartRec=1&Sort=2& Display=Page.

3   Métis National Council: *Who are the Métis?*
    http://www.metisnation.ca/who/faq.html

4   Permanent Mission of Canada to the United Nations *Statement by Ambassador McNee to the United Nations General Assembly on the Rights of Indigenous Peoples* http://geo.international.gc.ca/canada_un/new_york/statements/unga-en. asp?id=10373&content_type=2&lang_update=1

5   *Indian Country Today* Native Nations in La Paz on Draft Indigenous Rights Declaration
    http://www.indiancountry.com/content.cfm?id=1096415048

6   http://www.gov.yk.ca/news/2007/07-217.html

7   United Nations Special Rapporteur on adequate housing, Miloon Kothari *Mission to Canada*
    http://hic-net.org/content/press_release_onu_canada_oct2007.doc

8   Friends of the Lubicon Action Alert "TransCanada PipeLine's (TCPL) claim of no objections to a proposed new "jumbo" gas pipeline ripping through Lubicon Territory is false" http://www.lubicon.ca/pa/oilp/tcplp/po071123.htm

9   NWAC Media Advisory "Native Women's Association to attend conclusion of Pickton Trial." 2007. http://www.nwac-hq.org/en/documents/MediaAdvisoryreNWACtoattendPicktonconclusionNov23-07.pdf

10 Labrador and Aboriginal Affairs *Message from Beverly Jacobs*
    http://www.laa.gov.nl.ca/laa/naws/jacobs.htm

11 National Aboriginal Women's Summit Agenda
    http://www.laa.gov.nl.ca/laa/naws/agenda.htm

12 Native Women's Association of Canada, 2008: National Aboriginal Women's Summit Agenda
    http://www.nwac-hq.org/en/NationalAboriginalWomensSummit.htm

13 International Indigenous Women's Forum FIMI/IIWF's Participation at the V Continental Meeting of Indigenous Women of the Americas http://www.indigenouswomensforum.org/intadvocacy/vc07.html

14 Department of Indian Affairs and Northern Development, 2006: On-Reserve Matrimonial Real Property, Backgrounder http://www.ainc-inac.gc.ca/nr/prs/m-a2003/02329bk_e.html.

15 **Nicholas-MacKenzie, Lea, 2007**: Canada. In: *The Indigenous World 2007*. International Work Group for Indigenous Affairs

16 Native Women's Association of Canada *Matrimonial Real Property an Issues Paper* http://www.nwac-hq.org/en/documents/nwac-mrp.pdf

17 Assembly of First Nations National Chief says Ministerial Representative's Report on Matrimonial Real Property Offers hope for First Nations Families by Calling for Greater First Nations Control

18 Canadian Council On Learning: *Summary Report 2007 Redefining Success is Measured in First Nations, Inuit, and Métis Learning*
    http://www.ccl-cca.ca/NR/rdonlyres/156A9D63-F78B-4C9F-B720-4DD13F7C119C/0/Summary_Redefining_How_Success_Is_Measured_EN.pdf

Sharon P. Edmunds is a beneficiary of the Labrador Inuit Land Claims Agreement. She has worked for national and international Inuit organizations and currently works for Inuit Tapiriit Kanatami. Her interest in international policy is fostered by the International Training Centre for Indigenous Peoples in Greenland – an indigenous institute specializing in international law and sustainable development. Sharon is also a student of the University of the Arctic.

Lea Nicholas-MacKenzie is a member of the Walastakwewinowok (Maliseet) First Nation at Nekwotkok (Tobique) in New Brunswick, Canada. Lea has worked with First Nations organizations, international indigenous organizations and the federal government. She is a member of the International Indigenous Women's Forum and is currently a consultant focusing on international policy and relations.

THE UNITED STATES

According to the United States Census Bureau 2007[1], 2,151,322 people in the United States (minus Alaska) identified as Native American only, and 4,006,160 people identified as Native American in combination with another ethnic identity. These numbers add up to 0.75% and 1.4% of the total population respectively. There are currently around 335 federally recognized tribes in the United States (minus Alaska). More than half of American Indians live off-reservation, many in cities.

American Indian law includes individual treaties and federal Indian law, which is in flux and often dependent on individual U.S. Supreme Court decisions. Tribal governments' sovereignty is limited by plenary power of the U.S. Congress, which can unilaterally change historical treaty articles. Separate federal agencies, such as the Bureau of Indian Affairs and the Indian Health Service, are responsible for the federal government's trust responsibilities to Indian tribes. The political status of American Indian nations in relation to the United States has been defined as "that of a ward to his guardian."[2] This is best seen in land ownership. Some of the lands that are the property of American Indians are held in trust by the government; the government holds the title to the land, and is supposed to manage or at least extend oversight over the land's use on behalf of individuals or tribes. In addition to this, the government has treaty obligations, stemming from historical land sales by Indian nations to the federal government.

While there are widespread differences between indigenous nations, as a whole, American Indians have a lower life expectancy and higher poverty rates than the average U.S. citizens. Some of the main challenges they face are related to trust lands and sovereignty, unemployment, housing shortages, health problems and youth suicides.

1. Cheroqui Nation
2. Makah tribe
3. National Bison Range in Moiese
4. Walker River
5. Goshute tribe
6. Navaho Nation
7. Pine Ridge Reservation
8. San Francisco Peaks
9. Catskill Mountains

Developments in United States American Indian policies in 2007 were again influenced by the continued and extremely costly wars in Iraq and Afghanistan. Federal American Indian programs have seen budget cuts for several years, making it even harder to fulfill treaty obligations. The Bureau of Indian Affairs (BIA), for example, has lost $74 million over the last two years. The start of the presidential election races (elections will be held in November 2008) promised a limited amount of interest for American Indian issues.

With the office having been vacant for two years, Carl Artman was finally sworn in as the new director of the BIA. Artman is a member of the Oneida Nation of Wisconsin. As general counsel for his nation, he pursued a settlement for land claims that involved a possible off-reservation casino in New York (see *Indigenous World 2005*). This action delayed his confirmation to the United States Senate for two years, as the Republican majority had taken a stand against off-reservation gaming, which allows tribes to operate casinos away from their reservations as long as the land the casino is built on is Indian trust land.

Congress failed to pass a renewed Indian Health Care Improvement Act. It has been eight years since the last adjustment to the bill, and with the Indian Health Service (IHS) facing continuous budget cuts, the state of health care for American Indians, a trust obligation, is dismal. Not only do patients go untreated for lack of funds but the IHS also allocates only 1% of its budget to off-reservation clinics, even though around 60% of American Indians in the United States live off-reservation. There is hope that the bill may be passed in 2008. The federal government's per capita health expenditure on Native Americans came to $2,130 in 2005. This is about a third of the government's per capita expenditure on its Medicare program, the general social insurance program for older citizens.

Cherokee Freedmen

One of the most controversial American Indian issues in 2007 was the continuing question of whether the Cherokee Freedmen are members of the Cherokee Nation of Oklahoma (see *Indigenous World 2007*). On March 3, the tribe voted in favor of an amendment to its constitution that would restrict membership, excluding those Freedmen who cannot show a direct Cherokee ancestor in their lineage. Freedmen are descendents of slaves held by some Cherokee before the Civil War. When these slaves were freed, they were made members of the Cherokee Nation under a treaty with the United States in 1866. The case has once again brought to light several key issues that define the situation of American Indian nations within the United States, in particular, identity politics and the limitation of indigenous sovereignty.

The 1976 Cherokee constitution requires the approval of amendments, such as a restriction of membership, by the Secretary of the Interior. This necessary approval was withheld by the federal government which, under pressure from African American organizations, took a clear stand against excluding the Cherokee Freedmen. The Cherokee Nation argued that it had passed an amendment to the Constitution in 2003 removing the requirement for Secretarial approval to amendments. However, the BIA also withheld approval of this amendment, "concerned that approval by the Department of the 2003 amendment at this time would be used by some as a validation or evidence of legitimacy of the Cherokee Nation's removal of its Freedmen members from the tribe in apparent violation of the 1866 treaty."[3] In response, the Cherokee Nation held another referendum on June 23, 2007, again voting in favor of an amendment to their Constitution to remove the need for approval of amendments by the Secretary of the Interior. The BIA then approved that amendment but specifically stated that this could not be construed "as authorizing any action that would be contrary to Federal law."[4]

Since treaties with American Indian nations constitute federal law, and the BIA sees the exclusion of the Freedmen as a violation of a treaty, the approval of the amendment, from that legal perspective, has no impact on the issue of Freedmen membership. The Cherokee Nation, on the other hand, sees the BIA reaction as a violation of its sovereignty. The issue also raises the question of American Indian identity. Principal Chief Smith insists that "The Cherokee Nation simply wants to be an Indian tribe composed of Indians"[5], which would mean that Indian identity was defined by biological ancestry.

In response to the Cherokee vote, Congresswoman Diane Watson (Democrat, California) introduced a bill to the United States Congress that was aimed at stripping the Cherokee Nation of about $300 million of annual federal funding. The Congressional Black Caucus and the National Association for the Advancement of Colored People (NAACP) took a stand against the Cherokee Nation, calling the vote to exclude Freedmen racist, which had Principal Chief Smith concerned with the image of his nation. The U.S. House of Representatives voted in September to cut funding for Cherokee Nation housing development programs until the membership of Freedmen was officially restored. In the meantime, litigation on the issue is ongoing in the federal courts.

Ecological issues

Members of the Makah tribe in Washington State killed a whale on September 8, without tribal or federal permits. The Makah have been interested in reviving whale hunting for twenty years, and previously hunted a whale in 1999 with federal permission attached to certain conditions, such as the use of a traditional canoe. After protests by animal rights groups, the exception to the Marine Mammal Protection Act that had led to that hunt was revoked pending a more in-depth environmental impact statement. The Makah Tribe, who are working with the National Marine Fisheries Service on this process, immediately denounced the illegal hunt, pointing out that the "tribe has demonstrated extraordinary patience in waiting for the legal process to be completed in order to receive our permit to conduct a whale hunt".[6] The whale hunters argued that they were tired of waiting for federal permission. While the Makah have an explicit treaty right to hunt whales, United States courts have argued that they have to abide by federal laws. It is the latter that will be put to the test in the court cases against the whalers. The five crew members will be tried in both tribal and federal courts next year. In the meantime, the environmental impact statement will probably be delayed even longer and the tribe hopes that this illegal hunt will not sway public opinion against it and lead to a negative outcome.

A case that similarly poses questions for tribal sovereignty, federal oversight and the weight of public opinion is the ongoing issue of the National Bison Range in Montana (see *The Indigenous World 2007*). An agreement for shared management of the range between the Confederated Salish and Kootenai Tribes of the Flathead Reservation, upon whose reservation lands the range is located, and the U.S. Fish and Wildlife Service (FWS), was cancelled in 2006 after allegations concerning the tribes' management abilities. Several organizations had publicly doubted the tribes even before an agreement was signed in 2005, and had voiced concerns about the surrender of federal sovereignty to tribal governments as setting a precedent for other cases. Talks between FWS and the tribes continued throughout 2007. In December, the new director of FWS ordered his agency to have a new agreement ready by March 2008. While the tribes have welcomed this development, it will be extremely hard to convince those opposed to an agreement of its advantages and opportunities.

Nuclear policies

In April, the Walker River Paiute Tribe in Nevada blocked attempts to build a rail line across their reservation to the proposed federal nuclear storage facility at Yucca Mountain. The tribal council had been working with the Department of Energy on an environmental impact statement but adopted a resolution to discontinue that cooperation. The mayors of two major cities in the region, Reno and Sparks, expressed relief over the tribe's decision. The planned facility at Yucca Mountain has been causing concern in Nevada and along the proposed transportation routes to the site for years.

In a related case, the Skull Valley Goshute Tribe in Utah filed an appeal against a ruling by the Department of the Interior that blocked the tribe from operating a private storage area for nuclear waste. The tribe had signed an agreement with nuclear power companies to store the waste until a federal solution to the nuclear waste problem was found. The state of Utah and its powerful congressional delegation is at the forefront of opposition to the project which, in the eyes of the tribe, would bring much needed economic development opportunities to the Goshute reservation.

The Navajo Nation, in the meantime, has asked Congress to impose a moratorium on new uranium mining leases on Navajo trust lands until the existing mines have been cleaned up. The reservation has been experiencing a health crisis because of uranium mines; its lands hold a majority of the uranium deposits in the United States. While the Navajo Nation has imposed a ban on uranium mines on reservation land, it cannot stop mining on individually held trust lands that are located off the reservation. The BIA perceives itself as caught between following the wishes of the Navajo council and the desires of individual landowners to make money from mining leases. The BIA's inability to make a clear choice for the health of reservation communities follows a long history of federal agencies siding with economically powerful mining interests against the health interests of Indian communities, which often depend on drinking water that is being polluted by mining operations. In December, the Environmental Protection Agency (EPA) said that, while it planned to resume testing for contamination on the reservation, it did not have plans to clean-up the contaminated sites. Not only is groundwater being contaminated but erosion is also uncovering waste piles, and uranium ore has been used to construct houses. The Navajo government has asked for an initial $500 million to get the clean-up process underway.

A proposed expansion of uranium mining near the Pine Ridge reservation in South Dakota also led to protests there. Tribal groups are afraid that the in situ leach method used by Cameco at the Crow Butte mine in Nebraska would deplete the water resources and could contaminate the tribe's drinking water. Rumors about further uranium mining on Pine Ridge also led to an impeachment vote against the tribe's president. Since these rumors could not be confirmed, however, the action - brought by the Black Hills Sioux Nation Treaty Council - was unsuccessful.

While the Navajo Nation is asking for a clean-up of nuclear sites, it is also planning to build a massive new coal-fired power plant. This is opposed by many environmental groups and surrounding states. The proposed Desert Rock plant would sell power to the large cities of the south-west and potentially bring millions of dollars in taxes and profits to the Navajo. Environmental advocates, including Navajo groups, are protesting at the further use of coal to produce power, and are pointing to existing health and ecological problems. The Navajo government sees itself in the role of an underdeveloped nation, in need of jobs and income, pressured to conform to environmental rules made by privileged, developed nations who can afford to value ecology over economics.

Land issues

The Sherill decision (see *The Indigenous World 2006*), which legalized an historic land theft by the state of New York, is continuing to alter the judicial landscape of the United States. Referring to the decision, a federal judge threw out a land claim by the Shinnecock Nation of New York, citing "highly disruptive consequences" if the tribe were to be allowed to restore sovereignty over the land.[7] The specifics of the case involved a plan for a casino in the wealthy Hamptons area of Long Island, but similar decisions against tribes have become a trend. The courts are arguing that sovereignty over lands cannot be restored to Indian tribes if a restitution of land to tribes would disrupt economies and political systems that have been in place for decades. A loss of sovereignty cannot therefore be reversed, even if the lands in question were illegally taken. As such, the courts are legalizing historical illegal land transactions because upholding the law would create a burden for the majority that has been profiting from these acts. This is an extremely disturbing argument; its broader application means that the United States is not bound to uphold the law if doing so would create a disturbance to a customary, albeit illegal, status quo.

The Saint Regis Mohawk Tribe of New York in the meantime filed a lawsuit against the Bush administration. In February, the Department of the Interior completed an application by the tribe to have some lands turned into trust status, a requirement for building a casino on these lands. However, the Secretary of the Interior, who oversees Indian Affairs, had not granted the application by November. The Saint Regis Mohawk are trying to build a casino in the Catskill Mountains, a popular scenic tourist area within driving distance of New York City. Governor Spitzer of New York has agreed with the tribe's plans and supports the trust application. There are currently around 2,000 land-into-trust applications pending with the BIA. The backlog exists mainly because the Republicans put an unofficial moratorium on trust applications, for fear that tribes would only want to convert lands into trust in order to be able to build off-reservation casinos.

In March, the 9th Circuit Court of Appeals handed several tribes a victory in a lawsuit concerning the San Francisco Peaks, an area sacred to many southwestern tribes, especially the Navajo, Hopi, Hualapai and Havasupai. The tribes had sued the Forest Service in 2005 over the planned expansion of a ski resort in the Coconino National Forest that included a proposal for snowmaking using reclaimed wastewater. This ruling marked a tentative change in course; federal courts had previously shown a tendency to rule in favor of economic development over and above Native religious rights ever since the 1988 Lynn case. While the tribes welcomed the initial ruling by a three-member panel of the court, the full court decided to re-hear the case in December. A decision will be taken in 2008.

Political developments

In April, Amnesty International published a report highlighting the violence directed against native women.[8] The report documents how the judicial system ignores sexual assaults on Native women because of systemic failures. Tribal courts are limited in their sentencing to a maximum of one year in jail and $5,000. Under the Major Crimes Act, rape on Indian lands is a crime that falls under federal jurisdiction but federal agencies such as the FBI are chronically understaffed on reservations and often ignore what they consider to be less important crimes and investigations that have little chance of resulting in a conviction. Because investigation of crimes on Indian lands is dependent on whether the perpetrator and/or the victim are Indian, where the crime happened and how severe the crime is, the resulting confusion often leads to law enforcement agencies being incapable of bringing a case. Indian women suffer two and a half times more domestic violence and three and a half times more sexual assaults than average in the United States. According to some estimates, more than one in three Native women will suffer rape during their lifetime; the national average is a little less than one in five.

At the University of Colorado, ethnic studies professor Ward Churchill was fired from his tenured position. The university started an investigation into his research and writing in 2005 after right-wing media and politicians discovered his text on the events of September 11, 2001 in which he attacks the political system of the United States and its treatment of indigenous peoples. While Churchill's has been a very polemic and controversial voice in academia and in indigenous communities, there seems to be little doubt that it was his political opinion that was being punished. ❑

Notes and references

1   United States Census Bureau, 2007: *The American Community – American Indians and Alaska Natives: 2004.* American Community Survey Reports. Issued May 2007
2   *Cherokee Nation v. Georgia.* U.S. Supreme Court, 1831

3 Letter from the Assistant Secretary, Indian Affairs, Carl Artman to Principal Chief Chad Smith, May 21, 2007

4 Letter from the Assistant Secretary, Indian Affairs, Carl Artman to Principal Chief Chad Smith, August 9, 2007

5 "Bill could halt U.S. funds to Cherokees", *Tulsa World*, June 22, 2007

6 "Statement by the Makah Tribal Council", *Seattle Times*, September 10, 2007

7 *State of New York v. Shinnecock Indian Nation*. U.S. District Court, Eastern District of New York, Oct. 30, 2007

8 *Maze of Injustice. The Failure to Protect Indigenous Women from Sexual Violence in the USA*. Amnesty International USA: New York

Sebastian Felix Braun *is a cultural anthropologist. He is assistant professor with the Department of Indian Studies at the University of North Dakota (USA) and author of "Buffalo Inc. American Indians and Economic Development". sebastian.braun@und.edu.*

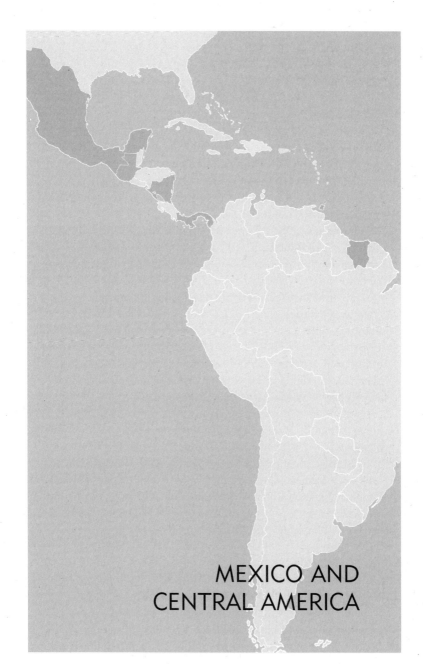

MEXICO AND
CENTRAL AMERICA

MEXICO

The indigenous population of Mexico is estimated at 12.4 million people, or 13% of the country's total population, spread across the country's 32 states. Sixty-eight indigenous languages were listed this year, spoken in 368 variants grouped together into 11 linguistic families.

The country ratified ILO Convention 169 in 1990 and, in 1992, Mexico was recognised as a pluricultural nation when Article 6 of the Constitution was amended. In 1994, the Zapatista National Liberation Army (*Ejército Zapatista de Liberación Nacional* - EZLN) took up arms in response to the misery and exclusion being suffered by the indigenous peoples. The San Andrés Accords[1] (add a footnote with some information on the Accords) were signed in 1996 but it was not until 2001 that Congress approved the Law on Indigenous Rights and Culture and, even then, this did not reflect the territorial rights and political representation enshrined in the San Andrés Accords. More than 300 challenges to the law were rejected. From 2003 onwards, the EZLN and the Indigenous National Congress (*Congreso Nacional Indígena* - CNI) began to implement the Accords in practice throughout their territories, creating autonomous indigenous governments in Chiapas, Michoacán and Oaxaca. Although the states of Chihuahua, Nayarit, Oaxaca, Quintana Roo and San Luís Potosí have state constitutions with regard to indigenous peoples, indigenous legal systems are still not fully recognised.[2]

Paramilitary intensification in Chiapas: tenth anniversary of the Acteal massacre

The atmosphere in Chiapas ten years ago was very similar to how it is now. Troop movements, a strengthening of paramilitary groups,

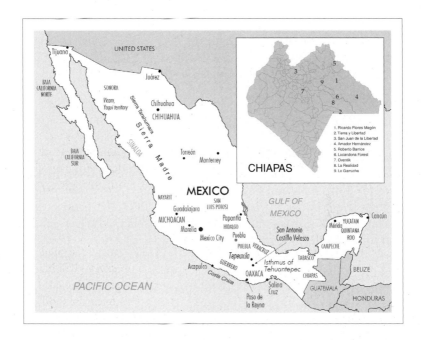

expulsions of whole families, displacements, death threats, evictions and the complicity of the authorities were all the prelude to a massacre in Acteal community on 22 December 1997. The mutilated bodies of 45 people, mostly women and children, belonging to a Catholic group known as "Las Abejas", were thrown just 200 metres from the police station. The police completely ignored the events. The local people were horrified. To this day, human rights organisations continue to demand a serious investigation from the federal and state governments. They stress that the then President Ernesto Zedillo and Governor Julio Cesar Ruiz Fierro should be held accountable before the courts, and that the state should accept that the act took place in an environment of counter-insurgency and paramilitary operations[3] aimed at bringing the EZLN and its autonomous governments to an end.

Huge controversy broke out in 2007 around this massacre due to a series of academic publications[4] that reiterated the official version[5] of a vendetta between communities to justify the state's action to "pacify" the area, absolving the state of all responsibility in creating paramilitary groups such as "Paz y Justicia", "Movimiento Indígena Revolucionario Antizapatista" and "Mascara Roja", and in the onslaught against the autonomous municipalities that took place after Acteal under Governor Roberto Albores Guillen.[6]

The war for Land and Territory

From 2006 on, and this last year in particular, land conflicts have intensified,[7] all of them along similar lines. The Organisation for the Defence of Indigenous and Peasant Farmer Rights (*Organización para la Defensa de los Derechos Indígenas y Campesinos* – OPDDIC) recruits peasant families who are waiting for their old land demands to be resolved and processes the property titles with the Agrarian Attorney (*Procuraduría Agraria*). The Attorney speeds up the process in a matter of months and certifies their land requests, including the lands recovered by the Zapatistas since 1994.[8] Shortly afterwards, agents from the Certification Programme for Ejidal[9] (explain in footnote) Rights and Land Titling (*Programa de Certificación de Derechos Ejidales y Titulación de Solares* - PROCEDE) arrive to issue land certificates and, once they have these, armed members of OPDDIC evict the Zapatista families and force non-Zapatistas to form part of their organisation, or lose their land. In the words of one inhabitant of the Zapatista community of Roberto Barrios, members of the Institutional Revolutionary Party (*Partido Revolucionario Institucional* - PRI), or the Party of the Democratic Revolution (*Partido de la Revolución Democrática* - PRD), "want to take our land from us, legalising it in the hands of just a few, that is to say, they want to conduct a new census in which they want us to replace the Zapatistas although ever since we recovered the land we have shared it equally among all inhabitants, Zapatista or not" (20 September 2007).

The escalation in conflicts, deaths, evictions, threats, bullet wounds, house destructions, injuries, troop movements, harassment and fear is reminiscent of 10 years ago. A strategy of creating dozens of local land conflicts can be seen, possible "hot spots" that could cause violent clashes thus justifying military intervention to "pacify" a violent situation between poor people or local vendettas. OPDDIC broke off dialogue with the Zapatistas and has this year strengthened its position. This process has been carefully documented by the Internal Displacement Monitoring Centre[10] and by the Centre for Political Analysis and Economic Research (*Centro de Análisis Políticos e Investigaciones Económicas*),[11] which have noted an increase in paramilitary activity and the entry of special troops. The most significant cases are found in the Lacandona Forest where the government has used a 1976 presidential decree to expropriate lands belonging to 60 local families, legalising OPDDIC members and sidelining the Zapatista communities. This strategy for legalising the lands recovered by the Zapatistas on behalf of non-Zapatista organisations is being extended to peasant farmer organisations that traditionally had co-existence agreements with the Zapatistas, such as the Union of Ejidos of the Selva (*Unión de Ejidos de la Selva*) which, for the first time, is in direct conflict with the successful coffee cooperative being run by the Zapatistas.

In this context, on 26 March, in the words of *Comandanta* Kelly, the EZLN launched the International Campaign for Land and Indigenous Territory in Chiapas and the World (*Campaña Internacional por la Tierra y Territorio Indígena de Chiapas y del Mundo*), with the support of one of the great leaders of the Brazilian Landless Movement (*Movimiento Sin Tierra*), João Pedro Estédile, and the coordinator of the International Campaign for Agrarian Reform of *La Vía Campesina*, the Honduran, Rafael Alegría. In October, an emergency network[12] was launched and the international human rights action network FIAN (FoodFirst Information and Action Network) based in Germany, published an urgent action after its visit to Chiapas.[13]

Elections and cabinet changes
A prelude to open war in Chiapas?

Local elections were held on 7 October and most of the successful candidates from the PRI, PRD and National Action Party (*Partido Acción Nacional* - PAN) in the indigenous municipalities were members of OPDDIC, which "puts the resources of institutions such as public security, the local authority and the three state powers at the service of a paramilitary organisation. They are empowering the paramilitaries; perhaps not even the government is clear as to what it is creating, and this may get out of hand".[14]

With the new municipal presidents and the actions of the federal army, civil society and the EZLN are predicting a situation of war. In his last presentation of the year, *Subcomandante* Marcos, EZLN spokesperson, emphasised the signs of war and announced his withdrawal to the mountains.[15] This was why the last part of his journey throughout the country in October was cancelled, in the second year of his efforts to build a national political, unarmed, peaceful, civilian movement by means of "The Other Campaign", which links hundreds of resistance campaigns and rural and urban struggles throughout the country based around indigenous peoples.

Ten years ago, there was a significant national and international response. The response to the events of today is very small and the indigenous movements spent all year making efforts to strengthen their links with the country's indigenous organisations and achieve solidarity with the world's peoples.

2007, the year of indigenous meetings

The indigenous peoples of Mexico held 10 meetings throughout the year with indigenous peoples from different parts of the world, 3 round tables and a conference with peasant farmer leaders and international thinkers. The events were covered by the alternative media, plus some newspapers and radio stations.

Meetings between Zapatista peoples and the peoples of the world
The Zapatistas held three meetings in the administrative centres of their autonomous regions known as *"caracoles"*. At the first "Meeting of Zapatista peoples with the Peoples of the World", held in January with more than 2,000 participants from 47 countries in the *caracol* of Oventik, members of the Zapatista communities and their autonomous governments gave a detailed report of their progress, achievements

and the challenges facing them in terms of autonomous government, justice procurement, health, agro-ecology and education.

The Second Meeting was held in the *caracoles* of Oventik, La Garrucha and La Realidad with 2,335 participants from 43 countries. In addition to reports from the Zapatista grassroots, special emphasis was placed on alliances with other rural movements throughout the world that are involved in *La Vía Campesina* international network of peasant movements. This organisation sent representatives from the peasant movements of Brazil, Canada, Korea, USA, Honduras, India, Indonesia, the Basque Country, Dominican Republic and Thailand. In closing the meeting in La Realidad, *Comandante* Tacho said, "It is an honour to be with you who are working for, fighting and suffering the same injustices. We have the same enemy, international capitalism, which aims to strip us of our lands, destroying our cultures."[16]

At the Third Meeting, Zapatista women organised and ran the meeting, which was dedicated to the late *Comandanta* Ramona, in the *caracol* of La Garrucha, with almost 3,000 women attending from 32 countries. The involvement of women and the struggle for their rights has been a factor since the start of the Zapatista movement and, although they have a long path to follow, the meeting bore witness to the changes in the lives of the different generations of the movement's indigenous women.

Meeting of indigenous peoples of America in Vícam

For the First Meeting of Indigenous Peoples of America, organised by the Sixth Committee of the EZLN, the National Indigenous Congress (*Congreso Nacional Indígena* - CNI) and the Traditional Authorities of the Yaqui tribe, four preparatory meetings were held at the start of October in four of the country's regions. The issues discussed at these preparatory meetings were: 1. The capitalist war of conquest of America's peoples; 2. The resistance of the indigenous peoples of America and the defence of Mother Earth, our territories and our cultures; and 3. Why we indigenous peoples of America are fighting.

Participants faced difficulties with military patrols on the road to Vícam; this military harassment caused the delegation of Zapatista *comandantes* to return to Chiapas halfway. A day before the meeting, the families of Vícam were harassed by an antidrugs operation. Vícam is

one of the eight villages in Yaqui territory whose forests were the setting for the last indigenous uprisings during the dictatorship of Por-
firio Díaz in 1900. During this time, the Yaqui people was one of the
most harassed, persecuted, massacred and dispossessed people in the
so-called "national territory", and the situation ended with the mass
deportation of families and an invasion of their lands.

In Vícam, 1,500 participants listened to Yaqui history reflected in the
voices of representatives from the 59 indigenous peoples of America
present at the meeting. From Canada to Paraguay, they heard tales of
dispossession of their lands, their cultures, the destruction of nature, the
separation of peoples, the co-opting of traditional authorities in order to
get natural resource exploitation contracts signed without their peoples'
authorisation. The agreement between the Governor of Sonora and the
Vice-Governor of Nevada (US) on plans to build a coastal highway
crossing the Yaqui territory was condemned, as was the destruction of
the territory of Canadian indigenous peoples for the 2010 Olympics.

In Mexico, hundreds of delegates from 29 peoples denounced the
relentless pursuit of their lands and the effects of the PROCEDE programme[17] and its indigenous version, PROCEDECOM[18], along with
the Mexican government's concessions to foreign companies for resource exploitation, the ecotourism projects planned on their territories, the ecological reserves, the divisions promoted between their peoples through the co-opting of authorities and the strengthening of *caci-
quismo* (the rule of local chiefs or bosses – *caciques*).

The meeting was one of the most representative of the National
Indigenous Congress (*Congreso Nacional Indígena* - CNI) and this organisation was confirmed as the coordinating body for Mexico's indigenous movements. Likewise, organisations that were experiencing
conflict amongst themselves in their own state were able to meet each
other. This meeting demonstrated the unity and vision of the native
peoples through its final declaration of 14 October.

Social movement and natural resources in Oaxaca

In September, a Forum for the Defence of Water in Oaxaca (*Foro La
Defensa del Agua en Territorio Oaxaqueño*) was held in San Antonino Cas-

tillo Velasco, Oaxaca. This meeting condemned the mechanisms for privatisation of water introduced by the National Water Commission. The commission makes extension of their concessions to agricultural wells conditional upon the indigenous Zapotec communities of Valle de Oaxaca installing water meters. The Chontal communities, for their part, were opposed to their waters being handed out in concessions to the Coca Cola company and the parastatal corporation Petróleos Mexicanos. The Chatin and Mixtec communities were opposed to the construction of the "Paso de la Reyna" dam, which the Federal Electricity Commission is intending to build on the Verde River, on the Oaxaca coast. In addition, Zapotec communities from Sierra Juárez criticised and opposed the Environmental Services Payment programme being promoted by the Ministry for the Environment and Natural Resources as it eliminates the communities' power of decision over their lands and territories, it displaces peasant farmers from farming land and forces them to undertake activities of supposed conservation for payments of less than was agreed, without considering the communities.

The organisations and peoples that participated in the third Meeting of Peoples of the Isthmus in Defence of the Land (*Encuentro de los Pueblos del Istmo en Defensa de la Tierra*), held in September, demanded the suspension of all neoliberal projects planned for the region of the Tehuantepec Isthmus, Oaxaca. This includes as the expansion of the "Benito Juárez" dam in Jalapa del Marqués, where the government wants to build a hydroelectric power station, widen the roads and implement a multimodal system for the movement of goods, among other things, including cancellation of the wind power project. Electricity generation projects using wind power on more than 20,000 hectares belonging to Zapotec communities of the Tehuantepec Isthmus are being supported by the state and federal governments, and will benefit transnational companies such as Iberdrola, Eurus, Gamesa, Preneal, Endesa, Unión Fenosa and Waltmart, among others. The indigenous Zapotec and Zoque communities, however, are opposed to them, as they are being dispossessed of their lands on payment of a miserable annual rent and the promise of social works, and because the right and capacity of the indigenous peoples of this region (Zapotec, Zoque, Mixe and Huave) to follow their own ways of life, taking into account their cultures, customs and sustainable use of natural resources, are not being respected.

In October, inhabitants of the Zapotec community of Capulalpam de Méndez, in the Sierra Juárez region, blocked the road to Oaxaca in opposition to the operations of the "La Natividad" mine, now owned by the Canadian company Continuum Resources, due to the contamination of the waters of the Grande River, which affects fifteen communities in this region and has caused the disappearance of nine springs. The said company holds concessions of around 54,000 hectares for prospecting in this region, without the communities' consent. A month later, Cuicatec communities stated their opposition to the 50-year concession granted to the Minera Zapatapor company to work 3,500 hectares in Tepeuxila municipality.

In November, Zapotec communities from Sierra Juárez attending the Globalisation and Natural Resources of Sierra Juárez Forum (*Foro La Globalización y los Recursos Naturales de la Sierra Juárez*) indicated that one of the main problems affecting the indigenous communities was migration. The low price of agricultural products after 13 years of the North American Free Trade Agreement (NAFTA) has caused more than six million people to migrate to the United States, most of them indigenous.

In addition, the Oaxaca state government denied that it had been violating the human rights of members of the Popular Assembly of Oaxaca Peoples (*Asamblea Popular de los Pueblos de Oaxaca* - APPO), an organisation that has since 2006 been demanding the resignation of the State Governor, Ulises Ruiz Ortiz, and which has been subjected to violent repression on the part of the local, state and federal police, as well as paramilitary forces, causing around 20 deaths and hundreds of injuries, along with members tortured or unjustly imprisoned. Complete impunity has followed this repression, as the actions have not been investigated. This is encouraged by the complicity existing between the State Governor Ulises Ruiz and the federal government of Felipe Calderón.

During 2007, numerous reports and recommendations were published by well-known human rights organisations and international figures, documenting the violent repression of the Oaxaca population. The International Civilian Human Rights Observation Committee

(*Comisión Civil Internacional de Observación por los Derechos Humanos*)
visited Oaxaca in December 2006 and January 2007; Amnesty International, headed by its Secretary General, Irene Zubaida Khan, visited in
July. The President of the Inter-American Commission on Human
Rights, Florentín Meléndez, visited in August, along with Roberto Carretón from the International Commission of Jurists (ICJ) in July 2007.
The Office of the UN High Commissioner for Human Rights published
its report, noting failings in the ability of Mexico's indigenous peoples
to access justice, taking Oaxaca as a case study.[19] The UN Rapporteur
on indigenous rights confirmed that poverty and marginalisation continue to be the most pressing problems facing Mexico's indigenous
peoples, and urged Mexico to give constitutional status to the recently
approved UN Declaration on the Rights of Indigenous Peoples.

Following its brutal and indiscriminate repression at the end of
2006, the Oaxaca social movement lost its capacity to mobilise during
2007, and the state and federal governments made the most of this to
intimidate Oaxaca's social leaders, including indigenous leaders,
through further selective arrests, threats of arrest or death of activists
and/or their families, kidnappings and accusations of belonging to
guerrilla groups.

Guerrero and Veracruz

Poverty and abandonment have turned Guerrero state into a guerrilla
zone since the 1970s. This is where the Popular Revolutionary Army
(*Ejercito Popular Revolucionario* - EPR) has its base. This year, the EPR
set off bombs in a number of Petróleos Mexicanos refineries, demanding the release of its members arrested last year during the demonstrations in Oaxaca (see *The Indigenous World 2007*).[20] Condemning the
explosions, the president of the National Human Rights Commission
(*Comisión Nacional de Derechos Humanos* - CNDH), José Luís Soberanes,
recognised the need for an amnesty for all of the country's political
prisoners. Earlier in the year, the CNDH was discredited following its
ruling that malnutrition was the cause of death in the case of Ernestina
Ascencio, a 73-year-old indigenous peasant farmer who was found
dead following her rape by soldiers in Veracruz state. Sexual violence

and rape of indigenous women has been used increasingly against communities and organisations in Oaxaca, Atenco and Chiapas and denounced by civil and human rights organisations such as the Mexican Commission for the Defence and Promotion of Human Rights (*Comisión Mexicana de Defensa y Promoción de los Derechos Humanos*). ❑

Notes

1   The San Andrés Accords are agreements reached between the Zapatista Army of National Liberation and the Mexican government, at that time headed by President Ernesto Zedillo. The accords were signed on February 16, 1996, in San Andrés Larráinzar, Chiapas, and granted autonomy and special rights to the indigenous population of Mexico. President Zedillo and the Institutional Revolutionary Party (PRI) however, ignored the agreements and instead increased military presence with the political support of the other important political parties Democratic Revolution Party and National Action Party (PRD and PAN).
2   **Aragón Andrade, Orlando, 2007:** Los sistemas jurídicos indígenas frente al derecho estatal en México. Una defensa del pluralismo jurídico. *Boletín Mexicano de Derecho Comparado*, Nueva Serie, Año XL, Num. 118, Jan-April 2007, pp. 9-26
3   **Centro de Derechos Humanos Fray Bartolome de las Casas:** *Acteal a diez años: Recordar para no olvidar*. Reporte. Chiapas, Mexico
4   **Héctor Aguilar Camín, 2007:** Regresar a Acteal I, II y III, *Nexos* 358, 359 and 360 October, November and December 2007; and **Alejandro Rosas y Hugo Eric Flores Cervantes,** Acteal la otra injusticia, Centro de Investigación y Docencia Económica (unpublished).
5   Attorney General's Office. *El Libro Blanco de Acteal*. 1998; **Armando G. Tejeda, 2007:** Estoy triste por los 45 indígenas muertos, pero la PGR actuó con seriedad: Zedillo. *La Jornada*, 7 November 2007. See also *Cronología de los eventos previos a la masacre de Acteal*, at: http://zedillo.presidencia.gob.mx/pages/chiapas/docs/crono.html
6   From October to December the *La Jornada* newspaper published a series of articles "Acteal Ten Years on", quoting reports made of the events at that time.
7   **Bellinghausen, Hermann 2007:** Se agudizan 'de repente' los problemas por tierras en municipios autónomos de Chiapas, *La Jornada*, 16 February 2007.
8   After the 1994 uprising, it was calculated that 250,000 hectares were taken throughout Chiapas by peasant farmers. The lands taken by the Zapatistas are called "recovered lands".
9   The Ejido is the traditional Indian system of land tenure that combines communal ownership with individual use.
10 **IDMC:** *Evictions of indigenous communities fuel displacement in Chiapas*, Norwegian Refugee Council. Available at http://www.internal-displacement.org/8025708F004CE90B/(httpCountrySummaries)/867BEAEE33C91435C1257 3D80033BF2F?OpenDocument&count=10000

11 CAPISE's detailed reports can be found at http://enlinea.capise.org.mx/node/24

12 http://www.landaction.org/spip/spip.php?article221

13 http://www.fian.org/cases/letter-campaigns/mexico-dispossession-of-indigenous-lands-chiapas/preview_lc

14 Interview with Ernesto Ledesma Arronte, director of the Centre for Political Analysis and Social and Economic Research (*Centro de Análisis Político e Investigaciones Sociales y Económicas*), San Cristóbal de las Casas, 15 December 2007.

15 Subcomandante Insurgente Marcos. "Ni el Centro ni la Periferia Parte VII. Sentir el Rojo: el calendario de la geografía y la guerra". Speech given at the conference Planeta Tierra: Movimientos Antisistémicos, San Cristóbal de las Casas, 17 December 2007. Available at www.primercoloquiointernacionalandresaubry.org

16 Comandante Tacho, Closing Speech, La Realidad, Chiapas, 28 July 2007

17 Program of Certification of Parcel and Titling Rights of Urban Lands

18 Program of Certification of Communal Rights

19 **OHCHR**: *Diagnóstico sobre acceso a la justicia para los indígenas en México: estudio del caso en Oaxaca.* http://www.hchr.org.mx/documentos/informes/oaxaca/InformeDiagn%F3sticoJusticia.pdf

20 **Roig Francia, Manuel, 2007**: Rebels Say They Are Behind Pipeline Blasts in Mexico, *Washington Post*, 12 July 2007, A20. **Jorge Ramos y Silvia Otero, 2007**: Sabotaje de EPR a Pemex, *El Universal*, 11 July 2007

María Elena Martínez Torres is a lecturer/researcher at the Centro de Investigaciones y Estudios Superiores en Antropología Social (CIESAS) *South-east Unit and a member of the National System of Mexican Researchers.*

Rosaluz Pérez Espinosa is studying social sciences at the École des hautes études en sciences sociales *in Paris, and has supported the organisational process of different indigenous peoples in her native Mexico since 1995.*

Aldo González Rojas is Indigenous Rights Coordinator of the Union of Organisations of Sierra de Juárez (Unión de Organizaciones de la Sierra de Juárez - UNOJSO), *Oaxaca.*

GUATEMALA

Six million of Guatemala's inhabitants (60% of the country's population) self-identify as indigenous. They are divided among the following peoples: Achi', Akateco, Awakateco, Ch'orti', Chuj, Itza', Ixil, Jacalteco, Kaqchikel, K'iche', Mam, Mopan, Poqomam, Poqomchi', Q'anjob'al, Q'eqchi', Sakapulteco, Sipakapense, Tektiteko, Tz'utujil, Uspanteko, Xinka and Garifuna. The indigenous peoples inhabit all over the country, although the highest population is found in the west and north. Despite some progress, they continue to suffer the worst living conditions, the result of historic processes of exclusion and marginalisation that have characterised Guatemalan society, manifested primarily in racism towards and discrimination of indigenous peoples.

87% of poor people are indigenous and 24% live in extreme poverty; child malnutrition stands at 34% among indigenous peoples but 11% among non-indigenous; average primary schooling is 3.38 years among indigenous peoples and 5.47 years among non-indigenous, and 41.7% of the indigenous population are illiterate as compared to only 17.7% of the non-indigenous. Similarly, only 5% of the indigenous population have access to healthcare.

According to the Political Constitution of the Republic, the country considers itself to be multiethnic and multicultural.

The year began with the entry into force of a national policy that was approved at the end of 2006 to eradicate racism and discrimination.

The general elections for President of the Republic, parliament and the local authorities once more demonstrated how the depth of racism and discrimination forms a check on a society that is seeking to resolve

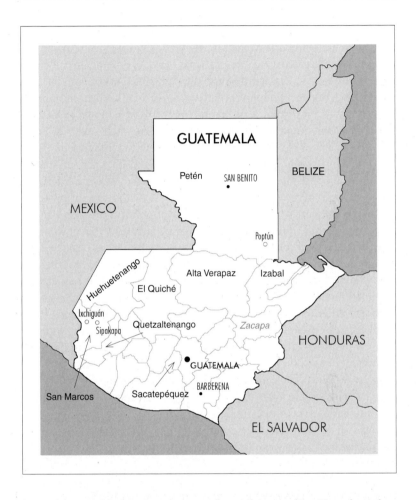

its serious problems of poverty and social inequality. Very few electoral manifestos focused on these problems and, instead, focused on addressing the violence and insecurity facing the country as a result of more than three decades of armed conflict (1962-1996), and as a consequence of a failure to respond to unemployment and the lack of opportunities for young people. After a costly and tense electoral campaign, the so-called "social democrat" option won, which was described by the international media as a triumph for the left.[1]

The fact that, for the first time in the country's history, an indigenous woman (Rigoberta Menchú, 1992 Nobel Peace Prize winner) ran for president created great expectations on one side, against a backdrop of the serious discrediting of political institutions of both left and right. The Winaq (People) political movement, which supported Menchú, was proposing a reconstruction of the Guatemalan state in order to make structural changes along a centre – left line. Although this proposal was initially well-received among the indigenous, peasant and rural organisations, it never managed to take off, partly through lack of resources but primarily due to the racist and defamatory campaign mounted by the country's mass media. One of the arguments put forward was the inadvisability of political proposals made by an indigenous identity base because they implied a risk of segregation. In fact, the most conservative sectors have tried at all costs to deny indigenous peoples recognition of their rights and, instead, continue to focus on an integration of all inhabitants in a nation that has neither ethnic differences nor attachments, and without significant changes in a power structure that is dominated by non-indigenous groups.

Although Menchú won no more than 3% of the vote, the foundations were at least laid for a more coherent and genuine indigenous involvement in the country's electoral processes, beyond the use of indigenous candidates and votes for the benefit of the country's dominant sectors. In fact, over the last four elections, it has been common for political parties to put indigenous leaders on their lists in order to attract voters, although they are usually placed some way down the list so that they have very little possibility of winning.

Indigenous participation in the electoral process

The indigenous turn-out was higher than in previous elections. It is estimated that 50% of those able to vote did so, primarily in the country's rural regions. The turnout was above the national average in 77 indigenous municipalities.[2] Analysts consider that this turn-out was decisive in the presidential result, whereby the winning candidate triumphed throughout the country with the exception of Guatemala City. This participation contrasts, however, with the scant representation achieved by indigenous peoples within parliament, as only 18 out of a total of 158 elected members are indigenous. In contrast, indigenous candidates for the local mayoral posts were successful in 129 out of 332 municipalities. These last figures show the clear strength of the indigenous movement at local level, although this is still far from extending to national level.

Turn-out among indigenous women increased in relation to previous elections, in part due to efforts made by women's organisations. Their representation in electoral posts was scant, however, as only 4 of the 19 women parliamentarians are indigenous and only 2 of the 8 women mayors.

As in previous elections, the indigenous organisations established an Indigenous Electoral Observation Mission with the aim of analysing how the electoral process was conducted in relation to indigenous populations. One of its main recommendations before the elections was the need for more information in indigenous languages, even the design of a ballot paper in these languages so that the population can have more information when voting. These recommendations were not taken up by the relevant authorities, however.

Despite having won the election with indigenous support, and despite including ethnic issues in its electoral discourse, the structure of the new government team did not include indigenous representatives in senior positions, indigenous individuals only being placed in middle-ranking posts. This does not augur well for the possibility of moving towards a more inclusive society.

Mining projects and consultation of indigenous peoples: unfinished business

There are currently 120 mineral exploration and exploitation licences approved by the government, most of them on indigenous territories in the north-west of the country. The indigenous communities affected by the expansion of mining, hydroelectric and agro-industrial projects on their territories have continued to raise their voices to the government authorities, not only because of the negative environmental and socio-economic effects on the communities but above all because they are in violation of the collective rights of indigenous peoples.

In more than 12 consultations organised by the communities and held throughout the year, the communities demonstrated their unanimous rejection of these projects. For example, on 13 June, the 42 communities of Ixchiguán municipality in San Marcos department gave an overwhelming NO to the establishment of open pit mining projects on their territory, due to the destruction and contamination of their water sources. Similarly, other consultation processes were held in communities in the departments of San Marcos, Huehuetenango, Quiché, Quetzaltenango, Zacapa, Izabal and Alta Verapaz, where mining projects were also rejected. The massive attendance of 46,000 people at the consultation conducted in Barrillas municipality, Huehuetenango department, rejected the imposition of projects and highlighted local concerns regarding mining projects.[3]

The results of these consultations were not taken into account by the government, claiming that they were of no legal validity, despite the fact that such consultations are provided for in the law that governs the functioning of the municipalities (Municipal Code), in the Constitution of the Republic and in ILO Convention 169, to which Guatemala is a signatory. Faced with a complaint of unconstitutionality lodged by lawyers of the mining companies against the community consultation held in Sipakapa municipality, San Marcos department, which established a ban on mining throughout the whole municipal territory, on 8 May the country's Constitutional Court ruled that the consultations were legal and legitimate and that they had to be considered as expressions of popular will and democratic participation. At the same time, however, it rejected the ban on mining in that municipality, given that the Constitution declares the technical and rational use of hydrocarbons, minerals and other non-renewable natural resources to be of public utility and necessity.

The indigenous organisations consider that by granting the mining concessions without consulting the communities, the state is not only in violation of the provisions of the country's Constitution and ILO Convention 169 but is also demonstrating a complete lack of respect for the local authorities, for municipal autonomy and for the people's rejection of this kind of activity.

One of the most significant cases was that of San Juan Sacatepéquez, a large territorial enclave of the Maya kaqchikel people where the country's largest cement company is trying to establish a production plant, for which it has received the government's backing. The local indigenous people are opposed to the factory because of the many environmental and social problems they believe it will entail and, at a community consultation held on 13 May, more than 8,000 people rejected it. The company subsequently unleashed a vast advertising campaign in the mass media in which it not only highlighted the importance and benefits of the investment but also attempted to discredit the indigenous opposition movement.

The recovery of indigenous territorial rights, an incipient issue

Approval of the Law on Land Registration and Information (in 2005) opened the door to a number of opportunities for indigenous organisations and related academic centres to commence efforts to defend indigenous rights to land and territories in the face of the land policies being promoted by the World Bank. An assessment was undertaken that demonstrated the importance and validity of the communal tenure system, particularly in the indigenous communities. It is necessary to have clear criteria with which to identify communal lands and recognise the historic rights of the communities over them. As a result of the indigenous organisations' proposals, the land registry office produced regulations for the measuring and titling of communal lands with the aim of ensuring recognition of ancestral rights to the land, particularly for indigenous peoples.

Despite these small steps in the right direction, however, there are still no administrative mechanisms to enforce recognition of communal and indigenous lands. On the contrary, indigenous communities expressed their fear in various fora that the land registry would legalise the dispossessions to which indigenous peoples throughout the whole country had been victim.

One case that set a legal precedent in this regard was the process of restitution of the titles and rights to land of the K'eqchi' indigenous community of Santa Cruz on the part of Poptún municipality, in Petén department. Despite the fact that this community had previously held the respective titles, under the influence of the military regime that governed the country during the internal armed conflict, the municipality appropriated the land and decided on its use. After five years of negotiations, and with the support of the Research and Projects Centre for Peace and Development (*Centro de Investigaciones y Proyectos para el Desarrollo y la Paz* - CEIDEPAZ) and the Ministry of Agrarian Affairs (SAA), the Santa Cruz community has managed to get its land titles returned, thus becoming the first indigenous community in the country to recover its lands from a municipality. This experience, unprecedented moreover, is both historic and instructive, in the sense that it shows the possibilities indigenous communities have of recovering lands taken from them by the local authorities, an action that was commonplace in the country from the end of the 19th century onwards. This case could also foster alliances between indigenous communities, civil society organisations, government bodies and cooperation agencies around the restitution of indigenous territorial rights.

Continental integration of indigenous peoples

In the last week of March, Guatemala's indigenous peoples hosted the 3rd Continental Summit of Indigenous Peoples and Nationalities, attended by representatives of indigenous organisations from all over the continent. The final declaration highlighted, among other things, the need to join forces in order to face up to the impulse of neoliberal policies, which are stripping the indigenous peoples of their lands and natural resources. The historic and ancestral right to territories and common assets was ratified, highlighting their inalienable, imprescriptible, non-seizable and non-transferable nature, and setting out a re-establishment of the national states, replacing the current mono-ethnic and mono-cultural structures with ones in which the indigenous peoples would have equality of conditions and opportunities with other peoples.

The Summit also stressed indigenous peoples' exercise of autonomy and self-determination, even without legal recognition of the nation states, and thus ratified its rejection of the free trade agreements given that they threaten the sovereignty of the peoples. Another aspect that was considered was the defence of food sovereignty and the fight against genetically modified crops. The construction of intercultural communication processes between peoples was also encouraged, with the aim of overcoming the isolation and fragmentation caused by European conquest and colonisation.

A warning was given with regard to the harm caused by the policies of large financial institutions such as the World Bank (WB), Inter-American Development Bank (IDB) or International Monetary Fund (IMF), illustrating this with examples of cases of dispossession and displacement suffered by indigenous peoples in the name of a supposed development that fragments and co-opts the autonomous and legitimate organisations of indigenous peoples and those of African descent.

Among its requests, the Summit called for a cancellation of the natural resource concessions in indigenous areas, an end to attacks on free movement and understanding between peoples, and an end to the use of indigenous peoples in armed activities.

Declaration on the Rights of Indigenous Peoples goes unnoticed

The approval of the Declaration on the Rights of Indigenous Peoples by the UN General Assembly on 13 September went virtually unnoticed by government bodies. A few indigenous organisations held activities to celebrate this momentous event but, generally, the declaration was given no analysis or publicity.

The country's mass media gave little coverage to the declaration at all although, according to analysts, Guatemalan legislation must be prepared to accommodate the changes that implementation of this declaration requires.

The International Day of Indigenous Peoples

"In Guatemala we have little to celebrate." With these words, the National Coordinating Body of Peasant Organisations (*Coordinadora Na-*

cional de Organizaciones Campesinas – CNOC) condemned the perpetuation of an exclusive state in which businessmen continue to accumulate wealth by exploiting the labour and natural resources of indigenous peoples. The absence of a land and rural development policy continues to favour a landholding minority that is opposed to any changes that would encourage recognition of indigenous rights.

Natural disasters, poverty, marginalisation and malnutrition thus continue to affect the indigenous population disproportionately, without there being any change in the priorities of a state that is accustomed to repression and neglect. Throughout the year, serious problems of hunger and malnutrition came to light in various indigenous communities, and only immediate and welfarist actions were mobilised in response, with no in-depth treatment of the issue that would address the problem of exclusion, which is at the root of these social injustices.

Indigenous children and youths, a dismal future

Given the socio-economic pressures weighing on families, indigenous children are pressured into taking badly paid work in order to contribute to the household. Many boys and girls are forced to abandon school and, often, their home, in order to make money to send to their parents. This practice not only encourages breakdown of the family and the social fabric whilst limiting young people's opportunities to study and overcome their circumstances but also entails risks to their physical integrity, as they are away from home. Statistics indicate that more than 500,000 indigenous children are forced to leave school and work in badly paid jobs far from their families.

Young people have found one of their main options to be international migration to the United States, albeit at a cost to their lives, because it is estimated that more than 200 young Guatemalans (at least half of them indigenous) die every year attempting to cross into this country.

In addition, the increasing number of deportations is increasing the risk that the families will not be able to recover the costly investment that migration signifies. This is why, although migration may mean an improvement in the lives of some families, albeit with the mentioned risks, for others it may mean total ruin and hence greater impoverishment. ❑

Notes

1 http://www.abc.es/hemeroteca/historico-06-11-2007/abc/Internacional/guatemala-gira-a-la-izquierda-con-el-triunfo-de-colom-en-las-presidenciales_1641295796008.html
2 http://www.miradorelectoral2007.org/documentos/informes/informe6.pdf? PHPSESSID=43b768e65777598c6741d2bc9fa29f7d
3 http://www.redmesoamericana.net/?q=node/630

Silvel Elías is an agronomist and lecturer at the San Carlos University in Guatemala. He is currently conducting research in Social Geography at the University of Toulouse-Le Mirail. He works as a researcher in the Latin American Faculty of Social Sciences (FLACSO) in Guatemala.

NICARAGUA

The seven indigenous peoples of Nicaragua live in two main regions: firstly, the Pacific Coast and Centre North of the country (or simply the Pacific), which is home to four indigenous peoples: the Chorotega (82,000), the Cacaopera or Matagalpa (97,500), the Ocanxiu (40,500) and the Nahoa or Náhuatl (19,000); and secondly, the Caribbean (or Atlantic) Coast where the Miskitu (150,000), the Sumu-Mayangna (27.000) and the Rama (2,000) live.[1] Other peoples enjoying collective rights in accordance with the Political Constitution of Nicaragua (1987) are those of African descent, who are known in national legislation by the name of ethnic communities. These include the Kriol or Afro-Caribbeans (43,000) and the Garifuna (2,000).

It is only in recent years that initiatives have been taken to establish regulations for and improve regional autonomy, such as the 1993 Languages Law; the 2003 General Health Law, which requires respect for community health models; Law 445 on the System of Communal Ownership of Indigenous Peoples and Ethnic Communities of the Autonomous Regions of the Atlantic Coast of Nicaragua and of the Bocay, Coco and Indio Maíz River Basins, which came into force at the start of 2003; and the 2006 General Education Law, which recognises a Regional Autonomous Education System (*Sistema Educativo Autonómico Regional - SEAR*).

The Sandinista National Liberation Front (*Frente Sandinista de Liberación Nacional -FSLN*) came to power in Nicaragua in 1979, soon after having to face an armed force supported by the United States. The indigenous peoples of the Caribbean Coast, particularly the Miskitu, formed a part of this force. In order to put an end to indigenous resistance, the FSLN created the Autonomous Regions of the North and South Atlantic (RAAN/RAAS)

in 1987, on the basis of a New Political Constitution and the Autonomy Law, 28). Three years later, the FSLN lost the national democratic elections in Nicaragua to the Constituent Liberal Party (*Partido Liberal Constituyente* - PLC) and an agriculture policy was implemented that promoted colonization and individual titling of indigenous territories, also commencing the establishment of protected areas over these territories, without consultation.

After winning the country's presidential elections for a second time in 2007, Daniel Ortega proposed establishing what he called

"Councils for People's Power" (*Consejos de Poder Ciudadano* - CPC) as the government's grassroots organisational structures. According to the Sandinista president, these councils are aimed at giving executive power to the people. For the opposition, however, they represent the long arm of the Sandinista National Liberation Front (*Frente Sandinista de Liberación Nacional* - FSLN). On top of this, they represent a risk to the democratic development of Nicaragua by sidelining existing spaces for civic participation and rolling back the few advances made in state institutionality. Unable to gain the votes necessary to pass his idea through the National Assembly, Ortega opted to implement it by Presidential Decree at the end of 2007, although a Supreme Court of Justice ruling has reduced the power of the CPCs to that of consultative bodies to the government. For the public, and the indigenous peoples in particular, this situation has led to confusion over the legitimacy of the CPCs and their own authorities, given that the way in which these councils' coordinators were selected followed neither traditional mechanisms nor a legally consolidated procedure. Consequently, in some cases, there are indigenous leaders who are fulfilling both the role of CPC coordinator and that of president of their indigenous territory and thus have to answer both to their community base and also to the national government. One of the first of the CPCs' initiatives within indigenous territories was to attempt to revive the forestry sector under the concept of community forestry without, however, revealing the initiative's source of funding or resolving the impossibility of marketing wood from indigenous territories that are protected areas, with no management plans.

As he took office, the main challenge facing Daniel Ortega in terms of indigenous affairs was that of implementing Atlantic Coast regional autonomy, granted by his own government some twenty years ago.

In an attempt to fulfil the commitments made to YATAMA, the political party of the indigenous Miskitu people, the Presidential Secretariat for the Atlantic Coast (SEPCA) was restructured to form the Secretariat for Atlantic Coast Development (*Secretaría para el Desarrollo de la Costa Atlántica* - SDC) during the 2006 national electoral process, with strong representation from the two autonomous regions. It has been established under the coordination of Comandante Lumberto Campbell and includes two historic Miskitu leaders: Brooklyn Rivera, a parliamentary representative, and Steadman Fagoth, who was appointed Director of the National Fisheries Institute, an extremely important economic sector for both Autonomous Regions. Similarly, for the first time, approximately 14 civil servants from the Autonomous Regions were appointed to senior executive posts. Whether this will promote further autonomy still remains to be seen.

Six months after the SDC was established, the "Nicaraguan Caribbean on the path to human development" plan was presented, focusing primarily on the demarcation, titling and defence of protected areas; the social sector (health, education and sports movements); development infrastructure (river transport, roads, airports and production access roads); renewable energy and water; and economic revival (food production and agroindustry, fishing, forestry and tourism).

Alongside these ad hoc initiatives, a working committee was established to reform the Autonomy Law (Law 28). YATAMA representatives were involved in this, together with mestizos from the mining triangle (Rosita-Bonanza-Siuna) and some Sumu-Mayangna, invited on a personal basis rather than as representatives. Given the controversy traditionally existing between the northern (RAAN) and southern (RAAS) regions, the absence from the committee of indigenous representatives from the RAAS was notable, particularly as the proposed reform considers turning the RAAN capital into the only capital in the future. In addition, a proposal has been made to change the name of the Atlantic Coast to that of the Caribbean Coast of Nicaragua, and to abolish the Regional Councils and replace them with a Regional Parliament with powers to draft and approve laws without these having to be debated by members of the National Assembly.

Although still at the design stage, these ideas for the political/administrative reorganisation of the RAAN and the RAAS may lead to discussions among various peoples on the restructuring and redistribution of political power at two levels: the urban municipal government and the indigenous territorial government. This will, where appropriate, be in application of the right to self-determination as envisaged in the recent UN Declaration, supported by Nicaragua. This proposal would also be in line with Nicaragua's Political Constitution (CPN), drawn up in 1987 during the Sandinista government's first period of office and which envisages two basic structures for the country's political/administrative organisation (CPN, Article 181). Paragraph IX of the Constitution is thus divided into two different sections: one on local councils, establishing the municipality as the basic unit of political/administrative division and the other on the Atlantic Coast communities, which are recognised the right to live and develop under forms of social organisation that are in line with their own traditions, with their own elected authorities and a special system of autonomy.

New legislative initiatives

The year commenced with the enactment of a new regulation on protected areas (Decree 01-2007), drafted by the previous government but published by the new President. Indigenous consultation on this proposal was conducted only with the Rama and Kriol Territorial Government (*Gobierno Territorial Rama y Kriol* - GTR-K), which made important observations as to the impossibility of recognising new titles in the protected areas. These observations were not taken into consideration, however. In the end, the GTR-K together with the indigenous and ethnic communities of the Laguna de Perlas basin had to lodge a constitutional challenge (*recurso de inconstitucionalidad*), primarily for failure to recognise rights established in the *sui generis* regime for their traditional lands on the Caribbean Coast. In this part of Nicaragua, these rights stem not from the state's granting of a property title but from constitutional recognition. Fortunately, the government amended the regulation in line with the provisions of Law 445, as requested by the indigenous people.

Another encouraging process is the draft Indigenous Law of the Pacific and Centre-North, which was introduced onto the National Assembly's agenda during 2006. Surprisingly, it received a positive verdict from the Commission for Ethnic Affairs and Indigenous Communities of the National Assembly (*Comisión de Asuntos Etnicos y Comunidades Indígenas*), in a decision taken but not published in 2006. With few observations and a recent openness towards Nicaragua's ratification of ILO Convention 169, at least in theory, this year has been spent considering the need to approve one or other of these legal instruments first, with little progress.

Among the new initiatives, the draft Coastal Law is noteworthy as this aims to nationalise lands throughout the whole country up to 200 metres from the tide line and hand responsibility for them over to the municipal councils. This is inconsistent with the process of titling indigenous lands and territories on the Atlantic Coast and the proposal is, moreover, unconstitutional in terms of indigenous rights. The GTR-K drew the attention of the committee responsible for the proposal to this, demanding a national consultation, which is now being conducted.

It has become fashionable throughout the whole Central American region to reorganize territory, land and natural resource administration. In Nicaragua, there is now a possibility of including indigenous and Afro-Caribbean lands as territorial entities on a par with the municipal authorities and also of recognising indigenous governments as territorial administrators within the official system. Various indigenous authorities put forward this possibility during a consultation in the National Assembly to which they had been invited. The current proposal promotes indigenous participation in territorial planning and administration only on an individual basis and through municipal councils, or as co-managers if their territories are also protected areas.

The process of demarcation and titling of indigenous and Afro-Caribbean territories

Conflicts still remain with regard to the ownership of indigenous lands in the Pacific and Centre-North of the country, as a consequence of authorities leasing land and issuing individual titles superimposed on collective indigenous lands without the power to do so. The internal conflicts caused by municipal validation of the wrong indigenous leadership are so serious that the indigenous community of Matagalpa had to request the intervention of the National Assembly's Ethnic Affairs Committee to resolve its disputes, which would otherwise have ended in a "blood-bath", they said.

In order to revive and complete the process of titling and demarcation based on Law 445, a very radical proposal was embarked on in the Atlantic Coast. Through the Secretariat for Development of the Atlantic Coast, it was proposed that the indigenous peoples and ethnic communities should recognise everything covered by Law 445 as a single title which, in fact, would have reconfigured the whole Caribbean Coast into the former Moskitia as it looked before this part of the country passed to the Nicaraguan state more than a century ago. The proposal was overwhelmingly rejected, however, except by the Miskitu themselves, with the argument that it would not resolve community and territorial jurisdictions and thus would not establish community control over natural resources, the main reason for implementing the law on community titling[2] in the first place.

Nevertheless, it did inspire the leaders of three territories, Tumarin Indígena, San Francisco and Desembocadura de Rio Grande, to sign an act of territorial unification entitled "Unity of the sons and daughters of Rio Grande" or "*Awal Tara Lupia Mairin Nani Aslakatanka*".

The first community property title (Mayangna Sauni As Territory) registered in 2006 on the basis of Law 445 ended up being cancelled due to irregularities in the titling process, including the transfer of indigenous property to the state. Later, in December of that year, the same title was again registered, along with four other Mayangna and Miskitu titles, all of which overlap with the Bosawas Biosphere Reserve. The issuing of the first valid titles after four years of existence of the law is undoubtedly an important step forward although the content of these titles still requires that all parts of the territories that overlap with the Biosphere's core area be jointly managed.

In accordance with its powers, the Commission for the Demarcation and Territorial Organisation of the Regional Autonomous Council of the North Atlantic (*Comisión de Demarcación y Ordenamiento Territorial del Consejo Regional Autónomo del Atlántico Norte* - CRAAN) issued a final decision on 15 February with regard to the border dispute between the symbolic Awas Tingni[3] Mayangna community and the Tasba Raya territorial block. Half of the area under dispute will be shared between the three Tasba Raya communities, with Awas Tingni receiving the other half (20,000 hectares). Along with the rest of the traditional territory it claims, this area will total 73,394 hectares. It is important to note that the area allocated to the Tasba Raya communities will exclude sites considered sacred by Awas Tingni. Just when the conflict seemed to have been settled, however, a problem arose with the Miskitu communities of the *Diez Communidades* territory, which is claiming to be the beneficiary of a real title covering the whole of the Awas Tingni community.

At its only working session of the year, the Intersectoral Commission for Demarcation and Titling of the RAAS (*Comisión Intersectorial de Demarcación y Titulación de la RAAS* - CIDT-RAAS) received a request to title the Rama and Kriol Territory, an area in which a large number of national infrastructure projects are planned. The request accompanied a long awaited technical-legal assessment which, in addition, envisages an innovative proposal for the co-existence of the indigenous population, Afro-Caribbean inhabitants and mestizo settlers in the territory. The Rama and Kriol territorial government aims to grant different types of titles to the mestizo population, depending on their place of occupation and proven behaviour.

International cooperation

Negotiations between the Nicaraguan government, international financial institutions and bilateral cooperation lasted several months in the hope of finding real strategies for poverty eradication in the country. After months of waiting, and still without a convincing strategy having been presented, the large financial institutions finally demonstrated once more that their interests in the country were too great for them to withdraw and so they prefer to remain, attempting to impose what little they now can through their loan and grant conditionalities.

However, Nicaragua's fourth largest bilateral donor, the Swedish cooperation agency SIDA, has finally decided to pull out gradually over the coming years (a decision apparently influenced by a lack of respect for human rights - and a Swedish requirement to reduce the number of countries in which it works). In addition, Germany was on the point of pulling out of its cooperation with Nicaragua, due to lack of government effectiveness. Indeed, if it were not for a commitment to civil society and, to a certain extent, to the indigenous peoples, it is highly probable that an even greater share of international donations and loans would have been cancelled.

Another issue, and one which partly explains the declining interest among traditional cooperation agencies, is that the Venezuelan government has been offering gifts (electricity generators to resolve the energy crisis, for example) on such attractive financial terms that other offers of cooperation melt into the background. In practice, not much has happened, but there are Venezuelan commitments to invest in the oil industry, with the construction of a refinery. Another oil-producing country and new donor committed to the Sandinista government is Iran, also interested in constructing oil infrastructure, in this case at Monkey Point in the Rama and Kriol Territory.

Changes in the indigenous movement's institutionality

The highest body of the Sumu-Mayangna nation, SUKAWALA,[4] seems to have ended a long-running dispute over its leadership. The conflict originally emerged a couple of years back following the irregular transfer of indigenous lands to the state in order to facilitate their titling process. Various assemblies were then held that were of limited legitimacy or representativeness, including one with a strongly partisan political leaning which, for a while, meant that there were as many as three parallel SUKAWALA boards in partial operation. Since the reconciliatory General Assembly held in December, we can now see that the communities' authorities and those of their nine Sumu-Mayangna territories are self-identifying as public legal subjects as provided by Law 445, and no longer as associations inappropriately covered by the civil code.

As an indicator of the success of recognition of the Chorotega indigenous identity, Ms Consuelo Rivera was elected president of the Indigenous Coalition in the Pacific and Centre-North (*Coalición Indígena en el Pacífico y el Centro-Norte*) and, instead of exacerbating a potential conflict with the Indigenous Movement of Nicaragua (*Movimiento Indígena de Nicaragua* - MIN) over leadership, the Coalition stated that it hoped to restructure and strengthen the MIN, recognising that unity could lead to the disappearance of the Coalition itself.

"Development" projects and natural resources

On 4 September 2007, Hurricane Felix, a maximum category 5 hurricane, hit the North Atlantic Coast. It hit first at Cayos Miskitos, where at least 300 fishermen and divers lost their lives, apparently due to a delay on the part of the National Disaster Prevention System (*Sistema Nacional de Prevención de Desastres* - SINAPRED) in issuing a red alert. Then the hurricane swept through the coastal community of Sandy Bay and, finally, now lessening in force, it affected 1.5 million hectares of forest to varying degrees, bringing down 10.7 million m³ of timber – all in indigenous territories.[5] The large volume of precious wood that came down has been devoted primarily to reconstructing houses but there is a real fear that the forests will be devoured by fire in the dry season, causing an uncontrollable inferno. A close link between YATA-MA membership and the beneficiaries of aid could be seen during the distribution of aid for emergency reconstruction. In addition, there has been a series of negotiations between the communities that own the forest resources and logging companies interested only in the precious wood. At the initiative of the Secretariat for Atlantic Coast Development, supported by a number of RAAN regional authorities, the year appeared to end with an initial agreement between a developmentalist company and the Miskitu authorities of the Tasba Pri territory to establish a joint limited company to make better use of the forest resources.

As a consequence of a constitutional challenge lodged against two contracts for oil exploration in the Caribbean signed by the Nicaraguan Energy Institute (*Instituto Nicaragüense de Energía* - INE), a consultation was conducted among the authorities of the Atlantic Coast regional governments. One of the companies, MKJ Exploraciones Internacionales S.A., managed to get its contract ratified while the other, Infinity Energy Resources Inc., was rejected because of the few social benefits it would bring and because of an alleged link between the company and the former president of Nicaragua, Arnoldo Alemán, who has been convicted of corruption charges.

Some regional councillors and territorial authorities are completely opposed to the oil activities due to the reported environmental risks they entail and because this activity was not submitted to a popular vote, as it was on the Caribbean side of neighbouring Costa Rica a few years back. As a result of this, oil activities were cancelled there, causing the industry to move to Nicaragua.

The indigenous peoples, for their part, have commenced a number of initiatives in the hope of finding a sustainable economic model for their development. The indigenous Nahoa de Sèbaco people are thus managing their collective lands via a transparent system of rental for national agricultural production, investing the income in university grants, indigenous health and bonds for the elderly.   ❑

Notes

1   Source: University of the Autonomous Regions of the Nicaraguan Caribbean Coast (URACCAN, 2000). Field studies undertaken jointly between URACCAN and the GTR-K 2005-2007, with funds from the Danish cooperation agency, DANIDA, as a contribution to the Rama and Kriol Territorial Assessment.
2   In fulfilment of a ruling of the Inter-American Court of Human Rights (IACHR, ·2001)
3   This is the ruling of the IACHR in 2001 on a forest concession in this community and against the State of Nicaragua, which led finally to the enactment of Law 445.
4   Sumu Kalpapakna Wahaini Lani
5   Source: Evaluación de Daños al Ecosistema Forestal Ocasionados por el Huracán Félix, Instituto Nacional Forestal (INAFOR), Gobierno Regional Autónomo Atlántico Norte (G-RAAN)

Claus Kjaerby has a Master's in International Development Studies and Civil Engineering. He is an indigenous affairs advisor to the Danish NGO Ibis in Central America. He has spent 11 years working as an advisor on processes of organisational development, joint management of protected areas, ecotourism and territorial management with indigenous peoples in the Amazon, the Andes and, more recently, on intercultural governance in Nicaragua.

PANAMA

The seven indigenous peoples of Panama are the Ngobe, Buglé, Bri-Bri and Naso in the western region, and the Kuna, Emberá and Wounaan in the eastern region. Together they total some 250,000 inhabitants, representing 8.4% of the national population. In constitutional terms, their right to indigenous territories is recognised in the form of indigenous *comarcas* (autonomous indigenous territories). There are currently only 5 recognised *comarcas*. In the case of the Naso, the Bri-Bri and part of the Emberá and Wounaan population, however, as well as two Kuna populations on the border with Colombia, the government is denying them legal recognition of their lands.

Despite the fact that the indigenous territories are home to a wealth of natural resources, there is alarming poverty among the indigenous population. This is shameful in a country that is characterized as having high levels of per capita income. Panama is listed as having the second worst distribution of income in the American region.

In terms of political participation, indigenous congresses are recognised as autonomous government entities and, through these, the indigenous people decide on internal regulations of all kinds. Indigenous involvement in central government bodies such as the executive, legislature or judiciary, however, is virtually nil.

Situation of the Indigenous Territories

The Constitution recognises indigenous peoples the collective right to their lands and territories. There are still indigenous peoples and communities who do not have this legal recognition, however, despite the corresponding legal and technical documents having been submitted and the necessary legislative procedures undertaken.

In 2007, the state embarked on a national coordination effort involving representatives of the indigenous peoples to discuss the autonomy of the indigenous *comarcas*.

The government and political party in power – the Revolutionary Democratic Party (*Partido Revolucionario Democrático* – PRD) – is refusing to discuss any law aimed at moving towards recognition of new indigenous territories, simply so that it can pave the way for projects that will be highly destructive to the indigenous peoples and their lands. Such is the case of the Naso, a highly vulnerable people with only 2,000 members, the Ngobe Bugle of Bocas del Toro, and the Embera, Wounaan and Kuna communities that live in the forests on the border with Colombia.

Territorial conflicts

The human rights situation of Panama's indigenous peoples deteriorated over the course of the year, communities were displaced, indigenous boys and girls imprisoned and territories destroyed.

The Naso indigenous people has called for approval of the law recognising their *comarca*. The government is opposed, however, because of the Bonyic hydroelectric power plant development. This dam will flood indigenous lands and destroy the land-based and aquatic animal and plant life associated with this indigenous people's traditional way of life. The Naso territory also coincides with the *Parque Internacional de la Amistad* (International Friendship Park) and the Palo Seco protected forest, both of which will be affected by the power station. The hydroelectric company began road construction in 2007, and the Naso tried to block them, with the result that more than 10 of their leaders were arrested for over 48 hours. The national government is also opposed to recognising Mr. Valentin Santana as King Naso and instead – against the people's will – supports Mr. Tito Santana, who - with the involvement of an indigenist NGO - illegally gave approval for construction of the power station, against his people's wishes.

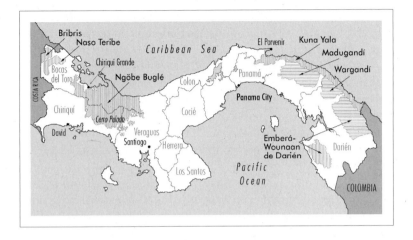

The Ngobe Bugle of the Valle de Risco and Esperanza communities, who live outside of the Ngobe *comarca*, are being displaced from their lands to make way for construction of the Chan 75, Chan 140 and Chan 220 hydroelectric power plants by the transnational company AES-Panama. These displacements are taking place by force, as in the case of Mr. Beker, an indigenous person whose house was destroyed. The Ngobe Bugle are suffering systematic violation of their human rights as they have not been duly consulted nor have they been permitted the right to prior, free and informed consent with regard to these projects. Some of the projects fall within the Clean Development Mechanism projects of the Kyoto Protocol.

In February 2007, there was a spillage of more than 5,000 barrels of oil in the Chiriqui Grande Bay which affected more than 50 indigenous communities who depend upon the sea for their survival. The waters were contaminated, thus affecting their health. The Petroterminal de Panamá company and other transnationals were responsible for this but they are refusing to compensate the indigenous communities.

The Embera and Wounaan living in Darién, who have no title to their lands, continue to be dispossessed of their lands and territories. The local authorities in the area are granting ownership rights over indigenous territories to non-indigenous farmers, causing the systematic seizure of their lands.

The situation of the indigenous *comarcas* is growing worse by the day, and includes violations of their autonomy and territories on the part of the government.

The Ngobe Bugle comarca is being affected by mining and tourism. In relation to mining, the state has granted a concession to the transnational company Aurum Exploration Inc. in the area of Cerro Pelado. The indigenous communities have protested very strongly as the Panamanian government did not obtain their prior, free and informed consent for this project. Moreover, there has been opposition in the Ño kribo sector of this comarca to the contract with the transnational Damani Beach S.A, signed by some of the region's indigenous leaders who are accused of failing to comply with the comarca's indigenous legislation and the need for the prior, free and informed consent of the Ngobe Bugle General Congress.

The Embera and Wounaan *comarca* is indirectly suffering from the instability in neighbouring Colombia. Complaints of human rights violations against the indigenous communities on the part of border police fail to get heard due to indigenous people's lack of access to the Panamanian judicial system. Moreover, indigenous people seeking refuge in Panama because of the armed conflict are given no humanitarian aid and are deported back to Colombia.

There are three Kuna *comarcas* recognised by law. The Kuna Yala *comarca* is calling for its territory to be extended by more than 7,000 hectares. This relates to an area known as Santa Isabel, which the communities own traditionally but which falls outside the limits of the currently legally recognised *comarca*. The Kuna Congress has lodged the relevant complaints but the government, while meeting with the indigenous people to find a supposed solution to the issue, continues to recognise private third party property titles over these lands. There are transnational companies who, taking advantage of the conflict between the government and the Kuna, are promoting the sale of the indigenous lands at conflict on North American and European markets.

In the case of the Kuna de Madungandi *comarca*, the violation of their human rights has now become intolerable. As in previous years, farmers are continuing to invade the *comarca*'s lands with the government's complicity, citing conditions of need, despite the fact that the Kuna de Madungandi Congress has made administrative and judicial complaints. Because of a supposed legal technicality, there is no authority that can enforce their rights and, despite the fact that the Congress is calling for the urgent appointment of an administrative authority in the *comarca*, the government has refused to do this, leaving the indigenous people legally defenceless and thus allowing their lands to be invaded. In October, the indigenous people of Madungandi held a peaceful protest on their territories but were suppressed by the National Police. The police used rubber bullets and tear gas, affecting women and children, and illegally arrested more than 100 indigenous people. ❑

Hector Huertas *is a Kuna lawyer. He has been involved for more than 20 years in negotiating laws on behalf of Panama's indigenous peoples and participating in international processes within the United Nations and the Organisation of American States.*

SOUTH AMERICA

SURINAME

The indigenous Amerindian and Maroon people living in Suriname's southern rainforest region (the Interior) are facing the most destructive period in their history. The Amerindian people are descendents of the original inhabitants of the Amazon. Maroons are descendents of African slaves who escaped from coastal plantations, fought a war of liberation, and today live in the rainforest far removed from the areas that are economically developed. Six culturally distinct groups of Maroons [Ndyuka (Aukaner), Saramaka, Paramaka, Aluku (Boni), Kwinti and Matawai], and four Amerindian groups (Wayana, Carib, Arowaks and Trio) live in more than 50 riverside villages. Suriname's interior region covers an area of approximately 24,000 km^2. This region constitutes about 80% of the Surinamese land area and is home to a population of approximately 50,000 people, indigenous and tribal, representing 8% of the population. Amerindian and Maroon communities rely on subsistence agriculture, hunting and fishing. Maroons, having a tradition of trade with the Dutch coastal colony, are more integrated into the cash economy than are indigenous communities.

On 28 November 2007, the Inter-American Court of Human Rights (IACHR) issued a ruling in the case of the Saramaka people versus the government of Suriname. Although the IACHR decision recognized the inextricable relationship between the land, including all of its natural resources, and the economic, social and cultural survival of indigenous and tribal peoples, it made it clear that international law subordinates tribal and indigenous land rights to the national community. In exchange for indigenous and tribal land conceded for economic development, the state must therefore consult the affected commu-

nities in the development planning process and they must receive reasonable benefits from the developments on their territory. The IACHR decision awarded the Saramaka people just US$75,000 for material damages from logging and mining concessions within their territory.

Three indigenous communities, Pikin Poika, Holandsecamp and Maho were predominantly in the press in 2007 because the Suriname government had conceded their traditional lands to third parties. In Pikin Poika, the Ministry of National Resources (NH) gave more than 500 hectares of land to Stichting De Eenheid, a private investment group, to develop an art and ecotourism resort. In 2007, De Eenheid erected a fence around their concession, running right through the village of Pikin Poika, and began the construction of an eco-resort. In a statement given to the Suriname Indigenous Health Fund, one woman from Pikin Poika claimed that her home had been burned and her garden destroyed while she was in the capital receiving medical treatment because it was on the De Eenheid concession. In a public meeting, community members stated that they had been cut off from homes, gardens and the land they depend on to live.[1]

Holandsecamp faces a government plan to move the village in order to accommodate the expansion of the Johan Adolf Pengel international airport. Village leaders stated that they had been fighting to gain title of their lands for 30 years. In 2007, they were informed of the planned airport expansion, which will permanently remove them from their traditional lands.

At Maho, a concession was awarded to Stichting Moshiro, a private investment group granted land by the Ministry of Environmental Planning, Land and Forest Management (RGB). Villagers in Maho staged a hunger strike in protest, gaining national attention, and this led to heightened tensions and fears of violence

Because all land in the interior of Suriname is considered to be the property of the government (domain land), the primary laws currently in place - known as the L-Decrees - as far as possible give the indigenous people "entitlements" to their villages and agricultural plots, unless there is a conflict with Surinam's general interest. The major problem with the L-Decrees is that the entitlements only apply to their villages and the current agricultural plots and do not account for their wider territories and other lands occupied and used for hunting, fishing and other subsistence and cultural activities.

Mining in West Suriname

In 2007, in cooperation with the Association of Indigenous Village Leaders in Suriname (VIDS), the North South Institute, a policy research charity based in Canada, issued a report in response to the BHP Billiton and Suralco joint bauxite venture, Bakhuys, in West Suriname. The concession in question covers 2,800 km^2 of primary forest, from which an expected annual production of 3.2 million tons of alumina will be extracted over 40 years.

This report states that the companies' actions have not met their own policy guidelines with regard to assessing impacts at all stages of the mining cycle. No Environmental and Social Impact Assessment

(ESIA) was conducted for advanced exploration. Affected communities were not included at the earliest stages of the ESIA, being excluded from the mine site scoping stage. The traditional rights of indigenous communities were not respected and the companies refused to negotiate. The companies argued that there was no legislative framework in Suriname that obliged them to abide by their own policy to respect indigenous rights.

The report urges the companies to study the environmental and social impacts of the exploration already suffered by the indigenous and tribal communities in question, and compensate them through good faith negotiations. It further demands that the companies cease advanced exploration until they have first explored ESIAs with the affected communities, including legally binding agreements to compensate communities for impacts on livelihoods.[2]

Land development policies cause public health crisis

The Maroon communities of Kwakoegron, Comisaris Kondre and Maki Kriki, all less than ten kilometers downstream from Cambior's IAM gold mine, have complained to the government of Suriname that they do not have access to clean water due to mining activities. The lack of clean water is causing acute diarrhea in children. The large-scale gold-mining operation periodically releases cyanide into the Saramaka River, the only source of drinking water during the dry season (August – October). Small-scale alluvial gold mining concessions, which mine sediments directly in the river, release mercury into the water. Mercury methylization leads to fish contamination, and fish are the primary source of protein for these communities. Two dredgers, or houseboats designed for the purposes of gleaning gold from river sediments, are in operation in the area. Dredging further leads to sedimentation and the accumulation of bacteria in the water. In the statements collected by the Suriname Indigenous Health Fund in November 2007, community members blamed the Ministry of Natural Resources, which has stated that the village is too far away to deliver clean water. Community members state that the river is not usable for drinking, dishwashing, bathing or fishing. The school and clinic that serve these three communities do not have adequate water to function properly.

Inter American Development Bank's Suriname Land Management Project cancelled

According to Annette Bettina, Natural Resource Specialist at the Inter-American Development Bank (IDB), the IDB Suriname Land Management Program (SLMP) was discontinued in 2007.[3] Since the project to strengthen the Ministry of Environmental Planning and Forest Management (RGB) was linked to preparation of the SLMP, this was also canceled. However, the RGB and the IDB's Project for the Sustainable Development of the Interior (SU-T1026) is continuing.

The Sustainable Development of the Interior Project (SDIP), initiated in April 2007, is poised to take up the goals of the discontinued SLMP. The stated aim of the SLMP was to replace the traditional land tenure system in Amerindian and Maroon areas with an "active market system for land". An assumption underlying this open land market is that it will provide equal access to land to all market competitors, with anyone able to buy or lease at the market rate. Maroon and Amerindian peoples are at a gross disadvantage in this model, since they do not enjoy legal rights to their traditional lands and they do not have the financial or social capital to compete on the open market. The discontinuing of the SLMP therefore benefits indigenous and Maroon peoples. The implementation of the SDIP could, however, have similarly negative consequences for interior peoples.

The SDIP aims to identify which lands in the interior are currently in use using GPS technology. This information will then form the basis on which to create legislation to clarify land ownership. An assumption underlying these goals is that there is some portion of the interior that is not currently in use. Suriname's resource-rich region is inhabited by people who live in and use the forest resources for food, shelter, medicines and cultural rites. There is no region that is not inhabited. Via capacity building, the SDIP aims to bring all stakeholders under the control of the bank, with the government, traditional authorities, local organizations and NGOs being trained in project management and loan application processes. An assumption underlying these goals is that all interior peoples wish to "develop", or become a part of the cash economy under the bank's supervision. Until now, the forest peoples of the interior have enjoyed self rule. Now, the aim of the SDIP is to replace self-rule with legislation defining the functions of tribal leadership, and to centralize authority under the central government.

The New Front, the current coalition government of Suriname, created the Ministry of Environmental Planning, Land and Forest Management (RGB) in order to allocate land resources along the lines of a neo-liberal program. Prior to this, the Ministry of National Resource had managed land policy. The Minister of the RGB, Michael Jong Tjien Fa, is currently the object of criticism with regard to corrupt practices. Parliamentarian Jiwan Sital has accused Tjien Fa of demanding large sums of money from individuals who are applying for domain lands. In December 2007, he argued before Parliament that more than 100 people had been the victims of the RGB's corruption. Based on these accusations, the Chairman of the National Democratic Party (NDP), Desi Bouterse, called on President Ronald Venetiaan to close down the RGB and return the state's land policy to the Ministry of Natural Resources (NH). The RGB is responsible for conceding traditionally held tribal and indigenous lands to third parties.

Interior villages are dependent upon their traditional lands for hunting, fishing, farming, medicines, shelter and daily necessities. As traditional lands are being taken away by the government, indigenous and tribal people are not given access to alternative sources of their basic necessities. Although current development practices tout an assimilationist model, indigenous and tribal people are, in fact, disenfranchised from the development process, and are not compensated for their losses with access to the benefits of the developed world.

Village leaders state that there is an urgent need for health services, education, transport and access to information because communities are unable to "assimilate" if they are not given the opportunity to replace their traditional practices with Western ones. Policies are being adopted, laws enacted and land conceded without village knowledge. Not only are forest peoples not consulted with regard to current development practices but they do not have an opportunity to participate in the process and, as a result, do not give their consent.

Notes and Sources

1   In collaboration with the University of Washington, Pudget Sound Partners for
    Global Health and Eclectic Reals, the Suriname Indigenous Health Fund gath-
    ered this testimony between November 2007 and January 2008.
2   **Weitzner V., 2007**: *Determining our Future, Asserting our Rights: Indigenous Peoples
    and Mining in West Suriname.* North-South Institute and the Association of In-
    digenous Village Leaders in Suriname. Paramaribo, Suriname. www.nsi-ins.ca
    Last accessed January 2008.
3   In collaboration with the University of Washington, Pudget Sound Partners for
    Global Health and Eclectic Reals, the Suriname Indigenous Health Fund gath-
    ered this testimony between November 2007 and January 2008.

Daniel Peplow is an eco-toxicologist and an affiliate Professor at the University of Washington Department of Forestry.

Sarah Augustine is a sociologist and grassroots organizer. Together, they run
the Suriname Indigenous Health Fund.

COLOMBIA

According to the official 2005 census,[1] there are eighty-seven indigenous peoples identified in Colombia, speaking sixty-four different languages and totalling 1.4 million people, or 3.4% of Colombia's total population. The country's indigenous organisations state that there are ninety-two indigenous peoples.[2] The most numerous are, in order of size, the Wayúu with around 300,000 members; the Nasa or Paez with 210,000; the Embera with around 100,000; and the Pasto with 80,000.

The vast majority live in the country's rural areas. They live across more than 30% of the Colombian territory and, to date, have obtained legal recognition of some 31 million hectares of land (310,000 km²). The map of indigenous territories largely overlaps with the areas of activity of armed groups which, since the early 1960s, have been pursuing an internal war. This has led to serious crisis among these peoples, especially in the Amazonian region.

The 1991 Political Constitution establishes that: "The State recognises and protects the ethnic and cultural diversity of the Colombian Nation". It also recognises the indigenous territories as territorial entities of the Republic. Since then, wide-ranging legislation has been promulgated but this has not, however, prevented the continuing loss of - and threats to - the indigenous territories.

Two contradictory political dynamics marked the events of 2007 in Colombia's indigenous world. On the one hand, the further dismantling of the rights gained by indigenous peoples over the last 40 years and, on the other, the revival of indigenous action to recover land and territories. This political tension was expressed in contradictory terms within the indigenous organisations: the continuing decline of the indigenous political parties in terms of their share of the vote in local elections, the formal breakdown in dialogue between the indigenous organisations and the government, and the absence of any in-depth consideration of the problems of the indigenous movement by the indigenous representative organizations are all indicative of the growing distance between the grassroots dynamics and their political expressions.

This backwards step has taken place despite a growing disenchantment with the government and its coalition parties, compromised by their links with extreme right paramilitaries and drugs trafficking. During 2007, around 40 parliamentarians allied to President Uribe, along with other government officials, were prosecuted for having made criminal alliances and undertaken criminal activities in order to ensure their election. And they were all people who had promoted constitutional change so that the president could be re-elected in 2006. The indigenous organisations have called for a purge of the government.

The pincer-like hold on information existing in the country, which has promoted a rightwards drift in public opinion, the fierce unity of businessmen and the traditional political parties around an alliance between financial capital and the large landowners, the unconditional support of the US government, the large-scale use of public resources to expand a clientilist base that in turn feeds on drugs money, and the systematic use of terror have all prevented this scandal from resulting in the fall of the government, as would have been the case in any other country.

Regulatory downgrading in relation to indigenous peoples

The signing of the Free Trade Agreement (FTA) with the United States

The signing of the Agreement in 2006 required its subsequent ratification by the Congress of the Republic in 2007. As the Democrat majority in the US Congress was opposed to approving the FTA, arguing systematic violations of the human rights of union members in Colombia and a lack of environmental safeguards, Bush unilaterally - and with-

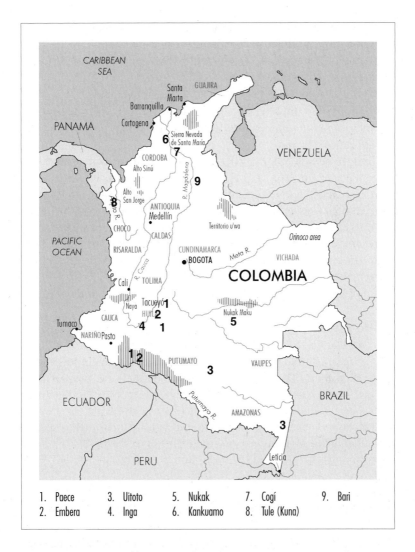

| 1. | Paece | 3. | Uitoto | 5. | Nukak | 7. | Cogí | 9. | Bari |
| 2. | Embera | 4. | Inga | 6. | Kankuamo | 8. | Tule (Kuna) | | |

out bilateral renegotiation with Colombia - incorporated new requirements into the Agreement in order to respond to his critics. As a result,
and fully aware of what it was doing, the Colombian government
processed an FTA text that was different to the one that was to be approved in the US, and submissively accepted all the new US require-

ments, leaving the door open for further unilateral changes. The pro-government majority in the Colombian Congress ratified the process, which not only represents a serious threat to sovereignty but was also blatantly unconstitutional.

And yet even the US Democrat Party's demands, stated in new letters of understanding that were subsequently signed, did not preserve the interests of the indigenous and Afro-Colombian peoples or rural communities. The most sensitive issues for the indigenous movement continue to be: a failure to protect their food security; the privatisation of intellectual property and application of patents to medicines, genetic resources, living beings, plants and animals; ratification of the International Convention for the Protection of New Varieties of Plants (UPOV); a lack of protection from environmental effects, including to their water; the non recognition of their territorial rights and indigenous authorities; a lack of protection for social participation and the control of public services; geographic designations for registering brands and the use of genetically modified organisms in the farming sector.

Alongside this, the government and Congress approved Legislative Act (change to the Constitution) No. 11 of 2007, which reduces public treasury funds to local administrative bodies, including indigenous *resguardos*.[3] This decrease will have a particular impact on those regions where both poverty and the indigenous population are greatest, especially the municipalities of the Colombian Pacific.

The government has indicated that it will insist on further actions to dismantle the legislative gains made during the 1990s. The Ministry of Agriculture is preparing to re-submit a new General Forest Law, which was previously declared unconstitutional because of a lack of prior consultation with the indigenous peoples. This new initiative that does not *formally* affect indigenous peoples although it is well-known that a large part of the forests they are hoping to turn over to the logging industry are to be found on the territories of indigenous and Afro-Colombian peoples. This will be accompanied by the submission of bills on the highland plateaux and on waters, the emphasis of which is on privatisation of resources by means of concessions; these resources are legally dissociated from the territory so that they can be transferred. The indigenous peoples' *coup de grâce* will be the ongoing processing of the draft "Organic Law on Territorial Organisation" that has been instigated by senators sympathetic to the government, and in which indigenous territorial rights will again remain unprotected.

The National Development Plan and revival of the large infrastructure projects

Such backward-looking proposals also materialised in the National Development Plan 2006-2010 (in effect since 2007). The Plan focuses on opening up the country to large investment, through an exhaustive inventory of the subsoil and an expansion of mining potential. The plan is to incorporate vast areas of territory into the market by expanding the agricultural frontier and increasing physical (transport, water, energy) and telecommunications infrastructure. These objectives are linked to the so-called Internal Agenda, which prioritises the extension of infrastructure, unprecedentedly fast energy production and legal security for investors.

The National Development Plan and Internal Agenda mean that the proposal for hydrocarbons is to inventory up to 450,000 km^2 by 2010 and 800,000 by 2019, almost 70% of the country's area and covering virtually all of the indigenous territories. To do this, the intention is to increase annual contracts with oil companies to 30 and to conduct 32,000 kms of seismic exploration. They hope to achieve a production objective of 475,000 barrels of crude oil and 1,000 million cubic feet of gas per day. The mining proposals are no less serious: 12,000 km^2 of geological exploration, 12,000 of chemical exploration and 90,000 of geophysical exploration, increasing the area under contract by 50% and producing 100 million tons of minerals per year. This is a most aggressive extractivist policy, the main backdrop to which will be the indigenous territories.

These two aims were widely applied in the indigenous territories throughout 2007. The Ministry of Mines held an auction for mining titles, most of which were allocated to the transnational company Kedahda, whose involvement in indigenous Andean areas began to affect dozens of communities of the Embera people in Antioquia, Risaralda, Caldas and Chocó; the same multinational has submitted requests for mining exploration and exploitation in Tolima, Huila and Vichada departments, which will directly or indirectly affect no less than 2 million hectares. In terms of oil, the areas allocated to seismic exploration cover almost 10 million hectares. Worthy of special note is the contract with Reliance Industries Limited for two areas of exploration in the Pacific: 804,000 hectares in all, covering virtually the whole of the indigenous territories of the Embera people of Chocó.

The Development Plan also finds expression in the Initiative for Integration of South American Infrastructure (*Iniciativa de Integración de Infraestructuras de Suramérica* – IIRSA). Of the 30 large projects being carried out in the country, 22 will be executed on indigenous territories. This includes the channelling and privatisation of the Meta and Putumayo rivers, the construction of more than 2,000 kms of roads across indigenous territories, the establishment of militarised border crossings in *resguardos* and implementation of the Archimedes Project, which aims to establish a waterway of more than 1,000 kms in the mangroves of the Pacific and connect it with the Atrato-Truandó Canal, which has been planned on several occasions. All these projects would mean a fundamental territorial and environmental breakdown for indigenous peoples.

Rural Development Statute

But by far the most serious regulatory and political blow to indigenous organisations in the last 40 years is the Rural Development Statute (Law 1152 of 2007). This is the culmination of a process of dismantling the legislative achievements gained by indigenous peoples throughout the 1990s that began with the imposition of the Mining Code in 2001. It also dismantles the territorial gains consolidated over the last three decades of indigenous struggle. It has been characterised as "the son of para-politics" as it was negotiated under the auspices of congressmen who are in prison or being investigated for their links with paramilitary groups.

The Statute's articles express the political project of landowners linked to the right-wing paramilitary groups and drugs traffickers. One of the most serious issues is the *legalization of fraudulent deeds*. A title, even if not issued by the appropriate authority, is considered valid if more than five years old, even if the land was taken by illicit or criminal means, something that is commonplace in Colombia. The State Comptroller recognises that more than 4 million hectares have been violently occupied by such groups. The "legalisation" of these titles means that former landowners whose supposed rights were denied in the processes of titling the *resguardos* in the 1980s and 90s because of their illegal or uncertain origin will now be able to claim that their deeds are valid and undertake actions to violate the territorial rights acquired by the indigenous peoples.

In order to guarantee such violations, the Statute was *approved illegally and unconstitutionally*: the agrarian reform bill promoted by the agrarian and indigenous organisations alongside the government initiative was not considered as the Constitution demands; there was no discussion of the amendments and alternative proposals made by the social agro-organisations in the Chamber of Representatives and there was no prior consultation with the indigenous peoples. The Vice-minister of Agriculture argued that consultation was not a requirement for legislative procedures and that it could even be conducted after a law had been approved in Congress; the government thus convened the Indigenous Territories Commission, the official body for discussing land issues with the indigenous organisations, in May 2007, when consideration of the bill was drawing to a close. The sole aim was to explain (and not to agree or consult) the content of the draft Law on the Rural Development Statute and thus to legitimise it, with which the indigenous committee members walked out of the meeting.

In particular, the content of the new Rural Statute wipes out all progress made with regard to the titling of indigenous peoples' lands and is in clear violation of the provisions of ILO Convention 169 (which has constitutional status in Colombia) relating to territorial rights. It expressly *prohibits forming or extending resguardos* in the whole Pacific Coast, an area of almost 3 million hectares with a high indigenous and presence and environmental value, as well as in "other areas of the country presenting similar conditions" to the Pacific. With this, the fundamental rights of the Wounáan, Embera, Eperara, Tule and Awáon peoples are openly ignored; and a cover is provided for the illegal process of allocation of the lands of Afro-Colombians, indigenous peoples and peasant farmers to the transnationals and paramilitaries that is being implemented by the government through enterprise development zones and the legalisation of fabricated deeds.

Another regulation *violently infringes the territorial rights of nomadic and semi-nomadic indigenous peoples*. Against all logic and in clear bad faith, it considers that these peoples must be *regular and permanently* settled (sic) in order to obtain the right to title to their lands, changing the expression "traditionally used" that appears in ILO Convention 169. This is a direct blow to the Nükák and other semi-nomadic and itinerant horticultural peoples such as the Yurí and Caraballos of Puré River in Amazonas department, the Yuhup and the Cacua in Vaupés and Amazonas, or the so-called Guahibos peoples, such as the Sikuani, Tsiripu, Wamonae, Yamaleros and Wayaberos, who have been forcibly settled but are claiming an itinerant territoriality across the whole Orinoco savannah.

The Statute also *criminalises legitimate actions of occupation and ownership*. It becomes a criminal offence for the legitimate owner to use his right to defend his ancestral property, as recognised in ILO Convention 169. The issue relates not only to future land titles and current situations but also to an historical and legal assessment of the past.

One fundamental step backwards is that the Statute's focus includes indigenous peoples within the concept of "ethnic minorities", in contradiction to the Political Constitution. The use of this term has political, legal and psychological consequences. By using the term "minority" the government is trying to impose projects on the indigenous territories that will damage the environment and the territorial integrity of indigenous peoples, arguing - as it has done repeatedly - that they are in the interests of the "majority".[4]

It can clearly be seen from the above assessment that the Rural Statute is dealing a serious blow to the rights of indigenous peoples. All the *resguardos* and collective territories established by Incora (the Colombian Institute for Agrarian Reform) and Incoder (the Colombian Institute for Rural Development) may suffer reductions due to fabricated deeds; their establishment and expansion will need to be in line with the POTs and will be prohibited on the Pacific Coast; five centuries of resistance will be criminalized. The degradation of indigenous territorial rights is absolutely clear, as is the flagrant violation of ILO

Convention 169 and the recommendations of the UN Committee on Economic, Social and Cultural Rights. The Statute does not stand up to the most minimal scrutiny in the light of the UN Declaration on the Rights of Indigenous Peoples.

The government's policy in relation to spaces for national and international consultation

Not by chance was the Colombian government the only Latin American government to abstain in the vote on the UN Declaration on the rights of indigenous peoples and, along with United States, Australia, Canada, New Zealand and Russia, to try to change its content with regard to issues as basic as self-determination, lands and territories, historic reparation and restitution, military presence on indigenous territories and so on. The government's public argument with which it justified its position was that there was a contradiction between the Declaration and domestic law.

The Colombian government's position within the UN was the trigger for virtually all spaces for consultation between the state and indigenous peoples - de facto or de jure - to suspend their operations. Once the Colombian government's vote in the UN became known, indigenous delegates to the National Committee for Consultation with Indigenous Peoples (Mesa Nacional de Concertación con los Pueblos Indígenas) unanimously suspended their participation, making their return conditional upon the state adopting the Declaration as legislation, which seems unlikely. In the National Indigenous Peoples' Human Rights Commission (Comisión Nacional de Derechos Humanos de los Pueblos Indígenas), the indigenous representatives refused to participate in the formulation of a National Human Rights Action Plan – promoted by the European states – as they considered that the Uribe government was giving no opportunity for any consultation in good faith. The same was the case in the National Commission for Indigenous Territories (Comisión Nacional de Territorios Indígenas),[5] organised by the national government to undertake the Prior Consultation to the draft Rural Development Statute in May 2007. As elsewhere, the government had initially refused to conduct this consultation, arguing that it was not compulsory. Then, under indigenous pressure, it convened the indigenous delegates, who later walked out of the Commission after condemning the fact that the law was already virtually approved in Congress and that the aim of the meeting was merely to legitimate a *fait accompli*.

Liberation of Mother Earth

The government's systematic policy of territorial aggression against indigenous peoples led the indigenous organisations to approve wide-ranging political action, in the context of what has been called the Liberation of Mother Earth, a concept born of the peoples of Cauca. At the same time as reclaiming the indigenous peoples' right to their territories, this states that life and natural heritage cannot be appropriated. The electoral campaign for local government that took place during 2007 and in which the indigenous peoples traditionally participate, the disagreements between some regional organisations and the National Indigenous Organisation of Colombia (*Organización Nacional Indígena de Colombia* – ONIC) in terms of establishing their appropriate involvement, meant that this protest did not have the necessary strength with which to overturn the Rural Development Statute. Even so, on two occasions over the course of the year, marches of condemnation and protest were undertaken from the indigenous territories to Bogota. The main one took place in June 2007 and culminated in the holding of an "Indigenous Parliament" at the seat of Congress, at which the indigenous peoples declared they would show civil disobedience of the Rural Development Statute.

This decision had an acid test at the end of the year, when the indigenous people began a day of recovering land from landowners in Cauca department.

Around 10,000 indigenous people were involved in recovering their ancestral lands and another 90,000 were ready to mobilise as of the end of December. The government's response was violence and harassment; in particular, the then governor of the department, Juan José Chaux Mosquera, now ambassador to Holland, used all institutional and communicational means to link the indigenous protest with the armed uprising. On 25 November, he publicly stated that the protest in Cauca was the work of criminals and indicated that the Jacobo Arenas guerrilla column of the Revolutionary Armed Forces of Colombia (FARC) was behind it. The security forces entered the communities with tanks, they arrested indigenous leaders without warrants in their houses, fired tear gas directly into the faces of the demonstrators, sent low-flying helicopters over schools and destroyed indigenous cultural centres. On 29 November, the official forces fired on the sheriff of the Town Council of Tacueyó, Lorenzo Largo Dagua, at point-blank range, leaving him in a coma and finally resulting in his death on 14 December. The situation remained tense until the end of the year and, during 2008, the indigenous people intend to intensify their Liberation of Mother Earth.

The actions in Cauca were accompanied by occupations of ancestral lands in other departments: in Tolima, where the Pijao have remained in a number of communities despite eviction orders from judges, and Caldas, despite pressure on the Chamí people from drugs traffickers. In addition, complaints and legal actions from the indigenous Wiwa, Kankuamo, Ijka and Kogi were revived in relation to the construction of the Ranchería and Besotes dams in the Sierra Nevada de Santa Marta, along with protests against mining in Antioquia on the part of the Embera. All these actions have taken place in the midst of severe military and paramilitary aggression. Although the number of acts of political violence has fallen, it continues to be a serious matter: in 2007, there were almost 190 cases, of which 143 were attributable to the public security forces, while the insurgency was responsible for 11 murders; in all, 36 indigenous people were murdered and 33 disappeared.

The Awá people of Nariño on the Pacific coast have been particularly badly affected. The transfer of large coca crops from the Amazonian foothills to the Pacific plains has, in turn, caused regular and irregular armed forces to move into the region, which has now become the main theatre for military operations to control the traffic in cocaine. In addition, the Belém do Pará – Tumaco roadworks are concentrated in this region, causing inflationary effects in economic and military terms. The result has been disastrous for the region's indigenous peoples: a *de facto* occupation of the indigenous territory on the part of armed players, a massive new displacement towards Ecuador on the part of around a thousand indigenous people, caused by bombing on the part of the state security forces, and at least 8 leaders and community members killed by the insurgency, a figure similar to that of 2006 when those primarily responsible were not identified. These violations have a huge impact on a people of only 17,000.

Local elections and the ONIC Congress

2007 was a year of local elections. As is often the case in these situations, there was a split within the indigenous movement between parties with an indigenous base and the traditional parties. The difference this year was the enrolment of large sectors of the indigenous movement in the *Polo Democrático Alternativo* (Alternative Democratic Pole), a recently established party of the centre-left. Nevertheless, the relevant phenomena were, once more, a concentration of indigenous votes in the Andes between the *Alianza Social Indígena* (ASI) and *Autoridades Indígenas de Colombia* (AICO), and greater links to the traditional parties – including those of the governing right-wing coalition – in the Amazon/Orinoco region. There was growing support among indigenous peoples in the Andean region, however, for the parties of the right. Various indigenous organisations and leaders at the time criticised the fact that these right-wing indigenous parties had adopted a general practice of supporting candidates from sectors that were in open contradiction to indigenous interests and that they had established alliances with parties close to President Uribe. The result of this erratic strategy and electoral dispersion was an ostensible decline in the indigenous vote and in indigenous representation on the legislative and council bodies, along with the election of officials who support the signing of the FTA and megaprojects on indigenous territories, overturning the movement's points of consensus as a whole.

The result in Cauca department went against the national trend, due to the state of permanent protest throughout the whole year. There the number of mayors elected with links to the community process increased.

The reflections and position of the regional and national indigenous organisations has taken another direction with regard to the situation of territorial dismantling. As noted, the indigenous organisations withdrew from all spaces for national consultation in 2007. In addition, they adopted consensus positions towards the government and its policies including, in particular, opposition to the Law on Justice and Peace, which gives free rein to impunity for paramilitary groups - responsible for most of the crimes against indigenous peoples.

ONIC's Congress, held in December 2007, was the main scenario for a reflection on a series of public policies aimed at indigenous peoples. Two issues interested the delegates in particular: the acute territorial problem and the growing regulatory threats to indigenous rights. As a result of the debate on these issues, the need for the indigenous peoples to rise up and continue the Liberation of Mother Earth was reiterated. Practical decisions with regard to this general uprising of indigenous peoples have yet to be taken, however.

Secondly, the exercise of autonomy and self-determination, in line with positions that had been maturing over the course of the year. The main expression of this was a call for civil disobedience and *de facto* application of the agrarian reform. As a path for the exercise of autonomy, ONIC's leaders particularly endorsed the initiative to transform the national organisation into a body of "own government" – the Council of Government – which would negotiate directly with the state on an equal footing, in the context of a reform that includes establishing an indigenous parliament and a National Council for Indigenous Justice. The significance of these transformations required the Congress to adopt a period of time for their implementation, the implications of which have not yet been fully discussed by the communities and local authorities. The main implication is undoubtedly their real capacity to exercise territorial control in the face of the armed players, to respond effectively to the state and its regulations and to neutralise the invasive presence of the large transnational companies. No less important, however, is the resulting relationship between a nascent national indigenous authority and the peoples' authorities that have not relinquished their positions as legitimate spokespersons, the implementers of own justice and territorial control. 2008 thus looks set to be

a year rich in theoretical and political discussions between indigenous
organisations, and a year of fierce protest.   ❑

Notes

1 República de Colombia. Departamento Administrativo Nacional de Estadística.
  October 2006. More information can also be found at www.dane.gov.co
2 The official 2005 census indicates that there are 87 indigenous peoples.
3 *Resguardos* is a legal concept that legalises the ownership of indigenous peoples
  over their ancestral territories. It is a private collective title that recognises the
  inalienable, imprescriptible and non-seizable nature of the lands.
4 The indigenous people had already indicated in the National Constituent Assembly that it was an incorrect classification, given that it referred to a popula-
  tion-territory correlation, and in the departments of Chocó, Guajira, San Andrés
  y Providencia, Vaupés, Guainía, Amazonas (with the exception of the municipal
  capital of Leticia) and Vichada (with the exception of the urban area of Puerto
  Carreño), and in the majority of territories where they are based, the Afro-Colombian and indigenous peoples form a majority. The same is the case throughout the Pacific Coast area, in Cauca department (if you exclude Popayán municipality) and in many of the countries' municipalities, such as Riosucio (Caldas), San Andrés de Sotavento (Córdoba) and several in Nariño.
5 The Committee for Consultation, the Territories Commission and the Human
  Rights Commission are consultation bodies created by decrees 1387 and 1396
  dated 1996, as a result of a huge indigenous protest.

*Juan Houghton is a researcher with the Centro de Cooperación al Indígena,
CECOIN, a research body of the Organización Indígena de Antioquia. He is
co-editor of the journal Etnias & Política, which is published by the Observatorio Indígena de Políticas Públicas y Derechos Étnicos. Since 1995, he has
been an advisor to the Organización Nacional Indígena de Colombia, ONIC,
to the Cabildos Mayores Embera Katío del Alto Sinú I, and to the Organización Regional Indígena del Casanare, ORIC. He is co-author of the book "Vio-
lencia política contra los pueblos indígenas de Colombia 1974- 2004", published by IWGIA-CECOIN in 2005.*

VENEZUELA

Venezuela is a multicultural country that recognises and guarantees the existence of its indigenous peoples and communities. The indigenous peoples in Venezuela are the Baniva, Baré, Cubeo, Jivi, Hoti, Kurripaco, Piapoco, Puinave, Sáliva, Sanemá, Wotjuja, Yanomami, Warekena, Yabarana, Yekuana, Mako, Ñengatú, Kariña, Cumanagoto, Pumé, Kumba, Urak, Akawayo, Arawako, Eñepa, Pemón, Sape, Wanai, Warao, Chaima, Wayuu, Añu, Bari, Yukpa, Japreria, Ayaman, Inga, Amorura, Timotocuicas and Guanono. Of the 26 million inhabitants in the country, 2.2% are indigenous.

The rights of indigenous peoples are enshrined in the 1999 National Constitution. Venezuela has also signed ILO Convention 169.

One of the most striking phenomena within the Venezuelan indigenous movement has been the gradual transformation of its character. The new Venezuelan legal framework (1999 Constitution) laid the basis for substantially increased indigenous involvement in national politics. There are currently three indigenous representatives in parliament (the National Assembly), along with a number of indigenous mayors and one governor. There are also numerous indigenous individuals holding decision-making power within ministries and in the military high command. In addition, a Ministry was created for indigenous peoples in January 2007. Alongside this, however, the organised indigenous movement has become weaker and the splits within it seem to be growing deeper. For example, the impossibility of reaching agreement meant that during 2006 there were two political groups claiming to be the National Indian Council of Venezuela (*Consejo Nacional Indio de Venezuela* - CONIVE), the national indigenous organisation.

A large part of the indigenous movement has changed its militant attitude of demanding rights from the government to one of implementing that same government's policies. The consequence of this change in profile is that the strategies used by indigenous peoples to promote their demands now differ from those of some years back when they were faced with difficulties in implementing their rights or the government's political opposition to those rights.

An increased indigenous involvement in state bodies, on the one hand, along with the fear of being associated with or manipulated by the opposition parties, on the other, rules out or minimises attempts to confront the government full on. The presence of indigenous individuals in the government also encourages strategies of "change from within", without challenging the President's political project. The government has moreover enlisted various leaders who have a greater tradition in and more experience of the indigenous movement, into its ranks, leaving the indigenous movement weakened while strengthening its negotiating power with the indigenous organisations.

In summary, although indigenous interests now have more representatives within government, this transformation is still emerging as a way of disarming or co-opting the indigenous movement, particularly when the government's stance is contrary to indigenous interests. The possible conflict of interests between the indigenous communities and peoples and the national government can be seen more clearly in the shape of the Ministry for Indigenous Peoples and in the person of the current minister (a Yekuana from the Upper Orinoco). Who does this ministry represent: the government or the indigenous peoples? What position does this institution take in relation to a conflict of interests between the indigenous organisations and the government?

A less structural and more welfarist trend can also be seen within the Ministry of Popular Power for Indigenous Peoples (*Ministerio del Poder Popular para los Pueblos Indígenas*) in its attitude towards public policies. The "achievements" announced by the Ministry for Indigenous Peoples range from the distribution of bags of food to visits to "highly vulnerable indigenous communities in order to... deliver food, clothes, hammocks, mosquito nets, along with inputs and materials for productive work... medical, dental, food, hygiene, school and productive care...".[1]

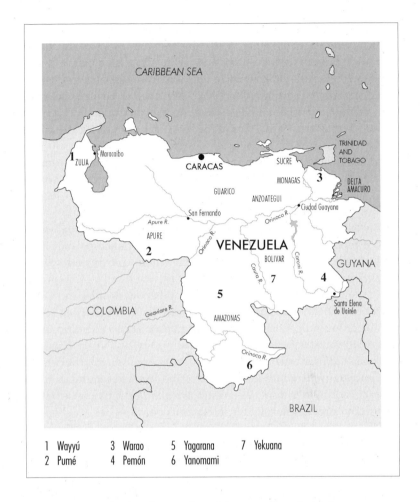

1 Wayyú	3 Warao	5 Yagarana	7 Yekuana
2 Pumé	4 Pemón	6 Yanomami	

There is undoubtedly a political interest in prioritizing care to a population group that has been historically considered as abandoned and highly vulnerable. Nonetheless, the choices for this care, often used to mitigate the severity of poverty among urban populations, are proving highly damaging to many indigenous communities, which are demanding or require structural policies aimed at achieving greater equality. We are talking of real transformations in the education system, for example, where there could be the possibility of indigenous peoples studying the ethnography of the white world, for example, as a cross-cutting issue. In other words, understanding it in its due measure, being taught the conceptual and technical tools necessary to understand it. Formal and informal education processes, both theoretical and practical, that encourage, extol and safeguard indigenous peoples' own traditions without underestimating the importance of serious educational processes, adapted to the social, linguistic and cultural reality.

There is an urgent need for an in-depth debate on alternative forms of sustainable development from a cultural, social, economic and environmental perspective for people who are crying out for the right to territory.

The absence of political training and of appropriate and high-level school processes, combined with welfarist-type public policies, will undoubtedly lead to more cultural and economic poverty among indigenous people.

Moreover, the draft Organic Law on Indigenous Peoples and Communities (LOPCI), formulated and presented by the Ministry of Popular Power for Indigenous Peoples, continues to attract attention. Various indigenous organisations that form part of CONIVE[2] (Consejo Nacional Indio de Venezuela) rejected its proposals, such as the change in terminology from indigenous habitat and lands to communal territories. In addition, it aims to abolish the legitimate and representative indigenous organisations of the indigenous peoples.

The Law is in contradiction to all of President Chávez' political proposals and the Bolivarian Constitution itself. It simply shows an immense confusion on the part of the staff of the Ministry for indigenous affairs.

Territory

In August 2007, 11 titles were issued to the Kariña communities of Anzoátegui (3), the Pumé communities of Apure (3), the Warao communities of Monagas (4) and the Cumanagoto communities of Anzoátegui (1).

None of these lands corresponds to the demarcation of the land of an entire indigenous people or group of peoples. This is despite the fact that there are plans for complete self-demarcations, such as that of the Yekuana-Sanema people of Bolívar and the Yekuana people of the Upper Orinoco. Given that the lands recognised have been relatively small in size and linked to requests from a community or group of communities, they are reminiscent of the provisional land titles once issued by the National Agrarian Institute (*Instituto Agrario Nacional - IAN*) on the basis of the 1961 agrarian reform. Whether they draw inspiration from the IAN titles or not, this kind of land recognition would seem once more to force indigenous communities and peoples onto a par with peasant communities, something thought to have been a thing of the past in Venezuela.

The standard title that has been issued to the above mentioned communities envisages recognition of the habitat, of the native rights to ancestral and traditionally occupied lands and of collective land ownership. It also envisages the inalienable, imprescriptible, unmortgageable and non-transferable nature of the lands and that the exploitation and use of the minerals and subsoil resources owned by the state shall be undertaken without damaging the cultural, social and economic integrity of the Indigenous Community.

In addition, it defines the boundaries and location of the lands in relation to the geographical administrative divisions (parishes, municipalities, etc.), it establishes that the Plans for Organisation and Regulation of Protected Natural Areas of Special Use shall regulate the use of the lands until such time as they are redrafted together with the indigenous peoples and communities, and it states that the legitimately acquired rights of third parties within the demarcated area shall be exercised in accordance with the law and "in a framework of respect for the habits and customs, world vision, values and spirituality of this indigenous community". Lastly, it commits the communities to promoting ethno-development and requires them to guarantee environmental conservation.

In fact, after the first lands were handed over in 2005, the different social ministries (e.g. health, education, housing etc.) were encouraged to send committees to define their contributions to the endogenous development projects that the communities with recently demarcated lands were going to propose. The content of the land titles and the establishment of this policy seem to suggest that, at some stage, they were hoping to promote the indigenous communities as exponents of the economic model of "endogenous development" being promoted by the national government as an alternative to the capitalist economic development model.

The climate of the demarcation process and a lack of political will

Problems of coordination between government bodies, a lack of clarity in the rules and a lack of funding have affected all the demarcation processes.

A weakening of the indigenous peoples and their non-indigenous allies can be perceived in the face of what, for some time, has begun to be interpreted as a lack of real political will to demarcate indigenous lands and habitats on the part of the National Executive.

There are various interpretations of this lack of will. Particular cases of indigenous leaders or communities who "misinterpret" the meaning of collective ownership of lands or who have been seen to be involved in cases of inappropriate resource use in protected areas (e.g. negotiation of logging permits) have often been cited. The increase in number and intensity of disputes between indigenous peoples and communities over land demarcation is also mentioned. The confusion of indigenous leaders' personal interests with the collective interests of defending rights is also given as a reason. All these perceptions of a supposed lack of indigenous capacity - whether in political terms, territorial management terms or in their understanding of the legal framework – have dissuaded the different government players responsible for territorial demarcation, affecting their efforts to make the indigenous peoples' constitutional rights to land a reality.

There also seems to be a lack of conviction among some key government players as to the appropriateness of demarcating lands. The weight of the "ownership" concept, combined with the idea of "handing over a lot of land to a few Indians" seems to make its mark, even among some whose job it is to promote demarcation. This lack of con-

viction even seems to stretch to the President, who is said to be uncon-
vinced of the virtues of demarcating large continuous stretches of land
(despite the fact that there is a constitutional mandate for this).

The demarcation proposal submitted by the Kuyajani organisation
for several million hectares corresponding to the Caura basin in Bolívar state seems to be the strongest evidence in favour of this interpretation. Different sources consulted agree that the proposal of the Yekuana-Sanema of Bolívar fulfils all legal requirements for demarcation; it
had the approval of the Ministry for the Environment but was rejected
by the President. In fact, the President had already previously publicly
stated that it was not possible to "hand over" large areas of land in
Bolívar as this would raise a problem of national sovereignty. For some,
this was an obstacle not only to the Yekuana-Sanema proposal but to
all national-level demarcation processes, by presidential order.

The last theory is that of a contradiction of the objectives of Latin
American development and integration projects and the demarcation
of certain indigenous lands, as may be the case of the Wayuu and Bari
lands in Zulia, which form the basis of the gas pipeline project to Colombia and hydrocarbon exploitation.

Current state of the demarcation processes

Given all of the above, it is difficult to assess the future of the demarcation processes in Venezuela. As of July 2007, the atmosphere was one
of "a paralysed process". However, a few months later, the Ministry of
the Environment seemed to have once more taken up some processes
with renewed interest. A large group of professionals (anthropologists,
lawyers) has been contracted to work on the land demarcations, and
priority has been given to ensuring a synergy with the National Strategic Plan for Defence, Development and Consolidation of the South
(PENDDCS) in the states of Apure, Amazonas, Bolívar and Delta Ama-
curo. The demarcation of the Yanomami in the Upper Orinoco has, in
particular, been prioritised and the plan is to establish a team from the
Ministry of the Environment in Upper Orinoco municipality at the end
of the year in order to take the process forward. It is difficult to interpret this new impetus against the backdrop of a political framework

that is unfavourable to the demarcation of large ethnic territories. There will, in any case, be a need to continue working to reverse the current political situation and to ensure that the technical work is ready for such time as when the political environment may be favourable to the demarcation of large continuous lands.   ❏

Notes

1 Taken from the document "Logros obtenidos por el Ministerio del Poder Popu-
   lar para los Pueblos Indígenas dentro de la defensa de los derechos constituci-
   onales indígenas", published by the Ministry of Popular Power for Indigenous
   Peoples.
2 Organización Regional de los Pueblos Indígenas de Amazonas (ORPIA)
   Confederación Indígena Bolivariana de Amazonas (COIBA)
   Federación de Indígenas del estado Bolívar (FIEB)
   Organización Indígena de la Cuenca del Caura (KUYUJANI)
   Unión de Comunidades Indígenas Warao (UCIW)
   Organización de Pueblos Indígenas de Anzoátegui (OPIA)
   CONIVE Sucre

*José Antonio Kelly is an anthropologist and member of the NGO Watani-
ba's governing board. This article was originally written for an assessment
conducted by Wataniba and the CCPY, with the support of Rainforest Norway.*

ECUADOR

There are 14 native or indigenous nations in Ecuador totalling approximately one million people.[1] In 1998, following intense pressure from the indigenous organisations, they managed to achieve constitutional recognition of the "pluricultural and multiethnic" nature of the country. In addition, in that same year, following protests from the indigenous movement, ILO Convention 169 was ratified by the National Congress.

Although almost a decade has passed since this framework of rights was guaranteed to indigenous peoples by the Ecuadorian state, these rights and the recognition of diversity are still not being enforced for lack of enabling legislation that would make their full implementation possible.

The mobilisation capacity of the Ecuadorian Confederation of Indigenous Nationalities (CONAIE) deteriorated following the presidential elections at the end of 2006, which saw Rafael Correa Delgado from the *Alianza País* (Country Alliance) movement - a coalition of social democratic and left-wing parties - elected.

This deterioration could be put down to a number of factors: the failed alliance initially proposed to the indigenous Pachakutik movement by Correa's Alianza País; the growing discontent among some of CONAIE's grassroots organisations, which chose to support Correa in the presidential elections; and the inward-looking focus of some other indigenous organisations, as explained by Delfín Tenesaca, president of the Chimborazo Indigenous Movement (MICH), which is affiliated to Ecuarunari:

The time came to turn back to our relationship with the grassroots and revive it. We have organised workshops and assemblies at which we dis-

cussed the situation of each second-level and provincial organisation. We have seen the need to make changes and adjustments that will enable us to consolidate and once more become the strong organisation that we were.[2]

The *Alianza País* government and popular expectations

Rafael Correa won the second round of the presidential elections with approximately 3.6 million votes. This also signified a third consecutive defeat for the banana tycoon, Álvaro Noboa, who obtained 43.3% of the vote. As the academic Alejandro Moreano commented: "It is an historic triumph because it offers the possibility of embarking on a new path to a recovery of sovereignty and South American integration".

Correa inherited two decades of structural adjustment policies, along with the enormous impact this has had on inequality within the country; a political and institutional system weakened by corruption and in need of urgent reform; and a vulnerable economy dependent upon market fluctuations in the prices of oil and agro-export crops such as bananas and flowers.

Correa has made his mark on some areas of national policy-making, including a greater state role in the economy and natural resource exploitation. Against an international backdrop of increasing crude oil prices, the government's policy is focused on obtaining more resources for the state and, specifically, for social programmes. Correa thus issued a presidential decree establishing that 99% of the windfall profits obtained by oil companies operating in the country would go to the state coffers and 1% to the companies.[3] The decree did not amend established contracts and the government subsequently explained how they would be renegotiated. "There is no room for negotiating the 99/1 and we call on the companies to migrate from the participation contract to the service provision contract. The state isn't trying to take anything from the companies. The Oxy company is acting irresponsibly by suggesting that Ecuador is confiscating assets when all it is doing is applying the law," stated Galo Chiriboga, Minister for Energy.

At the same time, the government has prioritised social policies targeting the most vulnerable rural and urban groups who have been affected by the negative impacts of adjustment policies. It has increased social investment by 15%, doubled the so-called "Human Development Benefit" for families on low incomes and in extreme poverty, and increased the "Living Benefit" for those same people by 100%.

The Ecuadorian economy is now the eighth largest in Latin America, after Brazil, Mexico, Argentina, Chile, Colombia, Venezuela and Peru. It also has one of the most unequal distributions of wealth on the continent, however. The richest 20% of the population hold 54.3% of the wealth and 91% of productive lands. At the other end of the scale, the poorest 20% have access to scarcely 4.2% of the wealth and only own 0.1% of the land. In other words, although Correa's government is focusing on achieving a level of economic stability, the bases of this are undeniably weak and it is therefore being forced through.

The government's social initiatives - increased welfare benefits, particularly for basic services, a credit programme for small-scale farmers and states of emergency declared in health and education - along with the decision to close the US military base in Manta and to shun involvement in the so-called "Plan Colombia",[4] have resulted in great support for the government and its policies. As of December 2007, the president commanded an average 75% popularity across the country.[5]

Another area of government action has focused on political reform of the state and this has taken place by means of a popular consultation around establishing a National Constituent Assembly.

The challenge is to re-organise the neoliberal development model, which has been seriously challenged throughout the whole region. The Constituent Assembly has thus, since November 2007, emerged as a way of facilitating a legal restructuring of the state's institutions, as demanded by a majority of the people.

However, relations between Correa's government, the Constituent Assembly – where the pro-government block has an 80% majority – and the social organisations are tinged with fear given the uncertainty among both poor (sceptical about any real possibilities) and rich (facing a future different to the confusing and muddy "state of affairs in which some flourished more than others, some lived in the shadow of others", as the writer Javier Ponce put it).

In this context, the indigenous organisations – headed by CONAIE – appear to be wrapped up in a dynamic of internal restructuring, amidst fierce regional conflicts resulting from expanding extraction projects, particularly in the Amazon region.

Conflicts, human rights and frustrated expectations

One of Correa's announcements that surprised the country's indigenous organisations was the proposal to leave oil from the country's largest heavy crude oil fields untouched in exchange for annual compensation of US$350 million. This is known as the "Yasuní ITT" initiative, an initiative sponsored by environmental groups when this oil field was discovered in the country's most important protected area, the Yasuní National Park and ancestral territory of the Waorani nation.

It must be recalled that, through the state company Petroecuador, the state had been promoting the so-called "Tiputini" project from 1983 up until 2004. This exploratory programme verified a total of 947 million barrels of crude oil. Exploitation of these wells was to take around 25 years and include options of building a refinery and a crude oil improvement plant, along with thermo-electric generation.[6]

According to *Alianza País* assembly member, Mónica Chuji, "The government's initiative must not be seen or considered in isolation, as a unique case, as this runs the risk of creating misunderstandings and disagreements, particularly given the reality of the Ecuadorian Amazon and the rights of peoples and nationalities". This statement is in line with that made by the Confederation of Indigenous Nationalities of the Ecuadorian Amazon (CONFENIAE) through its president, Domingo Ankuash, who expressed his reservations with regard to the government initiative thus: "It has to be considered as part of a wider, more integrated policy aimed at protecting and defending the territories, particularly the Waorani territory, where the Shuar, Achuar, Shiwiar, Kichwa, Andoas and Zápara nations still control more than 4 and a half million hectares of territory that is 90% native forest".[7]

CONFENIAE's fear is that if the US$ 350 million per year comes to an end then this will be the perfect pretext for the authorities to award concessions for 12 oil blocks affecting more than 2.5 million hectares.

But although the government favourably lived up to the people's expectations with the "Yasuní ITT" initiative, elsewhere indigenous communities faced repression throughout the year because of their resistance and opposition to various extraction projects on their territories. In June, there were strong protests at the activities of the transnational companies Petrochina and Petrobrás in the central Amazon.

The worst incident was at the end of November, however, in Dayuma, Orellana province, in the centre-north of the Amazon, at the very heart of the oil operations. Faced with the government's and Petroecuador's refusal to attend meetings proposed by the local communities, a road blockade was set up to demand that commitments be kept with regard to the construction of a road and the environmental rehabilitation of contaminated areas. According to official spokespersons, the demonstrators had threatened to block oil production. Instead of entering into dialogue, the government declared a state of emergency, suspended a number of constitutionally guaranteed rights and implemented the National Security Law, bringing civilians under military rule.

On 29 and 30 November, around 45 people were arbitrarily arrested by the Armed Forces, who entered homes in a violent manner. Some of those arrested were tortured. The release of 31 people under habeas corpus was ordered on 1 December but the security forces did not comply with this requirement.[8]

The events in Dayuma perhaps only served to reaffirm a constant truth in the region's conflicts: in the Amazon and other peripheral regions of the country, an increase in the price of oil and the news of greater resources leads only to increased expectations and frustrations.

The conflict and repression in Dayuma also led to questions regarding the government's relationship with the Constituent Assembly, which put a hold on complaints of human rights violations, appointing an investigative commission and abstaining from ruling against the government. The Dayuma case also demonstrated that the country's reforms, particularly those being promoted by the Correa government, would have to be achieved in the midst of social and political conflict.

In January 2007, in Pastaza region, various Kichwa communities of Villano seized the facilities of Agip Oil, holder of the concession to Block 10. In the neighbouring Kichwa community of Sarayaku, the harassment and terrorisation of leaders by people close to the Argentine oil company, *Compañía General de Combustibles* (CGC) has been constant. The list of human rights violations in this area is a long one, and can be found in the case pending before the Inter-American Court of Human Rights (IACHR).

According to the Sarayaku president, Dionisio Machoa, "To date, the state has ignored both the precautionary measures that the Commission passed in May 2003 and the provisional measures of the Inter-American Court of Human Rights passed in July 2004; it has failed to fulfil its previous year's commitment to end the contract with CGC

and we are still waiting for the pentolite (explosive used in oil exploration) left behind by the company to be removed".[9] There are 430 kgs of
high-powered explosives buried in the Sarayaku territory, distributed
along 640 points within Block 23 in the centre-south of the Amazon.

To these already well-known conflicts must be added those arising
as a result of mining activity (particularly gold and copper) in the region, affecting various Shuar communities in the Condor Mountains,
an inhabited area that is ecologically and culturally fragile.

In Morona Santiago, the Current Resources (Ecuacorriente, of Canadian origin) and David Lowell (US) mining companies have discovered large polymetallic deposits of copper and gold and, in the face of
community opposition, have commenced actions of terrorisation and
persecution of the community's leaders. The then member of parliament, Salvador Quishpe, from the Pachakutik movement, complained
that, "The illegalities being authorised by mining companies such as
Ecuacorriente, in complicity with the authorities, are causing persecution and harassment of indigenous peoples and other rural communities in the region".[10]

Similarly, in Intag, Imbabura province, in the Sierra Norte, the Canadian mining company Ascendant Cooper has been responsible for
committing a series of human rights violations, by contracting armed
groups to attack and terrorise the rural organisations and local authorities with guns and tear gas.[11]

These cases are scarcely the tip of the iceberg, extending to various
areas of the country and affecting indigenous communities in areas
under concession to mining companies. In Morona Santiago and
Zamora Chinchipe, in the settlements of Gualaquiza, El Bangui and
Yantzantza, an escalation of violence and repression was observed in
the middle of the year involving members of the Armed Forces.[12] "Ecuacorriente, Lowell Mineral Exploration, Ascendent Cooper and Iam
Gold Ecuador say there are no conflicts but confrontation is growing
amongst communities over mining activity".[13] In this context, in April,
the Minister for Energy convened the so-called "National Mining Dialogue", which resulted in few positive results or major commitments,
with the exception of a National Small-scale Mining Plan.[14]

These conflicts and the way in which they have been handled reveal the state's inability to deal adequately with them on the basis of

respect for human rights. There has been, and still is, a frequent delegation of tasks to private organisations, such as oil or mining companies, religious missions and NGOs, considerably affecting the legitimacy of such interventions and the sustainability of any agreements.

Constituent Assembly, collective rights and new expectations

Within the indigenous organisations, and particularly CONAIE, some grassroots sectors have been criticising the way in which the organisations are run, particularly in the Amazon and coastal regions.[15] Over the last few years, there has been a distancing of the leadership from the grassroots, and the state has gradually managed to co-opt the movement's dynamic by creating state mechanisms such as the National Council for Peoples' Development (CODENPE), attached to the Presidency of the Republic. This has had repercussions on the legitimacy both of the political system and the indigenous organisational set-up itself.

The critical voices, headed by the Sarayaku and Pastaza leaders, are effectively a cry for attention made to the indigenous elites in the face of the state's failures to comply with its agreements, but also in the face of the lack of organisational efficiency in the defence of territorial rights.

During 2007, the grassroots organisations of both Ecuarunari and CONFENIAE each organised internal discussion processes to articulate a proposal vis-à-vis the Constituent Assembly.[16] The proposals of CONAIE's organisations are focused around five basic themes, framed within the proposal of a unitary and plurinational state.

In this regard, Domingo Ankuash, CONFENIAE's president, explains: "We firstly want the construction of a plurinational state, which rejects once and for all the colonial and monocultural shadows that have accompanied the last 200 years.

Then we are proposing the nationalisation, not the privatisation, of the biodiversity and natural resources, in which the state must play an essential role in managing strategic areas and in promoting its inalienable sovereignty over the economy and natural resources". He adds that, "thirdly, we are proposing recognition of different forms of democracy and political participation, and that the main public social services must not be treated as commodities; access to all these services must be considered a human right. Finally, we are proposing the construction of a new state, a supportive socio-economic model, ecological, equitable, planned and inclusive".[17]

The Ecuadorian indigenous movement's prospects for the immediate future are going to depend on the Correa government's overall responses to various issues and to some criticisms, for example with regard to oil and mining, which is affecting territories in different areas of the country, particularly the Sierra Sur and the whole of the Amazon. The issue seems unpredictable because indications from the government point to a prioritisation of extractivist activities, given the direction of its economic model.   ❑

Notes

1   These are the Shuar, Achuar, Shiwiar, Siona, Secoya, Cofán, Waodani, Andoa, Zápara and Kichwas de Orellana, Sucumbíos, Pastaza and Napo, in the Amazon region; Awa, Epera, Chachi, Tsa'chila and Andean Kichwa migrants in the coastal region; and, in the Andean region, Kichwa identified as the Pasto, Natabuela, Karanki, Otavalo, Kayambi, Kitu kara, Panzaleo, Salasaka, Chibuleo, Tomabela, Kisapincha, Puruhae, Waranka, Cañari, Saraguro and Palta peoples.

2   "Diálogo entre agencias de cooperación y movimiento indígena. Informe Nacional Ecuador", Oxfam Amwrica/Hivos/Ibis/SNV, Quito, 2007.

3   *El Universo*, October 4, 2007.

4   The term Plan Colombia is most often used to refer to controversial U.S. legislation aimed at curbing drug smuggling by supporting different "War on Drugs" activities in Colombia. The Plan Colombia also refers to a wider aid initiative originally proposed by the Colombian President Andrés Pastrana Arango, which included but was not limited to the above piece of legislation. The plan was conceived between 1998 and 1999 by the administration of President Andrés Pastrana with the goals of social and economic revitalization, ending the armed conflict and creating an anti-drugs strategy. The most controversial element of the anti-narcotic strategy is aerial fumigation to eradicate coca. This activity has come under fire because it damages legal crops and has adverse health effects on those exposed to the herbicide. Critics of the initiative also claim that elements within the Colombian security forces that receive aid and training from it are involved in supporting or tolerating abuses by right-wing paramilitary forces against the population and left-wing organizations.

5   *Vanguardia*, 115, December 17, 2007, p.66.

6   Cf. Petroecuador, Estudio de Impacto Ambiental, Perforación Avanzada, Pozos 3 y 4. proyecto ITT, Quito.
7   Letter to President Rafael Correa, July 31, 2007.
8   "La FIDH condena la ola de represión en Orellana", Federation Internationale des Ligues des Droits de l'Homme (FIDH), December 3, 2007.
9   Personal interview, Puyo, October 28, 2007.
10   Cf. *La Hora*, February 17, 2007.
11   Cf. Observatorio de Conflictos Mineros de América Latina
12   Comunicado conjunto ante el atropello de los Derechos Humanos cometido por las mineras Ascendant Cooper y Current Resources, de la Comisión Ecuménica de Derechos Humanos (CEDHU), Coordinadota Zonal de Juntas Parroquiales de Intag, Coordinadora Campesina popular de Morona Santiago, Quito, December 15, 2006.
13   *El Comercio*, "Los conflictos llegan a cuatro mineras", p.10A, Quito, 15 November 2006.
14   Cf. *El Mercurio*, Cuenca April 5, 2007.
15   CONAIE has three affiliated organisations: Ecuarunari (Andean base), CO-NAISE (coastal base) and CONFENIAE (which comprises the Amazonian organisations).
16   As of writing this text, there is a document called "CONAIE's proposal to the Constituent Assembly. Principles, outlines for the new Constitution of Ecuador. For a plurinational, unitary, sovereign, inclusive, equitable and secular state", CONAIE, Quito, December 2007.
17   Intervention at CONFENIAE's Congress, in Unión Base, January 18, 2008.

Pablo Ortiz-T *is a researcher and academic from the Universidad Andina "Simón Bolívar", Area of Social and Global Studies. He holds a Master's in Political Science and a Doctorate in Cultural Studies. He works permanently with the indigenous organisations of the centre-south Amazon on issues of territorial planning and management, and has published various articles and texts on organisational processes and conflicts resulting from extractive policies. To contact him or for more information: mushukster@gmail.com*

PERU

The latest statistical information on the aboriginal population of Peru dates from the 1993 census, according to which there were 8,793,395 indigenous people, 97.8% of them Andean and 2.1% Amazonian. According to these figures, indigenous peoples thus represent a third of the 27 million inhabitants of Peru. In the Coastal and Andean regions, the majority of indigenous people are Quechua, followed by the Aymara who live primarily in the south of the country. In the Amazonian region, which covers 59.9% of the national territory, there are 16 ethno-linguistic families and more than 65 different ethnic groups, including no less than 11 living in voluntary isolation or initial contact.

Peru is a signatory to ILO Convention 169, which it ratified in 1993 by means of legislative resolution no. 26253. The indigenous peoples have never been accorded such recognition in their constitution, however. They were mentioned in the 1979 Constitution, but only as farming and native communities with a right to communal lands that were inalienable, unseizable and not subject to a statute of limitations. The Fujimori Constitution of 1993 severely weakened these powers in order to promote private investment in the natural resources existing on communal lands.

Public institutionality on indigenous peoples

On 23 February 2007, the government decided to abolish the National Institute for the Development of the Andean, Amazonian and Afro-Peruvian Peoples (*Instituto Nacional de Desarrollo de los Pueblos Andinos, Amazónicos y Afroperuano* - Indepa) and reduce it to a Native Peoples' Department within the Ministry of Women and Social

Development (MIMDES). With this measure, the government took a seven-year step backwards in terms of public institutionality on indigenous peoples given that, from being an autonomous ministerial-level decentralized public body that reported directly to the Presidency of the Council of Ministers, it has gone back to being hierarchically and functionally a much lesser body. The decision was taken suddenly, without consulting the indigenous peoples and by means of a Supreme Governmental Decree, despite the fact that Indepa had been created by a law issued by the Congress of the Republic. Indepa's abolition was a clear indicator of the little or no importance that Alan García's government gives to the need to promote inclusive and cross-cutting state policies on behalf of indigenous peoples and communities.

On 6 December, and at the insistence of Congress, a law cancelling the executive decree was passed. It nevertheless remains to be seen in 2008 whether the government will have the political will and make a real effort to establish Indepa and empower its public action.

Threats to the territorial rights of the communities

Opposition Congressmen and indigenous organisations described draft law 1770, presented by the government, as a veritable legal earthquake. This law aims to establish a temporary and extraordinary four-year system in which to formalise and title rural plots, peasant and native communities. Approval of this law would leave important regulations protecting communal rights in abeyance, such as Law 22175 on native communities and Law 24657 on the Demarcation and Titling of Peasant Community Lands.

The said bill was later complemented by draft law 1900 of the Peruvian Aprista Party (*Partido Aprista Peruano*), the party of the government, which aims to authorise the Institution for the Formalisation of Informal Ownership (*Organismo de Formalización de la Propiedad Informal* - Cofopri) to return lands not cultivated (*eriazas*) by the communities to the state for public auction to the highest private bidder. Both initiatives are in line with the theory stated in the articles on "the dog in a manger"[1] and other presidential declarations in which the indigenous communities – both Andean and Amazonian – are viewed as re-

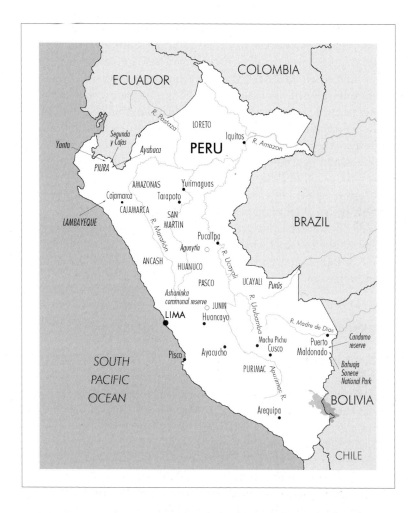

actionary institutions incapable of generating development because they leave lands "idle" and "unproductive" and "live in poverty".

Draft law 1770 even aims to disregard the property titles of communities who are duly registered in the Community Lands Registry section of the Peruvian public registers, and to revise community property titles in the Land Registry.

The Third Final Complementary Provision to draft law 1770 proposes that Cofopri – at the request of the peasant communities – will undertake to determine, convert and/or rectify the areas, boundaries and boundary measurements of the communal lands registered. But draft law 1900, introduced the following month, empowers Cofopri to do so "at its own initiative", that is, without requiring the permission of the communities, thus being able to issue new maps for already registered lands. This perspective will be even more dangerous and harmful to the communities if the Seventh Final Complementary Provision to the law is applied, as this establishes that the maps or graphic information issued by Cofopri will prevail over that held in the Land Registry.

The indigenous organisations indicate that such planned laws are the spearhead of an attempt to dismantle rights protecting the communities, to weaken collective ownership of the land and to create better conditions by which large-scale investment can access the natural resources found on the ancestral lands of the indigenous peoples and communities.

Weakened institutionality and environmental management

In March 2007, the government amended the regulations governing the Law on Protected Natural Areas and abolished the reference to Areas of Municipal Conservation as protected natural areas complementary to the National System for Protected Natural Areas (*Sistema Nacional de Áreas Naturales Protegidas* - SINANPE).[2] With this measure – described as highly damaging and unfortunate by the Peruvian Society for Environmental Rights (*Sociedad Peruana de Derecho Ambiental* - SPDA) – conflicts are being encouraged in these areas, which lack regulation and defined procedures.

Continuing in the same logic, a draft bill was introduced onto the agenda of the Council of Ministers with the aim of clearing more than 209,000 hectares of the Bahuaja Sonene National Park for a new hydrocarbon initiative. This decision would affect the area known as Candamo, a natural wonder declared by the National Geographic Society as one of the seven most emblematic sanctuaries in the world. The attempt failed due to an the immediate outcry on the part of national and international public opinion and the government's fear of hindering adoption of the Free Trade Agreement (FTA) with the USA at a time when Democrats in the US Congress were watching the country's environmental performance closely. However, the Peruvian government dismissed the Protected Natural Areas Superintendent because of his opposition to reducing the stated park. Although the government did not manage to get the draft bill sent to Congress, it did not rule out trying again at a later date.

The overlapping of hydrocarbon activities with Protected Natural Areas is a recurrent issue, given the short-term vision that the extractive industry promotes as a priority. One publication warned with alarm that one of the state's greatest weaknesses was its chaotic and dispersed environmental management, lacking any authority independent from productive activities or with sufficient political power to ensure respect for the legal environmental framework.[3]

Peru has a dispersed environmental institutional design, in which each sector has its own environmental area. Thus the Ministry of Energy and Mines itself has to promote investment in hydrocarbons, mining and electricity but also has to approve environmental impact assessments (EIA), establishing whether investment in the concession granted is feasible or not. The demand for an autonomous environmental authority grew to such a point that the President closed the year with the promise to create a Ministry for the Environment. The powers and functions of this authority will be one of the main areas of debate in 2008.

FTA: a severe blow to agricultural producers

Different press surveys conducted in the capital at the end of the year indicated that the signing of the Free Trade Agreement with the United States was the government's biggest achievement and more than 60% of Lima's inhabitants thought it was positive for the country's development. However, the same surveys indicated that most people had little or no information about the FTA, so their attitude can largely be summarised as one of hope amidst a deep lack of information.

The National Convention of Peruvian Agriculture (*Convención Nacional del Agro Peruano* - Conveagro), a body that groups together twenty-two business associations of agricultural producers, described the signing of the FTA with the US as a severe blow to agricultural producers and called for "the correction of elements which, if applied, could lead to social conflict", forcing those affected to migrate to the forest and resort to the illegal sowing of coca, with which "drugs trafficking would increase again". "The Peruvian agricultural majority who sustain internal demand and food security is condemned to unfair competition from North American products that receive millions in subsidies; it is therefore urgent to promote sector support policies that go beyond the compensation on offer," indicated its President, Luis Zúñiga.

The government's negligence and irresponsibility in the FTA negotiations was noted by specialists who questioned the inexplicable decision to unilaterally reduce tariffs to zero on more than 4,000 imported products just weeks before the US approved the FTA, and the possibility that this was a condition negotiated with the government has not been ruled out.

Mining: main source of conflict

The areas covered by mining concessions grew by 87.7% between 2002 and 2007. A report produced by the Peruvian Mining Conflicts Watchdog (*Observatorio de Conflictos Mineros en Perú*) reveals that 55% of the 6,000 peasant communities that own land in Peru are affected by mining activities.

Similarly, conflicts resulting from clashes between local populations and companies who are exploiting natural resources have been increasing and now rank first place, having displaced conflicts related to local authority performance. According to a report from the Ombudsman, there were 78 conflicts overall in December 2007, while in the same month in 2006 there were 97. However, while socio-environmental conflicts were only 20 in December 2006, they rose to 37 in December 2007, representing 47% of all conflicts.

85% of conflicts occurred in areas where a majority of the population live below the poverty line and these have polarised peasant and local communities against the state and business sectors. They are also involving a growing number of community, national and international players.

The government has been more than explicit in its support of mining activity to the detriment of civil rights. One concrete example is Supreme Decree 014-2007-EM by which the Ministry of Energy and Mines offers greater flexibility in the requirements for approval of mining exploration projects. This was strongly challenged by the Muqui Network, a collective of twenty environmental organisations, who indicated that this kind of regulation "constitutes a serious step backwards in the country's democratisation process and, undoubtedly, shows how attempts are increasingly being made to favour the interests of mining companies to the serious detriment of the rights of all citizens".

Another initiative that was strongly challenged was draft law 1640, which came directly from the government and by means of which it was attempting to declare twenty mining projects of "national interest", including the Majaz project in the northern region of Piura. One of its articles attempted to give the government the freedom to extend the list of beneficiary projects. This initiative was rejected by the two Congress committees to which it was sent.

Intolerance of the right to consultation and participation

One of the most active and significant conflicts of the year was that caused by the Majaz mining project of Monterrico Metals,[4] which was opposed initially by the peasant farming communities of Yanta and Segunda y Cajas, who were demanding the company's withdrawal from their communal territories, which had been included in the project without their consent. This struggle has drawn together a group of social organisations who fear the impacts of what could be the largest copper mine in the country on the water resources of the northern macro-region.

The municipalities of Ayabaca, Pacaipampa and Carmen de la Frontera organised a local consultation on 16 September to ascertain the local people's opinion with regard to mining activity. However the company, and particularly the government, embarked on an aggressive and intolerant campaign in opposition to the consultation, despite this forming a legitimate procedure for civic participation. Prime Minister Jorge del Castillo even threatened the council authorities and the broadcaster Radio Cutivalú for refusing to distribute a message that carried misleading information.

In the consultation process, the participants were asked to vote on the mining project. The "no" vote gained more than 94.54% of total votes cast and, despite the fact that the consultation was not obligatory and the government had unleashed a fierce campaign to discredit it, 60% of the electorate in these districts turned out to vote. On 16 December, in Piura, a huge march of approximately 8,000 people took place to demand that the government respect the local consultation. The march, initiated by community members and peasant farmers from Ayabaca, Huancabamba, Cajamarca and Lambayeque, was joined by agricultural producers, unions and other social organisations.

The climate of confrontation was stirred up by aggressive attitudes towards the organisations of communities affected by mining and the issuing of legislative decrees criminalising social protest and affecting the right to peaceful public demonstration. For this reason, the National Confederation of Communities Affected by Mining (*Confederación Nacional de Comunidades Afectadas por la Minería* - CONACAMI), along with the Human Rights Association (*Asociación Pro Derechos Humanos* - Aprodeh), began to gather signatures to get the Constitutional Court to declare the decrees approved on 22 July as unconstitutional. In addition, the Single Front in Defence of Life, the Environment and the Interests of Cajamarca (*Frente Único en Defensa de la Vida, del Medio Ambiente y de los Intereses de Cajamarca*) called for the establishment of a Truth Commission on Mining in Peru.

Problems in Amazonia

Under the slogan: "Peru, a country to invest in", the state ended the year with a record 24 hydrocarbon exploration contracts, surpassing the 16 contracts in 2006 and 15 in 2005. This initiative will mean that more than 80% of the Amazon is covered by oil or gas concessions.

A broad group of indigenous organisations, environmental NGOs and human rights defence organisations denounced the overlapping of hydrocarbon concessions with territorial reserves for indigenous peoples in isolation and protected natural areas.

Peoples in isolation

The national Amazonian indigenous organisation, AIDESEP, continued its work in defence of the peoples in isolation and found itself up against difficult people such as Daniel Saba, President of PeruPetro, a state-run private law company responsible for promoting investment in hydrocarbon exploration and exploitation activities.

Saba denied the existence of peoples in isolation in the press because, according to him, "nobody has seen them" and he announced that a consultant would conduct a study to contact the indigenous peoples in isolation in order to "obtain their opinion with regard to the development of hydrocarbon activity in these areas". "We do not know the position of these peoples in isolation, no-one has consulted them and in this study we are going to find out what they think in this regard," he said. Fortunately, this intention was ruled out by a resolution issued by the Fourth District Attorney's Office for Crime Prevention in Lima, which urged the PeruPetro's president to auction off the plots "without violating the fundamental rights of the Amazonian Indigenous Peoples in Voluntary Isolation, it being necessary to act within the relevant legal framework at all times".

The discussion around the existence or not of the peoples in isolation took an important turn in September when a technical expedition made up of INRENA and the Frankfurt Zoological Society verified beyond doubt the existence of nomadic indigenous groups in voluntary isolation in the south-east Amazon of Peru, whom they took photographs of from a light aircraft. The extraordinary findings ratified the position maintained by indigenous organisations such as Aidesep and contradicted government spokespersons who, in their desire to promote hydrocarbon activity, had repeatedly and irresponsibly denied the existence of indigenous peoples in isolation in Peru.

The Cacataibo in isolation and plot 107

In December, the Federation of Cacataibo Native Communities (*Federación de Comunidades Nativas Cacataibo* - FENACOCA) denounced the serious threat hanging over the indigenous Cacataibo in isolation due to the seismic exploration being conducted by the Canadian company Petrolífera Petroleum del Perú on plot 107. The Cacataibo are surrounded by settlers and loggers and this plot forms their last refuge. FENACOCA, the Institute of the Common Good (*Instituto del Bien Común* -IBC) and the Centre for International Environmental Law (*Centro para el Derecho Internacional Ambiental* - CIEL) have submitted a complaint to the Inter-American Commission on Human Rights (IAHCR) aimed at urging the Peruvian government to adopt measures to protect the life, health and personal integrity of the Cacataibo in isolation.

In fact, the IACHR granted a precautionary measure requested by the Native Federation of the Madre de Dios River and its Tributaries (*Federación Nativa del río Madre de Dios y afluentes* - FENAMAD) in favour of indigenous peoples in isolation and called on the Peruvian state to take concrete measures to put a stop to the illegal felling of mahogany within the Madre de Dios Territorial Reserve, where indigenous peoples in isolation are also to be found.

Indigenous coordination to protect the peoples in isolation

In April, the International Indigenous Committee for the Protection of Indigenous Peoples in Voluntary Isolation and Initial Contact (*Comité Indígena Internacional para la Protección de los Pueblos Indígenas Voluntariamente Aislados y en Contacto Inicial* - CIPIACI) was established in Lima with the involvement of AIDESEP (Peru), CIDOB (Bolivia), UNAP (Paraguay), ONHAE and CONAIE (Ecuador), ONIC (Colombia) and COIAB (Brazil), thus fulfilling a commitment made during the Regional Seminar on Indigenous Peoples in Isolation and Initial Contact held in Santa Cruz de la Sierra from 20 to 22 November 2006.

Antonio Iviche, from the Harakmbut people, was elected CIPIACI coordinator and headed a delegation to the sixth session of the UN Permanent Forum on Indigenous Issues where its proposed recommendations were accepted by the Permanent Forum, including the need to adopt supranational mechanisms to monitor how governments comply with requirements to protect peoples in isolation.

Other events related to land issues

The social and environmental impact of highways was noted by specialist Alberto Chirif, who expressed his concern at the new highway that will link the Pichis basin with the central highway, crossing the San Carlos mountain range, declared a protected forest in 1987 in order to preserve the quality of the tributaries forming the Pichis River. Similarly the indigenous association ECOPURUS, executing agency for the Management Contract for the Purus Communal Reserve, rejected the initiative to build the Purus - Iñapari highway because it would endanger the communal reserve and the Alto Purús National Park.

In addition, the Federation of Native Communities of the Corrientes River (*Federación de Comunidades Nativas del Río Corrientes* - FECONACO) documented Pluspetrol's responsibility for five new spills that occurred between 17 and 29 October 2007 on plots 1AB and 8, located on the banks of the Corrientes River. Similarly, the Camisea gas pipeline had its sixth leak in three years of operation on 2 April.

The 8th Congress of the Ashaninka Organisation of the Apurimac River (*Organización Ashaninka del Río Apurimac* - OARA), in the country's southern Amazon, condemned the constant invasions of and threats to their territorial integrity, which were putting them in a highly vulnerable situation. Invasions on the part of settlers from the Andean region are endangering the forests of the protected area in which the indigenous communities live. These forests adjoin the Ashaninka Communal Reserve and the Otishi National Park, areas protected for their specific biodiversity features.

Among more positive events was the Loreto regional government's decision to create the Ampiyacu – Apayacu Regional Conservation Area on 9 December, covering an area of 433,099 hectares. Likewise the public interest declaration made by the Ucayali regional government with regard to protecting indigenous peoples in isolation, with which it commenced the production of a Protection, Defence and Contingencies Plan.

Backwards moves, bad moves in intercultural and bilingual education

Education was one of the constant targets of indigenous organisations, who denounced the dismantling of Bilingual Intercultural Education (BIE) within the Ministry of Education and questioned the dreadful performance of the National Department for Intercultural, Bilingual and Rural Education.

First came abolition of the automatic renewal of contracts for BIE specialists, as a reprisal for having expressed their disagreement at the nationwide evaluation of second-grade primary school children purely in the Spanish language, even children whose mother tongue is an indigenous language.

Then there was the imposition of a single admissions examination for teacher training, applied by the Ministry itself and not the higher institutes as had previously been the case. This almost completely eliminated any indigenous presence by failing to assess cultural diversity and linguistic belonging. The centralised exam suspended and aborted the admissions process that was previously under the responsibility of the Loreto Higher Teacher Training Institute and the Training of Bilingual Teachers in the Peruvian Amazon (Formabiap) programme.

Finally, in November, the National Association of Bilingual Teachers of Peru (*Asociación Nacional de Maestros Bilingües del Perú* - AN-AMEBI) denounced the sector's lack of will and financial incapacity to execute the budget for bilingual, intercultural and rural education and warned that approximately US$10 million would be returned to the Public Treasury unspent.   ❑

Notes

1   There were two articles by Alan García in 2007: "*El síndrome del perro del hortelano*", on 28 October (http://www.elcomercio.com.pe/edicionimpresa/ Html/2007-10-28/el_sindrome_del_perro_del_hort.html) and "*Receta para acabar con el perro del hortelano*", on 25 November (http://www.elcomercio.com. pe/edicionimpresa/html/2007-11-25/receta_para_acabar_con_el_perr.html), published in the daily newspaper El Comercio.

His speech to the Annual Conference of Executives (*Conferencia Anual de Ejecutivos* - CADE) on 30 November (extracts at: http://ia360620.us.archive.org/0/items/Alancade2007/AlanCade2007.mp3) is also in the same vein.

2   Supreme Decree N° 015-2007-AG, enacted on 15 March 2007, which repealed article 41.2 and Chapter X of Section Two of the Regulations governing the Law on Protected Natural Areas

3   *"La gestión pública inconexa: el caso de la política ambiental a propósito de la superposición de lotes de hidrocarburos en las Áreas Naturales Protegidas"*, by Carlos Alza Barco and César Ipenza Peralta. Asociación Peruana para la Conservación de la Naturaleza (APECO), Lima, October 2007.

4   See *The Indigenous World 2006.*

Jorge Agurto is a social communicator and president of the NGO Servicios en Comunicación Intercultural Servindi. He is promoter and head of Servindi's Indigenous Information Service.
Website: www.servindi.org, e-mail: jorgeagurto@servindi.org

BOLIVIA

The official Bolivian census, conducted by the National Statistics Institute in 2001, indicates that 62% of the Bolivian population over the age of 15 is of indigenous origin. There are 36 peoples officially recognised, the largest being the Quechua (49.5%) and the Aymara (40.6%), who inhabit the western Andes; the Chiquitano (3.6%), Guaraní (2.5%) and Moxeño (1.4%) peoples, along with the remaining 2.4% corresponding to 31 other indigenous peoples, live in the country's eastern lowlands. Bolivia comprises four different eco-regions: the altiplano and valleys of the highlands and Chaco and Amazonia in the lowlands. It covers an area of 1,098,581 km², more than 50% of which is covered by tropical and subtropical forests. The indigenous peoples have managed to obtain title to 11 million hectares under the legal concept of Native Community Lands. Of these, 3.4 million hectares are in the highlands and 7.6 million in the lowlands. Bolivia has been a signatory to ILO Convention 169 since 1991 and, on 7 November 2007, through Law No. 3760, it became the first country in the world to ratify the UN Declaration on the Rights of Indigenous Peoples.

Constituent Assembly and approval of the New Political Constitution of the State

The Constituent Assembly was established by Law No. 3364 of 6 March 2006 with a mandate to completely revise the Political Constitution. In elections for its members, held on 2 June 2006, Evo Morales' party, the Movement to Socialism (*Movimiento al Socialismo -*

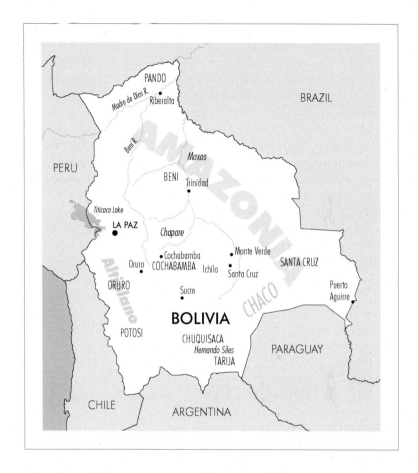

MAS), won an absolute majority (50.7%) of the votes, equivalent to 137 seats. Through alliances with members from another 10 parties, it was able to count on 164 supporters in all. The opposition held the remaining 90 seats, distributed among 6 political groups (although this did include some MAS members, just as the MAS also managed to win over some opposition supporters).

After an historic entrance to Sucre, where the assembly was situated, on the part of the 36 indigenous peoples, the Constituent Assembly was established on 6 August 2006 for a one-year period, at the end of which it was to deliver a new constitution to the country. Its work was characterized by political and social crisis and various interruptions. This meant that its mandate had to be extended to 14 December 2007.

One of the conflicts haunting the assembly was related to the system of voting and approval of committee reports and the constitutional text itself, which the government insisted should be by absolute majority while the opposition demanded a 2/3 majority. Finally, a mixed formula was chosen combining an absolute and a two-thirds majority. The discussions also related to the social conflict the issue was causing, particularly in Cochabamba in early January where, during a demonstration, two people died in street scuffles between government supporters and the opposition.

The 255 Assembly members visited all the country's regions between April and May 2007 in what were called "territorial meetings" where they met directly with the local population to hear their proposals for the new constitution. In some of these meetings, as in Santa Cruz for example, the committees on autonomies, natural resources, land and territory and legislative power were harassed by groups organised by the "Santa Cruz Civic Committee" and the private business associations, which refused to permit any proposals other than their own from being heard, particularly those coming from the social organisations.

In July, the deliberations began to harmonise the reports of the 21 committees in order to produce a text to be submitted to the plenary for discussion and final 2/3 approval.

This work got bogged down in the approval stage because the opposition presented minority reports at all turns and it was impossible to reach an agreement on one single document despite various attempts, even in large mixed committees structured around a common issue.

The issue of the country's capital

Shortly before the deadline for submission of the constitutional text, the opposition brought up the thorny issue of the country's capital in various committees, thus once again opening up an historic conflict that people thought had been laid to rest. They proposed changing the current seats of state power, currently divided between La Paz (executive and legislative) and Sucre (judiciary), which was also the seat of the Assembly. The opposition demanded a return to a position whereby all power was focused on Sucre, as it had been since the founding of Bolivia (1825) up to the so-called "federal war" of 1899, a military conflict whose consequences persist to this very day. This issue served to revive old rivalries between inhabitants of La Paz and those of Sucre. The discussion fuelled already exacerbated regional and ethnic conflicts yet further. The main political leaders of Sucre, coordinated around the opposition, used students from the San Francisco Xavier de Chuquisaca University and people from the Santa Cruz Youth Union (*Unión Juvenil Cruceñista de Santa Cruz*) as a strike force, implementing a strategy of physically blocking the place where the Assembly was being held, using threats, persecution and physical aggression towards Assembly members and thus preventing them from sitting.

On 4 August, given the imminent deadline for submission of the constitutional text, the Congress of the Republic extended the Assembly's mandate until 14 December, and also approved a referendum for issues that could not be agreed on, in addition to the already established referendum for overall approval of the Constitution.

On 15 August, the Assembly issued its final resolution with regard to the country's capital, although this was to prolong the conflict almost until the end of the Assembly's mandate. The plenary decided by a large majority to exclude this issue from the discussions and consider it separately, thus preventing the opposition from using it as a bargaining chip with which to reach agreements on other important issues, such as the autonomies or the natural resource system.

Approval of the new Constitution

During September, October and the first days of November, a number of *rapprochements* were attempted in order to agree on the issues to be included in the new constitutional text. The so-called "cross-party political committee" was formed, comprising representatives of all political forces in the Constituent Assembly. This had the task of reaching a consensus and completing the work within the extended deadline given. They managed to come to an agreement on only two of the seven issues proposed.[1] One of these was that of the capital. Having been discussed and approved by 13 of the 16 political forces, it was subsequently rejected due to the opposition of powerful sectors in the lowlands and the "interinstitutional committee" of Chuquisaca.[2] It was agreed to ratify the seats of power of the executive and legislative as La Paz, to maintain the judiciary in Sucre, to form a fourth branch known as the "electoral branch", and also to promote an integrated development plan for Chuquisaca department. The other agreements were on the country's economic system and vision.

Once all possible efforts to reach an agreement between the political forces had been made, the MAS struck up alliances with a large number of opposition Assembly members, who had distanced themselves from the more radical groups that openly wanted to abort the Assembly in order to find a solution outside of this forum. The government called his allied social movements to Sucre in order to ensure the Assembly's reactivation, with organisations of coca growers, peasant farmers and indigenous peoples from El Alto turning up in large numbers.

On 23 November, given the general crisis of several days in Sucre, now being openly organised and financed by the opposition and civic committees from the East[3] and which was preventing the Assembly members from entering the Gran Mariscal Theatre, seat of the Assembly, the Assembly's presiding officers decided to hold the session in a military school on the outskirts of the city, with a large military/police presence. The demonstrators, however, followed and clashed with the security forces for several hours. In the commotion, two people were shot dead; their murders have not been clarified to this day. In spite of all this, the MAS and its allies, totalling more than 150 Assembly members, approved the broad outlines of the New Political Constitution by 2/3 of those present, and in the absence of a part of the opposition.[4] The opposition condemned this approval "amidst rifles and bayonets" as ex–President Jorge Quiroga, leader of the main opposition group, put it and called for the session to be overruled.

Without the physical conditions being present to continue sitting in Sucre and having obtained authorisation to convene in another part of the country, endorsed by Congress in a law, the presiding officers called a session for 8 December in the town of Oruro – 288 kms to the south of La Paz – the Bolivian tin capital and President Morales' department of origin. In a session that lasted more than 17 hours, the 411 articles of the New Political Constitution were approved in detail, in the presence of 165 Assembly members.

This was submitted to the Vice-president of the Republic and ex-officio President of Congress, Álvaro García Linera, on 14 December and, the next day, in the midst of a great popular event in the Plaza Murillo, it was delivered into the hands of President Evo Morales himself.

After the failure of its hunger strike, organised to prevent the prefectures from having to accept lower hydrocarbons taxes, the opposition proposed rejecting the New Constitution, alleging irregularities in its formal approval. They labelled it "racist", "retaliatory", "separatist", "pro-MAS"[5] and began to gather signatures for a departmental referendum. This referendum, totally out of order as it was not authorised by the competent electoral authorities, had the aim of approving some autonomous statutes that were produced by the "Pre-autonomous Assemblies", meetings of deputies, senators, constituent assembly members and other regional representatives of the opposition. They have decided to commence *de facto* exercise of powers that are currently held at national level and, once these statutes are "in force", they will probably try to exercise *de facto* departmental autonomy, in open contradiction of the New Constitution, which will continue as the established institutional channel.

Pension funds

In the meantime, the government opened up another Pandora's box and one that would have direct repercussions for the Constituent Assembly. It proposed amending the source of funding for state retirement pensions. Previously, these were sourced from the profits of public companies that were privatised during the time of President Sánchez de Lozada. This pension was called the *"Bono Solidario"* (BONOSOL), and an amount of 1,800 bolivianos (in today's terms a little over US$200) was paid to the elderly once a year. President Evo Morales proposed creating the *"Renta Dignidad"* (Dignified Income), and granting a monthly payment of 200 bolivianos, to be funded from the lucrative oil profits Bolivia receives on sales to other countries, through the

"Direct Tax on Hydrocarbons" (DTH). In order to pay the retirement pension, the government would have to reduce the income from DTH that was being channelled to the regional prefectures. Prefectures allied to the opposition group, along with the Civic Committees, launched a fierce resistance campaign against the *"Renta Dignidad"*, with demonstrations and a well-publicised "hunger strike" that lasted until after the new Constitution was approved in detail. Against all odds, and in an eventful session, the Senate approved the Law creating the *Renta* on the same day as the new constitutional text was approved in principle.

Important factors for indigenous peoples in the new Constitution

The social movements, made up largely of indigenous peoples and peasant farmers, undoubtedly made significant advances in the Constitution. In terms of both structure and substance, it was these organisations that made the greatest contribution. The demands on which they have taken a stand are the most conflictive, even though they were approved unanimously in plenary. An essential boost came from the Congress of the Republic and the national government, which quickly ratified the UN Declaration on the Rights of Indigenous Peoples as law, thus enabling particular issues in the constitutional project to be strengthened or even put back in where they had been taken out. Nevertheless, the new Constitution will need careful legislative work to make the new institutions viable. The most important issues can be summarised in four areas, which formed the basis of the indigenous-peasant farmer proposal for the Constitution from the start:

Multinational State and the pre-existence of indigenous peoples
With the new Constitution, Bolivia recognises itself as a Social State of Community Multinational Unitary Law. It recognises the existence of indigenous peoples prior to the Spanish colonisation and elevates the 36 indigenous peoples to the rank of nationalities, with a right of respect for their own traditions, cultures and norms. Their languages are

official languages, on a par with Spanish. Defining the state as "Community" enables full effect and respect to be given to the social, economic and political forms current among the different indigenous and peasant farmer communities and peoples, on the basis of principles of solidarity, reciprocity and complementarity.

Three kinds of democratic participation in the state are recognised: 1) Participatory Democracy: by means of assemblies and councils, prior consultation, referenda, plebiscites, private legislative initiatives and possible revocation of mandate; 2) Representative Democracy: by means of representatives elected by universal and secret ballot, guaranteeing parity and alternance between men and women; and 3) Community Democracy; by means of the election, appointment or direct nomination of representatives according to local custom. The state takes up the values and principles of Andean and Amazonian indigenous cultures, such as the *ama qhilla, ama llulla; ama suwa* (don't be weak, don't be a liar, don't be a thief), *suma qamaña* (live well), *ñandereko* (harmonious life), *teko kavi* (good life), *ivi maraei* (land without evil) and *qhapaj ñan* (noble path or life).

Rights, duties and guarantees

The new Constitution devotes a special chapter to the rights of indigenous peoples, defining them as those who share a cultural identity, language, tradition, history, institutions, territoriality and world vision and whose existence pre-dates the Spanish colonial invasion.

Paragraph II of Article 30 of the text, in its 18 sub-paragraphs, establishes the rights to: cultural identity and its legal registration in civil documentation; to self-determination and territoriality; to indigenous institutions forming part of the state; to the collective ownership of their territories; to protection of their traditional knowledge; to respect for their sacred places and traditional systems; to the exercise and recognition of community justice; to prior, free and informed consent, in good faith and conducted by the state, in the case of any activity related to the non-renewable resources on their territories or if measures or projects are to be implemented that may affect them, along with participation in the profits of these activities; to the autonomous management of their territories and the exclusive use and exploitation

of the natural resources existing on them. In addition, it stipulates respect for and protection of peoples on the verge of extinction, as well
as those in a state of voluntary isolation, who enjoy the right to remain
as such.

Indigenous autonomies

Indigenous autonomies are covered in the chapter on state territorial
organisation. This was one area in which the opposition put up the
most resistance. These form part of a system of four levels of administrative decentralisation, namely: departmental, regional, municipal
and indigenous. The national level retains the strategic functions and
powers of the state such as legislation, jurisdiction, the monetary system, armed forces, overall control of natural resources, air space, etc.
All autonomous levels are of the same constitutional ranking and territorial jurisdiction and are not subordinate to each other. It is this last
detail, proposed by the indigenous and peasant farmer organisations,
that broke with the model of departmental autonomies proposed by
the opposition, which was endeavouring to return power to the regional level that had been lost in recent years to national government.
The indigenous autonomies will be established on the basis of their
ancestral territories, at the request of their members, and will exercise
full governmental, legislative and jurisdictional powers within the
sphere of their jurisdiction and under their own rules and procedures.
General powers have been established for each level. A large part of
the autonomous system was delegated to discuss a framework law in
which the drafting and approval of statutes would also be regulated.

New natural resource system

The chapter on natural resource regulation has endorsed the fact that
natural resources, whatever they may be and wherever they may be
found, are owned and directly controlled, indivisibly and imprescrip-
tibly, by the Bolivian people. The state ensures their management and
administration. Special sections have been included to cover issues
such as the environment, land and territory and, here, a broad definition of indigenous territories is established that goes beyond their right

to own the land and exceeds the current constitutional dictate that restricts them to native community lands (*tierras comunitarias de origen*).[6] In the case of the land system, the principles of the agrarian reform were ratified, namely that, to be retained, the land must be worked and must have a socio-economic function. The communities, the indigenous territories and small properties are indivisible, inalienable, imprescriptible and non-seizable. A ban on *latifundios* (large estates) is established, defined also as areas in which relationships of servitude are maintained, and indigenous and peasant farmers are given access rights to state lands, at no cost and only via collective title, giving women priority in this regard.

Indigenous territorial rights

Approval of implementing regulations for the RCRA Law
On 2 August, the day of the Agrarian Reform, the President of the Republic enacted Supreme Decree No. 29215 approving regulations governing the Law on Community Renewal of the Agrarian Reform No. 3545 dated 28 November 2006.[7] This decree represents a decisive step for the government towards implementing a law that has been fiercely challenged by the private agricultural and livestock sector, which considers it confiscatory and prejudicial to large-scale production. It is hoped that Supreme Decree No. 29215 will regulate all reasons for reversion, enabling the state to recover land titles without payment of compensation, for their redistribution to indigenous and peasant farmers, and expropriation, making it possible to re-establish the indigenous territories lost through bad implementation of the regularisation (*saneamiento*) process a few years ago, for their return to their legitimate owners. The more than 300 articles it contains mark out a speedier and simpler procedure for regularising agrarian rights and establish the key elements for the recovery of idle lands, for their subsequent redistribution. The procedure for expropriation of lands within indigenous territories where peoples are calling for their return is explained in detail, as well as reversion for reasons of servitudinal relationships, which results in a loss of ownership rights for the person in question.

Titling of indigenous territories

Regularisation of rights to the lands and territories of indigenous and peasant farmer communities, along with access to new lands for sectors without any, such as the Movement of Indigenous-Farm Labourers without Land (*Movimiento de los Trabajadores Indígena-Campesinos Sin Tierra* - MST) continued in 2007.

In July, more than three million hectares were titled solely for the Chiquitano people of Santa Cruz, amongst which was to be found the symbolic demand of Monte Verde, which received its title after 12 years of waiting. This territory gained national and international visibility due to the unending struggle of its communities, who were threatened throughout the whole process by landowners, loggers, miners and the authorities themselves, who conspired to prevent their success. Monte Verde has recovered the area of three logging concessions and almost half of its territory, claimed by illegal occupations on the part of land traffickers, thus consolidating an area of more than one million hectares.

Alongside this, territories that had been waiting years for the regularisation of their rights were titled.

Process for the release of captive families

Finally, one historic process that has begun aims to provide what is hoped will be a final solution to the problem of the so-called "captive" indigenous families, Guaraní families suffering in the Chaco region under different forms of forced labour, debt bondage or other methods of servitude, suffering violation of their most basic right: to freedom. To this end, President Evo Morales has declared the issue a national priority and has brought together five ministries,[8] international bodies such as the United Nations and the ILO, international cooperation agencies, local NGOs and indigenous organisations of the Guaraní people to work on this. The new guiding criterion is to re-establish the Guaraní territory. This territory can then be linked to actions to repay the workers' debts and obtain the release of these captive labourers so that they can start a new life as free citizens. In this regard, Supreme Decree No. 29292 dated 3 October was approved creating the Interministerial Council for the Eradication of Bondage, Forced Labour and

Other Similar Forms of Servitude". This contains a provisional plan 2007-2008 for the Guaraní people (art. 6).

In the context of this plan, Supreme Decree No. 29354 was approved on 28 November, stating that the area of Huacareta was of public need and utility. This area is located in the Chaco region, Chuquisaca department, Luís Calvo and Hernando Siles provinces, and covers an area of approximately 180,000 has, forming part of the ancestral territory of the Guaraní people and now densely populated with medium and large-scale cattle ranches that were consolidated under the distorted application of the land regularisation that took place over the period 1996-2006. The decree authorises the state to commence expropriation of these estates, for their return to their ancestral owners. In addition, three reversion resolutions were also issued in the area of the Cuquisaca Chaco, in which the state verified Guaraní families in a state of bondage. It is thought that this first part of the process, in which the lands will be returned to their legitimate owners, will last throughout 2008 and possibly part of 2009, giving way to stages of territorial consolidation, cultural recovery and social and economic development.❏

Notes

1   The issues were: Vision of country; Economic development; Land and Natural Resources; Autonomies; Legislative Power; Capital; Re-election; Election of judges by vote.

2   Refers to the assembly members from the PODEMOS (Poder Democrático y Social) civic group, the Santa Cruz Civic Committee and the business associations of the country's Eastern region, located above all around Santa Cruz de la Sierra.

3   A number of MAS assembly members were assaulted actually on the public highway and their homes looted for being considered "traitors" to the capital city cause.

4   In this controversial session, some articles regulating debates were also amended, aimed at speeding up the handling of issues, approving the constitutional text on the basis of the assembly members present and offering the possibility of sitting somewhere other than Sucre. This decision was justified insofar as the opposition's strategy was aimed at not attending the debates and blocking the Assembly's seat by force, thus preventing the sessions from being held.

5   As part of the strategy of discrediting the New Constitution, every time the opposition or private media (which in Bolivia represents 99% of the media) referred to the Constitution, they added that this was "the MAS Constitution" .

6   *Article 283: I. The integrity of the native and peasant indigenous territory is recognised
      and that of the communities, including the right to land, to the exclusive use and exploi-
      tation of renewable natural resources under conditions established by law, prior and
      informed consultation and participation in the benefits of exploitation of the non-renew-
      able natural resources on their territories; the power to apply their own rules, adminis-
      tered by their representative structures and a definition of their development in line with
      their cultural criteria and principles of harmonious co-existence with nature.*
      *II. The native indigenous territories and those of the communities comprise areas of
      production, areas of exploitation and conservation of natural resources and spaces for
      social, spiritual and cultural reproduction.*
      *III. The law shall regulate the way in which collective rights are exercised over their ar-
      eas of current occupation and traditional access, by means of procedures that will guar-
      antee their access and control, in favour of the native indigenous peasant peoples and
      communities, in accordance with that stipulated in this Constitution.*

7   The report of the Inter-American Commission on Human Rights (IACHR),
      which includes conclusions and recommendations to the state on its *in loco* visit
      conducted in October-November 2006, welcomes approval of Law 3545 and
      urges the government to undertake its rapid implementation.

8   Ministry of Justice, Ministry of Work, Ministry of Government, Ministry of For-
      eign Affairs and Ministry of Rural Development, Agricultural and Livestock
      Farming and the Environment.

Hernán Ávila Montaño *is a sociologist and member of the Advocacy Pro-
gramme of the Centro de Estudios Jurídicos e Investigación Social (CEJIS).
He has written a number of books on the indigenous peoples of the Bolivian
Amazon, including "El Ichini Moxeño ha despertado".*

Leonardo Tamburini *is an Argentine lawyer and executive director of CE-
JIS.*

Sebastián Ochoa *is a journalist and CEJIS' head of communications.*

BRAZIL

In a country with almost 180 million inhabitants and 8,514,215 kms[2] of land, Brazil's indigenous population numbers approximately 734,127[1] individuals, or around 4% of the national population and occupies 12.74% of Brazilian territory, with 96.61% of the Indigenous Lands being in the Amazon. Of the 734,127 Indians, 383,298 live in urban areas. Brazilian legislation establishes a series of rights for indigenous peoples and Brazil signed ILO Convention 169 in 2004.

2007 was marked by an intensification of the problems that arose during 2006 (see *The Indigenous World 2007*):[2] in the Mato Grosso do Sul region alone, violence increased by 214%, that is, 44 deaths as opposed to 14 in 2006.[3]

After a two-year delay, the President of the Republic recognised the National Commission for Indigenist Policy (CNPI)[4] as a consultative body of a deliberative nature. The CNPI comprises various ministries and indigenous representatives, including the Ministry of Justice, and its role is to propose guidelines for official indigenist policy.

Dissatisfaction is now widespread among the indigenous associations. They are accusing President Luis Ignacio Lula da Silva of being responsible for a worse erosion of indigenous rights than his predecessors by failing to recognise 272 territories claimed by the indigenous peoples, not meeting the legal deadline for the publication of 34 regulatory declarations for territorial demarcation, reducing the number of working groups to identify new indigenous territories (TI) and reducing the resources devoted to indigenist policy over the 2004 to 2006 period from US$ 23.55 million to US$ 20.3 million. A substantial part of these cuts were aimed at programmes regularising and protecting indigenous territories. In addition, the National Health Foundation (FU-

NASA) is abandoning indigenous health care, leaving indigenous children to die of malnutrition and, in some regions, causing a return of malaria.[5]

Faced with this reality, at the end of 2006, the President declared that environmentalists and indigenous communities formed an obstacle to the implementation of large infrastructural works and to the country's development. His second term of office is focused on the Accelerated Growth Programme (*Plano de Aceleração do crescimento*-PAC), which comprises various infrastructural works such as hydro-electric power stations and roads, affecting at least 21 indigenous territories and threatening the lives of communities, including 21 living in isolation.[6] Biofuel production incentives, particularly for ethanol, have caused a rush to buy land and this is blocking the possibilities for demarcating the indigenous territories yet more, and intensifying pre-existing situations of conflict.

Even so, on 21 September 2007, President Lula da Silva visited San Gabriel da Cachoeira (Amazonia) to launch the Indigenous Peoples' Social Agenda (PAC-*Social Indígena*). This relates to a series of inter-ministerial actions aimed at improving indigenous peoples' quality of life. It comprises three broad components: a) the protection of indigenous peoples; b) the promotion of indigenous peoples; c) the promotion of indigenous peoples' quality of life. The main goals are:

* To demarcate 127 indigenous territories and resettle 9,000 rural worker families occupying indigenous lands by 2010;
* To rehabilitate degraded areas of indigenous lands, to promote the creation of indigenous territories, to strengthen 11 fronts for the protection of indigenous peoples in isolation;
* To document and strengthen the use of 20 indigenous languages under threat of extinction;
* To bring federal government benefits to all villages and to the country's urban indigenous population, building the capacity of indigenous organisations to exercise social control over government actions.

To achieve the actions planned within the Indigenous Peoples' Social Agenda, the president of the National Indian Foundation (FUNAI),

1. Cinta Larga
2. Yanomami
3. Macuxi
4. Xavante
5. Guaraní
6. Ticuna
7. Guajajara

Márcio Meira,[7] announced that the institution's budget would increase by 44% in 2008. This money will come from the federal government itself, which has allocated US$ 152.5 million to FUNAI and US$ 100 million more to FUNASA, totalling US$ 252.85 million.[8]

According to the Yanomami leader, Davi Kopenawa, however,

The government has not explained the project properly; I do not find it clear. It speaks only in terms of 'works' and we don't want 'works' on our land. The government did not invite either the indigenous peoples or the institutions working with us to discuss this project. This is why I am concerned. This very project that wants to protect us is going to clash with another project, of Senator Romero Jucá, that wants to destroy our lands through mining.[9]

Most of the indigenous associations are tired of promises and know they are being treated with contempt and rhetoric. For an example of this we have to look no further than the rate at which FUNAI's president has been replaced since it was created in 1967: 32 times!

Lands approved and those in the process of approval

Parliamentary initiatives that are not favourable to indigenous peoples are continuing to pass through the National Congress; one of the main discussions has been the special situation under which bill of law no. 1610 of Senator Romero Jucá will be debated. This bill envisages regulating mining works on indigenous lands, despite the fact that an agreement exists with the National Commission for Indigenist Policy (CNPI) that this issue should be considered within the bill of law establishing the Indigenous Peoples' Statute. To this must be added the government plan for biofuel incentives, particularly ethanol, which is causing a rush for lands and delays in demarcating the indigenous territories.

Despite the promise to demarcate the indigenous territories, much more should have been accomplished during 2007. The total area recognised by the Minister of Justice, Tarso Genro, was 710,471 hectares, comprising 14 Indigenous Lands.

The delays in legalising the indigenous lands have led to intense conflict between the indigenous population and the ranch owners, loggers and mining companies, often resulting in deaths.

On 26 July 2007, permanent ownership of the Sururi'y Indigenous Land of 535 hectares was granted[10] to the Guaraní people of Maracaju municipality (Mato Grosso do Sul); this territory had formed the object of intense conflict since 1947, when it was handed over to the *Empresa Brasileira de Pesquisa Agropecuária*. At that time, the indigenous population was forced to spread throughout the surrounding region but, in

1984, some families decided to return. They were evicted once more but returned two years later and this cycle continued up until 1996, when 50 ranch owners, municipal authorities and thugs again threw them out. They returned for the last time in 1997, but settled on only 64 hectares of the 534 to which they had a right. It has taken 60 years for the process of land regularisation to come to its final conclusion.

On 28 August 2007, the Minister of Justice issued two regulatory declarations for lands that had been involved in one of the oldest territorial disputes, between Tupinquim and Guaraní Mbyá communities and the Vera Cruz Celulosa company. This issue had been dragging on since 1970. These declarations rule on the people's permanent ownership of the indigenous Comboios y Tupiniquim territory, located in Aracruz municipality, in Espírito Santo. The territory covers 18,027 hectares.[11]

In October 2007, 134,000 hectares of the traditional territory of the Guajajara people in Maranhão were identified and revised; they have been trying to extend this territory since 1980 as a number of age-old villages are located outside its boundaries.[12]

In 2007, the Xavante people obtained permanent ownership of the Maraiwatsede indigenous territory, located in the municipalities of San Felix do Araguaia and Alto da Boa Vista, in the north of Mato Grosso. This territory had been approved back in 1998. The dispute dates back to the 1960s, when the Xavante population in the area were evicted from their lands by Brazilian Air Force planes, with the help of missionaries and ranch owners, and taken to Xavante reserves in the south of the state. Scarcely had they arrived at San Marcos than 86 out of a total of 300 indigenous people died in an outbreak of measles.

According to a statement by FUNAI's former president, Mércio Pereira Gomes, the government's objective was to authorise 100 indigenous lands by 2006.

Violence caused by territorial disputes

According to Cláudio Beirão, advisor to the Indigenist Missionary Council (CIMI), between 2004 and 2006 there were a total of ten cases of summary executions of indigenous persons, and yet in the first 10 months of 2007 alone there were 15.[13]

According to information from CIMI, there were 76 murders of indigenous people in Brazil in 2007, 48 of which were in Mato Grosso do Sul.[14]
Mato Grosso do Sul has experienced the worst rates of violence, suicide and land conflict, becoming the great paradigm of the government's indigenist policy. For example, there was the eviction of 500 Guaraní-Kaiowá families from their Nhanderu Marangatu lands, followed by the murder of leader Dorvalino Rocha, whose self-confessed murderer is still at large. The history of this indigenous land is one of the greatest shames of Luis Inácio Lula da Silva's government. Title to the Guaraní-Kaiowá people was approved on 23 March 2005 with 9,316 hectares but the authorisation was suspended by a preliminary decision of the Federal Supreme Court, at the request of the ranch owners; to this day, they remain in conflict and a further life has been lost, that of the community's prayer leader, Hilário Fernades, on 25 November 2007.

The 37 Guaraní-Kaiowá families that camped along the road from Amambai to Coronel Sapucaia claiming ownership of the Madama ranch in Coronel Sapucaia are in the same situation. They consider this area to be an indigenous territory called Curussu Ambá. The region was invaded in 1976 by ranch owners who threw out all the indigenous people living there. On 8 July 2007, the 46-year-old indigenous leader, Ortiz Lopes, was murdered and, in November of that same year, a further four indigenous people were shot. The constant threats from the ranch owners and region's authorities mean that the indigenous population live in permanent fear.

The same thing is happening among the Pataxó-Hãhaãi in Taquari region, Pau Brasil municipality, Bahía. Here, another person was shot dead on 19 May 2007. Tension between indigenous people and ranch owners revolves around disputes over lands that are considered indigenous territories. The justice system is not working in favour of indigenous rights, however.

Mining and hydro-electric power: creating intense conflict

The 1988 Constitution opens up the possibility of mining exploration by national companies on indigenous lands. However, this will require approval of a law to regularise the activity, establishing who can ex-

plore, how they will do it, how the indigenous people will be compensated for damage and how they will be consulted to see if they allow
the exploration or not. However, the National Commission for Indigenist Policy (CNPI) wants this discussion to be undertaken within the
Indigenous Peoples' Statute that has been under consideration at the
National Congress for 13 years. "Mining exploration must be discussed
in the context of indigenous peoples' health, education, environment,
food security and so on".[15]

According to the organisation *Acampamento Livre*[16]:

> *The direct and indirect impacts of large undertakings such as hydro-elec-*
> *tric plants, roads, transmission lines, waterways and agribusiness on*
> *indigenous lands places the physical and cultural continuity of our peo-*
> *ples at risk, as well as the integrity of the environment and biodiversity.*
> *For this reason, it is essential that the government guarantees indigenous*
> *peoples the right to prior and informed consultation, as established in*
> *ILO Convention 169, and the right to exercise their autonomy, which*
> *even means not accepting that these undertakings be implemented on*
> *their territories. Such is the case of the transposition of the San Francisco*
> *River, the Belo Monte factory, the Estreito dam and the Madeira River*
> *hydro-electric power stations, which also cause increased conflict for the*
> *following reasons: illegal logging, reduced indigenous lands, the invasion*
> *of farm workers, ranch owners and mining companies, causing our rivers*
> *to dry up and an increase in the poisons used by agribusiness.*

The environmental impact assessment for the San Francisco River
transposition project anticipates direct impacts from the work on three
indigenous groups: the Truká, Pipipã and Kabiwá. The most serious
will be the deforestation of one of the few conserved areas in the region
and interference with animal movements.

The Estreito hydro-electric power works are at a standstill; the action questions the tender for the works, because the environmental
impact assessment conducted by the Estreito Energy Consortium gives
no analysis of the direct or indirect impacts on the region's indigenous
population. The same is the case for other hydro-electric plants on the
Madeira River (Rondonia).

The President of the Republic's insistent emphasis that these works are necessary for the country's progress does not convince the indigenous leaders, who are aware of the threat they represent. The greatest threat lies in the construction of five dams on the Xingu River.

The Belo Monte hydro-electric power station would be the first dam, followed by the Altamira, Pombla, San Felix and Montante Jarina; the total flooding could cover be between 8,000 and 12,000 km². And what would happen to the indigenous peoples on those lands?

In August 2007, *cacique* Raoni and other Kayapó Metyktire leaders from the Capoto-Jarina indigenous territory (Mato Grosso) protested at mining on their lands, citing the disastrous consequences this could have for their people's health and stating that they did not want gold diggers in their region. They are against the draft mining law on indigenous lands that is still under discussion.[17]

Indigenous health[18]

Since 2005, scandalous failings in indigenous health care have been a constant. Various indigenous protests bear witness to this, which could be considered a form of genocide. The continuing lack of technicians, medicines, along with a failure to transfer the most seriously ill to hospital, added to complaints regarding the diversion of funds and medicines, has left the indigenous population at the mercy of constant epidemics that had previously been eradicated, causing deaths in most cases among the children.

2006 and 2007 were marked by an even greater abandonment and chaos. According to the CNPI, indigenous health care was marked by the poor attention it received from the National Health Foundation (FUNASA). The situation deteriorated yet further because of the politicization of posts within the organisation and the increasing trend towards municipalising health care. This culminated in various complaints of corruption such as, for example, the prison sentence for Ramiro Teixeira, former coordinator of FUNASA in Roraima, for diverting public funds intended for indigenous populations.[19] The indigenous people ... "do not accept the municipalisation of health care, as many local authorities do not have the capacity to manage the resources and the prefectures tend to divert the funds for party-political purposes".[20]

One great disgrace is the return of malaria and hepatitis B and D in epidemic proportions to Valle de Javari (Amazonas). The number of victims has grown enormously. As many as 2,883 cases of malaria were noted during 2006/2007, suggesting that 90% of the population were suffering from the illness. Blood tests carried out by FUNASA discovered that 56% of the population was carrying the hepatitis B virus, whereas the World Health Organisation gives 2% as being an acceptable limit.

The great danger is among indigenous populations such as the Zo'é, who live in the state's Conservation Unit in the north of Pará, and who were contacted in 1991; in 2006, 80% of their population of 239 contracted malaria. The Matis of the Javari basin, a people who are on the verge of extinction following 25 years of fatal epidemics, are now suffering an epidemic of hepatitis B.

Hepatitis B and C is also spreading among the indigenous population of Polo-Base de Guajará Mirim (Rondonia). A study conducted in May 2007 of 836 blood tests showed the following: of a total of 100 people infected, 78 people tested positive for hepatitis B and 22 for hepatitis C.

The revolt of the indigenous organisations belonging to the Permanent Forum of Presidents of Indigenous Health Districts with regard to the national health policy resulted in an open letter condemning the urgent situation of indigenous health:

> *The tragic situation facing the indigenous population is exacerbated by the spread of hepatitis Delta among the indigenous peoples of Valle del Javari (Amazon) and the risk of a new wave of malaria among the Yanomami; these are the symptoms of a management crisis within the Sub-system for Indigenous Health Care, currently under the responsibility of the National Health Foundation-FUNASA.*[21]

Indigenous movements and organisations: main demands

During 2007, several meetings of indigenous organisations, communities and cooperations took place. The main concerns voiced at those meetings were the presence of ranch owners and the regulation of lands, the increasing influx of gold diggers and mining company and the government's Accelerated Growth Plan (PAC), as well as social problems, such as domestic violence, health issues and the preservation of culture and traditions.

Here we only mention a few of those meetings:

- Meeting of Cooperation and Alliance of the North-West Amazon (CANOA)[22] in San Gabriel da Cachoeira (Amazonas) held from 23 to 26 July 2007. The main aim was to support the situation of the Yanomami peoples on the border with Venezuela and to enter into dialogue with the Venezuelan organisation Wataniba (Association for the Multi-ethnic Human Development of the Amazon), in addition to discussing autonomy and land demarcation in Colombia and Venezuela.

- II Trinational Meeting of Indigenous Peoples from the Brazilian, Peruvian and Bolivian Borders – held in Río Branco (Acre) from 17 to 20 July 2007. The main concerns were related to the peoples in isolation, in addition to the movement of indigenous populations across borders between these countries. However, they also condemned the mining, hydro-electric, cattle rearing, logging, oil and gas exploration projects. The meeting was organised by the Organisation of Indigenous Peoples of Acre (PIN), from the south of Amazonas and northwest Rondonia, the Native Federation of Madre de Dios (FENAMAD), from Peru, and the Indigenous Federation of Native Peoples of Amazonia de Pando (CIPOAP), from Bolivia.

- *Campamento Tierra Libre* (Free Land Camp) - indigenous April – considered the largest movement in Brazil, its main strategy is to challenge federal government over its failure to keep its promises, such as: the 272 indigenous territories claimed by the indigenous peoples, the disregard of the Ministry of Justice, the failure to meet the legal deadline for publication of regulatory declarations for the 34 areas in the process of being demarcated, a failure to comply with the Constitution and ILO Convention 169 by not consulting the indigenous communities on various infrastructural works affecting them, some of which are listed in the Accelerated Growth Plan (PAC), and the insufficient attention given to their basic needs such as health, education and safety.

Conclusion

Another year has passed without autonomy or respect for indigenous populations. However strong the organisations become, it will be to no avail if there are no indigenous representatives with the power to intervene in discussions on public policies and the country's growth. The area of most concern is the Accelerated Growth Plan and its goals, which are the main focus of national government. This plan is reminiscent of past military government times; the slogan is no longer Security and Development but Progress and Development, at the cost of a weaker indigenous population and a declining biodiversity. We are witnessing, yet again, another "civilising" project. ❑

Notes

1 **IBGE – Instituto Brasilero de Geografia y Estadística, 2000:** *Demographic Census 2000*. The *Instituto Socioambiental* does not use the IBGE statistics and continues to state that Brazil's indigenous population totals around 370,000 inhabitants or 2% of the population.

2 CIMI – *A violência contra os povos indígenas no Brasil. 2003-2005*. The information previously given included data up to May 2006.

3 Folha de São Paulo, 8 January 2008.

4 The CNPI was created on 19 April 2007 in the Ministry of Justice in Brasilia and comprises 20 indigenous leaders.

5 www.socioambiental.org/noticias/nsa/detalhe?id=2447.

6 www.cimi.org.br/?system=news&action=read&id=2830&eid=293.

7 Marcio Meira was appointed FUNAI's president in March 2007.

8 www.socioambiental.org/nsa/detalhe?id=2532.

9 www.socioambiental.org/nsa/detalhe?id=2532.

10 Representatives of FUNAI, the Ministry of Justice and the Federal Attorney General's office.

11 www.socioambiental.org/nsa/detalhe?id=2523.

12 In 2003, *cacique* Zequinha Mendes was murdered in what the community considered to be a criminal attack. In 2004, an armed group invaded one of the ar-

ea's villages. In 2005, six armed men entered a village and killed 70-year-old *cacique* João Guajajara, raped his 16-year-old daughter and shot at bullet through the head of another son. In February 2007, a group entered another village and set fire to 30 homes.

13 www.cimi.org/?system=news&action=read&id=2844&eid=274.
14 www.cimi.org.br/?system=news7action=read&id=2963&eid=259.
15 www.cimi.org.br/?system=news&action=read&id=2836&eid=274.
16 Indigenous Movement, www.cimi.org.br/?system=new&action=read&id=250 6&eid=387.
17 www.sociambiental.org/nsa/detalhe?id=2515.
18 The National Health Foundation has been responsible for indigenous health since 1991. There are five indigenous leaders representing the Special Indigenous Health Districts (DESEI) on FUNASA's Consultative Committee, two directors of regional indigenous organisations and representatives from the Federal Attorney General's office, the National Indigenous Foundation (FUNAI) and the Intersectoral Coordinating Body for Indigenous Health, among others.
19 www.socioambiental.org/nsa/detalhe?id=2549.
20 www.cimi.org.br/?system=news&action=read&id=2506&eid=387.
21 www.socioambiental.org/nsa/detalhe?id=2412.
22 CANOA is a network of indigenous and non-indigenous organisations from Brazil, Colombia and Venezuela.

Maria de Lourdes Alcantara de Beldi is an anthropologist, scientific coordinator of the "Imaginary and Memory Group" and editor of the Revista Imaginário *of Sao Paulo University. For the last five years, she has been working with indigenous youth from the Dourados Reserve in Mato Grosso do Sul.*

PARAGUAY

The 2002 census of indigenous peoples gave a figure of 87,099 people, representing 1.7% of Paraguay's total population.[1] The National Census, however, through the question on ethnic belonging, recorded another 2,070 people who stated that they belonged to one of Paraguay's indigenous peoples. More than half the indigenous population live in the Western (Occidental) Region, also known as the Chaco.

The indigenous population has been classified into 20 ethnic groups, of which the largest numerically are the Mby'a guaraní, Avá guaraní, Paî tavyterâ, Nivaclé, Enlhet norte, Enxet sur and, to a lesser extent, the Manjui, Guaná and Tomaraho ethnic groups.

The situation of extreme poverty in which the indigenous peoples live is reflected in their lack of land ownership. The census indicates that there are 412 indigenous communities in Paraguay, of which 185 have no permanent property titles, 45 in the Western Region (Chaco) and 140 in the Eastern (Oriental) Region.

Paraguay has a legal framework that guarantees and recognises a fairly wide range of rights in favour of indigenous peoples. The approval of ILO Convention 169 should also be noted, transposed into law as Law 234/93.

Indigenous peoples living in voluntary isolation

The Paraguayan state has few coherent public policies for dealing with and protecting indigenous peoples in isolation.[2] Government protection measures are still limited to partial, isolated and generally totally insufficient interventions. An international mission of the International Committee for the Protection of Indigenous Peoples Living in Voluntary Isolation and Initial Contact (*Comité Internacional Indígena para la Protección de los Pueblos Indígenas Aislados y en Contacto Inicial - CIPIACI*) visited the north of the Chaco region in September 2007 and was able to observe the threats facing Ayoreo groups in isolation.

The case of the Totobiegosode is a longstanding one. This relates to a group of indigenous Ayoreo people who, in 1993, instigated a claim for the return of part of their former lands - an area of 550,000 hectares in Alto Paraguay department - with the support of a local NGO People Environment and Territory (*Gente Ambiente y Territorio - GAT*). The request is based, among other things, on a need to protect groups related to them who are living in isolation. Given the delays in the process and the constant threat of deforestation to the south of this area, the Payipie Ichadie Totobiegosode Organisation (OPIT) approached the United Nations Development Programme (UNDP) and requested that this organisation set up a body through which to dialogue and negotiate.

Representatives of the convened institutions and indigenous leaders decided to commence the process by establishing what was known as the Inter-Institutional Committee,[3] the main aim of which was to combine forces around the consolidation and legalisation of the estates of the Area of the Southern Zone of the Ayoreo Totobiegosode Natural and Cultural Heritage (PNCAT) in Alto Paraguay department, protecting the natural resources in that area and the rights of their related groups in isolation. Almost one year on since establishment of this body, however, the challenges still remain and the environmental threats are even greater.

The Union of Native Ayoreo of Paraguay (*Unión de Nativos Ayoreo del Paraguay - UNAP*) recently made a claim for the lands owned by the Umbú S.A. company in Boquerón department, stating its support for the protection of groups in isolation and calling for recovery of the control and use of their ancestral territory. The dispossession of their ancestral lands has received little public attention, and their respective rights are not respected in Paraguay. The Commission for the Self-Determination of Indigenous Peoples in Paraguay (*Comisión por la Autodeterminación de los Pueblos Indígenas en Paraguay - CAPI*) is taking up these challenges. In 2007, as in previous years, national and international private owners and public bodies continued to impose their

plans and projects on the ancestral Ayoreo territory without any consideration of the indigenous rights involved.

Exceptional emergency becomes the rule

The Paraguayan state's efforts to fulfil its commitments and avoid further prosecution and sentencing in relation to the indigenous peoples' cases being considered by the Inter-American human rights system has led to its partial compliance with the Inter-American Court of Human Rights' ruling in the Yakye Axa and Sawhoyamaxa cases, as well as the precautionary measures stipulated by the Inter-American Commission on Human Rights (IACHR) in favour of the Kelyenmagategma community in 2004. This compliance has focused primarily on areas of the ruling that related to providing the basic goods and services necessary for their subsistence, which has been implemented by the Ministry for National Emergencies.

Double standards have been perceived in this regard, however. In the first place, food aid has been focused on those indigenous communities that have formed the object of favourable international rulings, with greater implementation difficulties being noted in those without this protection. In addition, insufficient human, material and logistic resources for the aid effort throughout the country have led to a delay in responding to the pressing situation in many communities. Such is the case of the Payseyamexyempa'a community in Presidente Hayes department, whose members remain cut off due to the flooding that is surrounding them following bad weather. This is making not only movement outside the community impossible but also the provision of aid. Repeated communications were made to the Ministry for National Emergencies with regard to the extreme situation they were facing but aid was only provided once a constitutional appeal had been submitted and passed.[4]

The use of this constitutional guarantee has formed an effective measure by which to force the state to mitigate the urgent needs caused by this uncertain situation although it has not been a general rule. The issue of double standards in the provision of humanitarian assistance was identified by the Committee on Economic, Social and Cultural Rights as a violation of the right to food and water. Bearing in mind the urgency of the situation, rights are in some cases being violated by omission, by preventing quick "access to food aid of a humanitarian nature in [...] emergency situations".[5]

International justice: progress with compliance but no in-depth solutions

On 2 February 2007, the Inter-American Court of Human Rights decided to oversee compliance with its ruling in the case of the Sawhoyamaxa community vs. Paraguay, given the deaths of Rafael Martínez, Aurelia Montanía, Eulalio Yegros and Rodrigo Marcial Dávalos, Enxet members of the Sawhoyamaxa community. They had all received little or no medical care in their community. The Court considered that: "The state has not put a stop to the violation of the right to life of members of the Sawhoyamaxa community, it is still keeping them in a high-risk situation and has not adopted sufficient preventive measures to avoid loss of life".[6]

This ruling caused the Paraguayan state to take measures to comply with some points of the ruling and the precautionary measures taken against it in relation to indigenous peoples. Over the year, some noteworthy progress has been noted in this regard, the Office of the Attorney General being established as the new institutional point of contact responsible for promoting implementation mechanisms.

As previously noted, the need to provide food aid has been fulfilled in all cases,[7] albeit somewhat irregularly. The basic package does not provide sufficient food and water, however, and no clear indicators have been specified to establish the quantity and quality of food provided, despite the Inter-American Court's requirements in this regard.

A medical team was appointed by the state to investigate the cause of the above deaths and, in their report, its members clearly noted the low nutritional value of the food and identified elements aimed at preventing further deaths. The state has yet to take on board these recommendations from its own officials, however.

A communications system has been installed in the Sawhoyamaxa community enabling them to contact the relevant health authorities for assistance in emergency cases, in accordance with Point 10 of the Ruling. In addition, some compensation was paid for damages and costs.

Despite this progress, however, there has been no movement with regard to other issues of crucial importance, such as the return of traditional lands, which would enable other basic rights to be enjoyed, including cultural preservation. The deadline given by the Inter-American Court of Human Rights has not yet passed for the physical and formal handover of traditional lands but there has been a worrying lack of measures in this regard. The current Congress will have the power to adopt measures aimed at handing over land to the Yakye Axa community within the period established by the Court. If they do not do so, the Paraguayan state will be internationally compromised with regard to the national elections set for the coming year, given that the appointment of the legislative and executive representatives will take place outside the three-year period Paraguay has been given in which to return the ancestral territories.

On 1 June 2007, the Paraguayan state paid compensation and costs in line with the sentence passed against it in the case of Yakye Axa vs. Paraguay. On 13 July 2007, two years after notification to the state of the first international ruling against it in relation to indigenous peoples, leaders and delegates of the Yakye Axa community of the Enxet people made a proposal to the state with regard to complying with the rulings of the Inter-American Court in the cases of "Yakye Axa indigenous community vs. Paraguay" and "Sawhoyamaxa indigenous community vs. Paraguay".

Thousands of letters from people in Europe concerned at the situation of Yakye Axa families were at the same time sent to the President of Congress, in the context of an international campaign initiated by the Food First Information and Action Network (FIAN International) with the support of the local NGO Tierraviva. These letters reminded the Paraguayan state of its obligations arising from the international ruling.

Against a backdrop of intense lobbying, these actions led to significant progress with regard to the traditional territory of the Yakye Axa including, among other things: a request by the Attorney-General for a precautionary injunction to protect the status quo, and INDI's (Paraguayan Indian Institute - *Instituto Paraguayo del Indígena*) decision to request the expropriation of estates that overlap with the territory claimed.

On 24 July 2007, the Inter-American Commission on Human Rights ruled on the admissibility of petition 987-04 submitted by the Kelyenmagategma indigenous community of the Enxet people and its members[8] for alleged violations by the Paraguayan state of the rights to life, physical integrity, legal guarantees, protection of honour and dignity, protection of the family, the rights of the child, the right to property, movement and residence, legal protection and education, plus the state's obligation to respect rights and adopt domestic legislation to guarantee them.[9]

IACHR sessions and the presence of the Commissioner for Indigenous Peoples

The IACHR sat in Asunción from 5 to 7 September, in the context of its 129th special period of sessions. The presence of Commissioner Paolo Carozza, Rapporteur on the Rights of Indigenous Peoples, was of crucial importance because, prior to the sessions, he spent 3 and 4 September visiting the Xakmok Kásek and Yakye Axa indigenous communities in the Paraguayan Chaco, meeting the government authorities responsible for indigenous peoples' policy and holding working meetings on petitions and cases in which the alleged victims are indigenous communities. In addition, on 7 September 2007, Rapporteur Carozza and the president of the IACHR attended a meeting with representatives of more than 300 indigenous communities from the Eastern and Western regions of Paraguay. At this meeting, representatives from 14 indigenous associations described the serious and urgent situation facing their communities. They described the meeting as historic because "it was the first time there had been direct discussions, without intermediaries".[10]

In the context of the Kelyenmagategma case, the petitioners told the IACHR of the possibility of submitting a proposal to the state and that the working meeting would decide whether a friendly solution would be commenced or not. In the context of this agreement - a proposal from the community – a consensus had been achieved on the points raised by state representatives. However, unable to effectively comply with the proposal, the state representatives withdrew hours before it was due to be signed and so the friendly process was not initiated, due solely to the actions of the state.

Different ways of facing up to inequality

The emergence of indigenous peoples as social and political players in Latin America in recent years is an undeniable fact. Paraguay has been no exception in this, as participation in spaces for the protection of indigenous interests has increased and indigenous struggles have gained greater visibility.

Since the return to democracy, legislative advances have been made with regard to indigenous issues. And yet the communities continue to experience a context of discrimination, and are subjected to numerous forms of abuse, highlighting the gap existing between formal recognition of rights and their actual enforcement.

Strategies in 2007 were not limited simply to expressing their discontent and disapproval at state action through measures such as roadblocks. A constant vigil was held outside INDI, and Mbyá, Aché and Chupapou families set up camp in Asunción's squares to exert pressure on the authorities to guarantee their territories and the implementation of indigenist policies.

On 11 and 12 October 2007, in a day of protest and demands for the dignity of indigenous peoples, members of the Chaco communities closed the Rafael Franco road in the Sawhoyamaxa community demanding – among other things – enforcement of the international rulings and more funding for INDI, particularly for land purchases, whilst rejecting amendments to the Criminal Code.[11]

Indigenous organisations grouped together in the Coordinating Body for the Self-Determination of Indigenous Peoples (*Coordinadora por la Autodeterminación de los Pueblos Indígenas* - CAPI) also met with Juan León Alvarado, a Maya Quiché and president of the Working Group for the Declaration on the Rights of Indigenous Peoples of the Organisation of American States (OAS). He analysed the whole OAS Declaration process with his Paraguayan peers in the context of a *Workshop Seminar on Participation and Influence of Indigenous Peoples in International Spheres*, held from 27 to 30 March in Asunción. Among other things, the international instruments protecting and guaranteeing the rights of indigenous peoples were analysed and discussed.[12]

Indigenous organisations also gained prominence in other arenas, for example in the submission of alternative reports to the UN Committee on Economic, Social and Cultural Rights. The 39th period of sessions of this Committee was held from 5 to 23 November 2007 in its offices in Geneva, Switzerland. On behalf of civil society and along with other organisations, the Coordinating Body of Leaders of the Lower Chaco (*Coordinadora de Líderes del Bajo Chaco* - CLIBCh) and the

Coordinating Body for Self-determination of Indigenous Peoples (*Coordinadora por la Autodeterminación de los Pueblos Indígenas* - CAPI) presented this committee with an alternative to the official report on Paraguay's compliance with the International Covenant on Economic, Social and Cultural Rights, for the Committee's consideration.[13]

The recommendations adopted by this UN committee when making its final observations on the report submitted by the Paraguayan state were made known on 3 December 2007,[14] and they highlight the main concerns of the indigenous movement with regard to land, stating: "The Committee recommends that the state party step up its efforts to speed up the demarcation and recovery of the ancestral lands and territories of the indigenous peoples…". It also states its great concern with regard to other issues, such as the situation of extreme poverty in some areas, which has reached alarming proportions in recent years.

From 6 to 8 November 2007, the "Meeting of the Indigenous Peoples of the South American Gran Chaco" was held in Cerrito, Benjamín Aceval. This meeting is part of the ENCHACO initiative and is the culmination of a series of National Meetings of Indigenous Peoples of the Gran Chaco in defence of their access to water and to their traditional territories.[15] The eleven indigenous peoples of the Paraguayan Chaco attending this meeting accused the Paraguayan state of a massive structural violation of their collective rights, as guaranteed in the Constitution and ILO Convention 169. This is being exacerbated by threats against their autonomy as peoples, a massive dispossession of their territories and water resources and the deliberate dismantling of resources essential to their material and cultural survival. In turn, this is being aggravated by a rapid contamination of the drinking water and a constant, indiscriminate and aggressive marketing of resources and spaces, which is being conducted with no regard for legality in the three departments of the Paraguayan Chaco.[16]

Conclusion

This year was marked by emergencies that severely exacerbated the living conditions of indigenous peoples. The efforts made by the Paraguayan state to comply with obligations resulting from the rulings of international human rights bodies must be recognised, particularly with regard to the payment of compensation and the provision of goods and services. These actions merely alleviate the symptoms of extreme poverty being experienced by indigenous peoples, however, and do not cover all peoples throughout the country as they should.

These insufficient efforts are worrying, both in terms of the definitive return of the indigenous peoples' ancestral territories and in terms of the adoption of measures that are not in keeping with the principle of self-determination. Efforts to amend criminal legislation are also of concern, as this would enable indigenous persecution to be perpetuated in the context of their territorial demands.   ❑

Notes

1   **Dirección General de Estadística, Encuestas y Censos, 2002**: *Censo Nacional Indígena de Población y Vivienda 2002*. Available at: www.dgeec.gov.py.
2   These are groups that have not established contact with the rest of society and refuse to do so, even with members of their own people. The Ayoreo Totobiegosode confirm the existence of some of their relatives living in isolation. Other sources indicate the presence of up to five groups, making up a total estimated number of between 50 and 100 people. All belong to the Ayoreo people.
3   The Committee is made up of representatives of: the Payipie Ichadie Totobiegosode Organisation (OPIT), the Ministry for the Environment (SEAM), the Ethnic Rights Advisory Group and the Environmental Crime Unit of the State Attorney-General, the Paraguayan Indigenous Institute (INDI), the National Forestry Department of the Ministry of Agriculture and Livestock, the *Asociación Gente, Ambiente y Territorio* (GAT) and the Church Committee for Emergency Aid (CIPAE). The following are supportive observers: CODEHUPY, the *Red de Entidades al Servicio de los Pueblos Indígenas*, the *Red de Organizaciones Ambientalistas No Gubernamentales* (ROAM) and the *Asociación de ONGs del Paraguay* (POJOAJU), along with the *Coordinadora por la Autodeterminación de los Pueblos Indígenas* (CAPI) and P. Bartomeu Meliá.
4   Appeal for constitutional protection: Payseyamexyempa´a indigenous community vs. Ministry for National Emergencies No. 265/2007; ruling of 4 April 2007.
5   Committee on Economic, Social and Cultural Rights: *General Observation Nº 12 – The right to adequate food* (art. 11), para.19. E/C.12/1999/5.
6   Inter-American Court of Human Rights: *Supervising Compliance with Ruling in the case of " Sawhoyamaxa indigenous community vs. Paraguay"*, 2 February 2007, para. 13.

7   In this respect, the Ministry for National Emergencies maintains that "in the area of Pozo Colorado, the town councils receive 5,920 kilos of food every month. In Yakye Axa, 69 families benefit from one kit each, in Santa Elisa 52 families and at Km 16 27 families receive food". Available on the website: www.sen.gov.py

8   IACHR: *Report N° 55/07*. The case was given number 12629.

9   Articles 4, 5, 8.1, 11 , 1 7, 1 9, 21, 22 and 25 of the American Convention on Human Rights linked to articles 1.1 and 2 of the same and article 13 of the San Salvador Protocol.

10 Cf. Inter-American Commission on Human Rights (IACHR). Press Release N° 54/07, available at:
    http://www.iachr.org/Comunicados/Spanish/2007/54.07sp.htm.

11 ABC Color daily newspaper dated 10 October 2007, p. 33

12 A finished weblog of the seminar can be found at
    http://www.pci.org.py/capi/index.html

13 Available at http://www.ohchr.org/english/bodies/c/cescrs39.htm

14 Available at http://www2.ohchr.org/english/bodies/cescr/docs/cescr39/E.C.12.PRY.CO.3_sp.pdf

15 Meeting of Makxawaiya/Paraguay was held in August 2006, Meeting in Laguna Yema/Argentina in May 2007 and Meeting of Macharetí/Bolivia in September 2007.

16 Report provided by Cristina Vila from the Church Committee for Emergency Aid (*Comité de Iglesias para Ayuda de Emergencias* – CIPAE).

Mario Barrios *es abogado, miembro del área de casos y litigios de la ONG Tierraviva.*

ARGENTINA

Argentina is a federal state made up of 23 provinces. According to the official census, its total population was 23 million in 2001. The indigenous population is officially calculated to represent approximately 2.5 to 3% of this number, although indigenous organisations put this figure at closer to 5%. In 2004, an additional survey to the official census was conducted to estimate, by sampling, the number of indigenous people now living in Argentina. Although the criterion of self-identification was applied, the methodology used did not enable this figure to be taken as definite because a wide range of people did not admit their ethnic belonging through fear of discrimination, and because the survey was not carried out properly in urban areas, where a high number of indigenous people live. Even so, it has to be noted that there were 18 recognised indigenous peoples in 2001 and by 2007 there were 31. Legally, these peoples have specific constitutional rights at federal level and in various provincial states. ILO Convention 169 and other universal human rights standards such as the International Covenants on Civil and Political Rights and Economic, Social and Cultural Rights have constitutional strength within the country.

The country

Since Argentina's institutional, social and economic crisis of 2001 and 2002, there has been exponential economic growth each year, reaching up to 7-8% in 2007. This has been due, in part, to the advance of the agricultural frontier, which has preferred to focus on soya for the external market[1], hydrocarbon production and, to a lesser extent, the

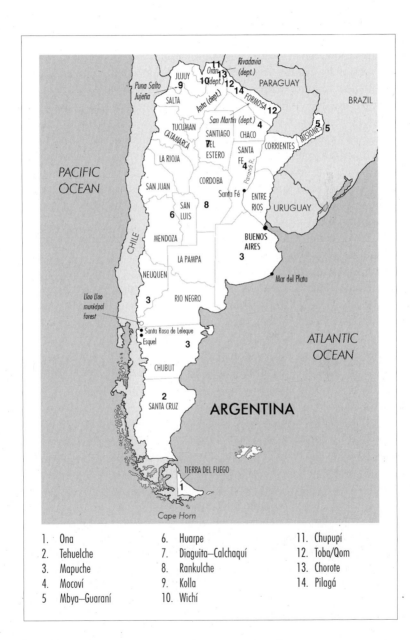

1. Ona
2. Tehuelche
3. Mapuche
4. Mocoví
5 Mbya—Guaraní
6. Huarpe
7. Diaguita—Calchaquí
8. Rankulche
9. Kolla
10. Wichí
11. Chupupí
12. Toba/Qom
13. Chorote
14. Pilagá

tourist industry. This has had a bearing in terms of a slight reduction in rates of poverty and unemployment and an improvement in the living conditions of the upper middle classes. Alongside this, there has been an increasing concentration of the land, the felling of native forest for conversion to farming affecting primarily the rural population, giving rise to new migratory processes from the countryside to the town, increased urban marginalisation, and discriminatory and xenophobic practices on the part of the city population towards the new arrivals. To remedy the critical situation of socio-economic exclusion and to reduce unemployment, the national government has put in place a policy of family subsidies which, far from favouring the poor, has provided easy pickings for a corrupt leadership whose main activity is restricted to establishing a client base essential for gaining support and ensuring electoral success, as we shall see later on.

This economic growth has led to violations of the collective rights of indigenous peoples and runs counter to the policy of recognition that the state claims to defend. On the one hand, this recognition has not resulted in an adaptation of the country's existing legislation to the specific features of indigenous peoples and, on the other, there are enormous failings in the correct implementation of those laws that have been passed. For example, there is no regulation governing the right to participation and consultation, nor are there effective legal means of safeguarding indigenous peoples' ancestral lands. In practice, many indigenous community members are intimidated, pressurised and persecuted to renounce claims to their lands; they are repeatedly removed from their territories by court rulings, or criminal proceedings are commenced against them for the crime of misappropriation. Meanwhile, infrastructural works and agricultural and livestock farms, mining and forestry operations continue to be developed in different areas of the country, endangering the territorial integrity, life and cultural survival of indigenous peoples.

In education, the state has not adopted a political framework that takes the linguistic, pedagogic and cultural features of indigenous peoples into account, nor has it implemented urgent and necessary reforms to the current curricular content aimed at the whole of society, which makes a mockery of the right to a bilingual intercultural education, as stipulated by law.

In terms of public information on the health status of indigenous peoples, there are notable deficiencies: although aware of the socio-economic vulnerability of these people, the state has not conducted an investigation that would enable it to gain a true assessment of the situation of their economic, social and cultural rights, nor has it adopted, within the social security system, special measures aimed at addressing the specific needs of these peoples, as shall be seen further on.

From an official perspective, 2007 was a year of economic growth and improvement in standards of living for the population, but for the indigenous peoples this signified an increasing loss of their lands and natural resources.

Deforestation emergency – Forestry Law

According to a report produced by Greenpeace Argentina on the basis of official data from the Ministry for the Environment and Sustainable Development of the Nation (*Secretaría de Ambiente y Desarrollo Sustentable de la Nación* - SAyDS), the country has lost 75% of its original native forests[2] to deforestation, calculated at between 280,000 and 300,000 hectares per year. The main reason is the expansion of the agricultural and livestock frontier.[3] The information used to produce the Greenpeace report came from forest maps produced by each province, updated until 2002 and published in March 2005, and from the report "Monitoring of Native Forests. Period 1998-2002, and 2002-2006. Preliminary findings." (*Monitoreo de Bosque Nativo. Período 1998-2002, período 2002-2006. Datos Preliminares.* Published in June 2007 by the Forest Evaluation System Management Unit - *Unidad de Manejo del Sistema de Evaluación Forestal*). The rate of deforestation in Salta, Santiago del Estero and Formosa doubled over this period. By way of comparison, Santiago del Estero and Salta have an annual rate five times and three times higher respectively than that calculated for the whole world over the period 1990-2000. In October, while debates on a forestry law were stepping up in the National Congress and an electoral campaign was in full swing in Salta province, the rate of deforestation increased to 101 hectares every hour.

Deforestation of large forest masses is taking place, among others, in the departments of San Martín, Orán and Anta, on indigenous ancestral territories. As has been noted in previous reports for *The Indigenous World*, the Route 86 communities in San Martín are physically preventing the advance of the bulldozers, patiently awaiting legislators to approve an expropriation project that would grant some of these communities titles to the territorial area on which the families are settled. This would not mean and automatic transfer of control because – as we know – the private owners appeal against legal rulings in order to gain time with which to continue the deforestation and their business. In contrast, the leaders are repressed by the security forces and taken to court.

Despite all this, the communities have commenced legal and political actions to prevent the continuing deforestation.

In July, the El Tabacal community, of the Guaraní people, in Orán department, managed to get the provincial courts to admit a constitutional challenge presented against the Seaboard Corporation, ordering it to abstain from "undertaking acts that involve predation, extraction of trees, plants, movements of land or desecration of graves on the La Loma lands" until the dispute over ownership of the lands between the multinational company and the community had been resolved.[4] Unfortunately, the company has failed to comply with the ruling and is continuing to destroy the forest, as noted by eye witnesses from the national newspapers.

The remaining native forests are located in the Chaco region which coincides - more or less - with Rivadavia department. The scarcity of rains makes it difficult to convert this area to farmland although the threat of deforestation is still present through the illegal felling of protected species such as the *palo santo* ("holy wood" or "lignum vitae"), which is used to make fencing posts and floors in luxury homes, and the carob tree, which is used to make furniture. In the northern section of Rivadavia department can be found more than 54 communities whose organisation, the Lhaka Honhat Association of Aboriginal Communities (*Asociación de Comunidades Aborígenes Lhaka Honhat*) managed in 2006 to get the Inter-American Commission on Human Rights (IACHR) to admit a complaint made in 1998 for violation of their right to land ownership and defence of natural resources.[5] Unfortunately, while the IACHR conducts an analysis of the facts in order to pass its ruling on an issue of law, the local government is making no efforts to put a halt to this dispossession of natural resources, and has allowed corrupt politicians to do business selling logging authorisations to third parties who, taking advantage of the indigenous people's poverty, give them chainsaws to cut down the trees of their ancestral territory in exchange for food, cigarettes and drink. Huge numbers of actions such as these and various complaints gained publicity through Greenpeace Argentina's campaign to obtain a million signatures in favour of approval of a Forest Law by the Congress of the Nation.

Law on minimum budgets for environmental protection of the native forests

This law establishes the minimum environmental protection budgets for the development, conservation, use and sustainable management of the native forests, and for the environmental services that these provide to society. It also establishes a regime and criteria for the distribution of funds. Among its objectives are: a) promoting conservation through the territorial regulation of native forests and regulating expansion of the agricultural and livestock frontier and any other change in soil use; b) implementing the necessary measures to regulate and control the existing native forest; aimed at achieving a sustainable area; c) improving and maintaining the ecological and cultural processes in native forests that are of benefit to society; d) enforcing precautionary and preventive principles, maintaining native forests whose environmental benefits - or the environmental damage that their absence would create - although they may not be able to demonstrate this with currently available techniques; e) encouraging activities of development, conservation, restoration, improvement and sustainable management of the native forests. For this reason, each province will need to present, within a one-year period, its plan for territorial regulation of the native forests in line with the sustainability criteria established in the law, according to different categories of conservation and depending on the environmental value of the different units of native forest and the environmental services they provide. The law, which will need to be enforced as from 2008, does not guarantee that the deforestation will stop; without an effective body to monitor the depredation, no law can stop it. And how many people would be needed to effectively monitor millions of hectares? We shall have to wait and see what happens over the coming months.

Mining ventures

75% of the country's area remains unexplored, and so the Ministry for Mining is inviting mining companies to conduct explorations in the 5,000 kms that includes the Andes mountain range.[6] In 2003, people – both indigenous and non-indigenous – from Esquel in Chubut province marched to say NO to the extraction activities of the Meridian Gold company in the area, with the result that it temporarily suspended its activity. The newspaper *Página 12* counts nine mining ventures being executed in the region on indigenous territories. Mining is one of the pressing problems in Jujuy province. Rock exploitation, acid rain and the cyanide used by these mines are contaminating the water that both animals and people drink in Puna Salto Jujeña, where children have been noted as having high levels of lead and other minerals in their blood.[7] In its Newsletter 532 in September, the NGO Ecologists' Action Network (*Red Acción Ecologista*), condemned the fact that there were more than forty metal mining explorations in Salta, with over one hundred claims of proven deposits of gold, silver, copper, lead, bismuth, iron, manganese, molybdenum, zinc, barium, lithium, uranium and thorium.

Oil contamination

Oil contamination continues to affect communities of the Mapuche people. For two months, the community of Lof Wentru Tahuel Leufu in Neuquén province paralysed the work of the oil company Piedra del Águila until a legal ruling authorised their access onto the community's territory. In December, the community condemned the burning of

. a vehicle, a *ruka*[8] and shots fired at them, blaming this action on the
provincial government and on Petrolera Piedra del Águila S.A.

A fundamental law in the making

In November 2006, Emergency Law 26160 on community ownership
was enacted.[9] This ordered a halt to the evictions of indigenous communities for a period of four years and the conducting of a survey of
the lands that "they traditionally occupy" during the first three years
of validity of the Law. When attempting to implement the law, however, the National Institute for Indigenous Affairs (implementing
body) came up against fierce opposition from the provincial governments with regard to the management of indigenous affairs within
their spheres of influence. Because of this, in 2007, after the law had
been in place for almost one year, the national government issued a
decree containing only two articles. One of them ratified the National
Institute for Indigenous Affairs, INAI, as the implementing body and
the Council for Indigenous Participation (*Consejo de Participación Indígena*) as the body working alongside the Institute supporting, advising
and, ultimately, validating the decisions it was to adopt. The Council is
made up of one representative from each town and province, chosen
by legally-constituted communities. Many of these representatives
have been rejected by the communities and organisations due to the
irregular manner in which the elections were held. This is why the
communities are not in agreement that it should be the Council that
supervises and ratifies the land surveys to be undertaken. The INAI
authorities, in contrast, consider that despite the difficulties encountered in undertaking the survey, the results thus far achieved are satisfactory and they cite, among other things, the progress in Jujuy province where nearly all indigenous lands have already been surveyed.
They are confident that progress will be made in Río Negro province
where the implementing agreement has been signed between INAI
and the Council for Indigenous Development (*Consejo de Desarrollo Indígena* - CODESI). This has been highly questioned by the Mapuche
communities of this province, who consider that this agreement re-

sponds only to official policy guidelines and not to the demands and political projects of the indigenous peoples.

Indigenous land recovery policy

In February 2007, Atilio Curiñanco and Rosa Rúa Nahuelquir, both Mapuche, returned to Santa Rosa de Leleque, from where they had been evicted in 2002 when a company of the Benetton Group denounced them for usurping its land. The response to this act of recovery was a court action on the part of the District Attorney requesting that the judge order their eviction from the land. The allegation of usurpation was based on the fact that, on entering, the Mapuche had caused damage to the area, and that their entry had taken place clandestinely; however, on physical inspection, the General Attorney noted that this was not the case and the General Attorney's office threw out the case.

In September 2007, members of this Mapuche community in Río Negro province set up a *ruka* in the area of Villa Tacul within the jurisdiction of the Llao Llao municipal forest, where a luxury international five-star tourist complex is located. According to information from the group's spokespersons, the area has been inhabited by their ancestors since before the 1900s but the conflict began with the creation of the National Parks, when the community ended up with no men due to the death of a grandfather and an uncle of the current members. It was under these circumstances that the eviction orders began, which the illiterate grandmother systematically refused to accept. They were finally chased out of the place until now, when the 126 community members decided to recover the land.[10]

For two weeks in December, community members of the Sacred City of the India Quilmes Community were in a state of alert and permanent assembly at the entry to the Sacred City, now a tourist attraction due to the archaeological ruins to be found there. The aim of the vigil was to get Tucumán Turismo to implement the decree cancelling the management concession for the Quilmes Ruins Tourist Complex, granted in 1992 for ten years to a private individual named Héctor Cruz. A ruling of the II Court of the Administrative Division ordered the state to involve the community in all issues relating to this cultural heritage, as recognised by the Constitution approved in 2006. Now the battle will begin to enforce the community's administration and management of the heritage.

Humanitarian disaster through abandonment and death through malnutrition and other avoidable causes

This was undoubtedly the most important event of the year, the scale of which was demonstrated by the front page of the liberal/conservative daily newspaper La Nación, which showed a photograph of a woman from the Toba-Qom people under an enormous crucifix of the cathedral of Chaco province. A few days later this woman died, in an advanced state of malnutrition, for lack of medical care. In only five months (July – November), 18 people died for the same reason and, at the time of writing this report (end December) this had gone up to 20. Some media and NGOs classed these deaths as extermination and genocide[11] and this led to the involvement of a number of national bodies: the Ombudsman lodged a constitutional challenge against Chaco province and the Nation in the Supreme Court of National Justice, which ordered both to provide drinking water, food and medical aid, and to provide the corresponding health teams in the respective health posts, with adequate means of transport to facilitate fluid communication with the communities. The Ombudsman's complaint stated that, according to the survey conducted and the reports produced by the Chaco Aboriginal Institute (*Instituto del Aborigen Chaqueño*) and the Ministry of Human Rights, "the aborigines of this area of the country are being affected by a serious socio-economic situation by virtue of which most of the population are suffering from endemic illnesses that are the product of extreme poverty (malnutrition, chagas, tuberculosis, donovanosis, bronchial infections, parasitosis, scabies, etc.), lacking in food, access to clean water, housing, necessary medical care and the defendants (national and provincial state) have failed to carry out the necessary actions aimed at reversing this serious situation".

In addition to admitting the requested precautionary measure, the Court called the parties to a hearing on 6 November so that they could publicly and orally inform the judges of their report and measures adopted.

The Nelson Mandela Study Centre published further details complementing the description provided by the Ombudsman. Referring to the death of a 52-year-old woman one month after the Supreme Court's ruling, its Director told a journalist, "She lived from making baskets and collecting things from the rubbish dump that was a kilometre from where she lived. In actual fact, the state's abandonment was all the greater because we are talking about [her] whole family ...living from rubbish. We are talking about an extremely poor family, without work, with no income, no plans, no food aid and who for a year and a half..., became ill....and was gradually losing weight until it resulted in a situation of acute illness that, in just a few weeks, caused her death. The health system again did not detect this illness in time and so what the Ministry says is untrue. There is no good health care and, above all, there is no social policy aimed at caring for and helping the most marginalised, poorest and most excluded sectors of the Chaco community, in particular the indigenous communities".

As noted above, these deaths, like those of the Mbyá Guaraní children in Misiones province in 2006, occurred as a consequence of a "false recognition" that paid lip service to indigenous cultural diversity but failed to implement concrete actions to protect and defend their differences, not granting them the most basic dignity, that of being the legal owners of their territories with the ability to control natural resources and lead a healthy life on them, in accordance with their own decisions.   ❑

Notes

1   47 million tonnes of soya were produced in the year, which represented a profit of 15,000 million dollars. For 2008, it is estimated that the area under cultivation will be 100 million hectares.
2   Although it is difficult to say what the total area of the country covered by native forests is, some authors estimate that it could be getting on for between 28,000,000 and 36,000,000 (Greenpeace Argentina, Ordenamiento Territorial de Bosques Nativos, pdf. From the site www.greenpeace.org.ar)
3   See www.greenpeace.org.ar

4   More information on this and other cases mentioned in this article can be found at www.indymedia.org ,on the web page of the journalists' collective, Pueblos Originarios, of this organisation.
5   Detailed information on this complaint and its process can be found in **IWGIA, 2006**: *Argentina: el caso Lhaka Honhat*. Report 1. Available in pdf form from www. iwgia.org
6   Página 12, op. cit..
7   According to the public complaint made by a Kolla leader from Abra Pampa, in la Jornada *Estado de Situación de los Pueblos Indígenas en la Argentina*, CELS-Defensoría del Pueblo de la Nación-IWGIA, Buenos Aires, 26 November 2007.
8   A traditional Mapuche dwelling
9   See *The Indigenous World 2007*.
10 More information can be found at www.azkintwe.org
11 More information can be found at www.centromandela.com.ar

Morita Carrasco is an anthropologist, lecturer and researcher at Buenos Aires University and advisor to the Centre for Legal and Social Studies (Centro de Estudios Legales y Sociales - CELS). She is working with the Lhaka Honhat Association of Aboriginal Communities (Asociación de Comunidades Aborígenes Lhaka Honhat) in their struggle for titling of their territory.

CHILE

According to the official Socio-Economic Survey (CASEN 2006), 1,060,786 people recognise themselves as members of indigenous peoples, a figure that corrects the 2002 census total of 692,192. Of these people, 87.3% are Mapuche, 7% Aymara and 3% Atacameño. The other peoples (Colla, Rapanui, Quechua, Yámana and Kawaskar) make up 2.7 % of the indigenous peoples. 70% of the indigenous peoples live in just three regions: 29.5% in Araucanía, 27.7% in the Metropolitan region and 14.7% in Los Lagos. More than half of the indigenous population are under the age of 30 and 64.8% of them live in urban areas as opposed to 35.2% in rural.

Chile has not ratified ILO Convention 169, and its Constitution does not recognise the pre-existence and rights of indigenous peoples. Indigenous affairs are governed by the Indigenous People's Special Law 19,253 of 1993. This indigenist legislation does not address indigenous rights but rather the development of indigenous "ethnic groups". In terms of lands and resources, Law 19,253 establishes a limited status of recognition and protection of indigenous lands but ignores rights to resources.

The year was characterised, in terms of indigenous peoples' collective rights, another year passed without ILO Convention 169 being ratified, despite repeated presidential announcements of "moving it along" to get it approved "as quickly as possible". The United Nations human rights bodies commented on Chile's failure to observe international standards but the government did not comply with their recommendations and continued to support harmful investment projects in indigenous territories and communities.

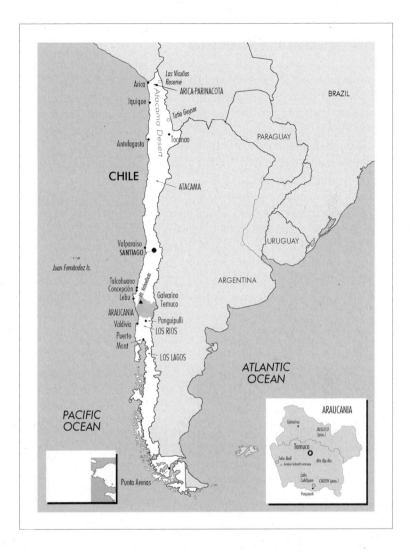

In terms of individual rights and freedoms, police violence continued against indigenous people and communities, and no solution to
the situation of the Mapuche political prisoners was sought. Further
indigenous complaints were admitted by the human rights bodies.

Social exclusion and a new pact

A number of social protests highlighted the shortcomings of the transition to democracy[1]: inequality, a lack of institutionality in processing conflicts and the absence of an Ombudsman to defend human rights. Social exclusion ended up taking the debate beyond the dictator/democracy focus that has structured Chilean politics for two decades, with a new "social pact" for governance being considered amongst the elites.

The CASEN survey published in 2007 corroborated the inequalities, and confirmed that indigenous peoples presented higher levels of poverty and misery than the Chilean population as a whole. At the same time, the survey revealed a growing discriminatory wage gap: the more years of secondary and higher education they have, the less indigenous people earn in comparative terms. Similar racist differences were highlighted in the International Labor Organisation (ILO)'s 2007 Labour Overview which, in this organisation's opinion, reflects the social exclusion of Chile's indigenous population.

The Chile file

The international file on Chile continued to grow in 2007. Two UN human rights treaty committees examined the state's fulfilment of its obligations, with particular reference to indigenous peoples.

In February, the Committee on the Rights of the Child (CRC) indicated in its report that: "the information received that young indigenous people have been the victims of ill-treatment at the hands of the police is worrying." The Committee recommended that the state: a) incorporate recognition of indigenous peoples and their rights into the Constitution; b) ratify ILO Convention 169; c) adopt measures to guarantee that indigenous children enjoy their rights, particularly with regard to education and health; d) ensure that young indigenous people are not the victims of ill-treatment at the hands of the police.[2]

In March, the UN Human Rights Committee (CCPR) indicated that the very broad definition of terrorism in Law 18,314 "has meant that members of the Mapuche community have been accused of terrorism for acts of social protest and demand," for which reason it recommended that this be amended. In its report, the Committee: "laments the information that the "ancestral lands" continue to be in danger due to the expansion of logging and infrastructure and energy megaprojects. (Articles 1 and 27)". In paragraph 19, it recommends that the state

a) make all possible efforts to (...) respect these communities' rights to land in accordance with articles 1 (paragraph 2) and 27 of the Covenant (...); b) amend Law 19,253, bringing it into line with Article 27 of the Covenant and revise sectoral legislation where the content contradicts the rights stated in the Covenant; c) consult with the indigenous communities before awarding licences for the economic exploitation of disputed lands and ensure that in no case shall said exploitation violate rights recognised in the Covenant.

The Committee gave Chile one year in which to implement this recommendation.

Both committees reiterated the need for Chile to establish an Ombudsman in order to monitor respect for human rights, in line with the Paris Principles[3], adding to the recommendations made in 2004 by the UN Committee on Economic, Social and Cultural Rights and the UN Special Rapporteur on indigenous peoples, Rodolfo Stavenhagen.

In August, the UN Committee for the Elimination of Racial Discrimination (CERD) received a complaint for "environmental racism", presented by Mapuche communities affected by rubbish dumps and wastewater treatment plants. The CERD also resolved to examine Chile regularly during 2008, given the delay in submitting its periodic reports.

In May, the Inter-American Commission on Human Rights (IA-CHR) declared two new complaints against the Chilean state admissible - the Ancalaf and Poluco Pidenco cases – for violation of fundamental rights, in cases opened during the Lagos government

(2000-2006), when the antiterrorist law was applied to Mapuche community members.[4]

Legislative agenda and indigenous rights

Indigenous affairs continued to be pushed down the legislative agenda, with only erratic initiatives taking place. The government presented a new plan for "constitutional recognition" that was condemned by the indigenous organisations as insubstantial and completely lacking in consultation. The indigenous organisations repeated their demand that ILO Convention 169 should first be ratified.

The only legislative progress in the year was the approval of the law on "Marine Coastal Spaces of Native Peoples" (EMCPO). Since 1990, the Lafkenche communities have been demanding recognition of their ancestral rights to their shores. The new law partly fills the vacuum left by the Indigenous Law and the Fisheries Law, both approved under former President Aylwin in the early 90s. However, as the name suggests, the EMCPO is simply a kind of system of concessions; it maintains state control and third party concessions - and hence the massive dispossession of indigenous shores that has occurred since 1991 - intact. As Lafkenche leaders indicated, the law had come at a time when there was little left to register, the horizon for the recovery of coastal rights at a later date remaining open.

The plans for educational reform, reform of the political system, and reform of the administrative division of a monolithically unitary state were all noteworthy on the country's agenda. In the first case, thanks to indigenous pressure, the draft general education law – which was the object of a national political agreement – included a small mention relating to incorporating "objectives referring to the indigenous mother tongue" into the school curriculum, which at least forms a first step. In terms of the electoral system, the Mapuche organisation *Consejo de Todas las Tierras* and a group of 10 parliamentarians proposed a bill that could establish quotas for indigenous parliamentary members and, alongside this, the Mapuche organisation *Wallmapuwen* continued the process for registering as a political party so that it could participate in elections.

Neoliberal expansion and territorial conflicts

The primary export model grew overwhelmingly over the year. Taxes received surpassed 8.7% of GDP thanks to the high price of copper, and the process for including the country in the Organisation for Economic Cooperation and Development (OECD), which comprises the world's 30 most stable economies, made progress. The most dynamic sectors – logging, salmon farming, mining, energy – have been exhibiting high rates of growth and new plans for expansion, with the resulting impacts on indigenous areas. In response, various social movements for territorial defence have gained in strength.

Timber exports increased by 27% on the previous year, to reach US$ 4,950 million; this means that the logging industry has doubled its sales over the last five years. Forest plantations are now penetrating into Mapuche communities, by means of individual contracts promoted by the logging companies. The conflict around the Celco-Valdivia cellulose project (see The Indigenous World 2007) continued in 2007 in relation to a waste pipe flowing into the sea along the Lafkenche coast. The government supported the project, extending the deadline for environmental studies, and the CELCO company has been offering cash bonuses to the fishermen, creating divisions between the unions and the local communities.

There were a number of noteworthy indigenous achievements in terms of mining conflicts, social protest being combined with the use of administrative mechanisms. In the south of the country, the communities of Lleu Lleu Lake have managed to neutralise one mining project and are standing up to other concessions covering an area of 60,000 hectares in the basin of the lake and the Nahuelb-uta mountain range. The local authorities have managed to get the area's lakes declared a Zone of Tourist Interest (ZOIT), which demands greater regulation of investment projects. In the north, Aymara organisations have managed to halt a mining project of the Copec group[5] in the Las Vicuñas world biosphere reserve. The case forced changes to regulations governing the environmental impact assessment system such that reserves are now included on the list of spaces requiring environmental assessment. In Atacama, Likan Antay communities in Toconao managed to get the Pampa Colorado project of the transnational BHP Billiton rejected on environmental grounds. This project was intending to extract more than a thousand litres of water a second from the Salar de Atacama water systems. The case of Pascua Lama de Barrick, which affects Diaguita communities, is quite the reverse: the company has obtained the necessary environmental authorisations and managed to prevent the establishment of a parliamentary investigation committee.

Geothermal energy projects triggered protests in the north and south of the country. Likan Antay communities, in the north, defended the Tatio geysers, petitioning the courts and the Inter-American system. In the south, Pehuenche communities mobilised to reject a project in the Valle del Queuco, Alto Bio Bio, organising marches and actions of force such as road blocks in October and November. Such projects are being implemented in the context of Law N° 19,657 "On Geothermal Energy Concessions", which establishes 120 areas that reopen to concession, including indigenous zones.

New conflicts arose in 2007 over hydroelectric projects in Mapuche basins. The Spanish company, Endesa, and the Chilean company, Colbun, have forcefully promoted their *Neltume* and *San Pedro* projects. A third group of three power stations is being promoted by the Norwegian company, SN Power, in Panguipulli in the areas of *Pellaifa, Liquiñe* and *Maqueo*.

The Mapuche communities of Panguipulli have been involved in a process of political/cultural revival and, in January 2007, thousands of community members joined together to commemorate the centenary of the "Coz Coz parliament", a landmark in Mapuche history. It was against this backdrop that the SN Power projects conflicts erupted, this being a Norwegian company that is a member of the Global Compact for Social Responsibility, and with resources in a state party to ILO Convention 169. In an area with a vocation for eco-tourism, an alliance was formed between the Mapuche, local authorities, businessmen and civil society. The conflict escalated due to the conduct of the SN Power's Chilean subsidiary - Trayenko SA –, which was reluctant to dialogue, and reached a climax in October when machinery was brought into the area without consent. It was removed by community members. The communities established alliances with Norwegian NGOs and unions and sent a Mapuche delegation to Oslo to meet with SN Power's head office and the Norwegian authorities. As a result, they have obtained the temporary suspension of the projects and the commencement of a dialogue.

Other protests took place during the year over planned infrastructure projects. Quepe communities in La Araucanía continued their opposition to the international airport being supported by the Ministry of Public Works. In July, however, the regional authorities granted environmental authorisation for this project, and tried to divide the communities with welfarist programmes. The communities affected by rubbish dumps and wastewater treatment plants led another protest in La Araucanía. In 2007, all the treatment plants were in operation; the communities continued their protest. In July, they prevented a new rubbish dump for Temuco city from being established in an area of environmental conservation and in August they managed to get the CERD to accept a complaint of "environmental racism".

The cases noted show the lack of an institutional framework for dealing with conflicts; in all cases, principles of indigenous consultation and consent have been transgressed. Without an Ombudsman, the communities are forced to stand up for their own rights by means of social protest; in the meanwhile, the government backs the infrastructure projects and maintains a harsh response in terms of police presence and criminal punishment.

Criminalisation of social protest

The government views indigenous protest as a security issue and an obstacle to investment, and it therefore follows a policy of social discipline, deploying the police force in areas of conflict, neutralising and criminalising protesters. The way issues were to be handled throughout 2007 was quietly made clear in January with the appointment of an authoritarian governor for La Araucanía, Oscar Eltit Spielmann. The *Consejo de Todas las Tierras* criticised the return of someone who, when holding the same post between 1994-2000, had instigated the criminalisation of the Mapuche movement.

Over the year, there were many episodes of police violence. On 31 January, Mapuche community members who were occupying the municipal building of Galvarino in protest at errors committed by CONADI in its land allocations were evicted and arrested; the mayor condemned the police action. In February, Mapuche from Lake Calafquen, Cautín province, who were claiming ownership of a Lican Ray peninsula that had been expropriated by the Treasury in 1940, were violently evicted. In Malleco, the Temucuicui community suffered four raids over the course of the year – in February, April, August and October –, disproportionate operations involving armoured cars and helicopters in search of their leaders

Evictions of community members claiming land and arrests of demonstrators were a constant. In October, Lafkenche community members claiming lands in the Teodoro Schmidt commune were evicted and arrested. In November, Mapuche student homes in Temuco and Valdivia were raided in the context of protests to free the Mapuche prisoners. In December, land claims in Arauco province were harshly repressed. In all, over the course of the year, at least 206 indigenous people were arrested in different protests in both town and countryside.

An international observer mission that visited La Araucanía in January 2007, involving Amnesty International and the UN Special Rapporteur on indigenous peoples, warned the authorities with regard to use of excess public force, lethal weapons, discriminatory treatment and harassment of human rights defenders.

Mapuche political prisoners. The end of the story?

At the start of the year, three symbolic indigenous leaders were released one after the other: Aniceto Norin, Pascual Pichun and Victor Ancalaf . Others took their place, however. Although the Antiterrorist Law 18,314 is no longer applicable, the proceedings commenced by the previous government continued, with all their consequences of arrests and trials.

In February, a new trial was held in the controversial proceedings relating to a fire at a forest plantation in 2001, on the Poluco Pidenco estate of the Mininco CMPC company. This time, José Llanquileo – arrested at the end of 2006 – was sentenced to five years in prison for "simple arson", thus ruling out the suggestion that these were terrorist crimes. This was the third different sentence passed by the court in this case. In 2004, the court ruled that the actions were "terrorist arson", sentencing six community members to 10 years in prison; in 2006, the court changed its mind, establishing that the acts were not "terrorism" and that there was insufficient proof for the perpetrators to be identified, absolving two community members. One of those absolved - José Cariqueo – even took Mininco CMPC to court and, in July, the company was required to pay compensation and make a public apology. In May, the complaint in the case of Poluco Pidenco was admitted by the Inter-American Commission on Human Rights for flagrant violations of due process.

On 21 February, a member of the Arauco Malleco Coordinating Body (*Coordinadora Arauco Malleco* - CAM), Hector Llaitul, was detained and, on 20 March, the leader of the CAM, Jose Huenchunao, was arrested. He had been in hiding since 2004, sentenced at the first trial of the Poluco Pidenco case. The arrest of Huenchunao was sensationally reported in the press, with inflated declarations from Governor Eltit and the Vice-Minister of the Interior, Felipe Harboe, who stated that the arrest of Huenchunao was "the end of the story". This episode, viewed with hindsight, was what marked the year, and revealed the distance between the Chilean and Mapuche political codes. The authorities' declarations and the media circus had an adverse effect on the Mapuche world, as they were considered as aggravating acts of inclemency and racism, eroding any incipient bridges of dialogue with the government.

During 2007, the Bachelet government maintained an inflexible position towards the Mapuche political prisoners, postponing any sentence remission. On 4 June, in Switzerland, on being questioned by European NGOs, the President stated that the Mapuche prisoners were "criminals", affirming that "there is a distorted view of the reality in Europe". In October, five political prisoners began a hunger strike in the Angol prison – the Mapuches José Huenchunao, Jaime Marileo, José Millalen, Héctor Llaitul and sympathizer Patricia Troncoso - demanding their release and the demilitarisation of the Mapuche region. The government maintained an implacable silence in the face of this protest, relying on the fact that the hunger strikers would fall, one after the other, defeated.

The strike took place amidst a communications siege and total isolation. Demonstrations of support organised by Mapuche students in Temuco, Santiago, Valdivia and Concepción were harshly repressed. As the months passed, the hunger strike took on a dramatic quality, becoming a harsh measure of strength. After 64 days, mediators from the Catholic Church ascertained that three of the hunger strikers were in a bad state of health - Huenchunao, Marileo and Millalen – and so they abandoned the protest, on the official promise of a committee for dialogue to review the prisoners' situation. The committee was never formed, as Llaitul and Troncoso - who continued the strike - feared. Two weeks later, after 81 days of hunger strike, and at the request of his family and children, Hector Llaitul stated that: "There being no alternative other than death, I will end my hunger strike", indicating that: "We will not consider the lack of response from the government as a failure but as a true declaration of war on the Mapuche movement". The year ended with only Patricia Troncoso still on hunger strike.

Indigenous policy at a crossroads

2007 began with an optimistic audience of the Coordinating Body of Mapuche Organisations (*Coordinadora de Organizaciones Mapuches* COM) with President Bachelet in the *Palacio de la Moneda*, at which she was presented with a proactive proposal focusing on the political rights of indigenous peoples. However, it quickly became clear that the government's focus was on the continuity of CONADI to maintain unrestricted support for investment projects, and to neutralise the indigenous movement. In a general context of growing social discontent, the government failed to fill the vacuum left by its lack of governance of indigenous affairs with any policies, thus deepening the crisis of legitimacy. At the end of the year, Bishop Goic summarised the country's situation by saying: "Social conflict is about to break out".

The indigenous movement retreated into sectoral issues and local, reactive resistance movements. With all political paths closed, proactive protest aimed at political change and improbable dialogue was not considered. The time for agreement has long passed. Faced with the hunger strike of the Mapuche prisoners, the government remained implacable, blind, deaf and dumb.

At the end of the year, during the night of 27 December, a Mapuche group, armed with shotguns and hunting instruments blocked the highway at Ercilla, and attacked a lorry, setting it on fire. A family car that was passing was also attacked and ordered to turn back, to the cries of slogans in support of the Mapuche prisoners. The car was being driven by Judge Karen Atala and historian Emma De Ramón. In a press interview, still dazed, the judge asked, *"Is this Chile?"*, to which the historian responded, *"I think these actions show the deep despair of a people that has not been listened to"* (El Mercurio, 30.12.2007). ❑

Notes

1 The Chilean transition to democracy (colloquially known in Chile as the *Transición*) began on September 11, 1980, when a Constitution establishing a transition itinerary was approved in a plebiscite. From March 11, 1981 to March 11, 1990, several organic constitutional laws were approved leading to the final restoration of democracy

2 http://www.unhchr.ch/tbs/doc.nsf/898586b1dc7b4043c1256a450044f331/a71 366158944313ec12572d500427fa2/$FILE/G0741435.pdf

3 Principles relating to the status and functioning of national institutions for protection and promotion of human rights

4 "Caso Ancalaf". Informe Admisibilidad N° 33/07, Petición 581-05, Víctor Manuel Ancalaf Llaupe V Chile, 2 May 2007, www.cidh.org/annualrep/2007sp/ Chile.58105.sp.htm; "Caso Poluco-Pidenco". Informe Admisibilidad N° 32/07, Petición 429-05, Juan Patricio Marileo Saravia Y Otros V Chile, 2 May 2007, ww.cidh.org/annualrep/2007sp/Chile.42905.sp.htm

5 Copec S.A. is the largest privately owned company in Chile. It leads all Chilean companies in the distribution of all types of fuels and owns several hundred gasoline stations operating under the Copec name. Its Arauco subsidiaries make

it the leading producer of forestry products in the country and, indeed, the largest forestry enterprise in South America.

Sources

www.azkintuwe,org
www.mapuexpress.net
www.politicaspublicas.cl
www.conadi.cl
www.observatorio.cl
www.mideplan.cl
www.emol.com
www.camara.cl

Víctor Toledo Llancaqueo is a historian from the Centre for Public Policies and Indigenous Rights (Centro de Políticas Públicas y Derechos Indígenas) in Santiago, Chile. He is also the Coordinator of the Working Group on Indigenous Movements and Democracy in Latin America of the Latin American Council for Social Sciences, CLACSO.

AUSTRALIA
AND THE PACIFIC

AUSTRALIA

Australia's growing indigenous community currently makes up two and a half percent of the total population, and more than half of these 460,000 indigenous residents live in urban and regional centres. However, compared to the non-indigenous population (2%), a far greater proportion (27%) still live in very remote areas. The vast majority of Aborigines have been violently dispossessed of their land, and all have been subjected to economic and political marginalization and oppressive state control. Today, indigenous life expectancy remains 20 years below the national average, and indigenous citizens are far more likely to live in poverty, be removed from their families as children and be incarcerated than the general population.[1]

Constitutional changes in 1967 led to all indigenous people being counted in the census and to the strengthening of their rights to vote, receive equal wages, own property etc, and a 1993 legal decision led to a limited form of native title. During the 1980s and 1990s, momentum was building for formal reconciliation and constitutional recognition in the form of a treaty; however, the election of the current conservative federal government in 1996 has halted this process.

"Shock and awe"

A year of indigenous policy drama ended in 2007 with a new Australian government promising and practising a new relationship with indigenous peoples. The Australian event that the world should really be aware of, however, is the use of the army, police and the suspension of Aboriginal civil rights in the Northern Territory (NT), announced and commenced on 21 June 2007. This "shock and awe" cam-

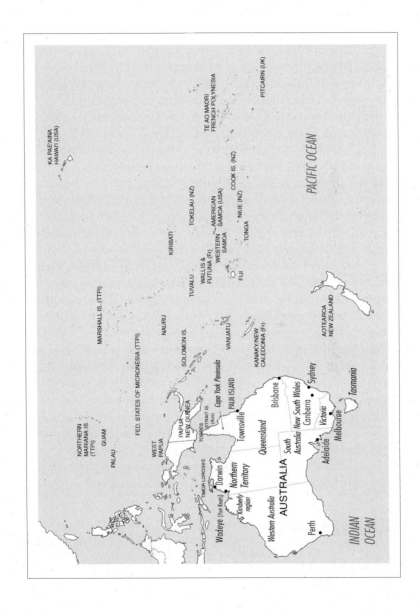

paign – to use the American term for the 2003 invasion of Iraq that some of Prime Minister Howard's supporters borrowed for the NT "Emergency Intervention" – was intended to save women and children from violent abuse in troubled communities but applied to all NT Aboriginal people.[2] At first, the army was going to ensure that children were medically examined for sexual abuse; doctors protested however, and this part of the plan was limited to more conventional health checks.

This military operation was imposed by Howard and his minister for indigenous affairs, Mal Brough, without consultation of NT Aboriginal people or the NT government. After all the recent years of fear-mongering and talk of Islamic terrorism by the government, along with the build-up of special military/paramilitary forces and anti-democratic powers, it was not dangerous tribes or armies in Central/Western Asia who were the target but the poorest, sickest, unfortunate people of the "First World" country of Australia itself who were now "the enemy". Fortunately, the general in charge was sensible and sensitive to Aboriginal opinion, even when minister Brough rushed around the country shouting excitedly and accusing anyone who had doubts regarding the anti-government "conspiracy" and "supporting child abuse"! Belatedly, Howard and Brough dragooned an Aboriginal lady from an appointed indigenous body to give the operation an Aboriginal face.

The alleged justification for the Intervention was an NT government report, *Little Children Are Sacred,* edited by Rex Wild and Pat Anderson, 2007.[3] This report stressed that, to succeed, any major social reform had to give Aboriginal people real control of the program. However, Howard and Brough preferred the drama of a D-Day-like show to appear "strong" and "decisive" before the election. Furthermore, Howard would never do anything to imply that Aboriginal peoples had distinct identity or indigenous rights, people with whom one might "negotiate" or "consult" in more than a token way.

Abuse and abusers

Since the NT Intervention, the government has been eager to extend the work to other areas of Northern Australia, notably the Kimberley region of Western Australia and Far North Queensland, e.g., Cape York

Peninsula. There has been little argument about the seriousness of the situation in many remote Aboriginal communities. Aboriginal voices often disagree about the style and the details of the NT Intervention but not about (1) the urgency of action and (2) the need for strong or even massive support from outside a given community.

Two leaders who supported the government Intervention were Noel Pearson of Cape York Peninsula in Queensland and Galarrwuy Yunupingu of Arnhem Land, east of Darwin in the NT. These two strong leaders have been very effective as power brokers in using their partial and public support for government to the benefit of their peoples and communities. But the government and its media supporters, notably the newspaper *The Australian*, have at best a limited view of the political and regional visions of these leaders. One cannot imagine either of these leaders abandoning their region's ethno-political autonomy under any White Man's government. Nevertheless, both government and Aboriginal leaders were able to work together and give Howard and Brough some much needed national credibility in the latter part of 2007.

The NT Intervention is reportedly draining medical and other skills from, e.g., Queensland, and there is already a well-known shortage of public service personnel in Aboriginal Australia. Indeed, some of the work done by national government pilot projects before the NT Intervention, e.g., in the large NT Aboriginal community of Wadeye (Port Keats), revealed that the census had underestimated the size of the Aboriginal population by up to 50%. In other words, if the actual number of children in Wadeye turned up at school, there would not be sufficient classrooms or teachers to cope with them. As many national critics – especially health and education authorities – point out, Australia is the one settler society among "First World" liberal democracies that has failed since 1945 to come to terms with its indigenous peoples.

However, there is one area in which Australia has been all too effective. Having been unable to bring rural and remote Aboriginal and Islander regions within the national socio-economic sphere of basic "First World" living standards, it has developed an unenviable reputation of tough policing and jailing. If you cannot solve the problem then "force the lid down on it" seems to be the plan. What's more, although reports and a Royal Commission demand that Aboriginal people be sensitively treated by the justice system, the state Premiers simply smile and receive these reports and then, on most other days, demand tough "law and order" policies. Translated into modern English this means locking up black youths who are unemployed and/or uneducated and/or unsuited to the modern Australian job market and likely to attract an official eye for disorderliness. After tiptoeing up to the proposal in recent years, Howard's government and friends finally began in 2007 to talk in earnest about moving Aborigines from their ancient territories and sending them into the industrial economy. Such a policy would be disastrous, as it has been everywhere else of course, and would leave Australia open to the charge of ethnocide.

However, in parallel with - or underlying - the NT Intervention was a report, *Lands of Shame* by Helen Hughes (Centre for Independent Studies, Sydney, 2007), a Right-wing plan that would re-create Aboriginal Australia as a white man's 1950s economy. Even most of the Aboriginal supporters of the NT Intervention worried about some of the details and, while Howard would not change them, the new Labor government is prepared to adjust them.

But so powerful is the image – and reality – of child abuse that no further public discussion was possible (although see below). Indeed, child care issues and abuse are a national focus in the white suburbs of Brisbane no less than in the black townships of the Far North. Strong Aboriginal advocates such as Prof. Marcia Langton – whose 1991 report for a Royal Commission, "*Too much sorry business*" is a classic study of NT Aboriginal social ills – have argued that no quibbles or qualifications should be allowed to detract from the momentum of Intervention-style change.[4]

The new Labor prime minister, Kevin Rudd, and indigenous affairs minister Jenny Macklin will review the NT Intervention. Indeed, on 15 December they met with NT Aboriginal leaders and had a good discussion and, when meeting the Premiers on 20 December, they set up a working group to develop national plans for tackling indigenous social ills, with a first report due in March 2008. They also promised action early in 2008 on other Aboriginal policy fronts.

Indigenous recognition at home and abroad

Whereas Australia, under the former government, was one of the four countries that did not vote in favor of the UN Declaration on the Rights of Indigenous Peoples, the new labor government has promised to sign it.[5] One of the reliable Right-wing press culture warriors respond-ed: "Labor's commitment to the UN declaration evinces a wilful igno-rance of indigenous politics and the law. It will have dangerous and divisive consequences, dragging indigenous people back into a vortex of victimhood politics premised on collectivism, separatism and trea-ties".[6] This is a clear expression of the sort of language that Howard and the Right have used for years. Aboriginal policy for these people has little to do with Aboriginal peoples or Torres Strait Islanders; rath-er, it is an intellectual preoccupation of whites in Australian cities try-ing to score points off each other.

On the eve of announcing the national election that was to end his own political career and his government, John Howard said that, if re-elected, he would lead a change to recognise Aboriginal peoples and Islanders in the Constitution's preamble: to promote black-white "rec-onciliation". This gesture was intended to surprise the public, who had stopped listening to him, his ministers revealed. As he explained, "This new Reconciliation I'm talking about starts from the premise that indi-vidual rights and national sovereignty prevail over group rights. That group rights are, and ought to be, subordinate to both the citizenship rights of the individual and the sovereignty of the nation." He went on to acknowledge that Aborigines had lived here before white settlement but that now they had to assimilate without any political or indigenous rights. As usual, the media missed the point and whooped and won-dered at this "new" departure, which would in fact be a death knell for indigenous culture and political autonomy.[7]

On November 24, both Howard and minister Mal Brough lost their seats in the election. Howard quietly vanished but Brough continued to haunt public conversations as if he were indispensable to indige-nous policy and progress. For a man whose fame rested on shouting at Aboriginal old people in desert shanty-towns and blaming anyone with a question or quibble of thereby promoting "child abuse", noth-ing could more clearly show Australia's inability to discuss intelligent-ly or confront its deepest domestic problem: the refusal to accept or respect indigenous peoples on their own terms, or to provide the offi-cial support they needed to overcome their problems.

Then a very strange thing happened. As Prime Minister Rudd sig-naled that he and Australia were rejoining the world community and its international networks by signing the Kyoto Agreement at the World Environment Conference in Bali, and making other moves to make Australia less a Howard time-warp of *good olde* Englishness in the sub-Antarctic like the Falklands, Howard's surviving ministers and other cronies began to throw off their costumes. Now, suddenly, they tried to look comfortable with Rudd's talk of "building bridges of respect" with indigenous Australia, and his talk of re-opening the national conversation to overcome division and inequality. Rudd was talking about and looking to a future in which fusty prejudices had no place and in which the accumulated knowledge, experience and goodwill of officialdom, universities and the thinking public would become assets in building a fine new Australia. As 2008 began, many Australians and their media were asking just what the Liberal and National parties were becoming, and what they believed. Not a few who had worshipfully followed Howard's worst detours into the archaic and the silly were now insisting that they had really believed it was all nonsense and that they were actually fine modern chaps. "And thus the whirligig of time brings in his revenges."   ❑

Notes

1   All statistics taken from Australian Bureau of Statistics National Aboriginal and Torres Strait Islander Surveys and the national census (2001;2002;2005). Available at www.abs.gov.au.
2   For Emergency Intervention website see http://www.facsia.gov.au/nter/. The Intervention is discussed and analysed in the most important Australian book of the year: **Jon Altman and Melinda Hinkson (eds.), 2007:** *Coercive Reconciliation: Stabilise, Normalise, Exit Aboriginal Australia,* Arena, Melbourne.
3   http://www.nt.gov.au/dcm/inquirysaac/
4   *The Australian,* 12-12-07.
5   14-9-07, Macklin, Labor party website
6   Albrechtsen, *The Australian,* 10-10-07
7   11 & 12/10/07, Transcripts, Prime Minister's Media Office

Peter Jull is Adjunct Associate Professor, Australian Centre for Peace and Conflict Studies (ACPACS), University of Queensland, Brisbane, Australia 4072.

WEST PAPUA

West Papua covers the western part of the island of New Guinea, bordering the independent nation of Papua Niugini (Papua New Guinea) and comprising the Indonesian provinces of Papua and West Papua (the latter changed its name from *Irian Jaya Barat* on 7 February 2007). 52 % of its 2.4 million inhabitants are indigenous, representing approximately 253 different peoples; the rest are Indonesian migrants.

The recent history of West Papua is a history of betrayal: the 1962 agreement between the two states handing over the territory from one colonial power (Netherlands) to another (Indonesia) without the consultation or consent of the indigenous peoples, a fraudulent "referendum" in 1969, in which a few hand-picked people were made to declare loyalty to Indonesia, and Indonesia's strong military presence, brutally suppressing any attempts by the West Papuan people to assert their rights to self-determination. While still demanding "rectification of history" and an investigation into the numerous human rights violations, the Papuan leaders also see the urgency of addressing widespread poverty, retarded development and untapped human resources. The majority of Papuans depend on natural resources for their livelihood. Injustices in natural resource management under Indonesian rule are a key aspect of the conflict in Papua. Under the Special Autonomy Law, all land is defined as community land and there is no "state forest" in Papua. One of the big challenges is how the natural resources can be used to improve the livelihoods of the indigenous peoples.

2007 saw little progress in Indonesia's goodwill to fully implement the Special Autonomy Law of 2001 (see also *The Indigenous World 2007*). Many feel that, through Presidential Decree No. 5/2007, the present administration of President Yudhoyono again bypassed the Papua administration by giving 11 central government ministers responsibility for Papua's economic development. This move is described as re-centralisation. However, 2007 also saw a further strengthening of Papuan forces.

Forests for life

Governor Barnabas Suebu (democratically elected in 2006) observed that, "The indigenous Papuans have abundant natural resources and yet they have become poor peoples on their own land". He declared a policy of People-driven Development[1] (representing a differing perspective to the UNDP's People-centred Development.[2] He aims to strengthen the capacity of Papuans to plan and manage the overall system, institutions and apparatus, to empower Papuans to assume key roles in development and to engage marginalized Papuans on an equal base in a discourse to better identify their needs and capacities. He has spent 2 months (July-August 2007) traveling around Papua by land, over water, flying in light aircraft and helicopters, and walking long distances to visit dozens of villages and listen to the people. Each village will receive and control a sum of US$10,000 dollars to improve the living standards of its communities.

In October 2007, Suebu was chosen by Time magazine as one of the "Heroes of the Environment" for his strong policy on protecting the province's forests, described by the magazine as "standing up to the deeply entrenched business and military interests that have richly profited from Papuan timber"[3]. Two months earlier, his progressive forest policy was described in the Wall Street Journal,[4] The governor is very well aware of the relationship between biodiversity and cultural diversity. During the 13th Conference of Parties meeting (COP 13) of the United Nations Framework Convention on Climate Change (UNFCCC) and the Convention on Biological Diversity (CBD) in Bali in December 2007, Suebu addressed the participants with a position paper entitled "From Forest Crimes to Forest for Life, The New Policy for Sustainable Forest Management in Papua". The main points of this

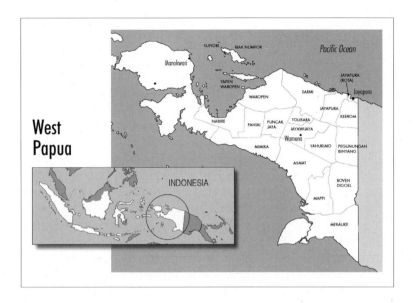

new policy are: 1) a return of forest ownership rights to the people; 2) a total prohibition of log exports; 3) an acceleration of home industry development and sustainable community logging; 4) forest concessions are to be extended only if they develop forest industries in Papua; 5) rewarding forest management and tree planting by local *adat* (indigenous) communities; and 6) law enforcement through deployment of well-trained forest rangers and improvement of community awareness. This policy is not welcome in Jakarta, where the central government still upholds Article 33 of the Constitution that establishes the exclusive right of the state over natural resources in the name of national interest and gives the state the arbitrary power to limit or abrogate the rights of indigenous peoples. Papua was further shocked by the announcement of Indonesian Forestry Minister Kaban that the transmigration program was to be revived because "the ongoing forest rehabilitation and conservation efforts had met with a labour shortage".[5] The government plans to send some 150,000 families to 436 locations in the forests of Sumatra, Kalimantan and West Papua.

Indigenous Congress

In July 2007, hundreds of representatives from all corners of West Papua gathered in Jayapura to participate in a congress of the Dewan Adat Papua (DAP – Papua Customary Council). This "Major Congress" is held every five years. The event provides a forum for decisions to be taken at inter-tribal level and for the council's performance to be evaluated. In 2002, the tribes selected Tom Beanal as council leader and Leo Imbiri as council secretary. The four-day congress in 2007 elected Forkorus Yoboisembut as the new Papuan Customary Council leader. He will hold the post until 2012. Imbiri will continue as council secretary. The DAP congress reiterated its stance on indigenous land rights:[6] "The land, the sea, the sky and all abundances of natural resources belong to the Papua indigenous peoples; the land, the sea and the sky are not sold and purchased to anybody else; the Indonesian government, investors and NGOs have to recognize, respect and guarantee the rights of Papua indigenous peoples, especially the rights of life, the rights of ownership and the rights of welfare". In line with Article 3 of the UN Declaration on the Rights of Indigenous Peoples, the Congress agreed in its General Statement that self-determination was the utmost right of the Papuan indigenous peoples. In reaction to Presidential Decree No. 5/2007, which is seen as an attempt to reduce the political conflict into an economic one, Congress stated: "The development and welfare in West Papua is of nothing if Indonesia continues to kill Papuan indigenous people each day. Papua indigenous peoples have been feeling threatened and insecure because of Indonesian military and intelligence operations. They execute force and silent operations throughout West Papua. Thus, Papuan indigenous peoples urge Indonesian President Yudhoyono to withdraw the military personnel and intelligence from West Papua". The Congress also rejected Jakarta's policy of administrative fragmentation and stated that Papua's land constituted one geographical, political, economic, social and cultural region. It urged Jakarta to stop dividing the region with the creation of new provinces until an agreement and consensus could be reached through public hearings with the Dewan Adat Papua, the Papua Consultative Assembly, the Papua Local Parliament and the

Governor of Papua. The DAP Congress called on the local government to develop rules and regulations concerning immigration from Indonesia, to oppose any transmigration programme and to stop the policy of manpower recruitment from Indonesia. In line with Governor Suebu, the Papua indigenous peoples called for an end to illegal logging throughout West Papua.

International observers

The active lobbying and advocacy efforts on the part of Papuans representing the indigenous peoples (DAP, NGOs, Presidium Dewan Papua) and by the provincial government, resulted in 2007 in major international visits to West Papua. In June, the UN Special Representative to the Secretary-General on human rights defenders, Hina Jilani, was invited to Indonesia.[7] In her report she expresses particular concern over developments in West Papua and mentions "credible reports of incidents that involve arbitrary detention, torture, harassment through surveillance, interference with the freedom of movement and in defenders' efforts to monitor and investigate human rights violations. [...] She is also concerned about complaints that defenders working for the preservation of the environment and the right over land and natural resources frequently receive threats from private actors with powerful economic interest, but are granted no protection by the police".

Following their meeting with Jilani, several Papuan representatives are facing ongoing attacks, intimidation, surveillance and threats, including death threats. In November, UN Special Rapporteur on Torture Manfred Nowak visited police lock-ups and prisons across Indonesia.[8] He concluded that torture in Indonesian detention centres was widespread. He singled out police lock-ups in Jakarta, and in Yogyakarta and Wamena in West Papua, for abusive behaviour towards prisoners or suspects. He said detainees in these places were afraid of talking to the team of investigators, and that the UN doctor found inmates bore serious injuries such as scars and bruises, suggesting that torture was routine.[9] Just before the year's end, US Congressman Eni Faleomavaega finally got permission to visit Papua. Afterwards, in a letter to the Indonesian president he expressed his disappointment at the restrictions he had met: "I was deeply disappointed that upon my arrival I was again denied entry into Jayapura and that my time was reduced from 5 days to only two hours of actual meetings with the leaders and people of Biak and Manokwari due to supposedly security concerns".[10] "It was a nightmare," Faleomavaega said. "I think it was a total waste of time for me to just be there and then say, 'I've got to go'. If the purpose was to intimidate me...it made me more irate because I don't think this is what the government or the President wanted. It is obvious the military is a problem". Indigenous leader Tom Beanal – who was initially prevented from attending the dialogue – urged Mr Faleomavaega to pay attention to the aspirations of a people who, he said, had never been allowed a voice in their own destiny.

The continuing situation of impunity, corruption, militarisation and weak enforcement of (international) law requires monitoring and sanction mechanisms for the protection and promotion of indigenous peoples' rights in West Papua to their natural and human resources.

The International Crisis Group predicts that Papua will remain a problem in 2008 because of "the cumulative impact of years of neglect of basic social services, unprosecuted past human rights violations, greedy security forces and uncontrolled migration from elsewhere in Indonesia, with a divisive and unnecessary process of pemekaran – administrative fragmentation – further roiling the waters. Governor Bas Suebu and his overstretched advisers are doing their best to move forward, but the obstacles they face are enormous".[11]

If there is to be positive change in Papua, the two governors need international support. Moreover, civil society organisations in Papua (NGOs, Community Based Organisations (CBOs) and indigenous organisations) need recognition and empowerment as they are indispensable for genuine development and structural change.   ❑

Notes

1   HS Dillon in Jakarta Post Opinion, *The Jakarta Post,* July 24, 2007
2   http://www.undp.or.id//papua/
3   *Time Magazine,* October 2007: http://www.time.com/time/specials/2007/article/0,28804,1663317_1663319_1669895,00.html
4   *Wall Street Journal,* August 10,2007: http://www.climos.com/articles/indonesianproposal.htm

5   *The Jakarta Post,* November 28, 2007
6   DAP Congress Manifesto: http://www.nieuwsbank.nl/papua-lobby/
7   Press Release:
     http://www.un.or.id/press.asp?Act=1&FileID=20070612-1&lang=en
8   Press Release:
     http://www.un.or.id/press.asp?Act=1&FileID=20071123-1&lang=1
9   Article in *Financial Times:* http://search.ft.com/ftArticle?queryText=nowak&aj
     e=true&id=071126000267&ct=0&nclick_check=1
10 Letter from Faleomavaega to Yudhoyono:
     http://www.etan.org/issues/wpapua/1207faleoletter.htm
11 Sidney Jones in Jakarta Post Opinion, *The Jakarta Post,* January 03, 2008

Viktor Kaisiëpo *is international representative of the Dewan Adat Papua –
the Papua Customary Council, and director of Papua Lobby.*

EAST &
SOUTHEAST ASIA

JAPAN

The two indigenous peoples of Japan live in the northernmost and southernmost islands of the country's archipelago. They are not recognized as indigenous by the government. Ainu territory stretches from Sakhalin and the Kurile Islands (now both Russian territories) to the northern part of present-day Japan, including the entire island of Hokkaido. Hokkaido was unilaterally incorporated into the Japanese state in 1869. Although most Ainu still live in Hokkaido, over the second half of the 20th century, tens of thousands migrated to Japan's urban centres for work and to escape the more prevalent discrimination on Hokkaido.

Okinawans live in the Ryukyu Islands, which now make up Japan's present-day Okinawa prefecture. Japan forcibly annexed the Ryukyus in 1879 but later relinquished the islands to the US in exchange for its own independence after World War Two. In 1972, the islands were reincorporated into the Japanese state, but the US military remained. The US relies on Japan's continued denial of Okinawans' self-determination to maintain its military forces there. Currently, 75% of all US forces in Japan are located in Okinawa prefecture, a mere 0.6% of Japan's territory.

Japanese government votes in favour of the UN Declaration

September 13, 2007 was a historical day for the world's indigenous peoples since the General Assembly of the United Nations adopted the Declaration on the Rights of Indigenous Peoples. The Japanese government voted in favour of the declaration, and delegate Takahiro Shinyo said,

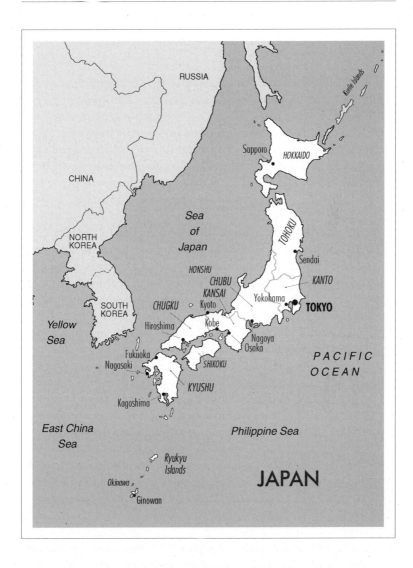

The revised version of article 46 correctly clarified that the right of self-determination did not give indigenous peoples the right to be separate and independent from their countries of residence, and that that right should not be invoked for the purpose of impairing the sovereignty of a State, its national and political unity, or territorial integrity. The Japa-

nese Government shared the understanding on the right and welcomed the revision.

Japan believed that the rights contained in the Declaration should not harm the human rights of others. It was also aware that, regarding property rights, the contents of the rights of ownership or others relating to land and territory were firmly stipulated in the civil law and other laws of each State. Therefore, Japan thought that the rights relating to land and territory in the Declaration, as well as the way those rights were exercised, were limited by due reason, in light of harmonization with the protection of the third party interests and other public interests.[1]

Right after the adoption of the Declaration, on 1 and 2 October 2007, the Ainu Association of Hokkaido, Japan's largest Ainu organization, requested that the Japanese government officially recognize the Ainu as indigenous people to whom the UN Declaration applies. The association also made a request to establish comprehensive measures, including new legislation, to improve the situation of the Ainu.[2]

Japan's Prime Minister Fukuda was not willing to make a clear commitment, however, and stated on 4 October 2007 in the Hokkaido newspaper Hokkaido Shimbun,

I recognize the fact that the Ainu are an ethnic group who has developed a unique culture, but it is not a situation to make a conclusion on whether or not the Ainu are indigenous peoples defined in the Declaration.[3]

Over the past years, the Japanese government's position on the Ainu issue has somewhat softened due to the relentless pressure of the Ainu and its supporters. Considering Japan's strong nationalist stance and the fact that, in the not-so-distant past, the government even denied the existence of the Ainu, the vote in favour of the declaration is a step forward in indigenous politics in Japan. Yet the Japanese government is still dragging its feet with regard to recognising the Ainu as an indigenous people, and the Ainu will have to keep up their pressure in order to achieve this goal.

Discriminatory statement by local politician

A statement made on 31 October by a politician belonging to the Democratic Party reflected not only a general lack of awareness of Ainu issues but also the extent to which discriminatory attitudes towards the Ainu still prevail within the political establishment in Japan. As the newspaper *Hokkaido Shimbun* reported in its November 1 issue, at a meeting held in Japan's Parliament during a discussion with a member of the Liberal Democratic Party on white skin colour, the Japanese politician from the Democratic Party stated, "we are savage people who descended from the Ainu".

He withdrew his comment later in a press conference saying that the comment was meant more as a joke and that he would like to withdraw the discriminatory statement. He apologized that it had led to a misunderstanding and added: "My comment meant that we are originally from Northern Japan. I meant we are strong and ordinary people. Regarding the recognition of the Ainu, the Ainu are indigenous people of Japan who are same as Japanese. I have not particularly thought about it so much."

The director of the Ainu Association of Hokkaido expressed his anger at the fact that a member of parliament had made such an ignorant comment about the Ainu right after the adoption of the UN Declaration on the Rights of Indigenous Peoples. He requested the Democratic Party's opinion on this matter.

The Okinawans

The six decade-long US military presence on the small island territory remains a primary source of the most pressing problems facing the peoples of Okinawa today. The Okinawans continue to suffer under the US militarization, with loss of land and subjection of their women to sexual harassment by US military personnel. Health indicators for Okinawans born after World War II show a negative trend which experts believe is largely due to the "modern" dietary and lifestyle habits introduced by the US presence.

In his 2006 report, the UN Special Rapporteur on Contemporary Forms of Racism, Racial Discrimination, Xenophobia and Related Intolerance called on the Japanese government to carry out a thorough investigation into the issue of whether the continued existence of the US military bases in Okinawa was compatible with respect for the fundamental human rights of the people of Okinawa. Until now, there has been little serious attention from the Japanese government in terms of understanding the social impact that the military presence has on the people.

Although tourism is Okinawa's largest industry, contributing roughly 23% to Okinawa's economy, the prefecture's overall economy remains heavily dependent on the US military presence. This presence contributes around 5.5% to the economy through employment on the bases, spending in the local economy and payments to those who lease their land (voluntarily or involuntarily) for use by the military. Most significant is the income that comes from central government in the form of monies for public works and extra grants to cities and towns adjacent to US bases. This economic dependence has, over the years, divided the people of Okinawa on the issue of the US military presence. In 2007, however, opposition to the US military presence deepened both within civil society and the local governments in Okinawa.

The continued militarization

A 2006 bilateral agreement between the US and Japanese governments to relocate US military personnel and construct new military facilities in Okinawa is seen by many Okinawans as a plan to further strengthen the US military presence.

The US-Japanese plans to construct several new facilities in Okinawa Island's rural northern region include new helipads in the Yanbaru forest (host to many native species) and a Marine Corps base in an offshore area inhabited by the world's remaining Okinawan *dugongs* (sea manatee, a large herbivorous sea mammal). Not only are environmentalists active in trying to save the dugong but this seagoing mammal is also considered an ancestor of human beings in Okinawan folklore and is still celebrated in songs sung by shamans and people who live along the bay that is home to the dugongs.

While the Japanese government is committed to delivering on their bilateral agreement with the US, many quarters of Okinawan society are not convinced that all the necessary environmental and social assessments are being properly conducted and many see the central government's action as aggressive and non-consultative. In many cases, anti-base activists have been able to prove that the legal procedure designed to maximize public consultation continues to be manipulated in order to evade public debate and supervision.

In a letter to the US Secretary of Defence, the Okinawa prefectural government conveyed its view on the military's plans, saying that the people of Okinawa had been shouldering the burden of US bases for a long time and that their presence continued to impact on people's lives, while the military facilities themselves were a hindrance to Okinawa's self-determined development. In December 2007, when presented with the environmental impact assessment documents for the construction of the new Marine Corps airbase, the prefectural government objected to the construction plans, arguing that they were too close to residential areas.

Although the Okinawa prefectural government has only recently taken a seat at the negotiating table, the situation is far from resolved and incidents continue to stir up anger and further resentment.

The continued behavior of US military personnel and the non-consultative approach of the Japanese government continues to anger the people in Okinawa and 2007 saw the Okinawan peace and anti-militarization movement grow. A number of campaigns and sit-ins have taken place over the years to show their dissatisfaction with the plans. However, the Japanese government's strategy to simultaneously initiate several base and helipad constructions in 2007 in different locations makes it difficult for Okinawan anti-base protestors to carry out effective campaigns.

The falsification of Okinawan history

For the past 25 years, Japan's high school text books have included the accepted historical fact that Okinawans were coerced by the Japanese Army to commit suicide rather than surrender to the US military during World War II. However, in 2007, the Education Ministry instructed that government-endorsed text books should eliminate all references to Japan's soldiers. According to the revision, the Okinawans simply committed mass suicide. Okinawa lost more than one-quarter of its population and its islands were devastated during the Battle of Okinawa at the end of World War II, but no memory is more bitter to Okinawans than that of their parents and grandparents being ordered to kill themselves and their loved ones.

Just one year before the text book revision, the UN Special Rapporteur recommended that history text books be revised to reflect an acknowledgement of the Japanese government's commitment to eradicate racial discrimination. However, this revision of Okinawa's history seems to be exactly the opposite and is perceived as an outrageous assault on Okinawa's collective memory. When an Okinawan delegation went to Tokyo to demand that the Education Ministry restore the deleted passages, no senior official would meet them and they were told that nothing could be done. Anger quickly spread and, in September 2007, more than 110,000 Okinawan people from all quarters of society protested in Ginowan City against the Japanese government's plans to revise history text books. Okinawa's Prefectural Assembly and all its 41 local governments were quick to pass resolutions demanding the text book revisions be overturned.

Okinawa's uproar over the history text book revision presents a serious challenge for Prime Minister Fukuda. Fukuda and his government need Okinawa's consent to carry out the reconfiguration of US military bases there. Fukuda pledged to seek a compromise on the new text books, which are expected to be introduced into classrooms at the start of the new school year in April 2008.

Changes in the political landscape

The 2007 protest in Ginowan was by far the biggest protest in Okinawa since it reverted to Japanese control in 1972. The second largest protest was in 1995, when 85,000 people protested at the rape of a 12-year-old girl by three US servicemen. This resulted in the US and Japanese governments agreeing that bases had to be reduced in Okinawa. While the protest in 2007 was against the Japanese national government, and the 1995 protests directed more against the US military presence in Okinawa, both protests have become part of the Okinawans' collective history and have united more Okinawans than ever before. As a result, the political landscape is also changing.

Over the past few years, progressive Okinawan candidates have suffered successive defeats in the House of Councilors' elections in Japan. Analysts agree that the elections have, over the years, been fought and won primarily on economic considerations. The bottled-up anger of the Okinawan people seems, however, to have finally reached its limit and, when given the opportunity, they delivered their verdict. In the July 2007 elections, two progressive Okinawan candidates won, including a veteran peace fighter and an activist associated with the anti-base and anti-militarization movement.   ❑

Notes

1   General Assembly adopts Declaration on Rights of Indigenous Peoples. http:// www.un.org/News/Press/docs/2007/ga10612.doc.htm October 22, 2007
2   Japan: Ainu People Seeks Indigenous Status, http://www.galdu.org/web/index.php?odas=2261&giella1=eng, November 1, 2007. See also Article "Recognize the Ainu as indigenous peoples," *Hokkaido Shimbun,* 3 October 2007
3   10 years of indigenous peoples, News No 138, 10 year citizen network of indigenous peoples, 2007, p. 2.

Kanako Uzawa holds a Masters in Indigenous Studies from the University of Tromsø. She is an intern with ILO in Geneva working on the project to Promote ILO Policy on Indigenous and Tribal People. As a member of the Rera Association, she is active in cultural preservation and furthering the indigenous rights of her people, the Ainu.

Mille Lund is a social anthropologist and works on IWGIA's Asia programme.

CHINA

According to the last census of 2000, there are 105,226,114 people belonging to ethnic minority groups, and they comprise 8.47 % of the total population of China. The government officially recognizes 55 ethnic minorities. There are 20 ethnic minority groups in China with populations of less than 100,000 people and, together, they number about 420,000 people. The Chinese government does not recognize the term "indigenous peoples". Although it has not been clearly established which of the ethnic minority groups can be considered as indigenous peoples, it is generally understood that they mainly comprise the ethnic minority groups living in the south-west of the country and a few groups in the north, east and on Hainan Island. Many of these belong to the category of small ethnic groups mentioned. They are mostly subsistence farmers belonging to the poorest segment of the country and they have illiteracy rates of over 50%. Twenty-five of the 55 officially recognized ethnic minorities live in Yunnan province. It is the province with the highest ethnic diversity in China. This year's report on China provides an update on developments with a focus on Yunnan Province.[1]

In February 2007, the China State Council announced a new national policy on development plans for ethnic minorities in the 11th Five-Year Plan on economic and social development for 2006 to 2010.

This is the first time since the People's Republic of China was established in 1949 that the State Council has formulated policies and plans specifically focusing on the development of ethnic minorities. The goal is to improve six key indices in order to meet the standards as set out in the Five-Year Plan. The six key indices comprise: ethnic minority income levels, nine years of compulsory education, infant mortality

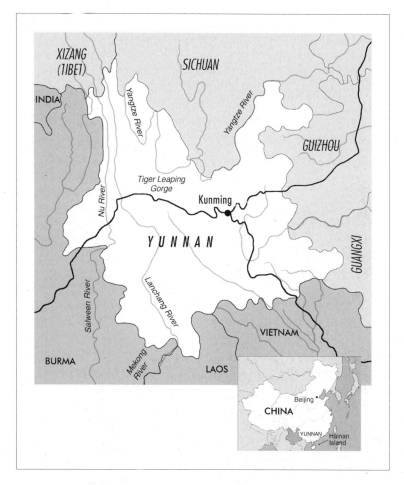

rates, ethnic minority language publications rate, employment and occupation talent[2] level, and the rate of urbanization in ethnic minority
autonomous regions.

While the Five-Year Plan for ethnic minorities appears to be full of
good intentions to narrow the development gaps, past experience of
policy implementation at the local autonomous government level indicates that there could be major shortcomings and deficiencies in the
administration and execution of these plans.

In 2007, China focused on policies to narrow the disparity (mainly income, education and employment) between ethnic minorities and the mainstream Chinese population. While Chinese government policies and plans may be well-intentioned in terms of benefiting the ethnic minorities in China, it is important that results and potential negative impacts are critically assessed in the coming years if China is serious about respecting the identity of its ethnic minority groups and avoiding simply another assimilation process.

Income

By tracking disaggregated data on income, the Chinese government aims to stop the growing gap between the average income of people living in urban and village areas of ethnic minority autonomous regions, and that of urban and village residents in the rest of China.

In Yunnan Province, economic and social poverty persists, especially in the three specially-designated categories: 1) the seven groups of numerically-small ethnic minorities,[3] 2) ethnic minorities living in "Direct Transition Districts" (including ethnic groups that lived under "the latter stages of primitive society conditions" during the 1950s) and 3) ethnic minorities living in "their cross-border traditional territories" close to China's borders. The continuing use of the term "primitive society conditions" by the government reveals that the approach underlying its policies is still very ethnocentric and assimilationist.

A set of policies collectively known as "Developing the Borderland, Enriching the Local People" is being implemented in the border areas of Yunnan Province. The majority of the funding from government is being used for transportation, roads, infrastructure, housing projects, small economic development, education, culture, health care and programs related to science and engineering training. In this way, a number of villages and small enterprises have been established as showcases of success, in line with the implementation of the "Developing the Borderland, Enriching the Local People" policies. However, most of these showcases are designed by government officials on the basis of the area's ethnic and cultural features, combined with what the government believes will be a good use of the surrounding environment to boost the local economy. Observers agree that there is limited involvement on the part of ethnic minorities in the design and decision-making processes. Furthermore, in spite of well-meaning policies and plans, problems persist in terms of misappropriation and abuse of funds for ethnic minority groups programs. Rooting out corruption, ensuring that state funds are actually reaching the poor and minorities, and ensuring people's meaningful participation in the decision-making process remain a big challenge.

Education

There are several key issues regarding the basic education system in China's western provinces and regions, which is where the majority of ethnic minority groups live. These include: insufficient state funding for education, persistent high drop-out rates for junior high school students in the rural villages, problems with implementing bilingual education programs in ethnic minority regions, and the need to raise standards for school teachers. Girls bear the brunt of the negative impacts.

The correlation between education and income disparities between rich and poor (including ethnic minorities) in China is becoming more apparent. The government found that the higher the education level among young people from ethnic minorities, the better prepared they were for the working and living conditions when they migrate to urban areas in pursuit of economic opportunities.

According to one study,[4] around 6.5 million ethnic minorities in Yunnan (approximately 47% of the total ethnic minority population in the province) are not able to communicate in Putonghua (the national Chinese language), limiting both access to higher education and to jobs. Those who are able to communicate effectively in Putonghua make up around only 12 % of the province's ethnic minority population.[5] The remaining 41% have some limited understanding of Putonghua.

Practical obstacles to implementing bilingual education include a lack of text books and teachers. There are many ethnic languages and writing systems used by Yunnan's ethnic minorities, some with linguistic sub-family branches and dialects, making the implementation of bilingual education an enormous challenge, even though a policy for this exists. There are currently 14 ethnic minority groups using 20 different systems of writing or phonetic spelling for bilingual education.

To deal with the challenges of text books and teachers, the provincial authorities trained 625 bilingual teachers in 2007. During 2007, the provincial government also completed the final editing of the publication of 276 different text books in 18 different ethnic languages. In total, 980,000 books were published and provided free to ethnic minority students in poor rural areas. The books are translations of officially approved standard Chinese text books and generally do not include content such as the histories and cultures of ethnic minorities.

According to official data, the province has instituted bilingual education programs in 3,687 schools in 66 prefectures under the 16 autonomous regional and city governments. Of these, a total of 127,046 students from pre-school or first grade up to sixth grade are receiving bilingual education.[6]

The aim of expanding bilingual education programs in Yunnan is to achieve higher schooling levels, reduce the drop-out rate and reach the target of nine years of national compulsory education.

Book publication

Of the 55 ethnic minority groups in China, many have their own language and writing systems. According to official figures from 2005, the total number of books published by ethnic minority groups was only 0.4 % of the national total. It appears to some observers that the Chinese government is starting to genuinely recognize the importance of preserving the languages and cultures of the ethnic minority groups. At the end of 2007, a character recognition system was successfully developed, and this establishes a platform for differentiating between the various ethnic minority languages in China. The central state authority is also providing additional funds for the publication of ethnic minority language books.

On 24 November 2007, the "Exhibition of Completed Projects on Ethnic Minority Languages and Writing Systems in China" took place in Beijing. Sixteen local units from 12 provinces and ethnic autonomous regions participated. Book publications and news articles on the ethnic minority groups of modern China were shown at the exhibition, along with the results of broadcasting and translation on ethnic minority groups, standardization of publications, information management, restoration of old manuscripts, calligraphy and text-writing books. The aim of the event was to enhance the general public's understanding of the issues related to the languages and cultures of China's ethnic minority groups. A "Compendium of the Cultural Heritage of the Yunnan Ethnic Minorities", which took five years to complete, was published in 2007 by the Yunnan government. It is popularly known as the "Encyclopaedia for All Ethnic Minorities of Yunnan" and contains more than 100 million words. Researchers and scholars involved in the project went to local communities and visited folk artists and audiences in rural areas to record and preserve the oral traditions of 26 ethnic minority groups, including Dai, Tibetan, Yi, Naxi, Bai, Zhuang, Hani and Miao. A total of approximately 250,000 items and forms of oral traditions and valuable cultural heritage were recorded and preserved. However, only 40% of these have been published for the general public. Approximately 30% have been recorded on mimeographic prints and another 30% held only in local offices and academic study centres on folk literature, scattered across the province.[7]

Employment

The aim of the Chinese government (in the Five-Year Plan) is for the employment level among ethnic minorities to equal that of the national population in order to boost economic development in all regions. One strategy is to ensure that human resources are developed so that individuals are able to enter the work force. Human resource development among ethnic minority groups in the western and hinterland regions continues to be lower than in the rest of China. A serious drain of young talent to urban areas, poverty and less economic development make it even more difficult to raise education levels and further human resource development in these regions.

Under China's new Five-Year Plan, the country's requirement for employment and skills is calculated on the basis of a national population census. Skilled employment of ethnic minorities increased from 7% in 1990 to 8% in 2000, averaging 0.1 % growth each year. Based on this figure the employment rate for skilled workers and trained personnel of ethnic minorities could increase by 0.5 % in 2010 as compared to 2005.

Although the government's objective of alleviating income poverty among ethnic minority groups may be achieved with a "human resource development approach", the approach also furthers the assimilation of the ethnic minority groups into mainstream Chinese economy and culture. Students from ethnic minority backgrounds continue to face financial and other difficulties in reaching university and college. Even those who graduate often face unemployment. This casts doubts for many ethnic minority communities on the value of pursuing a higher education, and this results in increased drop-out rates in schools and the belief that "education is useless".

Hydropower development

In late 2007, the government abandoned plans to build a huge dam on the Jinsha River (upper Yangtze) at Tiger Leaping Gorge in Yunnan after strong local opposition and international concern.[8] The project is located in the "Three Parallel Rivers Region" of north-west Yunnan, a UNESCO World Heritage Site (see *The Indigenous World 2007* for more information). The dam would have submerged one of the country's most renowned tourist areas and forced the relocation of 100,000 residents, mostly farmers from indigenous communities. However, preparatory work on a series of dams has begun on the nearby Nu River (upper Salween). According to news reports in 2007, the government has scaled down the project from a total of 13 to 4 dams in response to protests. The current project will displace at least 50,000 villagers from their traditional land, mostly indigenous peoples. The anti-dam campaign by environmental groups and local communities is on-going in its attempts to stop the construction of the Nu River hydroelectric dams.   ❏

Notes and References

1   When the PRC was established in 1949, a national project on "Ethnic Minority Identification" was initiated. At that time, Yunnan reported to the national government that there were around 260 "ethnic groups or minority peoples" within the province. On a national level, a total of 400 groups were reported. The government simplified this complexity by merging and classifying various ethnic groups under the 55 ethnic groups that were subsequently officially recognized. Yunnan also has the highest number of "autonomous prefectures" and "autonomous counties" in the country.

2   The term "Occupation talent" is a concept commonly used in the Chinese language - it refers to the skilled workers (and students finishing school) who are available for employment.

3   These include Achang, Blang, Deang, Dulong, Nu, Jinuo and Pumi.

4   Chen Shiao, quoted in news article: "47% of ethnic minorities do not understand national language, bilingual education has important responsibility", *China Ethnic Nationality Daily Newspaper*, Jan. 16, 2007

5   Ibid.

6   Li Sa-Ching, in news article: Free language textbooks given to poor ethnic minority students, in *Yunnan Daily*, Sept. 13, 2007.

7   Wang De-Hua, in news article: "Encyclopedia of Ethnic Minority Peoples Literature is Completed", in *Yunnan Political Bureau Daily*, May 30, 2007.

8   China abandons plans for huge dam on Yangtze, *The Guardian*, 29 December 2007 and Yunnan scraps Tiger Leaping Gorge dam, *South China Morning Post*, 21 December 2007.

*Huang Chi-ping is a lecturer in Ethnology Department at the National Cheng-chi University in Taiwan, where she is currently also studying for a Ph.D. Her article was translated from Chinese by **Jason Pan**, a member of the Executive Council of Asia Indigenous Peoples Pact.*

TIBET

Tibetans consider themselves an occupied people that shares problems with indigenous peoples around the world. Tibet was brought under the control of the People's Republic of China in 1959 when Tibet's political and spiritual leader the 14th Dalai Lama fled to India, where he and his followers were allowed to settle and establish the Tibetan Government in Exile. Evidence suggests that at least one million Tibetans have died as a result of occupation, imprisonment and starvation. Currently Tibetans number an estimated five million. They are outnumbered by at least 5.5 million Chinese, most of whom live in urban areas.

According to China's Law on Regional Autonomy, Tibetans are a minority with certain rights to autonomy and their own culture. In reality, Tibet is dominated by China. The Dalai Lama has long been asking for negotiations with China on "real autonomy". His approach has thus far not been successful in achieving any degree of self-determination. Tibetans are considered second-class citizens in their own country. There is little interaction between Tibetans and the increasing number of Chinese immigrants.

No rights for Tibetans

2007 brought no solution to Tibet despite a sixth meeting between representatives of the Tibetan Government-in-Exile and the Chinese Government in June. Because of the Olympic Games in Beijing in 2008, observers had hoped that this meeting would lead to sincere negotiations. It was described as "amicable" by the Tibetan delegation but nothing substantial seems to have been achieved. China may try to postpone decisions, hoping that material growth will disrupt the Ti-

Tibet Autonomous Region

Areas with Tibetan Autonomous Status in Quinghai, Gansu, Sichuan and Yunnan.

Additional territories claimed by the Tibetan Exile Government

betans' loyalty to the Dalai Lama. Reality paints a different picture. Every year, 2-3000 Tibetans cross the Himalayas, many of them to meet the Dalai Lama. Tibetans continue to celebrate his birthday in July, though forbidden, and most have not returned to wearing fur from endangered animals since the Dalai Lama asked them not to in 2006. When the Dalai Lama was awarded the US congressional medal in October, Tibetans all over Tibet celebrated the award.

Freedom of expression

An incident in August showed that the Tibetan population's rights to freedom of expression and basic human rights continue to be disregarded. During the annual horse festival at Lithang in Eastern Tibet, a nomad, Ronggye Adrak, took the microphone and asked for the return of the Dalai Lama. He was immediately arrested. In October, he was indicted on charges ranging from disruption of law and order to state subversion and colluding with "splittist groups" outside China. He was sentenced to eight years in jail. A local monk received a sentence of ten years, and an art teacher was jailed for nine years, both for attempting to pass information to "overseas organizations" about this case. A fourth person was sentenced to three years in prison. It is significant that two of the three Tibetans allegedly reporting on the event were sentenced to longer terms than the perpetrator. This may be intended to convey an intimidating signal to Tibetans about passing on news to the outside world prior to the Olympic Games. There has since been a military crackdown in the area. People have been required to engage in an intensified campaign against the Dalai Lama.

In September, seven boys from Eastern Tibet were arrested for scribbling "free Tibet" and calls for the return of the Dalai Lama on a wall. They were mistreated in prison and their parents had to pay large fines to obtain their release. A businessman from the Shigatse area was sentenced to three years in prison in February because the authorities found two forbidden Dalai Lama DVDs in his home. One of the longest-serving political prisoners, Ngawang Phulchung, one of the leaders of the peaceful demonstration in 1987, was released from prison in October. He had been incarcerated for 18 years and six months. There are currently an estimated 150 political prisoners in Tibet.

In April, Gedun Choekyi Nyima, who has been identified by the Dalai Lama as the reincarnation of the 10th Panchen Lama, turned 18. He and his family were taken into custody following his identification, and he has been missing for 12 years now. The Chinese government has not allowed any independent confirmation of his whereabouts.

Forced relocation and exploitation of natural resources

Human Rights Watch published a report in June documenting the forced relocation of Tibetan nomads. Beijing has announced that it will settle 80% of nomads before 2020. Many have not received compensation for the loss of their livelihoods and most find it difficult to sustain themselves in their new surroundings. They have at no point been involved in deciding the resettlement scheme. A similar development is taking place for other rural Tibetans. Families have been forced to build new houses along the roads. They are, in principle, given loans but they do not cover the expenses. Some families have been forced to leave their houses because they cannot pay back the loan. Families that have refused to comply have had their houses pulled down. There are also rumors that forcibly abandoned areas have been used for infrastructure projects. The housing scheme seems to have been devised to impress the increasing number of Chinese tourists but many houses have no modern conveniences. Observers accuse the authorities of not considering Tibetan livelihoods and poverty alleviation in their strive for urbanisation and modernisation. The exploitation of Tibet's natural resources continues unabated. According to Chinese law, they belong to the state. Tibetans are not involved in their exploitation in any meaningful way and benefit little from it. The local Government of the Tibet Autonomous Region has announced that it wishes to build a road to the base camp of Mt. Everest in order to make it more accessible to the team that will bring the Olympic flame to the top of the mountain in 2008 and to tourists. Mount Everest's base camp was the scene of embarrassment to China in April as a group of activists unfurled a banner with a slight change to the Beijing Olympic slogan "One World, One Dream. Free Tibet 2008". In September, another group of activists unfurled a similar banner at the Chinese Wall.

Tourist-style Buddhism

Tibetans warned that the new railway to Lhasa would increase the influx of Chinese into Tibet. It is too early to estimate its exact consequences but the number of Chinese tourists is said to have increased by 40% in 2007, many of these having used the railway to reach Lhasa. Tourism is considered a pillar of industry by the authorities and it is likely that Tibet received up to four million tourists in 2007. According to official sources, approximately 93% were from China.

The authorities present a picture of Tibet as a happy and exotic place. A tourist that is not informed about the political realities may be unaware of any repression and will fail to grasp that the survival of Tibetan culture, so critical to Tibetan identity, is facing its most severe crisis yet. Tourist guides are increasingly Chinese and the Chinese are remoulding Tibet according to their own perceptions, with Tibetan-style architecture, Tibetan-style souvenirs in Chinese-owned shops and Tibetan-clad "would-be-monks" in some monasteries hired by the tourist industry to show the tourists around. At the same time, the Chinese authorities go to extraordinary lengths to undermine Tibetan religious beliefs. The monasteries have, for example, been told that they must no longer rely on voluntary gifts from the communities but rather on tourism as their main source of revenue. The consequence is that monastic life in popular monasteries has been deeply affected by Chinese tourists.

A new report entitled "No faith in the state" by the Free Tibet Campaign documents the continued and strengthened repression of religion. The Chinese authorities announced new measures in June stating that they now had to approve the recognition of all reincarnated lamas. The measures indicate the Chinese Communist Party's agenda to undermine the Tibetan religious hierarchy and weaken the authority of legitimate Tibetan religious leaders. In May, they announced that all religious monuments in Tibet belonged to the Chinese state. They removed a large statue from Samye monastery. In September, similar destruction took place near Mt. Kailash. The authorities argued that placing large statues outdoors infringed a law from 2005.

International concern to no avail?

In November, a European Parliamentarian Conference for Tibet expressed deep concern at China's continuing violation of the rights of Tibetan people and called upon the European Union to push for a political settlement on the Sino-Tibetan issue. The Conference adopted two resolutions that highlight the ongoing risks to the sustainability of the Tibetan environment, resulting from Chinese government policies, social re-engineering that interferes with traditional livelihoods, rapid urbanization and the radical increase in Chinese settlers. The speaker of the Tibetan Parliament-in-Exile called upon the European Parliament to reaffirm its support for the dialogue between representatives of the Dalai Lama and the Chinese government. The conference participants called on China to promote freedom of press and independent reporting for journalists, including reporting from Tibetan areas.

Despite international political support for Tibet, to which the Chinese government always responds with vehement protests, most governments continue to prioritize business and choose not to let actions follow words. ❑

Charlotte Mathiassen is a social anthropologist and development advisor. She has been an active member of the Danish Tibet Support Group since 1989 and is currently its chairwoman, and is the Nordic representative on the International Tibet Support Network.

TAIWAN

The officially recognized indigenous population of Taiwan numbers 484,174 people (2007), or 2.1% of the total population. Thirteen indigenous peoples are officially recognized. In addition, there are at least nine Ping-pu ("plains") indigenous peoples who are denied official recognition.[1] Most of Taiwan's indigenous peoples live in the central mountains, on the east coast and in the south.

The main challenges facing indigenous peoples in Taiwan continue to be rapidly disappearing cultures and languages, low social status and negligible political or economic influence. A number of national laws protect their rights, including the Constitutional Amendments (2005) on indigenous representation in the Legislative Assembly, protection of language and culture, political participation, the Indigenous Peoples' Basic Act (2005), the Education Act for Indigenous Peoples (2004), the Status Act for Indigenous Peoples (2001), the Regulations Regarding Recognition of Indigenous Peoples (2002) and the Name Act, which allows indigenous peoples to register their original names in Chinese characters and to annotate them in Romanized script (2003). Unfortunately, serious discrepancies and contradictions in the legislation, coupled with only partial implementation of laws guaranteeing the rights of indigenous peoples, have stymied progress towards self-governance.

The legislation and enforcement of indigenous bills

The Indigenous Basic Law of 2005 demands that all related laws should be amended and promulgated by February 2008. To date, however, only one bill, the Indigenous Traditional Knowledge and In-

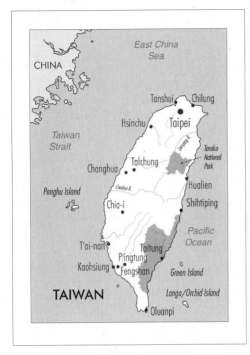

tellectual Property Protection Act, has been passed, and that was in December 2007. Another two bills – the Indigenous Self-Governance Act and the Indigenous Land and Ocean Act – are still in the drafting process. In light of the delay in the process and the problematic content of the current drafts, indigenous activists and NGOs are deeply concerned that the principles of self-determination and self-governance as embedded in the Basic Law will be enforced in a limited manner, and that, in the end, mere lip service will be paid to implementation of the Basic Law.

Despite an article in the Indigenous Basic Law that states that the Taiwan government should respect indigenous peoples' rights to land and natural resources, and that development projects in indigenous areas should obtain the Free, Prior and Informed Consent (FPIC) of indigenous peoples, this article has not been enforced. In cases such as the construction of a freeway, or the exploitation of water resources or scenic areas, indigenous peoples continue to suffer from the appropriation and exploitation of land. So far, national parks and other state resource management agencies have refused to develop co-management mechanisms with local indigenous communities, as enshrined in the Basic Law.

As the case of the utilization of forest resources by Tayal members in Smangus village shows, the executive and judicial branches of the state still fail to understand the meaning of indigenous traditional territories or indigenous customary law. The national Regulations on the Collection of Forestry Produce in Indigenous Peoples' Traditional Territories, published in October 2007, also fails to consider local indigenous peoples' institutions as part of the main management body. In addition, this Regulation completely disregards application of Tayal traditional customary law. Many indigenous communities and organizations have raised strong objections to this Regulation, for it not only ignores indigenous people's rights to self-governance but also fails to meet the principle of co-management.

How serious the impact of non-recognition of resource rights can be on indigenous communities is evident in the case of the Tao people living on Orchid Island off the east coast of Taiwan. The core of their culture, which revolves around flying fish, has been threatened by the commercial fishing conducted by non-indigenous people in recent years. As a result, the Tao culture now faces unprecedented crises. Conflicts between the Tao and non-indigenous fishermen have already broken out several times, but the government has not paid due attention to the matter and failed to propose any solution.

The third case illustrates how the imposition of conservation can violate the basic human rights of indigenous peoples. Taroko National Park was established on the Truku traditional territory.[2] The National Park Police Bureau has repeatedly conducted illegal searches of Truku individuals and their property in the park. Such a practice violates the basic human rights as well as the collective rights of the Truku people. Despite repeated protests from the Truku people, as of today the situation has not improved.

A fourth case concerns the Siraya – a Ping-pu group not yet recognized by the Taiwan central government. The Siraya National Scenic Area Administration Office was established in November 2005 and became the first national-level bureau to adopt the name of one of the Ping-pu groups. However, instead of supporting the Siraya's appeal for official recognition as an indigenous people, the Office interferes with their traditional decision-making process and organizes tours for visitors which intrude on the Siraya's traditional ceremonies.

Urban indigenous populations

Government plans have been revealed that demand the relocation of Shi-jou Community, an urban settlement of the Pangcah people (also known as Amis) that has existed for over three decades. The resettlement is supposedly being undertaken in the name of "city renewal" and was planned without adequate consultation with, or consent from, the Shi-jou Community. The Community rejects such a relocation program, which will disrupt their lifestyle and the social support mechanism that has been established by community members over the years. This includes community care for the elderly, the unemployed and single-parent households.

In December 2007, a response to the Shi-jou Community's petition from one of the candidates in the presidential elections exposed the deep–rooted discrimination towards indigenous peoples in Taiwanese society. Mr. Ying-Jiou Ma, the leader of the opposition party – the Chinese Nationalist Party (Kuo-ming-Tang) – outraged indigenous society by commenting in front of the petitioners that 1) indigenous peoples are not "genetically defect", but "only lack good opportunities", and 2) he has treated indigenous peoples as "human beings" and has meant to provide them with good care. Ma was pressured to apologize after making the comment, but the incident has revealed the prevalent discrimination towards indigenous peoples and the paternalistic attitude in indigenous policies in Taiwan.

Official indigenous status and the recognition process

Official recognition of indigenous group status continued to form a major issue of debate in Taiwan in 2007. In January, the Sakizaya people (formerly categorized as part of the "Amis" in official records) were officially recognized as a distinct indigenous group and became the thirteenth recognized indigenous people in Taiwan. Meanwhile, a decision on the application filed by the Seediq/Sediq/Sejiq people,[3] who are currently categorized as part of the "Tayal" but identify themselves as a distinct group, is still pending due to delays in the administrative procedure and the political concerns of the Council of Indigenous Peoples, the highest body overseeing indigenous affairs in the executive branch.

Following the Japanese colonial method, recognition is based on the level of "civilization" and lineage. This means that one still needs to have a father or mother who was recognized as indigenous by the Japanese to have the status of an indigenous person. The Kavalan and Sakizaya – two recognized groups – are both considered as Ping-pu (which are generally not officially recognized as indigenous), but some of them were mistakenly categorized as Pangzah and their descendants therefore hold indigenous status. Although they recently succeeded in obtaining distinct group status, those Kavalan or Sakizaya people whose ancestors were not mistakenly categorized as Pangzah are still not considered as indigenous. Most Ping-pu peoples have never received official recognition as indigenous – either as a group or as individuals. After a decade of Siraya's struggle for official recognition, the Tainan County Government established the Siraya Indigenous Affairs Commission in 2005, which granted collective rights to the Siraya people in Tainan County. However, this recognition does not stretch to the individual level. While Tainan County recognizes the Siraya as an indigenous group and has established institutions to promote its culture and language, the county does not have the authority to give individuals indigenous status. In the national administrative and political system, the Siraya people are still not considered as indigenous individuals. The Siraya people are therefore now asserting their own right to self-determination, at least on the issue of group membership. In 2007, the Siraya Communities Alliance started to design a mechanism to assign membership without seeking approval from the county and central government, and they aim to start actually assigning membership in 2008. This initiative has inspired other indigenous groups to assign their own membership based on the principle of self-determination.

On a national level, Ping-pu activists and group leaders formed the Working Group on Ping-pu Peoples' Issues and requested meetings with the Council of Indigenous Peoples to demand basic support for cultural, language and educational projects. This Working Group met twice with government officials in 2007 to hammer out constructive policies and priority projects. However, by the end of the year, there was still no decision as to their implementation.

Reinstating traditional names of indigenous communities and natural landmarks

One clause in the Treaty of New Partnership between Indigenous Peoples and the Government of Taiwan, signed in1999,[4] referred to the intention to "reinstate traditional names of indigenous communities and natural landmarks". This clause was thought to be the easiest of all objectives in the treaty to achieve. However, it has taken the government seven years from signature to finally making a first, and still only small, step towards reinstating the Cou name of a township co-inhabited by the Bunun and the Southern Cou tribes to Namashya. Other indigenous areas are expected to follow suit.

Reviving indigenous cultures

To revitalize the *dadala* (Tao longboat) culture, the Tao people spent seven months building a large longboat of over 10 meters. More than 100 Tao members took turns to row the *dadala* from Orchid Island to Taipei, on the north-western corner of Taiwan, and they completed the 600 kilometer-long journey in four months. With the arrival of the *dadala* in Taipei, the Tao people were able to introduce their culture to Taiwanese society at large, and to express their hope to be able to reconnect with the oceanic peoples from whom they have been divided by national boundaries, such as their closest neighbors on the Batan Islands, which now belongs to the Philippines. Since 2002, two Ping-pu groups, Kahabu and Pazeh, have started revival programs for their endangered languages. Although the Ministry of Education supported these programs, facilitated the publication of related text books and, in 2007, sponsored a text book, due to the Ping-pu groups' unrecognized status at national level these text books cannot be adopted for use in mother-tongue education in primary schools.

Since the late 19th century, the Siraya language has been an all-but-dead language. It was, however, documented in a Siraya–Dutch bilingual part of the Bible (Book of Matthew) in the 17th century. From this document, a Bisaya-speaking Filipino, a son-in-law of a Siraya family, found that Siraya was closely related to Bisaya. In 2002, he and his Siraya wife started to edit a Siraya dictionary based on the Bisaya language and this ancient Book of Matthew. In 2004, they began to teach local children the Siraya language. In December 2007, more than 20 children staged an opera in a theater in the Siraya language only. They were able to proudly announce that the Siraya language was back.

Research ethics and indigenous rights

The Kavalan people are the first group ever to publicly file an objection to medical research targeting them. The Kavalan's complaint has received due response from both the research team and the government. The Kavalan collectively protested against the research project because it violates the Free, Prior, Informed Consent (FPIC) principle and they demanded that their saliva samples be completely destroyed . Meanwhile, the funding agency for the research project, the National Science Council, responded to the Kavalan's demand and, for the first time on record, issued a corrective notice to the research institute. This represents important progress in indigenous peoples' rights, after decades of neglect on the part of academia.

On the positive side, the first case of a community-reviewed research ethics case took place in an indigenous community in Taiwan. In order to meet the provisions of Article 20 of the Indigenous Peoples' Basic Act, which states that no academic research should violate the FPIC principle, a research team held a public hearing in a Siraya community in December 2007 and obtained its permission before the research began.   ❑

Notes

1   The officially recognized groups are: the Amis (aka Pangcah), Tayal, Paiwan, Bunun, Pinuyumayan (aka Puyuma or Punuyumayan), Tsou, Rukai, Saisiyat, Tao (aka Yami), Thao, Kavalan, Truku and, since January 2007, Sakizaya. The nine non-recognized Ping pu groups are: Ketagalan, Taokas, Pazeh, Kahabu, Papora, Babuza, Hoanya, Siraya, Makatao.
2   aroko and Truku both refer to the indigenous group and the same geographical area. Taroko is the official name of the National Park, which comes from the Japanese pronunciation of Truku.
3   The Seediq/Sediq/Sejiq includes three subgroups who are all now under the same umbrella and who filed an application together to be recognized as a distinct people. Seediq, Sediq and Sejiq all have the same meaning – human-beings, but are pronounced and spelt differently according to each subgroup.
4   The treaty was signed in 1999 by presidential candidate, Sui-Bian Chen, and was reconfirmed during Chen's first term of presidency in 2002.

Shun-ling Chen, Mag Chin, Rebecca C. Fan, Pasang Hsiao, Shu-ya Lin, Ciwang Teyra, Jolan Hsieh, Yayuc Napay, Siyat Ulon, Echo Lin, Shu-juo Chen and *Jason Pan* are members of the Taiwan Indigenous Peoples' Alliance (TIPA) mailing-list (tipa@googlegroups.com <mailto:tipa@google-groups.com>), via which the report was developed and discussed.

Bauki Anao, Besu Piyas, Hong-kuan Duan(Alak), Echo Li-Pun Chang, Chia Tek-Khiam, Ong Tsan, Stephen Ta-Ho Pan and *Paichuan Tsai* are not TIPA mailing-list members but participated through other channels.

PHILIPPINES

Of the country's current projected population of 90.4 million,[1] indigenous peoples are estimated to comprise some 10%, or around 9 million. There has been no accurate comprehensive count of Philippine indigenous peoples since 1916. They generally live in isolated areas with a lack of access to basic social services and few opportunities for mainstream economic activities. They are usually the people with the least education and the smallest income. An abundance of valuable natural resources in their areas makes them vulnerable to development aggression.

The different indigenous groups in the northern mountains of Luzon (Cordillera) are collectively called Igorot while the different groups in the southern island of Mindanao are collectively called Lumad. There are smaller groups collectively called Mangyan in the central islands as well as even smaller, more scattered groups in the central islands and Luzon.[2] They generally cannot be differentiated physically from the majority population, except for a few bands of dark-skinned people collectively called Negritos.

The year 2007 commemorated the tenth year of the promulgation of the Republic Act 8371, known as the Indigenous Peoples' Rights Act (IPRA). The law calls for respect for indigenous peoples' cultural integrity, right to their lands and right to self-directed development of these lands.

Ten years of the Indigenous Peoples' Rights Act (IPRA)

Supporters and critics alike have been watching the IPRA's implementation closely over the years and, in observance of its tenth

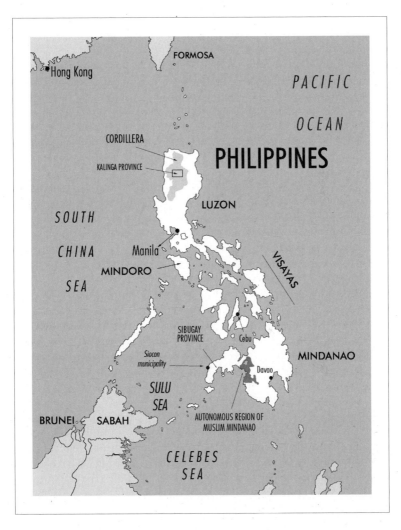

year, assessments of how the IPRA had fared were undertaken.[3] In 1997, the adoption of the IPRA into law had been greeted with much elation as it was regarded as landmark legislation showcasing a government's response to indigenous peoples' decades of struggle for their rights.

One assessment was that indigenous peoples' concerns have not been sufficiently mainstreamed within government agencies. In most cases, there is a continuing conflict between different laws and their implementing agencies, for example, between the National Commission on Indigenous Peoples (NCIP)[4] and the Department of the Environment and Natural Resources (DENR) regarding access to and management of forests. Sometimes the problem is indifference rather than conflict, as with the Department of the Interior and Local Governments (DILG) regarding the responsibilities of local government units (LGUs) in upholding indigenous peoples' representation in local bodies.

Regarding the NCIP, the observation is that this institution is still in great need of institutional strengthening. Frequently, the NCIP is perceived as addressing the interests of government or of business rather than those of indigenous peoples' communities, resulting in many expressions of disappointment from them and indigenous peoples' support groups. Instead of following the spirit of the law, the NCIP is seen to have succumbed to a more bureaucratic interpretation of the law's provisions.

This can clearly be seen in the NCIP's performance in one of its three core programs: the delineation and titling of ancestral land. Since 2003, when the first Certificate of Ancestral Domain Title (CADT) was granted, the NCIP has processed only 57 CADTs, which is 9% of the titling applications it has received. Just two certificates were approved in early 2007 (see paragraph below). The titling procedures have been criticized for being unnecessarily costly and lengthy, and lacking in cultural sensitivity. These criticisms were also leveled at the NCIP projects aimed at assisting indigenous peoples' communities to develop their community development plans which, according to the IPRA's Implementing Rules and Regulations (IRR), come under the Ancestral Domain Sustainable Development and Protection Plan (ADSDPP).

Very few CADTs were approved by the NCIP in 2007 because of a lack of appointees to complete the seven-member Commission En Banc (CEB), the highest governing body of this agency. The terms of six of the Commissioners expired in February and, by the end of the year, only five had been reappointed or replaced. Yet the NCIP, as of November 2007, was able to issue 62 Certificates of Compliance to the FPIC Process and Certification that the Community Has Given Its

Consent for development projects, including for mining claims and for plantations to produce bio-fuels. A total of 118 such certificates have been issued since 2004, when the first one was granted.[5]

According to the assessments, civil society groups, both NGOs and indigenous peoples' organizations, have fared better in furthering the rights of indigenous peoples embodied in the IPRA and in delivering services to the indigenous peoples' communities.

Violations of indigenous peoples' rights

As expected, one of the most violated of indigenous peoples' rights is the right to their ancestral domain and its development. Mining continues to be promoted by the Philippine government. Indigenous peoples' communities continue to oppose this as they have observed how other communities have suffered loss of access to and control over the land, as well as environmental degradation, without the promised benefits. A landmark case is the almost decade-old battle of the Subanen in Siocon municipality, south-western Philippines, to stop the activities of the TVI Resource Development, Inc., a Canadian mining company. In August 2007, the Subanen filed a complaint with the United Nations Committee on the Elimination of Racial Discrimination (CERD) under its urgent action procedure. The CERD has directed the Philippine government, a signatory to the Convention for the Elimination of All Forms of Racial Discrimination, to respond to the complaint. The CERD also reminded the government that the last time it had submitted a report to the Committee, something it is supposed to do every two years, has been in 1997, before the IPRA became law.[6] The CERD is to consider the Subanen case at its 72nd session in Geneva from 18 February-7 March, 2008.[7]

In 2006, a particular form of human rights violation that gained notorious prominence was the extrajudicial killing of civilians, including a number of indigenous peoples, allegedly by the military. The victims were identified as critics of President Gloria Macapagal-Arroyo's administration, including some who were against her business interests, including mining. The number of killings of indigenous people appears to have been less in 2007: ten by June 2007 in contrast to a total of 43 in 2006. Of these ten, nine were indigenous farmers (including four elderly, one blind woman and one minor) who were massacred by military and police forces while demolition was going on as a consequence of a land dispute in Kalinga province, Cordillera. In this case, the land claimants, who belonged to different indigenous groups, were using varying tenure systems to support their claims.

Indigenous peoples' representation

The small number of indigenous peoples in the Philippines in relation to the total population makes it hard for them to have meaningful representation on relevant bodies and thus exacerbates their difficulties in pursuing recognition of and respect for their rights.

One strong opinion that became clear from the assessment of IPRA's implementation was that, in retrospect, indigenous peoples' rights advocates should have engaged more with the local government units, or assisted the indigenous peoples to mainstream their concerns within the local political environment. The local elections that took place in May 2007 could have provided an opportunity for indigenous peoples to become more involved. By the end of 2007, the NCIP still had no data as to how many indigenous peoples had won in local elections held mid-year. However, the consensus is that there were very few,[8] most of them in areas where the indigenous peoples still constitute a majority of the population. There were attempts to get some indigenous peoples elected to Congress through the party list system but the candidates identified were not acceptable to a significant number of indigenous peoples. In the party list system, a sectoral candidate can get elected if able to garner a minimum of 2% of the total votes cast. However, because of their small number and when they are not able to rally support for common candidates, the chances of electoral victory for indigenous peoples remain slim.

The representation of indigenous peoples has not been considered in the ongoing peace talks between the government and the Moro Islamic Liberation Front (MILF), even though there are large indigenous peoples' groups, especially the Teduray, in the Autonomous Region of Muslim Mindanao (ARMM). While there is an indigenous person assigned to the Technical Working Group providing support to the government panel, there is no indigenous peoples' voice on the negotiating panel itself. In 2007, the indigenous peoples were in uproar over the MILF's September 2006 statement calling for recognition of a Moro ancestral domain. In theory, this would not take into consideration the ancestral domain claims of indigenous peoples within the ARMM. Reports on the exploratory talks between the government and the MILF in November 2007 stated that the impasse had been broken but precisely how it was resolved has not been revealed.[9] When indigenous peoples ask why their grievances are not heard within the peace talks, they are told by the government that it is because the protesting indigenous peoples do not have an army, and the MILF forces do.[10]

Ancestral lands where the population density is relatively small are currently being considered for inclusion in the government's agrarian reform program. Tensions were already high in 2004 when the NCIP was attached to the Department of Land Reform (DLR, formerly Department of Agrarian Reform). In 2007, the tension manifested itself in specific cases, such as when the boundary delineation survey for the CADT of the Buhid Mangyan on the central island of Mindoro was continually disrupted because the DLR issued Certificates of Land Ownership to non-indigenous farmers within the ancestral domain claim. By the end of 2007, negotiations were still ongoing to settle this amicably, although at this point it is the DLR that is presenting a hard line.

In the face of the growing intensity of the rights and development issues confronting the indigenous peoples in the Philippines, the call for unity among indigenous peoples and their support groups grew even stronger over the year. One manifestation of this call was the agreement not to field any party list candidates rather than put forward a controversial one.

Prospects and challenges for the coming year

After considering what has or has not been accomplished following 10 years of the IPRA, indigenous peoples and their support groups are seemingly torn between feeling that there is no further point in supporting its implementation, or that something constructive can still be done. Calls for the IPRA's abolition grew in number throughout 2007. At the same time, there are those who recognize the weaknesses inherent within the law and in its implementation by government but would still like to use it as a springboard for furthering indigenous peoples' rights.

Data on how indigenous peoples fared in the May 2007 local elections is expected by March 2008, in preparation for a discussion of the NCIP's Commission En Banc on planned guidelines for mandatory representation of indigenous peoples on local legislative councils and other policy-making bodies.[11] Several of the NCIP guidelines issued in previous years – on titling, on the formation of a Consultative Body, on the procurement of the FPIC, on the formulation of the Ancestral Domain Sustainable Development and Protection Plan (ADSDPP) – have already been criticized both in their substance and in their implementation, with the criticisms not yet leading to any acceptable revisions in the guidelines. As a result of a study it commissioned in 2007, the World Bank has approved a project for the institutional strengthening of the NCIP, including better procedures for titling (CADT), community development planning (ADSDPP) and ascertaining the free and prior informed consent of indigenous peoples for projects on their ancestral domains. The project is to be undertaken in 2008-2009, and the results are expected as early as 2010. Among the results expected are: approval of 75% of CADT applications and a significant reduction in the time and cost needed to obtain a Certificate of Compliance.[12]

During 2007, indigenous peoples in the Philippines and their support groups joined in the international celebrations when the United Nations General Assembly passed the Declaration on the Rights of Indigenous Peoples. One of the ways in which it is thought the Declaration could effectively be used in the Philippine context is in upholding cultural integrity, including its application to environment-related issues. This may sum up what lies ahead for advocacy of indigenous peoples' rights in the Philippines – the search for new or innovative ways to be pro-active with regard to longstanding issues.   ❏

Notes and References

1   Figure from http://www.census.gov.ph/ accessed 13 February 2008.
2   Data in this section is taken from **Sabino Padilla, Jr. 2000**: *Katutubong Mamamay-an*. Manila/Copenhagen: International Work Group for Indigenous Affairs (IW-GIA).
3   The major sources of information regarding the assessment are the following: **PANLIPI, 2007:** *Initial Assessment of the Extent and Impact of the Implementation of IPRA* (Manila: International Labour Organization for South East Asia and the Pacific, 2007)**; Indigenous Peoples Rights Monitor, 2007:** *The Situation of Human Rights and Fundamental Freedoms of the Indigenous Peoples in the Philippines: January 2003 to November 2007* (Manila: Indigenous Peoples Rights Monitor, 2007); **Josefo B. Tuyor et al., 2007**: Philippines Indigenous Peoples Rights Act: Is It Protecting the Rights of the Indigenous Peoples?, Study commissioned by the World Bank, April 2007; and Masli A. Quilaman (Director of the NCIP's Office on Empowerment and Human Rights), Status: Issuance of CADTs/CALTs, ADSDPP Formulation, & CP Issuances, report presented to the "Subanen Elders and Leaders General Assembly and Environment and Indigenous Peoples' Concerns", Springland Resort, Pagadian City, 18-20 November 2007. As of writing, the NCIP does not yet have its own assessment of the 10 years of IPRA but it is said that one is being planned with Tebtebba, a research NGO on the IP situation in the Philippines, and the UN Permanent Forum on Indigenous Issues, according to mobile phone communications with Quilaman on 18 February 2008.
4   The NCIP was established in 1998 to oversee implementation of this law.
5   Ancestral Domains Office, NCIP, "List of Issued Compliance Certificate as of February 2008 (Certificate of Compliance to FPIC Process and Certification that the Community Has Given Its Consent)".
6   A good summary background on this can be found in **Lina Sagaral Reyes,** "RP in hot seat as tribal folk sue government at UN agency, http://newsinfo.inquirer.net/inquirerheadlines/regions/view/20080209-117846/RP-in-hot-seat-as-tribal-folk-sue-govt-at-UN-agency, first posted 19:47:00 02/09/2008. See also: Ibid.: Human Rights and Fundamental Freedoms of the Indigenous Peoples in the Philippines, pp. 24-25; The CERD and Indigenous Peoples Rights, PowerPoint presentation prepared for the conference entitled "Celebrating the Adoption of the UN Declaration on the Rights of Indigenous Peoples and Strengthening Partnerships for its Implementation", organized by Tebtebba et al., held in Quezon City, Philippines, 21-22 October 2007; and http://www.tviphilippines.com/milestones.html, accessed 6 March 2008.
7   Cf. Endnote 6.
8   Mobile phone communications with Quilaman on 18 February 2008.
9   Carolyn O. Arguillas, 2007: Peace panels resolve territorial scope of ancestral domain, *MindaNews*, 25 October 2007; **idem, 2007**: MILF ok Ancestral Domain issues; IMT stay likely extended, *MindaNews*, 15 November 2007; and **idem,**

2007: Dureza: best-case scenario in GRP-MNLF and GRP-MILF talks by March 2008, *MindaNews*, 23 November 2007.

10 As discussed in "Panagtigum: A Gathering of Indigenous Peoples Leaders and Advocates", Samdhana Retreat Center, Cagayan de Oro City, 20-22 August 2007. The source for this particular item in the discussions requested not to be identified.

11 Mobile phone communications with Quilaman on 18 February 2008.

12 "Terms of Reference – Consultancy Service: Enhancement of Standard Systems and Procedures for Data Gathering and Analysis", part of the project on "Strengthening the Institutional Effectiveness of the National Commission on Indigenous Peoples", n. d.

Ma. Teresa Guia-Padilla and Mynabel T. Pomarin are staff og Anthropology Watch, which is a non-governmental organization (NGO) composed of anthropologists and other social scientists who work with and for indigenous peoples in the Philippines. It engages in assistance to land titling, culturally appropriate community development planning, capacity-building and advocacy on indigenous peoples' issues.

INDONESIA

Indonesia has a population of around 220 million. The government recognizes 365 ethnic and sub-ethnic groups as *komunitas adat terpencil* (geographically-isolated customary law communities). They number about 1.1 million. However, many more peoples consider themselves, or are considered by others, as indigenous. The national indigenous peoples' organization, Aliansi Masyarakat Adat Nusantara (AMAN), uses the term *masyarakat adat* (the term used to refer to indigenous peoples). A conservative estimate of the number of indigenous peoples in Indonesia amounts to 30-40 million people.

The third amendment to the Indonesian Constitution recognizes indigenous peoples' rights. In more recent legislation there is an implicit, though conditional, recognition of some rights of peoples referred to as *masyarakat adat* or *masyarakat hukum adat*, such as Act No. 5/1960 on Basic Agrarian Regulation, Act No. 39/1999 on Human Rights, MPR Decree No X/2001 on Agrarian Reform.

However, government officials argue that the concept of indigenous peoples is not applicable, as almost all Indonesians (with the exception of the ethnic Chinese) are indigenous and thus entitled to the same rights. Consequently, the government has rejected calls for special treatment by groups identifying themselves as indigenous.

The Third Congress of Archipelago's Indigenous Peoples

In March 2007, some 1,000 indigenous representatives gathered in Pontianak, West Kalimantan to attend the third Congress of Archipelago's Indigenous Peoples. Representatives participated from all over

Indonesia to discuss the priorities of the indigenous peoples and to choose the new leadership for their alliance, AMAN.

The opening was attended by Indonesia's Minister for the Development of "Neglected Regions", Mr. Syaifullah Yusuf. An indigenous representative from Bangladesh, Mr. Raja Devasish Roy, and the Chairperson of the Cordillera Peoples' Alliance – Philippines, Ms Joan Carling, also attended the Congress.

Eleven parallel workshops were held as part of the congress, focusing on key issues such as politics, corporate accountability, education, economy, indigenous women, community-based forestry, oil palm plantations, environment, land and policy reform, environment, customary law and human rights.

The alliance's agenda for the next five years was agreed in the work plan entitled "Toward Indigenous Peoples' Sovereignty, Prosperity and Dignity"". The work plan covers a range of programs such as policy advocacy, economic empowerment, indigenous women and youth empowerment, education and political empowerment.

Policy Status on Indigenous Peoples

During 2007, progress was made in terms of recognising indigenous peoples' rights in Law No. 27/2007 on Coastal and Small Islands Management. The law recognizes the rights of indigenous peoples to manage coastal and small islands and recognizes indigenous knowledge as an important aspect in the protection of the coastal areas and small islands. However, another law, No. 25/2007 on Foreign Investment, also passed in 2007, allows foreign or domestic investors the right to cultivate plantations for a period of up to 95 years. Law 25 also provides clear incentives for the investor, such as tax relief and free repatriation. In reality, this means that indigenous peoples whose lands have been occupied for plantations have very limited chances of getting their land returned. Meanwhile, conflicts over land for plantations have increased dramatically over the past few years. The new law on Foreign Investment will put Indonesia in a new colonial model, not recognizing indigenous peoples' rights to land. Civil society activists see the

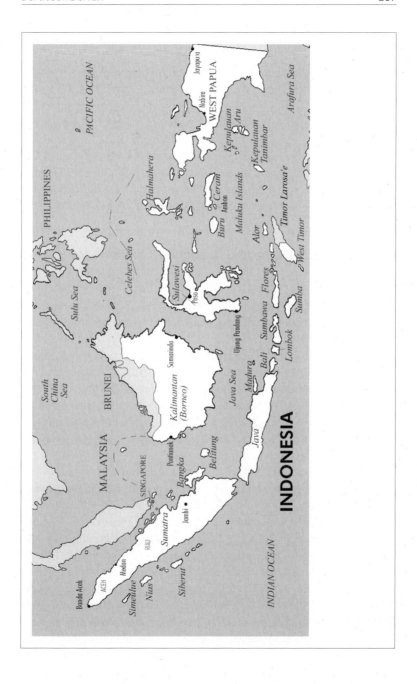

law as extremely problematic and are actively following the ongoing judicial review by the Constitutional Court.

In addition to the Foreign Investment Law, other policies, inter alia, the Spatial Layout Plan Law, the Plantations Law, Water Resources Law, Forestry Law and the Mining Law, are also seen as highly problematic with regard to violating the rights of indigenous peoples in Indonesia.

Indigenous peoples in Indonesia welcomed the adoption of the UN Declaration on the Rights of Indigenous Peoples by the UN General Assembly on 13 September and furthermore appreciated the Indonesian government's decision to vote in support of the Declaration.

The Agrarian Reform and worsened conflict over natural resources

On paper, one of central government's priorities in 2007 was to operationalize the principle of "land for justice and prosperity of the people" under the agrarian reform agenda. On 28 September 2006, President Yudhoyono called upon the services of the Minister of Forestry, Minister of Agriculture and the Head of the National Land Agency and announced the allocation of 8.15 million hectares of existing converted production forests to the poor. The president's policy is in accordance with Agrarian Law No. 5/1960 and is aimed at addressing poverty and unemployment. However, by the end of 2007, the agrarian reform plan was yet to be implemented.

From an indigenous perspective, the agrarian reform seems to further threaten indigenous lands. The allocated lands may include indigenous land because most of the so-called "state forest" land in fact belongs to indigenous communities.

Such land re-distribution as the government is planning may also trigger conflicts between indigenous peoples and other sectors of society since it is associated with old-style transmigration programs, which the government is also planning to re-launch. Transmigration is the facilitation of settlers moving from densely populated areas to areas that are less populated. Most of the less-populated areas in Indonesia belong to indigenous peoples. In addition, the government recently launched the so-called *Kota Terpadu Mandiri* (KTM) initiative that includes providing additional financial support to enable transmigration areas[1] to become more economically independent by focusing on modern development initiatives.[2] The transmigration program is also believed to advance the situation of less developed areas.[3] Indigenous peoples, however, are put in a situation where they are forced to compete with transmigrants for their livelihoods. Experience in transmigration areas shows that most often conflicts break out because of a competition over resources. Conflicts are also caused by extreme cultural differences. Mita Noveria from the Indonesian Science Institute (LIPI) shows that there have been seven conflicts in the Central Kalimantan Province due to the impact of the massive expansion of oil palm plantations.[4]

According to data summarised by the Agrarian Reform Consortium (*Konsorsium Pembaruan Agraria*/KPA), violence against indigenous farmers increased over the period 2005-2007. In 2007, there were at least 80 cases of conflicts over natural resources reported to the police all over Indonesia, as documented by the KPA. The majority of the conflicts occurred in the plantation and forestry sectors.

Meanwhile, the report of *Sawit Watch*, an Indonesian network against palm oil plantations, shows that as of 2007 there had been 514 indigenous communities in conflict with oil palm plantations, involving 141 companies, in 14 provinces alone.

To avoid permanent large-scale conflicts, the government needs to engage with indigenous peoples to find solutions when indigenous and state forest is involved. Furthermore, implementation of any plans that could have an impact on indigenous communities, including the land distribution plan, should respect indigenous peoples' free, prior and informed consent.

Threat of government established institution

The National Secretariat for Protection of Constitutional Rights of the Indigenous People was inaugurated on 11 December 2007 (declared on 9 August 2006). Institutions such as the Constitutional Court, the Social Department, Forestry Department, Coordination of Survey and

Mapping National Agency and the National Commission on Human Rights are all included.[5] Several Indonesian Ministers and Governors have special positions in the Secretariat. This process has also been supported by UN agencies such as the United Nations Development Program (UNDP) and the International Labour Organization (ILO). The Secretariat of Malays Indigenous Institution (*Lembaga Adat Rumpun Melayu*) in Riau Province has been agreed as the National Secretariat-ad interim.

AMAN - the indigenous peoples' alliance in Indonesia - is not in favour of the initiative since it was established without indigenous peoples' full participation and its members are not legitimate indigenous representatives (former military and government officers).

Indigenous peoples welcome recommendations from the Committee on the Elimination of Racial Discrimination (CERD)

Palm oil production for food and agro-fuels is resulting in widespread indigenous peoples' human rights abuses in Indonesia. Oil palm companies often use violent tactics to grab indigenous land, with the support of the police and the authorities. Self-reliant indigenous peoples, who were previously able to meet their own needs, have been tricked into giving up land with the promise of jobs, financial aid, educational support and other infrastructure facilities. Instead, indigenous people have ended up locked into debt and under-paid work, while the bounty of the rainforest is replaced with large oil palm plantations. Pollution from pesticides, fertilisers and the pressing process is also leaving some villages without clean water. Furthermore, related water pollution has also caused reproductive problems among indigenous women.

In August 2007, AMAN and 11 NGOs in Indonesia submitted a report to the Committee on the Elimination of Racial Discrimination's Urgent Action and Early Warning Procedures on a Consideration of the Situation of Indigenous Peoples in West Kalimantan. The request was submitted in relation to Indonesia's plan to expand oil palm plantations over some 850 kilometres along the Indonesia-Malaysia border in Kalimantan as part of the Kalimantan Border Oil Palm Mega-Project. This area is part of the traditionally-owned territories of the indigenous peoples of this region. The project will cause irreparable harm to indigenous peoples' territories, traditional means of subsistence, cultural, territorial and physical integrity. Indeed, it is no exaggeration to say that an intrusion of this magnitude will threaten the indigenous peoples' very survival. In 2007, the United Nations Special Rapporteur on the situation of human rights and fundamental freedoms of indigenous people and two Special Rapporteurs appointed by the UN Permanent Forum on Indigenous Issues reached the same alarming conclusion.

In response to the report, CERD has noted its concern and made some recommendations to the Indonesian government. Of those recommendations, three have direct implications for indigenous peoples:

The State Party is encouraged to take into consideration the definitions of indigenous and tribal peoples as set out in ILO Convention 169 of 1989 on Indigenous and Tribal Peoples, and to envisage ratification of this instrument.

The State party should recognize and respect indigenous culture, history, language and way of life as an enrichment of the State's cultural identity and provide indigenous peoples with conditions allowing for a sustainable economic and social development compatible with their cultural characteristics.

The State party should review its laws, in particular Law No. 18 of 2004 on Plantations, as well as the way they are interpreted and implemented in practice, to ensure that they respect the rights of indigenous peoples to possess, develop, control and use their communal lands.

Although the third recommendation needed to be followed up within a year, there has been no follow-up or response by the government to date. A letter sent by the Indonesian Ministry of Foreign Affairs mentioned that the government was producing a report in response to the CERD recommendations.

Lack of inter-departmental coordination seems to be part of the reason for the government's slow response. There is no clarity as to which department/s should take responsibility. While the Ministry of Foreign Affairs is producing a report, the Ministry of Forestry and Ministry of Plantations, supported by the Governor, are moving forward with the expansion of oil palm plantations, especially in relation to climate change mitigation schemes. In Papua, for example, some 1 to 3 million hectares of land have been allocated for oil palm plantations,[6] although the plan was opposed by civil society.[7]

Climate change mitigation - REDD and the World Bank Forest Carbon Partnership Facility

From 3-13 December 2007, the United Nations Framework Convention on Climate Change (UNFCCC) was held at Nusa Dua, Bali. The international community hoped that the Convention would set the stage for the formulation of climate change mitigation and adaptation policies and schemes. Activists agree, however, that no appropriate or sustainable solution was identified. Furthermore, no social justice solution was agreed to, as demanded by indigenous peoples. As was forecast, many activists agree that the Convention was merely an arena for manipulative concession practices benefiting only the carbon-producing countries and the multinationals trading in carbon credits.

As the host, instead of taking a critical or at least neutral stance, Indonesia was involved in promoting the initiative for *Reducing Emission from Deforestation and Degradation* (REDD) and the World Bank's Forest Carbon Partnership Facility (FCPF).

During the UNFCCC meeting, Papua's Governor, Mr. Barnabas Suebu, stated that Papua was allocating half of its productive forest for *Reduction Emission from Deforestation and Degradation* (REDD). Meanwhile, a quarter of Papua's "converted forest" has been allocated by the Governor for initiatives under the *Clean Development Mechanism* (CDM). The policy is in accordance with a Provincial Regulation (*Perda*) and is planned to come into force in January 2008.[8]

Indigenous peoples in Indonesia feel threatened by the extent of climate change mitigation and adaptation efforts. People fear eviction in the name of conservation or climate change. Experience has shown how indigenous peoples have been forcibly evicted in the name of conservation and such evictions still occur, against the wishes of the indigenous peoples. Indigenous peoples have lost their land to oil palm plantations and will certainly suffer further to meet the bio-fuel targets of Western nations.   ❏

Notes and References

1   Transmigration areas were originally established by the Indonesian state, main-
     ly in the 1970s, for the resettlement of large numbers of migrants from the
     densely populated islands, mostly from Jawa Island.
2   http://infokito.wordpress.com/2007/11/28/kota-terpadu-mandiri-sumsel-
     butuh-rp42-m/
3   http://www.suarapembaruan.com/News/2008/01/05/Nusantar/nus06.htm
4   **Mita Noveria et al., 2004:**   *Berbagai Ruang dengan Masyarakat: Upaya Resolusi
     Konflik Sumberdaya Hutan di Kalimantan Tengah.* Jakarta: LIPI Riset Competitif
     Pengembangan Iptek, Subprogram Otonomi Daerah, Konflik dan Daya Saing.
5   The initiative was proposed and agreed upon as a joint Secretariat of these gov-
     ernment institutions. The heads of these state bodies are on the Board of Trus-
     tees of the Secretariat.
6   www.kompas.com/kompas-cetak/0305/12/daerah/307204.htm,
     http://202.173.64.197/newsdetail.php?id=382&marchid=2006,   http://www.
     seputar-indonesia.com/edisicetak/nusantara/investasi-kelapa-sawit-papua-2.
     html, http://64.203.71.11/ver1/Nusantara/0704/20/124808.htm
7   http://mediatani.wordpress.com/2007/10/25/pembukaan-perkebunan-saw-
     it-tak-mampu-sejahterakan-masyarakat-papua/
8   http://64.203.71.11/ver1/Iptek/0712/06/160820.htm and http://www.repub-
     lika.co.id/koran_detail.asp?id=316200&kat_id=3

Abdon Nababan is the General Secretary of the Aliansi Masyarakat Adat Nusantara (AMAN), the nationwide alliance of indigenous peoples of Indonesia.

Mina Susana Setra, Director of International Advocacy and Foreign Affairs, AMAN

Rukka Sombolinggi is an indigenous person from Toraja in Indonesia. She worked with AMAN from 2000 to 2006 and She currently works as a consultant on indigenous peoples' issues.

MALAYSIA

In all, the indigenous peoples of Malaysia represent around 12% of the 28.6 million people in Malaysia. The Orang Asli are the indigenous peoples of Peninsular Malaysia. They number 145,000, representing a mere 0.5% of the national population. Anthropologists and government officials have traditionally regarded the Orang Asli as consisting of three main groups comprising several distinct tribes or sub-groups. The main groups are the Negrito (Semang), the Senoi and the Aboriginal-Malay. In Sarawak, the indigenous peoples are collectively called Orang Ulu or Dayak and include the Iban, Bidayuh, Kenyah, Kayan, Kedayan, Murut, Punan, Bisayah, Kelabit, Berawan and Penan. They constitute around 50% of Sarawak's population of 2.3 million people. The 39 different indigenous ethnic groups in Sabah are called natives or Anak Negeri, and make up approximately 60% of the 2.4 million population of the state. In Sarawak and Sabah, laws introduced by the British during their colonial rule recognizing the customary land rights and customary law of the indigenous peoples are still in place. However, they are not properly implemented, and even outright ignored by the government, which gives priority to large-scale resource extraction and plantations of private companies over the rights and interests of the indigenous communities.

The plight of the Penan in Sarawak

In July 2007, the nomadic and semi-nomadic Penan people from Sarawak finally managed to obtain much-needed attention when the fact-finding mission of the Human Rights Commission of Malaysia (Suhakam) issued a statement identifying seven key areas requiring "drastic improvement"

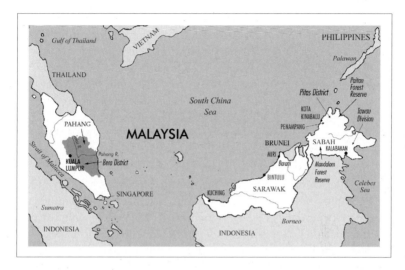

by the government in order to improve the situation of the Penan. The mission listed the following issues of main concern: land rights, Environmental Impact Assessment (EIA) reports, poverty, personal identification documents, education, health and the duty of the Sarawak state government to protect the rights of the Penans. On land rights, Suhakam claimed that the Sarawak Land Code of 1958 has no provision on the rights of the Penan to land ownership and, as such, recommended that the legislation be amended to take into consideration the Penan's unique way of establishing land ownership and stewardship.

In the same month, the Penan community of Long Lamai, on the upper reaches of the Baram River, filed a new court case against the Sarawak state government and the Malaysian logging giant, Samling. In the representative action case, five plaintiffs are claiming Native Customary Rights to 31,000 hectares of primary rainforest and farmlands on behalf of the community of Long Lamai.

On June 2, a road blockade was re-erected by some 50 Penans in Long Belok and Long Sayan, in the Apoh region of middle Baram, to prevent Rimbunan Hijau, another Sarawak-based logging giant, from entering and extracting timber within communal forest reserves in the upper reaches of the Belok River. In August, another new blockade was erected by the Penans in Long Nen, Sungai Layun, together with the nomadic Penans from Sungai Marong, in upper Tutoh, to stop logging activities on their land by Samling and their sub-contractor, Jumbo Green. The nomadic Penan said that the two groups decided to join forces because they could not handle the pressure from the company on their own.

Blockades have been set up by Penans at different sites in the upper reaches of Baram for the last 14 years. Upper Baram is regarded as one of the last remaining primary forests in Sarawak and the last frontier to be exploited by the logging companies. The upper Baram blockades, often associated with the Long Benalih villagers, have been dismantled by the authorities on numerous occasions. On July 4, the authorities destroyed the barricades again but the villagers re-erected them shortly afterwards. In mid-July, the Benalih blockade was dismantled once more by timber company workers, together with the military's General Operations Force (GOF) personnel. The people were warned that they would be arrested if they continued with the blockade.

As Jok Jau of the Sarawak branch of Friends of the Earth, Malaysia stated, "The continuous dismantling and rebuilding of the blockades has received much attention in recent years, particularly after the concession's inclusion into the controversial Malaysian Timber Certification Council scheme whose legal and sustainable claims have been questioned by national and international civil society groups." (see *The Indigenous World 2007*). As in the past, when the Penans have received high-level publicity, retaliation from the authorities and companies was inevitable. On October 9, 2007 Sarawak's Natural Resources and Environment Board (NREB) controller stated that the Penans could be easily manipulated by NGOs if they were allowed to participate in Environmental Impact Assessment (EIA) studies since they do not have a high level of education. He was, in fact, trying to cover up an embarrassing situation whereby the NREB had passed an EIA for the Shin Yang Forest Plantation in Murum, claiming that people did not reside within the area in question when there were seven Penan villages there. Furthermore, on November 7, the Sarawak Attorney-General announced to surprised representatives from Suhakam, state and federal agencies and several NGOs that the state government has plans to resettle the Penan.

At the height of the conflict in November came the sad discovery of the remains of a Penan headman from Long Kerong, KK Kelasau, who had been opposing the logging companies for a very long time. Villagers have reason to believe that the death of KK Kelasau was not an accident as the community had previously received numerous death threats. This is not the first time that a death from around the upper Baram has been linked to logging companies operating in the area, as thugs sometimes used to threaten them. Because of their close relationship with and dependence on the forests, Penan communities have vehemently opposed the incursion of logging companies. Many Penans have been arrested and jailed for their actions. Many supporting activists who carried out fact-finding missions, or spoke out against the atrocities committed by logging companies, police and GOF personnel, or who were investigating police reports have been banned from entering Sarawak.

Suhakam's recommendation to the government to balance the country's economic development and exploitation of resources with the promotion and protection of the basic human rights of its citizens seems to have fallen on deaf ears.

In the Courts

Two landmark court judgments were made in 2007 in Sarawak and Sabah.

On October 8 in Sarawak, Dato' Arifin bin Zakaria and two other Federal High Court judges concluded a civil appeal case between the Superintendent of Lands and Survey, Sarawak and the Sarawak government and Madeli bin Salleh (on behalf of his late father, Salleh bin Kilong, and representing several indigenous groups with customary land rights). This was an appeal against the decisions of the Court of Appeal of April 2005. In this case, two important decisions were made: one with respect to native customary rights (NCR) to land, and one with respect to the reservation of NCR lands for commercial purposes. On the former, Federal High Court judge Dato' Arifin bin Zakaria emphasized in his judgement that " ... common law [native customary law, ed.] is not a mere precedence for the purposes of making a judicial decision. It is a substantive law which has the same force and effect as written law" (page 22). This is also judged to be applicable to both individual and communal rights to land. In this case, the judges in the Court of Appeal recognized that the late Salleh bin Kilong had already established native customary rights to his land prior to the Land Settlement Ordinance of 1920 and that this Ordinance does not purport to nullify native customary rights, which had been acquired or recognized prior to the Ordinance. The court also judged that absence does not mean that the owner is no longer in control of the land, and ruled that as long as the land is cared for, the owner must have due recognition of rights to the land. In this case, Salleh's continued maintenance of the fruit trees on the land strengthened his claims as it did not constitute abandonment or non-occupation. Even though the land was reserved to the Miri District for the operations of Sarawak Oilfields Limited under the 1921 Order, the judges decided this should not extinguish customary rights since this was not clearly spelled out: "...the Order could not be construed to have the effect of extinguishing the rights of the native over such land which had been in existence prior to the coming into force of the said Order. Such a drastic measure needs to be expressed in clear language and cannot be derived by mere implication" (page 40).

The other landmark judgment was that of Justice Ian Chin at the Kota Kinabalu High Court in Sabah in July. Justice Ian Chin presided over two judicial reviews and one civil suit, all inter-related, between Rambilin binti Ambit (a woman of the Dusun indigenous people) and the Assistant Collector of Land Revenue of Pitas District, the Director of Lands and Survey, Sabah, and local entrepreneur Ruddy Awah. Apart from important decisions upholding Native Customary Rights over land, very similar to the civil appeal case in Sarawak mentioned above, the case also revealed several weaknesses in the land registration system and the fraudulent ways in which companies - and even indigenous peoples themselves - pursue their own interests. The court pointed out that "... native 'customs and laws' in Sabah (formerly known as North Borneo) were explicitly acknowledged and recognized as far back as 1881 and in the subsequent two pieces of land legislation" (i.e. the Proclamation of December 23, 1881, and the Land Proclamation of 1885) (page 7 of the judgment). As the judgment continues, the further passing of land rules to register lands did not automatically extinguish the rights of the natives to land but only required them to register their claim, without setting a time limit within which to do so and that native rights to land continued even though not registered as they have not been extinguished by any legislation. Additionally, Justice Ian Chin pointed out that natives do not need permission from the authorities even today to enter any "state" land to establish customary rights through residential occupation or cultivation for three or more consecutive years.

Meanwhile in Peninsular Malaysia, the headmen of two Semelai villages in Bera, Pahang, and four other villagers, in their representative capacity, filed a suit in April against the state and federal governments as well as the Department of Orang Asli Affairs (JHEOA) in the Temerloh High Court for failing to gazette their lands and for not doing enough to protect their well-being and advancement.

Forest Reserves for logging and plantations

Despite repeated appeals from the Serudung Murut in Kalabakan, in the southern part of Sabah, to gain recognition of their traditional lands, the state has given the lands which lie within the Kalabakan Forest Reserve to several companies. In another area, residents from Kampung Kaibiton at the Paitan Forest Reserve in the northern part of Sabah reported the destruction of fruit and rubber trees. Such drastic actions are often taken by the Forestry Department, which considers cultivation of the land illegal. Many indigenous communities have moved to establish settlements and farms in forest reserves as more lands are being taken for oil palm plantations. The growing number of incidents in the country reflects the slow process of demarcation and recognition of customary lands, compared to the alienation of large areas for plantations, logging and protected areas.

The National Human Rights Commission, Suhakam, stressed that state assemblymen should resolve the problem of settlers in Forest Reserves as all laws relating to state administration, including the Forestry Enactment, are enacted and amended by the State Assembly. Villagers from Kg Bonor, Kg Karamtoi Laut, Kg Malaing, Kg Sinalut and Kg Pengaraan, mainly Murut communities, want to have their village excised from the Mandalom Forest Reserve which encompasses their villages. Suhakam urged the government to consider the problems faced by the villagers, who have been residing in the area since before it was gazetted as a Forest Reserve.

Bakun Dam

On August 7, Australia-based Rio Tinto Aluminium signed a deal with Malaysian conglomerate Cahya Mata Sarawak, whose principal stakeholders are family members of the Sarawak Chief Minister, for a joint study to build a US$2 billion smelter in Similajau, near Bintulu, 80 km inland from the Bakun Dam. Expected to open in 2010, it will be one of the largest in the world. Its initial production capacity is projected at 550,000 tonnes a year, with the capacity to expand to 1.5 million tonnes later. This resuscitation of the controversial Bakun Dam is the latest chapter in a long-running saga to push forward the environmentally sensitive project. There was apparently no open tender for the aluminium smelter project or public announcement. The mammoth dam, one of the mega-projects of former Prime Minister Mahathir Mohammad, has already destroyed 23,000 hectares of virgin rainforest and displaced 9,000 indigenous people.   ❑

References

www.thestar.com.my/news.nation dated 12 Dec 2007
Various articles in 2007 under "Land Rights" in www.rengah.c2o.org
Various articles in 2007 from www.newsabahtimes.com.my
Articles submitted by PACOS Trust, Malaysia

Jannie Lasimbang is a Kadazan from Sabah, Malaysia. She has been Vice-Chairperson of the PACOS Trust, Sabah, since 1987. She has also been involved in the Indigenous Peoples' Network of Malaysia (JOAS-IPNM) since its inception in 1992, and is currently the Secretary-General of the Asia Indigenous Peoples' Pact Foundation based in Chiang Mai, Thailand.

THAILAND

The indigenous peoples of Thailand mainly live in two geographical regions of the country: indigenous fisher communities (the chao-lae) and a small population of hunter-gatherers in
the south of Thailand, and the many different highland peoples
in the north and north-west of the country (the chao-kao). With
the drawing of national boundaries in Southeast Asia during
the colonial era, many peoples living in highland areas were
divided. Nine so-called "hill tribes" are officially recognized:
the Hmong, Karen, Lisu, Mien, Akha, Lahu, Lua, Thin and Kha-
mu. Other indigenous groups, such as the Palong, Padong and
Kachin are not included. According to the official survey of
2002, there are 923,257 "hill tribe people" living in 20 provinces
in the north and west of the country.

All indigenous peoples of Thailand share similar experiences caused by discriminatory policies. A widespread misconcep-
tion of indigenous peoples being drug producers and posing a
threat to national security and the environment has historically
shaped government policies towards indigenous peoples in the
northern highlands. Despite positive developments in recent
years, it continues to underlie the attitudes and actions of government officials. 480,000 indigenous persons in Thailand still
lack full citizenship, which restricts their ability to access public
services such as basic health care or admission to schools.

Political situation: developments since the military coup

Dissatisfaction with the Thaksin regime created political turmoil in
2006 and paved the way for a military coup in September of that
year. But the coup resulted in the emergence of a strong "anti-coup"
movement and the ensuing political uncertainty resulted in a down-

turn in economic growth, which was further aggravated by higher oil prices and led to increased unemployment and the closing down of factories. There was also an increase in violence in the conflict zone of the three provinces of the deep south. All these problems resulted in the resurgence of a spirit of nationalism, and policy makers sought to protect the nation from destructive influences. The military appointed the National Legislative Assembly (NLA) which, in 2007, passed a new Constitution as well as a number of laws that have an impact on the indigenous people and their struggles.

The 2007 Constitution does not explicitly recognize the identity of indigenous peoples. This is despite the fact that, during the drafting of the new Constitution, indigenous peoples' representatives participated in different constitution-drafting discussion forums at provincial as well as national level. Even though the Constitution does not specifically mention indigenous peoples' rights, Part 12 on Community Rights refers to the "traditional community" and indigenous communities can benefit from the recognition of economic, social and cultural rights guaranteed to "local" or "traditional" communities under articles 66 and 67 of Part 12 of the Constitution.

On 20 December 2007, the National Security Act was passed by the NLA, just a few days before the parliamentary elections and in the face of strong opposition from civil society. Under this law, an Internal Security Operations Command (ISOC) will be responsible for implementing the Act and, according to Article 15, can exercise legislative power and issue laws without any checks or balances. Under Article 23 of the Act, the ISOC is provided with "immunity" from criminal and civil charges as well as disciplinary action while exercising the powers provided by the Act. It is feared that such powers may be exercised with the aim of restricting the rights of vulnerable groups. Under the present draft, while the prime minister will be the nominal director of the ISOC, real power is likely to reside with the Army Chief, who will serve as deputy director and have hands-on command of the organisation.

On the same day, the NLA also passed the Nationality Act, which gives absolute authority to the Minister of the Interior to grant or withdraw Thai nationality and to issue related rules and regulations. In the past, the Cabinet has been involved in decisions regarding the provi-

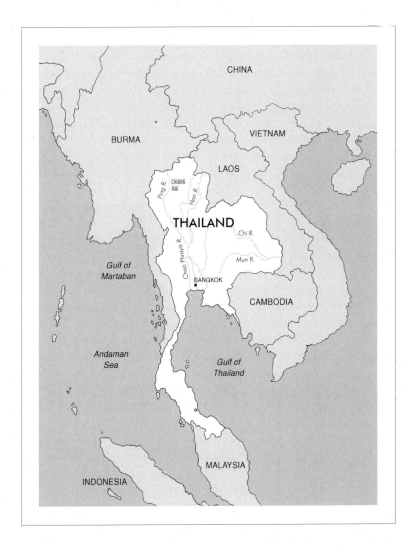

sion of nationality. A Civic Registration Act was also passed granting authority to the Director of Public Administration to take action in freezing applications for Thai nationality without first informing the people concerned for reasons of national security.

Community Forest Act passed

The Thai state has, over the years, enacted various laws to protect and conserve forests and wildlife and brought virtually all forest land under state control. In one stroke, these laws - the objective of which was essentially to curb illegal logging – have thus de-legitimized the indigenous people who had been living in the forests but had no title deeds to their land. Subsequently, other laws have declared more areas as national parks, reserved forests or wildlife sanctuaries and have restricted the use of such land by communities. Today, 28.78% of Thailand is categorized as protected areas.

On 21 December 2007, the Community Forest Act was passed, again in the face of much opposition from civil society. The law has been long awaited. But the final version deviates substantially from the original people's proposal. Many provisions in the final draft dismantle the rights of numerous communities that have been protecting the forests for a long time. The contents of Sections 25 and 34 are no different from the conventional forest laws aimed at curbing people's rights to use forests and which, in fact, led to conflicts of interest and the demand for a Community Forest law in the first place. Indigenous people's groups believe that the Act will result in further violation of the communities' right to manage natural resources such as land, forest and water. Article 25 of the Act states that, to be recognized under the Act, a community has to prove that it has been managing the forest area for more than 10 years prior to 2007. Indigenous people feel that it would be quite difficult for them to satisfy such a requirement. The law will definitely make it impossible for most IP communities to participate fully in community forest management and it thus contradicts the provisions for community resource management rights included in the new Constitution (see more below).

Windows of opportunity

Despite the state policies that seem to be directed towards assimilating the indigenous people into mainstream Thai society, there have been some positive developments over the past decade as well. A first recognition of some rights of forest-dwelling peoples is contained in a Cabinet Resolution of 1997. The resolution provides that when there is a petition by the people to revoke the declaration of a particular area as forest land by the cabinet, the cabinet shall refer the matter to sub-committees at provincial levels, which will be responsible for categorization of that land. However, another Cabinet Resolution passed in June 1998 makes it very complicated to claim rights over areas declared as protected. After protests by the people, a Commission was established to resolve these issues and the Commission recommended that the state should adopt a problem-solving approach and involve the villagers in the process.

As mentioned above, the new Constitution recognizes "traditional communities". Article 66 of Part 12 also provides for the right of "persons so assembling as to be a community, local community or traditional community" to "participate in the management, maintenance, preservation and exploitation of natural resources and environment, including the biological diversity, in a balanced sustainable manner".

The 2007 Constitution also contains other encouraging provisions. Article 78 (3) provides for the decentralization of powers to local government for the purposes of independence and self-determination of local affairs, in order to encourage local governments to participate in implementing fundamental state policies, developing public facilities, infrastructure and local economies. The indigenous peoples' networks are thereby also given a space to participate in national-level decision-making.

Article 82 states that the government shall respect and fulfil Thailand's human rights obligations under the international human rights treaties it has ratified. This article empowers civil society to hold the government accountable for violating people's basic human rights. Over the years, the indigenous peoples' movement has grown stronger and, with the help of civil society organizations and institutions such as the National Human Rights Commission, communities have, for example, been able to successfully stall and resist the state's forced eviction programs.

Celebration of Indigenous Peoples Day

For the first time, International Day of the World's Indigenous Peoples was publicly celebrated in Thailand on 9 August 2007. More than 40 indigenous peoples' organizations took part in the celebrations. The idea to celebrate their indigenous identity was expanded and the Thailand Indigenous Peoples Festival was celebrated from 5-11 September at the Art & Cultural Exhibition Center at Chiangmai University. Ms Pinita Kapu na Athyutaya, Director of Social Development and Social Welfare within the Ministry of Social Development and Human Security, and Mr. Thonchai Wong-rien-thon, Vice Governor of Chiangmai Province, chaired the opening sessions. Mr. Joni Odochao, Chairperson of the Organizing Committee of the festival and a local Karen intellectual, while speaking at the opening session on 6 September 2007, said:

> *We have a distinct way of life, settlement and cultivation - practices that are intricately linked with nature, forests and wildlife. Our way of life is sustainable and nature friendly and these traditions and practices have been taught and passed on from one generation to the next. But now because of State policies and waves of modernization we are struggling to preserve and maintain our traditional ways of life. The objective of organizing this festival is to celebrate the diversity of Thai society and specially promote understanding about the culture and way of life of the Indigenous Peoples in Thailand.*

The festival, which involved people from all walks of life, including state agencies, can be seen as a step towards achieving these objectives. But the struggle of indigenous peoples to gain recognition and respect for their identity is not going to be easy.

Government response to the UN Declaration on the Rights of Indigenous Peoples

The government delegation that participated in the Indigenous Peoples Festival said that Thailand had voted in favor of the United Nations Declaration on the Rights of Indigenous Peoples on the understanding that the Declaration did not create any new rights and that benefits flowing from the Declaration would be subject to the laws and Constitution of Thailand.

Such an understanding, taken together with the overall legal and policy framework governing indigenous peoples in Thailand, negates the fundamental principles recognized in the Declaration. The indigenous peoples' movement in Thailand will have to overcome considerable obstacles to gain respect for their dignity and way of life.

The progress of the Na-on case

As reported in *The Indigenous World 2007*, towards the end of 2006 the Lisu villagers of Na-on community in Vienghaeng District, located in the Chang Dao National Park, Chiangmai Province, were accused of encroaching upon 200 rai (32 hectares) of land within the National Park. The authorities, accompanied by the military, threatened to evict them and resettle them on a new piece of land. With the intervention of civil society groups and the National Human Rights Commission, the eviction was stopped and the people are still currently in their village. But there is a chance that they may nevertheless eventually be evicted. The people of Na-on are worried that, in the absence of any title deed to the land on which they have their houses, they may be uprooted and forced to move from their land. They are also afraid of losing their cultivable land. If the villagers are evicted from their land, they will have no option but to migrate to the cities in search of employment.

The people of Na-on point out that the whole district of Vienghaeng is covered by the National Park and, if the conservation laws were applied in an equal manner, then all the people living in Vienghaeng district should be evicted.   ❑

Wiwat Tamee is a Lisu from Chiangrai Province. He is currently working as Project Manager for the Highland Peoples' Taskforce (HPT), the secretariat for a network of 12 indigenous and highland peoples in Thailand.

Pornpen Khongkachonkiet is a women's human rights activist experienced in defending the rights of refugees, migrant workers and indigenous peoples in Thailand. She has worked with the Highland Peoples' Taskforce since 2006 and is also working with the Cross Cultural Foundation based in Bangkok.

CAMBODIA

Compared to its neighbours in Southeast Asia, Cambodia has the smallest indigenous population, both in relative and absolute terms.[1] The country's majority ethnic Khmer account for approximately 90% of the population.

The 1998 Cambodian Population Census identified 17 different indigenous groups. Based on spoken language, the census estimated the indigenous population at around 101,000 people, or 0.9% of the then total population of 11.4 million. Empirical research, however, suggests that the figure is most likely underestimated and could be as high as 190,000 people, or 1.4% of Cambodia's population.[2]

The Cambodian Constitution (1993) guarantees all Cambodians[3] the same rights, regardless of race, colour, language or religious belief. There is little recognition of the specific rights of indigenous peoples in Cambodian legislation, however. Nonetheless, the promulgation of the 2001 Cambodian Land Law has marked an unprecedented period of explicit legal recognition of collective indigenous land rights on the part of the state. The 2002 Forestry Law also makes explicit reference to the rights of indigenous communities although it still alienates the majority of forest lands from indigenous peoples' control and re-classifies them as "state public land".

Cambodia is signatory to a number of international instruments that protect the rights of indigenous peoples.[4] Cambodia is a party to the Convention on Biological Diversity (1992), which recognizes the role of indigenous peoples in protecting biodiversity. The Cambodian government also voted in favour of the UN Declaration on the Rights of Indigenous Peoples.

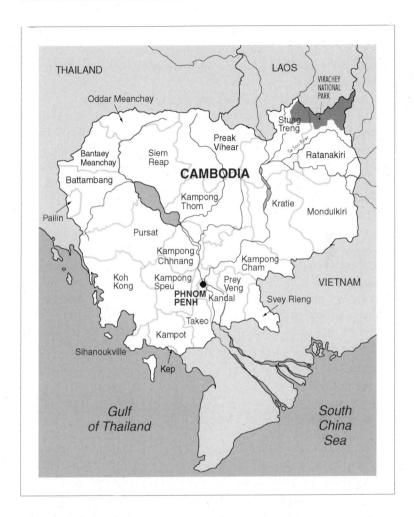

Land concessions

During 2006 and 2007, indigenous peoples' alienation from land and natural resources continued on an increasing scale. Although fewer large Economic Land Concessions (of over 1,000 ha) were granted over the past year, numerous smaller ones (less than 1,000 ha) continued to be granted across Kratie, Stung Treng, Oddar Meanchay,

Preah Vihear, Ratanakiri, Kampong Thom and Mondulkiri provinces. For example, ten concessions of less than 1,000 ha each were granted in Mondulkiri in late 2006 while Kratie Province is presently considering 22 new small-scale concessions. Many of these new concessions have been actively resisted by the local indigenous communities.

Although the Chinese company Wuzhishan continues to operate its pine tree plantation in Mondulkiri (see *The Indigenous World 2007*), of greater concern is the recent re-allocation of 75,000 ha of forested land from the Mondulkiri Protected Forest to small-scale concessions, primarily for rubber plantations. Although information is as yet unverified, approximately 5,000 indigenous Bunong will be affected and reports are being received by human rights groups that companies have been allocated concessions over existing villages and agricultural fields. Local communities who have tried to protect their land have been threatened. In Preah Vihear Province, the Chinese company Sui Gang announced that it would not develop a rubber plantation (which would have impacted on Kui communities) as planned because the plan was so unpopular. Conversely, development of a tourism concession in an area sacred to the Suoy people in Kompong Speu Province by the Chinese company New Cosmos is continuing despite local resistance.

Land title registration

The 2001 Land Law potentially provides a mechanism by which to safeguard indigenous communities' land rights in the form of communal land titles. However, not a single title has yet been granted.

In 2006, the Ministry of the Interior worked on developing by-laws for three pilot communities that would serve as the basis for guidelines, to be applied across the country, enabling indigenous communities to register their lands. These three communities received formal recognition as legal entities in 2007 and the approach used is now being applied to other indigenous communities. During 2007, the Ministry of Land Management, Urban Planning and Construction (ML-MUPC) focused on finalizing two other pieces of legislation relevant to indigenous peoples' land rights: the Policy on Indigenous Peoples'

Communal Land Registration and a yet un-named sub-decree also addressing communal land registration. Consultations on the draft policy held by the MLMUPC with indigenous peoples were not successful as community representatives did not agree with (among other things) size limitations put on the agricultural, burial and spirit-forest areas that they would be able to register, as this undermines the no-limit provisions of the 2001 Land Law. Civil society groups have been involved in ongoing negotiations with relevant government agencies to ensure that the policy's content is in line with existing legislation. As of November 2007, the draft sub-decree had not yet been publicly released although government representatives had informally stated that they intended to approve both sub-decree and policy before the end of 2007.

In the meantime, indigenous communities in Preah Vihear and Kompong Thom provinces continue to map their own lands in preparation for the submission of claims for communal titles. Many, however, do not have high hopes that official recognition actually delivers land security, particularly when there is a very poor record of governance and implementation of even the most basic laws of the country.

Illegal land alienation

Illegal alienation of indigenous land for commercial and state interests is continuing unabated all over the country, although it is still particularly acute in the north-east. In the communities under most stress, this has already led to the dissolution of a number of communities, and social disintegration.

One of the most disturbing patterns evident is the trade in land by indigenous peoples themselves, many of whom have lost hope in the future. Some have not known about the laws, some have been encouraged to sell and broker sales by outsiders, others have lost faith in social and legal systems that are meant to protect the rights of indigenous peoples. Many people have decided to sell the land rather than lose it, as they have seen happening in neighbouring communities and as they have been told will happen by local authorities. In some cases the problem has become so severe that the majority of indigenous villagers have been involved in selling off their community land and even the land of neighbouring communities.

Indigenous peoples' attempts to tackle land grabs have been hampered by the courts and by many people in government. In a notable case in Ekapheap commune of Ratanakiri Province, a court upheld a land grab of land belonging to a Tampuen community. At the beginning of 2007, indigenous villagers from Gong Yu village in Ratanakiri Province launched a legal challenge against a family member of the Minister of the Economy and Finance and the Secretary of State for Land, who, they claim, illegally bought some of their land. Since the case began in February, the villagers and their lawyers have been threatened on numerous occasions, and supporting NGOs have been accused of incitement by government authorities and less-than-independent-journalists.

Mining

Since 2006, the government has issued seven licenses for large-scale mining exploration in indigenous areas in Mondulkiri, Ratanakiri, Kratie, Preah Vihear and Kampong Speu provinces. These include concessions for gold, bauxite and iron ore. Five of the companies are Australian, one is Vietnamese and one is Chinese. In mid-2007, Indochine Resources was given a concession for 180,000 ha, or 54% of Cambodia's Asean-heritage listed Virachey National Park for the exploration of unnamed minerals.[5] Not only an essential area for biodiversity conservation, Virachey National Park also forms the traditional lands of several indigenous groups. In addition to the large concession, there are 25 further companies with licenses for small-scale mineral exploration or extraction.

The granting of mining concessions over areas of indigenous peoples' lands is a relatively recent trend, and one that indigenous communities have not yet found ways to deal with effectively. The Land Law provides no protection against mining concessions and, under the Law on Environmental Protection and Natural Resources Management, the Ministry of Environment (MoE) must approve an Initial Environmental and Social Impact Assessment (IESIA) before the Ministry of Industry, Mines and Energy (MIME) can grant a license. However, this step is frequently ignored; IESIAs are not always required, or are conducted after the license has already been granted.

Hydro-electric dams

Over the past year, the Cambodian and Vietnamese governments have signed agreements for the construction of two hydropower dam projects to be built on the Sesan River in Cambodia. A feasibility study was carried out for the 3000 MW Sambor dam in Kratie Province and an environmental impact assessment has been conducted for the 240 MW Don Sahong dam in Lao PDR. All of these dams planned for the Mekong River system would have devastating impacts on fisheries, seriously affecting the livelihoods of indigenous people throughout Cambodia.

Education

There are still very few indigenous people with high levels of formal education and a recent study in Mondulkiri Province found that 97% of Bunong women and 86% of Bunong men were unable to read or write.[6] Similar situations are found in other provinces and there are at present only around 20 university students who are indigenous.

The Ministry of Education, Youth and Sport continues to actively support the expansion of bilingual education in formal education. As a stepping stone to policy formulation, guidelines on implementing bilingual education have now been developed for formal education. In Stung Treng, Mondulkiri and Ratanakiri, the Ministry has set up bilingual community schools and, in Ratanakiri, a number of state schools have adopted bilingual education in the Kreung, Tampuen, Phnong and Kavet languages. The Royal Academy and the Ministry of Education, Youth and Sport have approved over 75 readers in different languages to be used in formal education.

Despite these positive developments, as in non-indigenous areas of Cambodia, much more needs to be done to reach the Millennium Goals for education by 2015. The EU has donated US$57 million for the Fast Track Initiative funds to speed up this process. A proportion of these funds have been allocated to ethnic minority education.

Health

Data available from the latest Cambodia Demographic and Health Survey (CDHS 2005), published early 2007, confirms that the health status of minority groups is still considerably lower than the national average. One example is the under-fives mortality rate of 165 per 1,000 live births in Mondulkiri and Ratanakiri provinces, compared with the national average of 83 per 1,000 live births.

The right to health and well-being, according to the World Health Organisation (WHO), not only means being free from disease but also having access to preventive health education and counselling. Here, language barriers and cultural discrepancies between indigenous people and the public health service providers form major obstacles. Money, transportation, language, discrimination, low levels of education and traditional beliefs/obligations have all been cited as the main barriers to accessing health services and information.

There is still a significant imbalance in the distribution of public health service staff, with most staff in these provinces coming from the majority population. An obvious impact of this imbalance is the continued restrictions on access to health services and information. Observations in Ratanakiri also indicate that some of the previous indigenous staff in health centers have been replaced by majority Khmer staff. In Mondulkiri Province, where the Phnong make up a majority of the population, only 27 of 121 health service staff are Phnong, and most of these are employed as "floating staff", not necessarily in full-time employment, at the health facility.

In early 2007, the United Nations Population Fund (UNFPA) funded extensive research in Ratanakiri into priority issues as seen from the indigenous peoples' perspective. Over a three-month period, nine priority health issues were identified and agreed upon by consensus. The priority issues included social issues such as domestic violence and inter-generational conflict (as younger people no longer or rarely use traditional medicines), as well as issues more strictly associated with health such as maternal health and malaria. In Ratanakiri and Mondulkiri provinces, advocacy has now begun with regard to health. Indigenous people are seeking ways of gaining a voice in relation to public health services and, with NGO support, have begun to create associations representing the many ethnic groups in the provinces, as a first step.

Indigenous peoples' organizations and networking

The national-level Indigenous Rights Active Members (IRAM) network significantly increased its involvement in advocacy and policy-making during 2007. IRAM worked closely with NGOs in Cambodia and regional indigenous peoples' advocacy groups to organise a national forum in February 2007 on "Indigenous Peoples and Access to Land in Cambodia". The Asia Caucus preparatory meeting for the 6th UN Permanent Forum on Indigenous Issues (UNPFII) was also held in Cambodia during February 2007, with indigenous networks such as IRAM helping to facilitate it. Finally, two representatives of IRAM were the first Cambodian indigenous people to attend the 6th UNPFII.

IRAM and the Cambodia Indigenous Youth Association (CIYA) also began working closely together during 2007, co-hosting a number of press conferences and co-organising the National Indigenous Peoples' Forum held in Phnom Penh in December 2007.

IRAM have also begun to work very closely with non-indigenous community networks across Cambodia in order to build solidarity with other marginalised peoples (actually the majority of Cambodians). These groups are able to significantly strengthen each others' activities through sharing lessons learned, combining resources and providing support structures during times of crisis.

Security

Security continues to be of increasing concern to indigenous (and non-indigenous) activists as many of them are being arrested, often illegally, for resisting attempts to alienate land and forests on the part of rich and powerful people and companies. A worrying trend during 2007 was that provincial authorities were increasingly preventing indigenous community representatives from participating in workshops, forums or training activities. Civil society groups across Cambodia will remember the tragic death of Mr. Seng Sarom, an indigenous community forestry and fisheries activist from Stung Treng who was killed in cold blood at his home in July 2007. At the time of writing, there has been no resolution to this case and a number of civil society groups maintain that the killing was related to Mr. Seng Saron's opposition to a land concession.   ❑

Notes and references

1   **Ovesen, J. and I.-B Trankell, 2004:** Foreigners and Honorary Khmers. Ethnic Minorities in Cambodia. In: Duncan C.R. (ed.): *Civilizing the Margins. Southeast Asian Government Policies for the Development of Minorities*, pp. 241-269. Ithaca: Cornell University Press.
2   According to the Statistical Year Book, Cambodia's total population was 13.8 million in 2005.
3   In the English translation, the term used in the Constitution is "Khmer citizens", but it is generally recognized that this term applies to Khmers and minority groups alike.
4   This includes the International Covenant on Economic, Social and Cultural Rights (ICESCR), the International Covenant on Civil and Political Rights (ICCPR) and the International Convention on the Elimination of All Forms of Racial Discrimination (CERD).
5   **Gillison, Douglas, 2007:** Cambodia Braces for a Mining Invasion. Gillison, *Asia Sentinel* 21 September
6   **International Cooperation Cambodia, 2003:** *An Assessment of Khmer Language Skills and Literacy Levels within the Adult Hilltribe Population of Mondulkiri Province*. International Cooperation Cambodia: Phnom Penh.

The article was prepared by a group of people working in consultation with indigenous peoples, who all prefer to remain anonymous.

LAOS

Laos is the most ethnically diverse country in mainland Southeast Asia, with a population of over 6 million. The ethnic Lao, comprising around a third of the population, economically and culturally dominate the country. Another third consists of members of other Tai language speaking groups. The final third have first languages in the Mon-Khmer, Sino-Tibetan and Hmong-Ieu Mien families. These latter groups are sometimes considered to be the "indigenous peoples" of Laos. Officially, all ethnic groups have equal status and therefore the concept of "indigenous peoples" is not generally recognized. The Lao government recognizes over 100 ethnic sub-groups within 49 ethnic groups. Some researchers have estimated there to be well over 200 ethnic groups throughout the country.

The indigenous peoples of Laos reside predominantly in mountainous areas. They are generally economically worse off than Lao groups, and form a majority in Laos' 47 poorest districts. They experience various livelihood-related challenges, and their lands and resources are under increasing pressure from government development policies and commercial natural resource exploitation (tree plantations, mining concessions and the construction of large hydroelectric dams). There is no specific legislation in Laos with regard to indigenous peoples.

New Participatory Poverty Assessment for Lao PDR released

In 2000, the Asian Development Bank (ADB) funded a "Participatory Poverty Assessment" (PPA) of the most impoverished parts of Laos.

This demonstrated the serious livelihood problems facing indigenous communities as a result of the Lao government's internal resettlement program and the land and forest allocation, which restricts communities' access to land and forest[1] (see *The Indigenous World* 2001-2002).

In 2006, Dr. Jim Chamberlain, team leader of the 2000 PPA, organized a second PPA with the National Statistics Center, which was completed in October 2007.[2] The study found that while Laos has nationally experienced a considerable reduction in poverty, from 39% to 33% in recent years, these achievements have been very uneven, with a much larger proportion of rural and ethnic minorities being "poor" compared to Lao-Tai language speakers and urban dwellers. The study revealed that the primary cause of poverty in all regions of the country was a lack of access to land as a result of land allocation and the relocation of villages. The study also found that governance problems are becoming more commonplace as local officials attempt to control the economies of villagers, restricting their access to free markets, and to collaborate with private companies.[3] Furthermore, the study reported that,

> [C]ompared to the PPA of the year 2000, the original villages that were revisited in 2006 were found generally to be either about the same or worse off. The policy environment in the provinces has not changed noticeably and access to land remains the major concern of villagers who view agricultural solutions as the only way to alleviate poverty.[4]

Indigenous people have been widely reporting that critical natural resources are being seriously degraded, threatening the livelihoods of many. The study criticized efforts to resettle villages, eradicate swidden agriculture and impose restrictive land and forest allocation, claiming that while these strategies are often promoted as a means of reducing poverty, the reality is that they do not work.

Confirming the results of the PPA II, the World Food Programme conducted a food security and vulnerability analysis in 2007.[5] They found that farmers without sufficient opportunities for fishing and hunting were most likely to have malnourished children. Sino-Tibetan ethnic groups have the highest proportion of food insecure households, followed by Hmong-Ieu Mien and Mon-Khmer language-

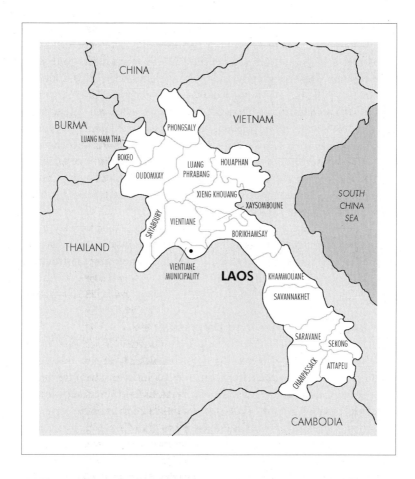

speaking groups. The report linked these problems with bans on opium production and shifting cultivation and associated internal resettlement.

Draft Forestry Law - bad news for local rights

During the latter part of 2007, the Lao PDR government completed a draft Forestry Law, which the National Assembly is expected to approve in the coming months.[6] Unfortunately, the new law will do little for Laos' indigenous peoples. In fact, the new legislation does not recognize local rights over forests but reaffirms the state's control of all lands and forests, and empowers the state to make all decisions regarding who uses forestlands and for what. Under the legislation, locals do not even have any particular rights over forests directly adjacent to their communities. Instead, communities are only allowed to manage forest areas if they are allocated to them by District Governors. District Governors can arbitrarily revoke those rights as well. The concept of "community" or "village forests", or *pa mai ban* in Lao, is not recognised in the new legislation. No mention is made of customary rights over lands and resources, and there are no possibilities for communal land or forest rights.

Recent bad experiences with attempts to implement forestry management systems more favorable to local people indicate that the government is not committed to empowering indigenous peoples to manage local forestry resources.[7]

Plantations and other land concessions

Over the last couple of years, the question of land concessions being granted to Lao and foreign companies to plant trees and other crops has become one of the most important and contentious issues for indigenous peoples in Laos. 2006 saw a significant increase in forest investment, especially from China, Vietnam and Thailand, in various kinds of tree plantations (see *Indigenous World* 2007). That trend continued in the first half of 2007.

Plantations of eucalyptus, agar wood, teak and rubber are being developed throughout the country. Large cassava concessions have also been granted. In total, there are around 75,000 hectares of plantations in the country. Most are reportedly not performing as well as expected, with many experiencing low growth rates. However, the Lao government plans to expand plantations in Laos to 500,000 hectares by 2020,[8] even though a study of land concessions in Laos conducted in June 2006 found many serious problems with the way in which they are currently granted and monitored.[9]

With particular reference to rubber, a 2006 survey by the Forestry Research Center found that, nationwide, a total of 11,778 hectares was already under rubber tree cultivation, with a total of 181,840 hectares of new plantations planned in all provinces in the country. Most of this expansion in rubber is being driven by high demand from China.[10]

In the province of Bokeo, the government plans to increase the area under rubber plantations to 16,000 hectares by 2010. Twelve Chinese companies have been granted concessions to cultivate rubber. Officially, swidden cultivators living in the area (mainly indigenous peoples) have to become rubber growers. They are supposed to join with the companies in order to become rubber plantation planters and tappers, whether they like it or not. As one NGO observer wrote, "Now I am not completely against rubber farming – it should just be one component of a livelihood system and not a forced livelihood."

Many people in Laos are becoming increasingly concerned about the rapid changes occurring as a result of the increased prevalence of large land concessions in the country. One concerned individual wrote,

The concessions are granted most often for plantations, but in many instances these are fictitious excuses for simply gaining title to large tracts of land. Such land grabs are most successful where the original owners are indigenous people who are least capable of protesting or having recourse or any semblance of a legal system.

Indicative of the fact that concerns have reached the highest levels of government in Laos, on May 9, 2007 Laos' Prime Minister, Bouasone Bouphavanh, announced a moratorium on the granting of new land concessions of more than 100 hectares, including those associated with industrial trees, perennial plants and mining.[11] The moratorium was meant to give the government time to review its policies on granting large-scale concessions and to address the shortcomings of its previous land management strategies.[12] [13] However, the moratorium stopped short of revoking any problematic concessions and, in some places, concessions have continued to be granted.[14]

Mining

The mining sector in Laos continued to attract considerable interest from foreign investors in 2007 (see *The Indigenous World* 2007) although there is concern that such investment is at the expense of the environment and the livelihoods of indigenous communities. The moratorium on land concessions mentioned above affected mining concessions as well.[15] There appears to be inadequate systems in place for ensuring that those who receive large mining concessions do not abuse the interests of local people. Despite the moratorium, the Lao government appears to be open to further foreign investment, in particular from China. The Director General of the Department of Planning and Investment in Laos was quoted as saying, "Although our government wants to suspend investment in the mining sector, to allow for more comprehensive research on the possible negative impacts, I believe that China will remain the number one investor in Laos if Chinese businesses invest more in other sectors."[16]

Over the last year, a number of new mining projects were initiated in various parts of the country, including many areas where indigenous people live. One of the largest investments involves the Hongsa lignite-fired power plant in Xayaboury Province. Expected to generate 1,000 MW of electricity, the Thai government recently agreed to import all of the power generated by the plant.[17] The Mae Moh lignite power plant in northern Thailand has already caused serious environmental and human and animal health problems in the surrounding area, leading to numerous local protests.[18] This is probably one of the reasons why importing lignite-produced electricity is attractive to the government of Thailand: they can obtain the electricity without having to deal with the associated risks.

Large hydroelectric dam development

Foreign interest in investing in large hydropower dam development in Laos continued to increase throughout 2007, driven by high oil prices and higher demand for electricity in neighbouring Thailand and Vietnam, after most dam projects in Laos were put on hold in the wake of the Asian financial crisis of the late 1990s. A large number of feasibility studies have been initiated, some projects have been approved and the construction of others has begun (see *The Indigenous World* 2007). Since many serious environmental and social problems caused by large dams remain unresolved, it seems likely that this new push will come at considerable cost to indigenous communities.

The largest dam project in Laos, the Nam Theun 2 project in Khammouane and Bolikhamxay provinces, is facing various difficulties, including problems with the resettlement of indigenous communities[19] and unresolved issues related to the thousands of people who will be seriously affected once water is released from the dam's reservoir into the Xe Bang Fai River, changing the downstream hydrology significantly. There are also serious concerns about the dam's reservoir becoming contaminated with mercury, resulting in downstream contamination of the Theun and Xe Bang Fai rivers. [20]

Vang Pao and Hmong colleagues charged in the USA

On June 4th, the ethnic Hmong former military leader, General Vang Pao–an important ally of the US Central Intelligence Agency (CIA) during the 1960s and early 1970s war in northern Laos–and ten other Hmong, along with a former U.S. Army Ranger, were arrested in California and charged with plotting terrorist attacks and violating US arms export laws. Potentially faced with life in prison, Vang Pao and the other defendants are accused of conspiring to ship hundreds of AK-47s, C-4 plastic explosives and Stinger missiles to Thailand. The weapons were allegedly destined for Hmong armed groups in Laos so that they could be used to assassinate government officials and attack administrative buildings in what was expected to be a heavy assault on Vientiane.[21]

Problems for Lao Hmong in Laos and Thailand continues

Meanwhile, in Laos, there were unconfirmed reports of Lao military attacks against what some Hmong call "US Secret War veterans and their families", in the Xaysomboun area, Vientiane province, in June and July 2007.[22]

On August 31, 2007, the US-based NGO, Human Rights Watch, criticized the Thai government for planning to forcibly repatriate approximately 7,000 Hmong from the Huay Nam Khao camp in Petchabun province in northern Thailand to Laos (see *The Indigenous World 2007*), where Human Rights Watch believes they are likely to face persecution. However, the Lao government has rejected any suggestion of international monitoring of the repatriations, claiming that it is a bilateral arrangement between Laos and Thailand. At the end of 2007, most of the Hmong remained at the Petchabun camp, although it is expected that they will be repatriated to Laos soon. The Lao government has reportedly prepared a resettlement site in Kasi district, Vientiane province.[23] The situation in Petchabun remains tense. .   ❑

Notes and references

1   **State Planning Committee, 2000:** *Poverty in the Lao PDR. Participatory Poverty Assessment (PPA).* Vientiane, Lao PDR, 26 pp.
2   **Chamberlain, James R., 2007:** *Participatory Poverty Assessment II (2006). Lao People's Democratic Republic.* National Statistics Center and the Asian Development Bank, 99 pp.
3   **Chamberlain, 2007:** *Ibid:* 10.
4   **Chamberlain, 2007:** *Ibid:* 11.
5   **World Food Programme, 2007:** Lao PDR Comprehensive Food Security and Vulnerability Analysis, Vientiane, Lao PDR, November 2007.
6   National Assembly 2007. Forestry Law (draft), Vientiane, Lao PDR, 44 pp.
7   See, for example, **Hodgdon, B., 2007:** No success like failure: policy versus reality in the Lao forestry sector. *Watershed* 12: 37-46.
8   TERRA, World Rainforest Movement, Oxfam, NGO Forum on Cambodia 2007. Mekong Regional Conference on Tree Plantations Proceedings, Kratie, Cambodia, November 2007.
9   German Agency for Technical Cooperation (GTZ) 2006. Study on State Land Leases and Concessions in Lao PDR, Vientiane, Lao PDR, June 2006.
10 **McCartan, B., 2007:** China rubber demand stretches Laos. *Asian Times Online*, December 19, 2007.
11 *Vientiane Times, 2007:* Govt suspends land concessions. May 9.
12 *Vientiane Times, 2007:* Laos: Authorities voice concern over concessions. May 8.
13 **Hanssen, C.H., 2007:** Lao land concessions, development for the people? Paper presented at the International Conference on Poverty Reduction and Forests: Tenure, Market and Policy Reforms, RECOFTC, Bangkok, 3-7 September 2007.

14 Mike Dwyer has prepared a useful summary report about land concessions in Laos for the International NGO Network in Laos. **Dwyer, M., 2007:** *Turning Land into Capital. A review of recent research on land concessions for investment in Lao PDR. Part 1 of 2 (existing literature).* A report commissioned by the INGO Network in Lao PDR, Vientiane, 53 pp.

15 **Dwyer 2007,** *Ibid.*

16 *Vientiane Times,* 2007: China top investor in Laos, June 6.

17 *Thai News Agency,* 2007: Thailand signs MoU to buy more hydro and coal-fired power from Laos, December 22.

18 *Watershed,* 1999: Pollution disasters continue at Mae Moh. *Watershed* 4(2): 5

19 **Ganjanakhundee, S., 2007:** Relocation at Laos giant dam nearly completes. *The Nation,* December 14.

20 **Ryder, G., 2007:** Lao dam impact policies a 'shambles'. *The Nation,* December 13.

21 **Schou, N., 2007:** Hero or Heroin? Alleged coup-plotter Vang Pao's shady past eludes mainstream media, *OC Weekly,* June 14.

22 FactFinding.org., 2007: Report from the jungle of Laos: 45 children, 17 over the age of 10 killed in June and July.

23 **Pongern, S., 2007:** Hmong refugees in Thailand believe they will be repatriated to Laos soon. *Voice of America,* December 14, 2007.

Ian G. Baird, originally from Canada, has been working on natural resource management and ethnicity issues in mainland South-east Asia for 20 years. He is Executive Director of the Global Association for People and the Environment, a Canadian NGO active in Laos.

BURMA

Burma is a very ethnically diverse country, with over 100 different ethnic groups. The Burmans make up an estimated 68 percent of Burma's 50 million people. Other major ethnic groups include the Shan, Karen, Rakhine, Karenni, Chin, Kachin and Mon. The country is divided geographically into seven, mainly Burman-dominated, divisions and seven ethnic states. It is usually the non-Burman ethnic groups that are considered Burma's indigenous peoples. In accordance with more general usage in the country itself, in this article they will be referred to as "ethnic nationalities".

Burma has been ruled by a succession of military regimes dominated by ethnic Burmans since the popularly elected government was toppled in 1962. After decades of low-intensity conflict in ethnic nationality areas, the military regime negotiated a series of ceasefire agreements with various groups in the early and mid 1990s. The military regime has justified its rule, which is characterized by the oppression of ethnic nationalities, by claiming that the military is the only institution that can prevent Burma from disintegrating along ethnic lines. While the ceasefires resulted in the establishment of special regions with some degree of administrative autonomy for the ethnic nationalities, the agreements also allowed the military regime to progressively expand its presence and benefit from the unchecked exploitation of natural resources in ethnic areas.

Continued militarization and displacement

The aggressive policy of Burma's military regime, the State Peace and Development Council (SPDC), towards ethnic nationalities

has resulted in military build-up and increased attacks on civilians.

The regime's military offensive in Eastern Burma, which began in November 2005, continued unabated throughout 2007. The SPDC Army deployed 273 infantry and light infantry battalions on active service in Eastern Burma. This was an increase of 35% on the previous year. SPDC Army units in Eastern Burma now represent more than 30% of the Army's battalions nationwide. Approximately 76,000 people in Eastern Burma have been forced to leave their homes as a result of the armed conflict. Over the past year, the SPDC Army displaced at least 167 villages, in addition to the destruction or forced relocation of 3,077 villages between 1996 and 2006. Forced migration has mostly taken place in the northern Karen State and eastern Pegu Division where the regime's ongoing offensive has displaced approximately 43,000 civilians. Human rights violations committed by the SPDC Army as part of their military operations against ethnic armed opposition groups remain a key cause of displacement.[1]

In June 2007, the International Committee of the Red Cross (ICRC) lashed out at the regime's continued abuse of civilians in ethnic areas. The ICRC drew particular attention to the abuses committed by the regime against civilians in Eastern Burma, including violence, arbitrary arrest, displacement and forced labor.[2] In addition, 25,000 people face starvation as a result of the regime's military operation in Eastern Burma because of the large-scale destruction of food supplies and farm crops.[3]

Women and girls in Karen State have been particularly vulnerable to the abuses committed by SPDC Army soldiers. Karen women and girls continue to be killed and raped by SPDC soldiers, subjected to forced labor, and are displaced from their homes.[4] In December 2007, the ethnic armed opposition group the Karen National Union (KNU) released a statement accusing the SPDC of waging a "genocidal war" against Karen villagers.[5]

Emboldened by the political protection provided by China and Russia, the SPDC has ignored calls by the international community to stop its attacks on civilians in ethnic areas. In January 2007, China and Russia vetoed a proposed UN Security Council resolution which called on the SPDC "to cease military attacks against civilians in ethnic minority regions and in particular to put an end to the associated human rights and humanitarian law violations against persons belonging to ethnic nationalities, including widespread rape and other forms of sexual violence carried out by members of the armed forces."[6]

The National Convention

On 3 September 2007, the SPDC concluded the 11th and final session of the National Convention, 14 years and 8 months after it first convened with the task of adopting the guidelines for Burma's new constitution.

In the months leading up to the last session of the Convention, the SPDC stepped up its intimidation campaign in order to ensure the ethnic nationalities' compliance with the junta's constitution-drafting agenda. However, many ethnic organizations continued to boycott or express their strong opposition to the National Convention for its lack of inclusiveness, transparency and freedom. In addition, various ethnic organizations denounced the junta's attempt to legitimize military rule through the new constitution and called for a more inclusive constitution-drafting process. They warned that the outcome of the National Convention would cause greater instability in the country.[7]

Some of the ethnic ceasefire groups also proposed amendments to the guidelines for the new constitution. As with the previous sessions, the junta ignored the amendments tabled by ethnic organizations, including the 19-point proposal submitted by the ethnic ceasefire group, the Kachin Independence Organization (KIO). The KIO complained that basic principles adopted for drafting the new constitution ignored the rights of ethnic nationalities and the emergence of a genuine national union. The KIO's 19-point proposal envisaged the creation of a federal system that clearly demarcates the powers of the central government while enhancing the legislative power allotted to the states.[8]

Ethnic nationalities support anti-junta protests

On 15 August 2007, the SPDC increased fuel prices by up to 500% overnight, affecting the cost of essential commodities and transport. People from all walks of life participated in nationwide protests against the SPDC's protracted mismanagement of the economy. By September, tens of thousands of Buddhist monks had joined, and led massive anti-junta rallies in the largest show of peaceful protest against the military regime since 1988. Demonstrations were held across all Burma's states and divisions, including urban centers in Arakan, Kachin, Mon, Chin and Shan states.

Many of Burma's ethnic political leaders and several of Burma's ethnic armed opposition groups voiced support for the Buddhist monks' peaceful protests against the military junta. Ethnic leaders that joined the demonstrations included representatives from the Arakan League for Democracy, the United Nationalities League for Democracy, and the Mon National Party.[9]

The regime reacted to the peaceful protests by killing, attacking and arresting key activists and peaceful demonstrators. The United Nations estimated that the regime's security forces arrested 3,000 to

4,000 people during the crackdown. In addition to the arrests during the protests, the regime's security forces conducted night time raids on dozens of monasteries throughout Burma. Monasteries affected by the SPDC's security forces included those in Akyab, Arakan State, and Bhamo and Myitkyina in Kachin State. On 26 September, U Thilavantha, the deputy abbot of the Yuzana Kyaungthai monastery in Myitkyina, Kachin State, was allegedly beaten to death in detention.[10]

The ethnic nationalities' support for the anti-junta demonstrations strengthened the alliance between the pro-democracy movement and the ethnic groups. Daw Aung San Suu Kyi, the detained leader of the National League of Democracy (NLD), stressed the importance of the ethnic nationalities in the process of national reconciliation. On 8 November, in a statement read out by the UN Secretary-General's Special Advisor on Burma, Ibrahim Gambari, Daw Aung San Suu Kyi indicated that any dialogue with the SPDC required taking into consideration "the interests and opinions [...] of the ethnic nationality races."[11]

Daw Aung San Suu Kyi's 8 November statement received widespread support from Burma's ethnic nationalities.[12] However, her statement angered the SPDC, who immediately began a campaign of harassment of ethnic ceasefire groups to denounce Suu Kyi's statement. On 20 November, SPDC authorities arrested and briefly detained Chin political leader and chairman of the Zomi National Congress, Cin Sian Thang, Kachin leader, Hkun Htoo, and Arakan leaders Aye Thar Aung and Tin Ohn. On 24 November, the regime arrested eight KIO members.

Despite the regime's intimidation, major ethnic ceasefire groups, notably the United Wa State Army, the KIO and the New Mon State Party, refused to release any statement against Daw Aung San Suu Kyi.

Infrastructure projects and commercial agriculture

In 2007, the regime inaugurated two large-scale hydropower projects in areas inhabited by ethnic nationalities. The construction of dams has raised concerns among local communities because of their devastating impacts on the environment and the widespread human rights abuses usually associated with the regime-sponsored infrastructure projects.

At the end of March, Thailand's MDX Group began construction of the Tasang hydropower dam on the Salween River in south-eastern Shan State.[13] The Tasang dam is the biggest of four planned dams on the Salween River. The 7,110-megawatt, 228 meter-high dam will be the tallest dam in Southeast Asia. The US$6 billion project will generate 7,110 MW, mostly for sale to Thailand. Over 300,000 people have been forcibly relocated from the area since feasibility studies on the project began in 1996. The dam's reservoir will flood an area covering 870 square kilometers. The project will drive thousands of people from their homes and will result in more forced relocations by the regime.[14]

In May, the SPDC held a project-launching ceremony for the Irrawaddy Myitsone dam, located where the Irrawaddy River begins in Kachin State. The Irrawaddy Myitsone dam is the first in a series of seven large dams to be built along this waterway by Chinese companies. The 152-meter-tall hydropower dam will generate 3,600 megawatts of electricity, most of which will be transmitted to China. The regime will pocket an estimate US$500 million per year. An estimated 47 villages will be inundated in a region recognized as one the world's eight "hottest hotspots of biodiversity". In addition, approximately 10,000 people will be displaced, losing their livelihoods and exacerbating the existing problems of unemployment, drug addiction and HIV/AIDS in the area. Roads linking major towns will be cut off by the floods, impeding communication, transportation and trade.[15] Concerned about the dam's negative impact on local communities, civil society groups across Kachin State have promoted petitions against the dam project. The regime has ignored these appeals. On 14 November, SPDC authorities in Myitkyina detained five activists for two days for their involvement in the petition campaign. Despite the regime's harassment, university students with the All Kachin Students Union have continued to protest against the Myitsone dam project through graffiti, poster and leaflet campaigns.[16]

Over the past year, dam projects have also resulted in increased militarization of many communities in ethnic areas. Additional troop deployments to the Hutgyi dam site on the Salween River in Karen State during September have further undermined local livelihoods in areas surrounding the proposed hydropower dam project.[17] Similarly, the presence of SPDC Army troops has accompanied the construction of the first in a series of three hydropower dams on the Shweli River, a main tributary of the Irrawaddy River in northern Shan State. Militarization has resulted in forced labor, extortion and sexual abuse of the ethnic Palaung villagers.[18]

In addition to the regime-sponsored infrastructure projects, local communities in ethnic areas have been negatively impacted by the regime's drive to promote commercial agriculture. The regime's promotion of castor oil plantations to produce bio-fuel has become more pervasive, and has been accompanied by widespread land confiscation, extortion and forced cultivation, especially in southern Shan State. Palm oil and rubber plantations operated as joint ventures between local SPDC Army commanders and foreign investors have resulted in similar abuses in Tenasserim Division.[19]   ❑

Notes

1   Thailand Burma Border Consortium (TBBC), October 2007: Internal Displacement in Eastern Burma, 2007 Survey
2   ICRC, 29 June 2007: Myanmar: ICRC denounces major and repeated violations of international humanitarian law http://www.icrc.org/Web/Eng/siteeng0.nsf/html/myanmar-news-290607!OpenDocument
3   Asian Tribune, 26 June 2007: 25,000 face starvation – appeal made for regional and international action of human rights abuses perpetrated in Burma
4   Karen Women's Organization (KWO), February 2007: State of Terror,
5   AFP, 10 December 2007: Myanmar stepping up attacks on insurgents: rebel group
6   UN Security Council, 12 January 2007: Security Council Fails To Adopt Draft Resolution On Myanmar Owing To Negative Votes By China, Russian Federation, http://www.un.org/News/Press/docs/2007/sc8939.doc.htm
7   National Council of the Union of Burma (NCUB), 15 July 2007: Former National Convention delegates urge boycott; IPS, 19 July 2007: Burma: New constitution in two months Junta
8   Irrawaddy, 19 July 2007: KIO to challenge regime's National Convention appeal
9   Irrawaddy, 24 September 2007: Ethnics join protests
10 Human Rights Council, 6th Session, 7 December 2007: Report of the Special Rapporteur on the situation of human rights in Myanmar, Paulo Sérgio Pinheiro, UN Doc. A/HRC/6/14
11 AP, 8 November 2007: Text of Aung San Suu Kyi's statement released by U.N. envoy

12 *International Mon News Agency (IMNA),* 12 November 2007: Ethnics welcome Daw Su's message
13 AFP, 5 Apr 2007: Myanmar, Thailand begin work on controversial dam
14 Shan Sapawa Environmental Organization, 2006: Warning Signs
15 Kachin Development Networking Group (KDNG), October 2007: Damming the Irrawaddy
16 Kachin News Group, 16 November 2007: Five anti-Irrawaddy dam detainees freed in Myitkyina
17 Thailand Burma Border Consortium (TBBC), October 2007: Internal Displacement in Eastern Burma, 2007 Survey
18 Palaung Youth Network Group (PYNG), December 2007: Under the boot,
19 Thailand Burma Border Consortium (TBBC), October 2007: Internal Displacement in Eastern Burma, 2007 Survey

Andrea Martini Rossi is a human rights researcher from Italy. He has worked in Europe, Latin America and Asia and is currently a Research Officer at the Bangkok-based ALTSEAN-Burma.

NAGALIM

Approximately 4 million in population and comprising more than 45 different tribes, the Nagas are a transnational indigenous people inhabiting parts of north-east India and north-west Burma. The Nagas were divided between the two countries with the colonial transfer of power from Great Britain to India in 1947. In the absence of democratic mechanisms and platforms to address their demands, Nagas residing in the federal units of north-east India (Assam, Arunachal Pradesh, Nagaland and Manipur) and Burma (Kachin state and Sagaing division) forged a pan-Naga homeland, Nagalim, transcending modern state boundaries in order to assert their political identity and aspirations as a nation.

The Naga people's struggle for the right to self-determination dates back to the colonial transfer of power from Great Britain to India. Armed conflict between the Indian state and the Nagas' armed opposition forces began in the early 1950s and is one of the longest armed struggles in Asia. A violent history has marred the Naga areas since the beginning of the 20th century, and undemocratic laws and regulations have governed the Nagas for more than half a century.

Indo-Naga Peace Process

The ongoing political negotiation between New Delhi and a section of the Naga armed opposition group, the National Socialist Council of Nagalim (NSCN), this year entered its 11th year. In this political negotiation, the Nagas have actively engaged in the peace process, demanding a peaceful solution to end the armed conflict between the Naga armed opposition groups (the two factions of the National So-

cialist Council of Nagalim) and the government of India. In 2007, the public debates and discussions on the Indo-Naga peace process resonated with deeper and more serious ethical and political issues with regard to the negotiation between the Naga armed opposition groups and the government of India. Naga civil society was demanding that political negotiation should not simply mean a cessation of hostilities but should represent a peace process that truly demonstrates the vibrancy of Indian democracy in negotiating with diversity and multiplicities.

Political events in Nagalim were no different from other years in terms of peace rallies, dialogues and demonstrations pressing the government of India to expedite the political negotiation. On the other hand, there were consultation meetings between the Naga people and the armed opposition groups around issues of factional violence, cessation of factional hostilities and appraisals of ongoing talks between the National Socialist Council of Nagalim, led by Isaak and Muivah (NSCN-IM), and the government of India. In 2007, the Naga human rights organizations, student bodies and peace activists sought support from both the national and international communities in order to expedite the political negotiation between the government of India and the NSCN-IM. On that note, on July 19, 2007 delegates and representatives of the Naga People's Movement for Human Rights (NPM-HR), the Naga Mothers' Association (NMA) and the Naga Students' Federation (NSF), along with several mass-based Indian movements, academics and concerned citizens, held a national convention on the Indo-Naga political dialogue. There were concerns over the deliberate and uneventful progress in the Indo-Naga ceasefire, declared on 25 July 1997. The Naga People's Movement for Human Rights (NPH-MR) and other Naga delegates presented the Naga people's demand for peace and justice before the British Houses of Parliament on December 10, 2007. By making the British colonial policies and administration a party to the division of the Naga inhabited areas, the Naga representatives from Nagalim were seeking the British government's support for the Indo-Naga political talks and the demand for a peaceful solution.

Human Rights Abuses

Human rights abuses continued in the Naga areas of India in 2007. There were particular concerns about the continuing human rights abuses meted out by the law enforcers. On August 22, 2007, the 7th Manipur Rifles assaulted innocent civilians at Moren in Chandel district. Again, on August 23, 2007, the 21st Assam Rifles and the Manipur state Commandos assaulted the residents of Tokpa Ching in Thoubal. On October 31, 2007, the 5th Bihar Regiment killed a Naga man and wounded another person. In a joint statement, the Naga People's Movement for Human Rights and the Naga Students' Federation condemned the Indian security forces' atrocities against the Naga civilians. The Naga organizations also condemned the increasing activities of state and security informers. The Naga People's Movement for Human Rights also reported the forced use of 140 child labourers by the 1st Assam Rifles at Kamjong, Ukhrul district. The NPMHR reported that on November 2, 2007, the 1st Assam Rifles used unarmed school children and women as human shields, thereby seriously injuring and wounding three children in a bomb explosion. Due to the lack of health care infrastructure, the injured could not be provided with immediate first aid or medical care. Due to the militarized conditions, most of the village administration is under the military and security control of the paramilitary forces, which continue to terrorise and abuse ordinary villagers.

Human rights awareness initiatives

2007 witnessed a series of human rights awareness meetings and consultations among various human rights groups. On October 13, 2007, the Naga People's Movement for Human Rights organized a one day "Human Rights Conference on the United Nations Declaration on the Rights of Indigenous Peoples" in Ukhrul. Participants at the conference discussed the significance of the declaration, the concept and definition of indigenous peoples and the right to self-determination. On this occasion, the NPMHR released the translated version of the Universal Declaration of Human Rights in the Tangkhul Naga language. Raising the issue of accountability, the participants noted that the international community had a moral responsibility to be more proactive and support the Naga people's demand for a peaceful settlement to the Indo-Naga political talks.

The growing conflict over resources between the state and indigenous groups also featured high on the agenda for the Naga people in 2007. On this note, the NPMHR organized a two-day consultation in October with various Naga indigenous groups and elder forums to discuss the United Nations Declaration on the Rights of the Indigenous Peoples. The participants were critical of the Indian government's "Look East" policy, which focuses on the economic growth of the region and envisages establishing trading relations with Southeast Asia. The NPMHR stated that the policy compromised its democratic stand on the issue of restoring democracy to Burma and, at the same time, suppressed the democratic aspirations of the peoples of north-east India. The "Look East" policy will have serious repercussions on the environment and economic sustainability of the region because of its emphasis on aggressive developmental projects that will greatly affect the natural resources of the region's indigenous people. The consultation also took serious note of the problem of land alienation and loss of resources and other issues such as Joint Forest Management (JFM) and the new proposed definition of forest, which is against the principle of free, prior and informed consent of the people in question.

One of the important campaigns that continued to bring people together during the year was the demand for the repeal of the Armed Forces Special Powers Act (AFSPA), a draconian law that allows the Indian security forces to kill innocent civilians on the mere grounds of suspicion and permits arbitrary arrests and detention; it is a law that grants impunity to those security forces who are involved in torturing and killing innocent civilians. Some of the dreadful results of the AFSPA have been decades of militarization and the intensification of structural violence among indigenous societies ravaged by armed conflict, as in the Naga case. The Nagas joined the national campaign against AFSPA and observed November 19 as a nationwide day of protest against the continuation of the AFSPA, alongside the rest of India's civil and political rights groups. The Nagas criticised the fact that the decade-long ceasefire between the government of India and the Naga people had not led to the repeal of the AFSPA or a reduction in the deployment of security forces in Nagalim. There were protests at the systematic violence meted out to the Nagas by the armed forces in terms of increased vigilance of people and groups in the villages and towns. The systemic expansion of the intelligence and state local spy networks within communities led to frequent conflicts and violence among communities and groups.   ❏

Dolly Kikon is a Lotha Naga and at present a PhD student with the Department of Cultural and Social Anthropology, Stanford University, California.

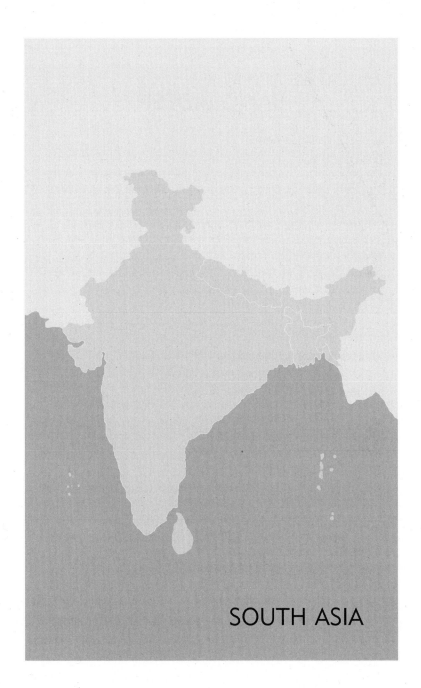

SOUTH ASIA

BANGLADESH

The majority of Bangladesh's 143.3 million people are Bengalis, and approximately 2.5 million are indigenous peoples belonging to 45 different ethnic groups. These peoples are concentrated in the north, and in the Chittagong Hill Tracts (CHT) in the south-east of the country. In the CHT, the indigenous peoples are commonly known as Jummas for their common practice of swidden cultivation (crop rotation agriculture) locally known as jum. There is no constitutional recognition of the indigenous peoples of Bangladesh. They are only referred to as "backward segments of the population".

Indigenous peoples remain among the most persecuted of all minorities, facing discrimination not only on the basis of their religion and ethnicity but also because of their indigenous identity and their socio-economic status. In the CHT, the indigenous peoples took up arms in defence of their rights. In December 1997, the 25-year-long civil war ended with a Peace Accord between the Government of Bangladesh and the Parbattya Chattagram Jana Samhati Samiti (PCJSS, United People's Party), which led the resistance movement. The Accord recognises the Chittagong Hill Tracts as a "tribal inhabited" region, its traditional governance system and the role of its chiefs, and it provides building blocks for indigenous autonomy.

Caretaker government and State of Emergency in Bangladesh

The fate of Bangladesh's indigenous peoples has been closely tied to that of other Bangladeshis throughout the year, as the elections planned for January 2007 were stalled amid accusations of corruption

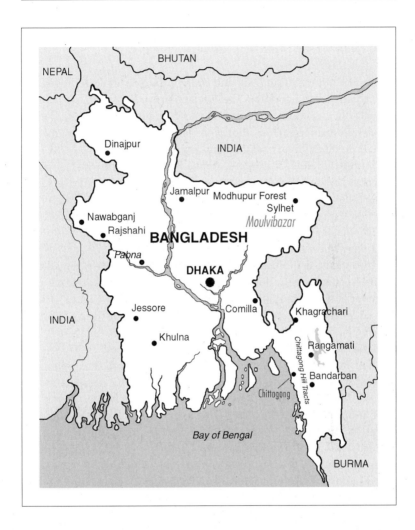

and cheating, and outbreaks of violence between the two main political parties.

   With the end of its five-year term, the coalition government left office on 28 October 2006. It left a "controversial" caretaker government
(read more about this in *The Indigenous World 2007*) in power. The opposition alliance rejected the caretaker government and demanded,
among other things, the formation of a "neutral" Election Commission

for free, fair and credible elections. This resulted in a serious political crisis, with violent confrontations between the caretaker government and opposition parties.

In order to maintain "law and order", the President deployed the military across the country. This deepened the crisis and, on January 11, 2007, the President declared a State of Emergency under the Constitution and resigned. This situation paved the way for the formation of a new caretaker government on January 12, 2007.

Under the State of Emergency, the Army has been given special powers to crack down on corruption and prepare for free and fair elections in Bangladesh. One of the Army's first moves was to call off the elections completely while broadening its power base. On 15 July 2007, the Election Commission published a roadmap for the elections, promising an official election call before the end of 2008.

The extension of Emergency Powers to the Army was deemed necessary to tackle corruption in politics. The focus of the caretaker government and the Bangladesh military has been on political figures involved in financial corruption and abuses of power. Corruption involving human rights abuses such as those faced by minorities and indigenous peoples continues to be largely overlooked.

A glance at Bangladesh's human rights record indicates a complex picture. Bangladesh was identified by the South Asian Association for Regional Cooperation (SAARC) as the number one human rights violator among the SAARC countries in December 2006. This was because of systematic attacks on the opposition and the high number of extrajudicial killings by the Rapid Action Battalion (RAB) during peacetime. Bangladesh was also the number one human rights violator in terms of persecution and safety of journalists and minorities.

Chittagong Hill Tracts

Forthcoming elections and voter lists in the CHT
There is still concern over the current electoral rolls in the Chittagong Hill Tracts (CHT) as they include non-permanent Bengali residents, such as Bangladesh Army and Bangladesh Rifle Division personnel stationed in the region, settlers and seasonal workers, along with more

than 300,000 Rohinga refugees from Burma. The region remains one of the most militarised in the world, and the votes of over 100,000 troops would have a significant impact on the results of an election and the ability of the Jummas to elect their representatives as Members of Parliament from the CHT districts.

Targeting of indigenous leaders and activists in the CHT

The indigenous peoples, their leaders and activists have been targeted since the formation of the interim caretaker government. By the end of 2007, more than 20 indigenous political activists had been arrested and, in some cases, had received lengthy sentences on allegedly false charges. Cases of courts failing to follow due process have been reported, with indigenous peoples denied access to legal counsel.

Although the State of Emergency has extended the powers of the military to counter possible threats to national security, the powers are also allegedly being used to target political dissent. Mobile telecommunications have been banned in the CHT on the grounds of alleged terrorist activities, and arrests of democratically elected indigenous leaders took place during January and February 2007. Journalists are also affected by the ban on mobile telephone networks, leaving them unable to report on the current situation.

In February 2007, the Joint Security Forces in Bangladesh arrested a number of key leaders and activists, many of them involved in the Parbattya Chattagram Jana Samhati Samiti (PCJSS, United People's Party). Furthermore, the international community received reports of torture, along with appeals to the UN Special Rapporteurs. One activist, Ranglai Mro, received such severe injuries that he had to be treated at Chittagong Medical College Hospital, under armed guard.

While it is important that the Security Forces clean up corrupt politicians, it is essential that they do not target indigenous peoples' representatives, working for legitimate democratic movements. Satyabir Dewan, one of the people arrested, is the Secretary General of the PCJSS and was a key person involved in the drafting and signing of the Peace Accord. In August 2007, Satyabir Dewan and Ranglai Mro received jail terms of 17 years each, which their supporters maintain were based on false charges. Since his imprisonment, Ranglai Mro has once again been brutally beaten and required further treatment at Chittagong Medical Hospital.

Continued militarisation, communal violence and human rights abuses

The continued presence and even expansion of the military bases, and the influx of settlers are reportedly contributing to the ongoing human rights abuses, including gender-based violence in the CHT. The impunity that exists for such crimes has led to this culture of violence becoming acceptable within the military. The lack of access to justice for indigenous people has long been recognised as a serious issue by international human rights organisations. The issue of impunity has been exacerbated by the State of Emergency.

Dialogue meeting between Khasis and government administration in Moulvibazar

The Khasis have been facing the threat of eviction from their land by the Eco-park and social forestry project planned by the government without their consent. More than 10,000 Khasis have been living in 65 villages in Moulvibazar district for many years but do not hold land registration documents. In July 2007 the administration, led by the Deputy Commissioner in Moulvibazar, organised a meeting with indigenous leaders, headmen and women. He assured them that steps would be taken to resolve the land ownership problem.

Eco-park movement murder case: court order to record case after three years

A court in Tangail district has ordered the Officer-in-Charge of Modhupur police station to record the murder of Piren Snal. Piren, a young Garo, was allegedly killed by police and forest guards during a protest rally against the Eco-park project in Modhupur Forest on 3 January 2004 (see *The Indigenous World 2004* and *2005*). Forest guards and police were accused and yet in 2004 the judicial enquiry report acquitted both. Piren's father did not accept the report and appealed to the court. In 2007, three years later, the court finally ordered that the case be recorded.

The killing of an indigenous activist

On 18 March 2007, Cholesh Ritchil a young *Garo* activist and human rights defender from Modhupur, was killed by Army-led Joint Forces. Cholesh was an outspoken leader of the Garo indigenous people, campaigning against the construction of a so-called "Eco-park". It is alleged that Joint Forces personnel tortured Cholesh for several hours before taking him to Modhupur Thana Health Complex, where he was declared dead. On 20 March, thousands of indigenous peoples and local Bengalis attended Cholesh's funeral in his home village of Magontinagar, while the military threatened people in the area. Garo leaders have identified three people as being primarily responsible for killing Cholesh and have filed a petition. The wife of Cholesh has also filed a General Diary (GD) accusing three people of primary responsibility for the killing and torture of her husband and other Garos.

The killing of Cholesh Ritchil was covered extensively by the media. On 5 May, in response to pressure from human rights activists, journalists, lawyers, NGO activists and high-level foreign representatives, including the former US Ambassador and Ambassador of the European Commission, the government formed a one-member judicial commission to investigate the death. On 16 May, the Forest Department suspended six forest officers for negligence of duties. Although the judicial commission has submitted its report, indigenous peoples do not have any information as to its content. On 10 October 2007, the Army donated 50,000 Taka (approx. 700 US dollars) and two sewing machines to the family of Cholesh Rotchil in compensation.

Indigenous elders and youth dialogue

On 25-27 October 2007, in association with the Asia Indigenous Peoples' Pact (AIPP), the Bangladesh Adivasi Forum organized a national dialogue on "Exchange of Indigenous Knowledge from Elders to Youth" with more than 75 youth and elders participating. The dialogue took place in Modhupur Forest where indigenous peoples have been struggling for their ancestral land rights for many years. The elders described how they protect the forest, trees, nature, environment and Mother Earth and called upon the youth to work hard to learn the skills and pass the knowledge on to the next generations.

Destruction of indigenous villages in North Bengal

On 5 November 2007, more than two hundred miscreants attacked indigenous neighbourhoods in Naogaon district and injured 15 Santal villagers while burning their houses in an effort to evict them from their land.

Twenty-two indigenous families have been living on the highlands of two traditional ponds for generations. Four indigenous peoples own the ponds, but the adjacent depositories are Khas land,[1] supposed to be allocated to landless indigenous peoples. Two villagers from nearby reportedly led the attack on the village, in collaboration with the local police and government administration, after they failed to gain ownership of the land adjacent to the ponds.

Indigenous organizations such as the Bangladesh Indigenous Peoples' Forum, Jatyo Adivasi Parishad, civil society organizations and the Deputy Commissioner of Naogaon have visited the place, and indigenous organizations have demanded relief and rehabilitation of the peoples, punishment of the miscreants and legal allocation of the Khas land to indigenous peoples. No legal or administrative action has been taken against the miscreants.

International action

The alarming events of the 2007 Emergency Rule have led to a number of protests regarding the situation of indigenous peoples in the CHT. In Sri Lanka, Jumma Buddhist monks protested at the land grabs taking place in the region with a petition to the Bangladesh High Commission in Colombo. Peaceful protests were also held in London in October 2007. The tenth anniversary of the signing of the Chittagong Hill Tracts Peace Accord (signed 2 December 2007) was marked by indigenous peoples in Bangladesh and by the Jumma diaspora internationally. The Jumma Peoples' Network co-signed a letter of concern along with international NGOs to draw attention to the current situation and the lack of implementation of the Peace Accord. The Government of Bangladesh refuted some of the allegations made. Bangladesh was one of the few countries to abstain during the vote on the adoption of the UN Declaration on the Rights of Indigenous Peoples.

While it is essential that Bangladesh is supported in its attempts to clean up corruption in politics, it is also essential that the methods employed are not used to silence political opponents and those involved in representing the most marginalized of society's groups.   ❑

Notes

1   Khas land refers to the common lands of the indigenous community with shared rights of access. The government does not formally recognise the rights of indigenous peoples to common land, but regards these lands as state-owned. The forest department classes them as unclassed state forests. Ref. **Rajkumari Chandra Roy, 2000:** *Land Rights of the Indigenous Peoples of the Chittagong Hill Tracts, Bangladesh.* (p.61)

Sources

Amnesty International (http://amnesty.org/)
Asian Centre for Human Rights (http://www.achrweb.org/)
International Work Group for Indigenous Affairs (http://www.iwgia.org)
Jumma Peoples' Network UK (http://www.jpnuk.org.uk/)
Parbatya Chattagram Jana Samhati Samiti (PCJSS) (http://www.pcjss.org/)
Peace Campaign Group
Unrepresented Nations and Peoples Organisation (http://www.unpo.org/)
Vanishing Rites (http://vanishingrites.com/)

Ina Hume is a consultant on indigenous issues and a cultural recording artist. She established Vanishing Rites in 2004 to develop collaborative media and advocacy projects in the UK and internationally (www. vanishingrites.

*com). She has written the section on the Chittagong Hill Tracts in cooperation with the **Jumma Peoples' Network UK**, a human rights organization aimed at promoting the rights of Jummas living in the Chittagong Hill Tracts and abroad.*

Sanjeeb Drong *is a Garo from northern Bangladesh. He is a columnist and freelance journalist and currently editor of the indigenous magazine Solidarity. He has published more than 400 articles and four books on indigenous issues (sdrong@bangla.net).*

NEPAL

Nepal is a pluralistic country with many castes and ethnicities, cultures, languages, religions and practices. The total population of Nepal is 22.7 million, and over one hundred castes/ethnic and religious groups, and ninety-two mother tongues were listed in the Census 2001. Indigenous nationalities (*Adivasi Janajati*) comprise 8.4 million, or 37.19% of the total population. However, indigenous peoples' organizations claim they have been under-represented in the census, and their actual populations comprise more than 50% of the total population. Fifty-nine indigenous nationalities have been legally recognized under the National Foundation for Development of Indigenous Nationalities (NFDIN) Act 2002. The NFDIN Act defines Indigenous Nationalities (*Adivasi Janajati*) as communities who perceive themselves as distinct groups and have their own mother tongue, traditional culture, written and unwritten history, traditional homeland and geographical areas, and egalitarian social structures.[1] Numerous indigenous communities are yet to be recognized. Nepali society is highly stratified, with the state imposed and protected Hindu caste system's self-declared upper castes (*Bahun* and *Chetri*) holding key positions in the state, and indigenous nationalities, Dalits and Terai caste groups experiencing subjugation, exclusion, discrimination, oppression and exploitation.

Indigenous movement in transitional stage

In 1996, the Nepal Maoist Communist Party began its so-called "People's War". The Maoist movement had no significant impact, however, until it began to raise indigenous issues, including the right to self-determination. A number of indigenous peoples then joined its army, which eventually controlled 80% of the country's territory. The twelve-year-long armed conflict ended with a power-sharing pact between the Seven Party Alliance (SPA) and the Maoists on 22 November 2006.

The restructuring of the nation was identified as crucial for addressing the problems of all sectors of society in Nepal, including the indigenous peoples, and a commitment was made in the pact to hold elections for a Constituent Assembly. The SPA and the Maoists collectively urged all interested parties, including indigenous peoples, to join the Second People's Movement against the King's autocracy in order to restore democracy and reinstate Parliament, which was dissolved by the King in 2002. Indigenous peoples' organizations actively participated in the movement, demanding a secular state, the restructuring of the nation, the right to self-determination for indigenous peoples as well as other political, social and cultural rights. The nineteen-day-long movement forced the King to step down, and he then urged the agitating political parties to recommend the next Prime Minister on 5 April, 2007. This, however, did not pacify the movement and the unrest continued until the dissolved parliament was reinstated on 24 April, 2007. This was an historical turning point in Nepalese politics.

In the same month, the reinstated parliament announced that a new Constitution was to be drawn up by a Constituent Assembly. It declared Nepal a secular state, and this was later incorporated into the Interim Constitution. The Interim Constitution also – if only partially – addressed some of the issues raised by the indigenous peoples. Since the end of the armed conflict, various agreements, such as the Twelve Point Agreement of November 2006, the Eight Point Agreement of June 2007, the Comprehensive Agreement of November 2007, the Resolution of the SPA and Maoists Meeting of October 2007, reaffirmed the agenda of including excluded groups, including indigenous peoples, and abolishing the continuing racially discriminatory policies and practices. Ironically, the collaboration between political parties and indigenous peoples established during the movement was sabotaged when the Interim Constitution Drafting Committee (CDC) was formed without the participation of indigenous peoples. This was in clear disregard of the mandate of the people's movement and the ruling parties' own declared commitment. Later on, three new members

of the CDC were appointed, including three indigenous advocates. However, the appointments were made by political parties, and were not selected or nominated by the indigenous peoples themselves. The exclusion of indigenous peoples from the CDC was a clear message that indigenous peoples had to continue their struggle if they wanted to ensure that their rights were recognized in the Nepal of the future. As the indigenous advocates Shanti Kumari Rai and Kumar Yonjon stated, indigenous rights were largely ignored during the Interim Constitution-making process due to the overwhelming representation of the dominant Hindu groups.

The Interim Constitution

Parliament passed the Interim Constitution in November 2007. It was highly criticized by legal experts, civil society, the *Madhesi* (Hindu minority in the Terai region bordering India), the *Dalit* (Hindu consider them as "untouchables") and indigenous peoples. The fundamental issue of free and full proportional representation in the electoral system for the Constituent Assembly, based on ethnicity, language and region, was totally disregarded. Indigenous peoples thus felt compelled to respond with a peaceful demonstration.

Both Article 63 of the Interim Constitution and Section 58 of the Constituent Assembly Election Act 2007 fail to provide the much-desired free representation of indigenous peoples in the Constituent Assembly but grant powers to political parties to select candidates, even for the proportional representation seats. These are supposed to be elected or selected by indigenous peoples which, however, is not going to happen under the present status quo. This perpetuates the divide-and-rule policy over indigenous peoples who, for their emancipation, depend on political parties that are overwhelmingly controlled by conservative forces of the dominant groups.

Furthermore, the discriminatory policy on language, culture and religion of the previous Constitution is, although cloaked in new wording, perpetuated in the new Constitution. Rights to land and natural resources are not recognized even though Article 35 clearly stipulates that, in mobilizing the natural resources and heritage, priority should be given to the local communities.

In protest at the failure of the drafters of the Interim Constitution to address their concerns, indigenous peoples gathered in Mandala, Kathmandu, on January 17, 2007 and burned a copy of the Interim Constitution. They subsequently intensified their peaceful movement in various parts of the country, organized by the Nepal Federation of Indigenous Nationalities (NEFIN), demanding free representation in the Constituent Assembly, the collective right of communities to elect constitution-makers through a proportional electoral system, Constituent Assembly elections, federalism, regional autonomy based on ethnic identity and the guarantee of human rights and fundamental freedoms. They demanded the immediate amendment of the Interim Constitution. So far, the Interim Constitution has been amended three times but has not heeded the demands of the indigenous peoples.

The Constituent Assembly

In light of the above, the drafting of the new Constitution will be critical for the future of indigenous peoples. Elections for the Constituent Assembly have been postponed twice and the new date announced by the government is now 10 April 2008. A number of non-indigenous

political organizations representing minorities, such as the Tarai Lok-
tantrik Party, have already made it clear that, under the current conditions, they will not take part in the Constituent Assembly elections.
Similarly, indigenous political organizations such as the Federal Democratic National Forum, the Federal Limbuwan Council and Tambasal-
ing, Khumbuwan Mukti Morcha have called strikes demanding the
free participation of indigenous peoples in the Constituent Assembly,
and political assurances of autonomy based on region, language, ethnicity and history.

However, the Seven Party Alliance, which is in government and
likely to obtain a majority in the Constituent Assembly, has responded
negatively to these demands, labeling them an avenue for the disintegration of the nation. The Prime Minister publicly denied the right to
self-determination of indigenous peoples or other groups. Similarly,
the Secretary General of the Communist Party UML (one of the largest
parties in the country) also expressed same view in response to the
Madhesi minority's demand for the right to self-determination.

Another major concern of the indigenous organizations is that Article 67 of the Constitution and Section 3 (d) of the Party Renunciation
Act 1998 prohibit Members of Parliament from taking up issues in Parliament which are not authorized by their party. Decision-making
within the Constituent Assembly is thus undemocratic since – in the
name of consensus building – decision-making power ultimately rests
with the political parties. If consensus cannot be achieved, a two-thirds
majority is necessary for a decision to be taken. Since indigenous representatives in the Constituent Assembly are not expected to hold more
than 20% of the 601 seats, it is not likely that any of their key issues of
concern will find their way into the new Constitution.

Restructuring of the nation

Significantly, the historical injustices suffered by excluded groups, including indigenous peoples, are recognized and the need to restructure the nation is stipulated in the Interim Constitution. Article 33 declares the Nepalese state to be democratic and federal, and Article 138
states that all discrimination based on class, ethnicity, language, gen-

der, culture, religion and sector is to be prohibited. These provisions have thus far not been translated into practice, however, and all voices of concern were disregarded. For example, the Lawyers' Association for Human Rights of Indigenous Peoples (LAHURNIP) filed a complaint to the Special Parliamentary Hearing Committee against the government's recent appointment of ambassadors mostly from the dominant groups, thus violating Article 33(d)1, which clearly states that marginalized groups must be included in the appointment of such positions. However, no action was taken.

Nepal's indigenous peoples continue their struggle for self-determination. The historical movement for the restoration of autonomy of the Limbu people, or the movements for autonomy of Khumbuwan, Tamsaling, Newa Mandal, Tharuwan or Tamuwan, for example, are encouraged by and determined to seize the historical opportunity offered by the drawing up of a new Constitution and the restructuring of the state.

Positive developments: ratification of ILO Convention 169

Over the past months, the indigenous movement has undoubtedly also made considerable achievements. In general, indigenous issues have made it onto the national political agenda, and this is reflected in various provisions of the Interim Constitution. Most significantly, Convention No. 169 was ratified by Parliament on August 22 and formally submitted to the ILO on September 5, 2007 by the Minister for Local Development, Dev P. Gurung. ILO Convention 169 is so far the only legally binding international instrument focusing on the rights of indigenous peoples, and Nepal is the first Asian country to have ratified it.

Bitter experiences in the indigenous movement

Ironically, at this crucial juncture in the history of Nepal, the indigenous movement has been weakened by the political maneuvers of the United Marxist and Leninist Party (UML) and the Maoist Party. For instance, the indigenous agenda of full proportional representation and right of self-determination was dropped in the Twenty Point Agreement that was made between the government and the Nepal Federation of Indigenous Nationalities (NEFIN) on August 6, 2007. Furthermore, indigenous leaders in Parliament and the government are not taking a strong stand on indigenous peoples' issues, which creates conflict among indigenous peoples and severely weakens the movement. The main reasons for this are the influence of the political parties they belong to, personal interests and the lack of conceptual clarity and accountability within the leaderships.   ❏

Notes

1   The Foundation for Development of Indigenous Nationalities (*Janajati Utthan Rastriya Pratistan*) is a focal governmental organization under the Ministry of Local Development with a mandate to make suggestions to the government for the improvement of the situation of the indigenous peoples of Nepal. The NF-DIN mainly works in the areas of preserving cultures, language, belief system and history. It also provides scholarships for education and works for the economic development of indigenous peoples.

Shankar Limbu is an Advocate, who acts as Secretary of the Lawyer's Association for Human Rights of Nepalese Indigenous Peoples (LAHURNIP), as well as Campaign and Policy Advocacy Coordinator for the Asia Indigenous Peoples Pact (AIPP) Foundation.

INDIA

In India, 461 ethnic groups are recognized as *Scheduled Tribes*, and these are considered to be India's indigenous peoples. In mainland India, the Scheduled Tribes are usually referred to as *Adivasis*, which literally means indigenous peoples. With an estimated population of 84.3 million, they comprise 8.2% of the total population. There are, however, many more ethnic groups that would qualify for Scheduled Tribe status but which are not officially recognized. Estimates of the total number of tribal groups are as high as 635. The largest concentrations of indigenous peoples are found in the seven states of north-east India, and the so-called "central tribal belt" stretching from Rajasthan to West Bengal. India has several laws and constitutional provisions, such as the Fifth Schedule for mainland India and the Sixth Schedule for certain areas of north-east India, which recognize indigenous peoples' rights to land and self-governance. Indigenous peoples continue to face civil and political rights violations, land alienation, displacement and false prosecution for accessing minor forest produce. As India's booming economy requires more resources, indigenous peoples' land and resources have been grabbed, resulting in a strong sense of alienation among the indigenous peoples and further exacerbating conflicts. The laws aimed at protecting indigenous peoples have numerous shortcomings and their implementation is far from satisfactory. India has a long history of indigenous peoples' movements aimed at asserting their rights.

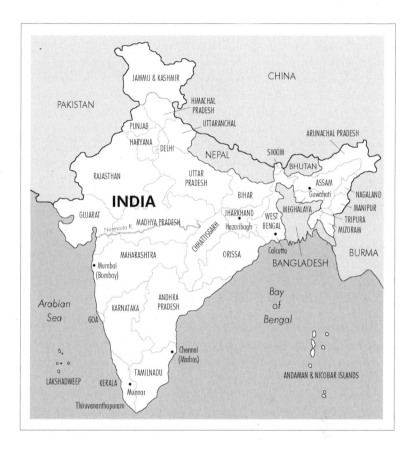

Legal rights and policy developments

On 31 October 2007, the government published the National Reha-bilitation and Resettlement Policy of 2007. The policy was sup-posed to be an improvement on the Draft National Rehabilitation Pol-icy of 2006, addressing the failures of the 2004 National Policy on Re-settlement and Rehabilitation for Project Affected Families. Unfortu-nately, the 2007 policy fails to address one of the key issues relating to conflicts: forcible acquisition of lands by the state in the name of the "public interest". In India, the "public interest" has come to mean the forced acquisition of land for private companies whereby the state often silences protests by tribal peoples through the indiscriminate use of firearms and militarization. The 2007 policy upholds the sovereign power of the state to apply the concept of "eminent domain" in order to forcibly acquire any private property in any part of the country in the name of "public purpose" under the Land Acquisition Act 1894.

Although the Scheduled Tribes and Other Traditional Forest Dwellers (Recognition of Forest Rights) Act was adopted in December 2006, it came into effect only on 31 December 2007. The Forest Rights Act continues to be marked by controversy, among other things because of the inclusion of "other traditional forest dwellers". Many of the "other traditional forest dwellers" are landlords who have been responsible for the pauperization of the Adivasis in many areas. In 2007, the Ministry of Tribal Affairs failed to deliver a final draft of the National Tribal Policy although a revised draft has been public since July 2006.

Indigenous peoples engulfed by armed conflicts

In 2007, the national government and various state governments of north-east India continued to engage in peace processes with a number of armed opposition groups seeking autonomy and the right to self-determination. However, although peace processes continue in the north-east, more and more indigenous peoples find themselves engulfed in low-intensity armed conflicts. At present, 20 out of 28 states of India are affected by armed conflicts (see details in *The Indigenous World 2007*).

The areas under pressure from the Naxalites, ultra-left wing armed opposition groups also known as Maoists and claiming to represent the poor, are inhabited mainly by indigenous peoples yet the Naxalite movement is neither an Adivasi movement nor is it led by the Adivasis, although Adivasis form a majority of its cadres. According to the Asian Centre for Human Rights (ACHR), at least 384 persons were killed in the Naxalite (Maoist) conflict over the period January to September 2007. These included 129 civilians, 162 security force personnel and 93 alleged Maoist cadres. The majority of the civilian victims were indigenous peoples. The state of Chhattisgarh continued to remain the epicenter of the Naxalite conflict, as a direct consequence of the counter-insurgency Salwa Judum campaign, which involved Adivasi civilians to counter the Maoists.[1]

Human rights violations against indigenous peoples

According to the 2006 Annual Report of the National Crime Records Bureau of the Ministry of Home Affairs, a total of 5,791 cases of crimes against scheduled tribes were reported in the country as compared to 5,713 cases in 2005, showing an increase of 1.4%. This is notably less than the increase of 3.2% reported in the period 2004-2005. Of the 10,495 accused persons who stood trial after being charged with crimes committed against Scheduled Tribes, only 20.8% were convicted.[2] This is less than the conviction rate of 24.4% reported in the 2006 Annual Report.

Impunity

Impunity contributes to further torture by the security forces and denies justice to tribal victims. With regard to the extrajudicial killings of 14 Adivasis by the police in Orissa on 2 January 2006, the state government of Orissa set up a judicial commission headed by sitting Orissa High Court judge Justice A.S. Naidu. However, on 9 April 2007, the Supreme Court annulled the Commission on the ground that a sitting judge of a High Court could not head an Inquiry Commission. On 10 April 2007, the Orissa Chief Minister promised to set up a new commission headed by a retired judge. As of the end of 2007, the new commission had yet to be established.

Similarly, two judicial inquiry commissions were set up to inquire into the extrajudicial killings of at least nine tribal students in Meghalaya on 30 September 2005. The final reports were tabled in the State Assembly of Meghalaya on 19 April 2007. While the Justice D.N. Chowdhury Commission stated that security personnel fired from close range and that the security personnel started firing again when the people were moving away from the field,[3] the Justice (Retd) D.N. Baruah Commission defended the police action as "just and proper" and added that "the question of fixing responsibility does not arise at all".[4]

Violation of humanitarian laws by the armed opposition groups

2007 continued to see armed opposition groups involved in gross human rights violations. Naxalites continued to kill innocent tribal peoples on the charge of being "police informers", members of anti-Maoist civilian militias such as Salwa Judum, and for not obeying their rules. In Chhattisgarh, innocent tribal civilians were killed for participating in the anti-Naxalite Salwa Judum campaign, irrespective of whether they had participated of their own volition or had been forced to by the anti-Naxalite Salwa Judum.

Violence against indigenous women and children

Indigenous women are especially vulnerable to violence, including rape, from non-tribals, the security forces and members of the armed opposition groups. In its 2006 Annual Report, the National Crime Records Bureau recorded a total of 699 cases of rape of tribal women in 2006 as against 640 cases in 2005, showing an increase of 9.2% in 2006. Out of these 640 rape cases, 40.6% were reported from Madhya Pradesh alone.

The security forces continue to take part in violence against indigenous women and children. On 9 January 2007, the police arrested three Paharia tribal women and several tribal men in Godda, Jharkhand on charges of murder. While the men were detained in the police lock-up, the women were detained in the residential quarter of the police station's officer-in-charge, where they were allegedly tortured and raped by the officer-in-charge and the assistant sub-inspector.[5] On 24 May, a 16-year-old tribal girl was raped by two Home Guards in the Harda District Collector's office in Madhya Pradesh. The accused have been arrested.[6] And on 20 August, 11 tribal women were allegedly gang raped by Greyhound policemen during anti-Naxalite operations in Andhra Pradesh. According to the victims, 21 policemen entered the village, raided houses on the grounds that family members were associated with the Naxalites, and raped women.[7] The police allegedly tried to hush up the incident and failed to conduct an identification parade of the suspects, although the victims claimed they could identify the rapists. On 30 August, the National Human Rights Commission took *suo motu* cognizance of the incident and sent notice to the district Senior Superintendent of Police and the Director General of Police, Andhra Pradesh to submit a factual report within four weeks. To date, no action has been taken to identify and prosecute the rapists.

On 11 December, an under age tribal girl was allegedly raped by the sub-inspector in the Bisramganj police station in West Tripura. After a public outcry, the government suspended and arrested the accused police officer and handed the case over to the Criminal Investigation Department for investigation.

Non-tribals also continue to take part in violence against tribal women and girls. On 9 April, a tribal woman was raped by a priest of a Hanuman temple in Gwalior district of Madhya Pradesh.[8] On 24 November, an Adivasi woman was stripped naked and beaten in public by non-tribal residents in Guwahati, the capital of Assam. The Adivasis were holding a procession demanding Scheduled Tribe status in Assam when it turned violent. As the police watched, local residents tortured at least one Adivasi youth to death.[9]

The armed opposition groups were also accused of the rape of indigenous women in 2007. On 9 July, a 20-year-old tribal woman was raped in her home by two alleged members of an unidentified militant group in Churachandpur district of Manipur.[10]

Land alienation

The rate of alienation of tribal land in India is alarming. In the state of Andhra Pradesh, non-tribals presently hold as much as 48% of the land in Scheduled Areas of the state. Since the Andhra Pradesh Scheduled Areas Land Transfer Regulation came into effect in 1959, 72,001 cases of land alienation have been detected involving 321,685 acres of land in the state. As of January 2007, around 300 cases were pending in Andhra Pradesh High Court, involving approximately 2,500 acres of land under the Andhra Pradesh Scheduled Areas Land Transfer Regulation.[11]

Similarly, the tribal group of All Assam Tribal Sangha has accused the state government of Assam of illegally transferring lands to non-tribals in violation of the Assam Land Revenue Regulation Act 1886. The non-tribals buy plots of land individually or in the name of private schools, societies or trusts and then subsequently use the plots for commercial purposes.[12] Furthermore, false cases have been filed against the tribals by non-tribals who try to forcibly grab tribal lands, and by police accusing the tribals of being "Naxalite sympathizers".[13]

For the poor and disadvantaged tribal peoples, the legal battles involving land are too difficult to be won. In February 2007, the Supreme Court allowed a tribal petitioner to file a fresh petition before the Jharkhand High Court for recovery of his land from a mining company. In its order, the Supreme Court held that the Jharkhand High Court was wrong to dismiss the petition of Surendra Dehri, a tribal who alleged that over 10,000 acres of "notified tribal land" had been usurped by mining contractors in connivance with government officials. The High Court had dismissed his petition saying that it involved only "private interest". However, the Supreme Court stated that blatant violation of the constitutional guarantees given to the tribals could not be held to be related to "private interest".[14]

In Jharkhand, cases of alienation of tribal land have been on the rise despite two state laws – the Chotanagpur Tenancy Act and the Santhal Parangan Tenancy Act to prevent the sale of tribal land to non-tribals. As of January 2007, 3,789 cases had been filed by tribals with the Special Area Regulation Court.[15]

The steel project planned by Korean Pohang Steel Company (POSCO) in Jagatsinghpur district in Orissa is expected to displace 4,000 tribal families.[16] On 29 November 2007, anti-*POSCO* tribal activists were attacked by supporters of the steel project in Jagatsinghpur district.[17] The attackers hurled crude bombs, injuring 15 protestors and burning their tents.[18] Instead of taking action against the attackers, the state government deployed armed policemen around Dhinkia village, where the tribal-led *POSCO Pratirodh Sangram Samiti* (Committee for Resistance Against POSCO) has its headquarters.[19] By the end of 2007, the villagers of Dhinkia were being detained in their homes, as all exits were manned by pro-POSCO activists and state armed police.[20]

In November 2007, the ruling Communist Party of India (Marxists) (CPI-M) cadres in the state of Kerala forcibly took over land earmarked for distribution to indigenous peoples in Munnar. Some 200 tribal families had built makeshift huts on government land in protest at not being allocated land as promised in 2003 by the government.[21] In the November incident, over 2,000 CPI-M cadres captured a 1,500-acre stretch of prime government land in Munnar's Chinnakkanal area and forced the 200 Adivasi families to flee. The huts of the Adivasis were destroyed and huts were constructed for the CPI-M cadres. On 27 November, an all-party meeting was called by the Munnar Additional District Magistrate, at which it was decided that both the CPI-M and Adivasis should move out of the area within 48 hours.[22] After the meeting, Adivasi leader C.P. Shaji was attacked by alleged CPI-M cadres.[23]

Development-induced displacement

Tribals make up the majority of development-induced displaced persons. According to a recent survey conducted by the NGO ActionAid and the Indian Social Institute, over 1.4 million people have been displaced in the four states of Andhra Pradesh, Chhattisgarh, Orissa and Jharkhand because of large-scale development projects such as mines, industrial plants and dams in the last decade. Out of all the displaced persons in these four states, 79% were tribals.[24]

Although the Narmada Control Authority claimed that all 32,600 families affected by the Sardar Sarovar dam at a height of 121.92 metres in Maharasthra, Madhya Pradesh and Gujarat had been resettled, thousands including tribals had not been rehabilitated by the end of 2007. In November, the Narmada Bachao Andolan (the movement to save the Narmada River) claimed that more than 1,100 affected families were yet to be resettled in Maharashtra alone.[25]

In Lohandiguda of Bastar district of Chhattisgarh, tribals have been protesting against the forcible acquisition of their land for the establishment of a steel plant by the Tata group. The state government of Chhattisgarh signed an MoU with Tata Steel in June 2005, requiring 1,784 hectares of private land and 278 hectares government land, including ten villages in the Lohanigunda area.[26] On 10 December 2007, over 100 tribals were detained by the police in Bastar for protesting against the steel plant. Several other tribal activists were allegedly booked on false charges.[27]

Apart from displacement, development projects also negatively affect the cultures and traditions of the tribals. On 23 November 2007, the Supreme Court of India barred the UK company Vedanta Resources Plc from mining bauxite in the sacred Niyamgiri hills in Orissa. The hills are considered sacred by the Dongria Kond tribe and 10,000 Dongria Kond tribals live by farming in the forests of the Niyamgiri.[28]

The tribals of Jharkhand have been protesting against the implementation of Koel Karo hydroelectric project on the part of the National Hydroelectric Corporation. If implemented, the project would submerge as many as 256 villages, 50,000 acres of forest area, 40,000 acres of agricultural land, 300 forest groves (considered sacred by the tribals), 175 churches and 120 Hindu temples.[29]

Conflict-induced displacement

Indigenous peoples constitute the majority of over 600,000 conflict-induced displaced persons (IDPs) in India. The conflicts include intra-indigenous peoples' conflicts, conflicts between different armed opposition groups and state governments' counter-insurgency operations and security measures.

Indigenous IDPs continue to face discrimination in terms of access to basic humanitarian services. Kashmiri Pandits[30] are currently provided with cash assistance of Rs 1,000 per head per month up to a maximum of Rs 4,000 per family per month both at Jammu and Delhi relief camps, in addition to basic dry rations. On the other hand, a Bru tribal adult gets only Rs 2.90 per day (i.e. Rs 87 per month (approx. US$ 2) and 450 grams of rice per day. Furthermore, the central government has provided millions of rupees to construct concrete buildings for the Kashmiri Pandits in Jammu, while the Brus cannot get funds to repair their bamboo huts. In education, the benefits enjoyed by the Kashmiri migrant students include the reservation of seats in technical/professional institutions while Bru children only get primary education. In 2007, a survey[31] in the six relief camps found that over 94% of the Bru

IDPs in the relief camps possessed documents issued by the state government of Mizoram to prove that they were residents of Mizoram. Yet, the government of Mizoram refuses to take them back.

Repression under forest laws

Due to delays in implementing the Forest Rights Act of 2006, tribals were deprived of their forest and land rights throughout 2007. In Jharkhand alone, around 12,000 cases had been filed by the state's Forest Department against tribals as of 12 August 2007. Most of these cases relate to claims of land rights by tribals, guaranteed under the Scheduled Tribes (Recognition of Forest Rights) Act.[32]

Tribal peoples are often arrested on false charges and, at times, have to pay a heavy price for accessing minor forest produce. For example, on 17 June 2007, a 35-year-old tribal was allegedly beaten to death by forest officials in the Hazaribagh National Park accused of cutting a tree to make a bed.[33]

On a positive note, in April 2007, the government of Chhattisgarh decided to drop criminal charges against 108,890 Scheduled Tribes and 36,298 Scheduled Castes registered under various forest and wildlife protection laws.[34] Similarly, on 12 August 2007, the government of Jharkhand ordered the release of tribals who had been held in various jails in the state in connection with cases registered by the Forest Department, and for compensation to be paid to all the villagers who had lost paddy fields and vegetable farms due to the forcible plantation undertaken by the state's Forest Department.[35]

The indigenous peoples continue to face eviction from their traditional habitat under the Forest Conservation Act of 1980. On 13 March 2007, as many as 118 Adivasi families were evicted by the Forest Department from reserve forest land under Haltugaon Forest Division in Kokrajhar district of Assam. The state government failed to provide alternative resettlement.[36] On 19 April 2007, the state government of Madhya Pradesh tried to evict tribals from forestland in Rewa district. The state government served notice on around 3,000 tribals who were allegedly encroaching on forestland.[37] When the tribals resisted the eviction drive, the police opened fire injuring many, including women and children.[38]

Affirmative actions

Affirmative action programmes for Scheduled Tribes and Scheduled Castes exist in India, including reservation in parliament, education and employment. Although affirmative action has been instrumental in bridging the social, political and economic disparities, experts believe they could have shown better results had officials been committed to implementation.

The tribals continue to lag behind in educational achievements. The literacy rate among tribals in India was only 47.1% against the national average of 65.38%, according to the 2001 census of India. Literacy among scheduled tribal women (34.8%) is approximately 20% lower than among the female population in general (53.7%).[39] In September 2007, a report released by the National Council for Educational Research and Training (NCERT) found "institutionalized discrimination" against students belonging to Scheduled Tribes and Scheduled Castes in schools. This is resulting in their alienation from schools and high levels of child labour.

The NCERT report provides examples of how tribal students face discrimination, e.g. teachers in Madhya Pradesh felt that teaching the "Korku" tribal children was equivalent to "teaching cows".[40] Earlier, the Thorat Committee headed by University Grants Commission (UGC) Chairperson S. K. Thorat also found gross discrimination against Scheduled Tribe and Scheduled Caste students and doctors at the premier medical institute, the All India Institute of Medical Sciences (AIIMS) in New Delhi.

Due to non-issuance of Scheduled Tribe certificates to tribal peoples, many tribals are not only denied their right to access affirmative action programmes but also their rights under the Constitution. With no tribal certificate, human rights violations against tribals are not registered by the police as cases under the Scheduled Castes and Scheduled Tribes (Prevention of Atrocities) Act of 1989.

The Madhya Pradesh government has refused to issue tribal certificates to the tribal children of the Barela, Bhil, Bhillala, Patelia and Nagwanshi tribal communities living in 13 villages of Chhattarpur district and three villages of Damoh district, although they are recognized as Scheduled Tribes in the state of Madhya Pradesh. In 2007, a survey[41] in these villages found that the majority of the tribals possessed legal documents such as ration cards, voter identity cards, land *patta* (deed) issued by the government, educational certificates, and even in some cases court documents proving their land ownership (documents establishing that they are residents of Madhya Pradesh). However, the state government has turned down several pleas for the issuing of tribal certificates.

In Andhra Pradesh, many villages are still not recognized as tribal areas for inclusion in the Fifth Schedule to the Constitution despite being tribal-majority villages. Because of the non-inclusion of tribal-dominated villages under the Fifth Schedule, nearly 200,000 Adivasis spread over 805 villages in nine districts of Andhra Pradesh do not enjoy Constitutional protection.[42]

Mismanagement of tribal welfare funds continues to be a serious problem. While various state governments do not use the funds meant for the tribals, the tribals across the country remain without basic needs. As of 31 August 2006, the state government of Assam had failed to utilize Rs 706 million (approx. US$ 17,500,000) of a total of almost Rs 3.4 billion (approx. US$ 84,900,000) released by the Ministry of Tribal Affairs from 1999-2000 to 2006-2007.[43] Similarly, the state government of Delhi reportedly siphoned off Rs 9.6 billion (approx. US$ 239,90,000) meant for the welfare of the Scheduled Castes and Scheduled Tribes of Delhi during 2006-2007. This was revealed to the public through the Right to Information Act in 2007.[44]

Vulnerable tribal communities

Seventy-five tribal communities have been identified as "Primitive Tribal Groups" by the government of India in 17 states and one Union Territory with a registered total population of 2.4 million in 1991.[45] Although the central government allocates assistance to these vulnerable communities through the Tribal Sub-Plan and Special Central Assistance, the communities have not benefited substantially.

Today, many tribal communities such as the Singphos of Assam;[46] the Birhores, Chero, Paharia and Malpahari in Jharkhand; the Abuj Madias and Baigas of Chhattisgarh; the Karbongs of Tripura, the Great Andamanese, Onges, Shompens, Jarawas, and the Sentinelese of the Andaman and Nicobar islands are on the verge of extinction due to the government's apathy. By the end of 2007, the government had still failed to implement the directive of the Supreme Court of 2002 to close down the Andaman Trunk Road that runs along and through the Jarawa Tribal Reserve. The trunk road continues to threaten the survival of vulnerable Jarawa tribals.

On 13 September 2007, ten persons belonging to the nomadic tribe of Kureris were beaten to death by a mob at Dhelpurwa village in Vaishali district of Bihar for alleged stealing. An inquiry conducted by the National Commission for Denotified and Nomadic Tribes found that the tribal victims were innocent. In a letter to the Bihar Chief Minister, the Commission stated that: "They (the tribals) were not caught red-handed, in fact the scene of theft was nearly five kilometres away from the scene of mob violence."[47] The police neither conducted postmortems nor did they ensure that last rites were carried out. Instead, the half-burnt bodies were reportedly dumped into the Ganga River by the police.[48]

Denial of voting rights to Chakmas and Hajongs

In June 2007, the state government of Arunachal Pradesh formed a high-level committee to find an amicable solution to the Chakma-Hajong issue[49] (see *The Indigenous World 2007*). Both the All Arunachal Pradesh Students' Union (AAPSU) and the Committee for Citizenship Rights of the Chakmas and Hajongs of Arunachal Pradesh (CCRCAP) have welcomed the formation of the high-powered committee.

However, despite specific guidelines from the Election Commission of India on how to revise the electoral rolls in the areas, the electoral officers in question have not yet enrolled all eligible Chakma and

Hajong voters. Consequently, the Election Commission of India has suspended the publication of the electoral rolls of Changlang, Lohit and Papumpare districts since 2005. Although a team from the Election Commission of India visited the four Chakma/Hajong-inhabited Assembly Constituencies in December 2007 to resolve the issue, the Chakmas and Hajongs, whose total population is estimated at 65,000, continue to be denied enrolment.   ❑

Notes and references

1   The Naxals get lethal. Chhattisgarh continues to be the epicenter of the conflict, *Naxal Conflict Monitor*, Vol-II, Issue-III, Asian Centre for Human Rights, 3 October 2007

2   2006 Annual Report of National Crime Records Bureau, Chapter 7: Crime Against Persons Belonging To SCs / STs, available at http://ncrb.nic.in/cii2006/cii-2006/CHAP7.pdf

3   Probe holds Tura firing "irresponsible", *The Assam Tribune*, 20 April 2007

4   Probe holds Tura firing "irresponsible", *The Assam Tribune*, 20 April 2007

5   Gang rape slur on Godda cops, *The Telegraph*, 29 January 2007

6   Teenager raped in Collector's office premises, *The Pioneer*, 26 May 2007

7   Eleven Girijan women allege gang-rape by policemen, *The Hindu*, 21 August 2007

8   Tribal woman raped, *The Pioneer*, 11 April 2007

9   Shame on Guwahati streets, *The Telegraph*, 27 November 2007

10 Gunmen rape housewife in Churachandpur, *The Kanglaonline*, 10 July 2007

11 Half of tribal land grabbed, *The Deccan Chronicle*, 29 January 2007

12 Concern over transfer of tribal lands to non-tribals, *The Assam Tribune*, 1 February 2007

13 Cases against tribals withdrawn, *The Hindu*, 15 August 2007

14 SC snubs land order, *The Telegraph*, 12 February 2007

15 Tribal land grab cases on rise in Jharkhand, *The Pioneer*, 14 February 2007

16 Atrocities at Singur, India: A matter of rights of the dispossessed, *ACHR Review* No. 144/06, Asian Centre for Human Rights

17 Opposition to POSCO mounts, *The Hindu*, 1 December 2007

18 Divide over Posco plant turns violent, yet again, *The Telegraph*, 1 December 2007

19 Uneasy calm at POSCO project site, NDTV, 9 December 2007

20 Posco protesters held hostage, *The Hindustan Times*, 10 December 2007

21 After CPM men attack activist, tribals refuse to vacate Munnar land, *The Indian Express*, 29 November 2007

22 After Nandigram, red terror in Munnar, *The Indian Express*, 28 November 2007

23 After CPM men attack activist, tribals refuse to vacate Munnar land, *The Indian Express*, 29 November 2007

24 79 per cent land oustees tribals, *The Hindustan Times*, 20 December 2007
25 NCA admits illegality of Sardar Sarovar Dam Height Increase to 121.92 m, Narmada Bachao Andolan, press release dated 14 November 2007, http://www.narmada.org/nba-press-releases/november-2007/Nov14.html
26 Trouble at Tata Bastar plant, now survey team attacked, *The Indian Express*, 1 March 2007
27 CPI says tribals being ousted for Tata plant, *The Indian Express*, 12 December 2007
28 Supreme Court bars British company from mining sacred hills, Survival International, 29 November 2007, http://www.survival-international.org/news/2696
29 Koel Karo: Tribal surge that stalled a dam, *The Times of India*, 5 June 2007
30 Person from Kashmir belonging to a Hindu sect. Many Kashimi pandits have fled because they are targeted by militants in Kashmir.
31 Survey conducted by AITPN, 2007.
32 Relief nod after forest eviction, *The Telegraph*, 13 August 2007
33 Man cuts tree to make cot, beaten to death, *The Deccan Chronicle*, 19 June 2007
34 Tribal-friendly, eco-unfriendly, *The Indian Express*, 5 April 2007
35 Relief nod after forest eviction, *The Telegraph*, 13 August 2007
36 118 Adivasi families evicted from Saralpara, *The Sentinel*, 15 March 2007
37 Tribals, police clash in Rewa district, *The Pioneer*, 20 April 2007
38 Governor's intervention sought in Rewa firing, *The Pioneer*, 24 April 2007
39 2006-2007 Annual Report of the Ministry of Tribal Affairs, Government of India, page 27-28.
40 Tribals face bias in schools, *The Asian Age*, 24 September 2007
41 Survey conducted by AITPN, 2007.
42 Apathy denies tribals statutory rights, *The Deccan Herald*, 16 October 2007
43 Over Rs 70 crores Central fund for tribals unspent, *The Assam Tribune*, 7 December 2007
44 Rs 965 crores for SCs/STs misused: RSP, *The Tribune*, 9 November 2007
45 Annual Report 2006-2007, Ministry of Tribal Affairs, Government of India
46 Singphos, an aboriginal tribe nearing extinction, *The Shillong Times*, 11 June 2007
47 Probe doubts guilt of 10 lynched for stealing, *Rediff News,* 23 September 2007, http://www.rediff.com/news/2007/sep/23bihar.htm
48 Bihar Street Justice - Fingerprints of victims not taken, *The Tribune*, 19 September 2007, http://www.tribuneindia.com/2007/20070919/nation.htm
49 The Chakma and Hajong tribals in Arunachal Pradesh have been denied registration on the electoral roll because the state government has not processed their citizenship applications.

Paritosh Chakma is Coordinator of the Asia Indigenous and Tribal Peoples Network (AITPN) based in Delhi, India.

SRI LANKA

Sri Lanka is home to diverse indigenous cultures that have combined to influence its societal make-up for over two thousand years. Of these, the historically recognized *Vyadha* ("huntsmen/ archers") or *Vadda*, as they are now commonly referred to, were among diverse other social or occupational indigenous groups who served a defined role, recognised by royal decree, and who owed allegiance to the King.[1] With European colonisation, however, the different indigenous groups, including the Vadda, came under threat as a result of social transformations that ended up isolating them. The norm among European and other travel writers of the colonial era was to depict hunter-gatherer groups such as the Vadda as "uncivilised" or "barbarous".

The Vadda comprise independent groups who originally coexisted alongside their non-Vadda neighbours and were once widespread in the south-eastern and eastern coastal belt, the northern tracts and the central part of the island where they are, however, less known.[2] Of these, a comparatively few Vadda groups – particularly those of the south-east - are recognised by certain cultural traits, such as *varige* (Sinhala term for clan name) and ancestor worship.[3] The majority, however, compare with their neighbours, the long-term Sinhalese sedentary agriculturalists, and some with Tamil-speaking populations. While colonial census reports portrayed the Vadda people as a distinct ethnic group and gave population figures of between 1,229 and 4,510 people, census surveys of the last three decades have not distinguished them as a separate ethnic group.[4]

Current issues

The Vadda, as traditional forest-dwelling hunters, are suffering from extreme poverty as a result of state interventions since the European colonial and post-colonial era, for example, modern development schemes (including forced resettlement) and the establishment of conservation policies that ignore the intrinsic sustainability of Vadda lifeways.[5] Their enforced adaptation to mainstream scenarios has adversely affected the once free-spirited Vadda people, their traditional lifeways and cultural values, and has intensified their marginalisation and enhanced their dependency. Their primary occupation of hunting is now prohibited by national law. In some cases, where protected forest resources are used by forest-dependent communities, including the Vadda, arrests are made and major conflicts and legal battles ensue between the stakeholder groups. One key livelihood transition has been the adoption of sedentary agricultural practices. This shift has led to an increased dependency on external inputs, e.g., chemical fertilisers and pesticides, and has restricted access to seasonal water sources. As a result, the traditional livelihood strategies of the Vadda, which helped to preserve forest resources, are being eroded. The price the Vadda people has paid is a high one. They are facing undue pressures and are struggling to maintain livelihood security. An erosion of traditional values, in exchange for material aspirations, influenced by external economic, socio-cultural and religious influences, is distinctly evident.

The rights of the Vadda people are incorporated within broader national policies focused on the rights of forest-dependent communities in general. These policies have deprived traditional forest-dwellers such as the Vadda people of their economic mainstay and livelihood through displacement and a denial of the right to access forest resources.

Policy advocacy

The Inter-Agency Working Group on the Livelihood Recovery of Traditional/Indigenous Forest-Dwelling People (IWGLRIP-2005) was established in response to the livelihood insecurities being experienced

by modern forest-dependent communities. The Working Group committee, facilitated by the United Nations Development Programme/ Global Environment Facility-Small Grant Programme (UNDP/ GEF-SGP), comprises representatives from the Biodiversity Secretariat of the Ministry of Environment and Natural Resources (BS-MENR) and the Centre for Eco-Cultural Studies (CES), operating as the joint secretariat, and the Department of Wildlife Conservation (DWLC).

The Working Group's main objective is to facilitate the recovery of forest livelihoods and to preserve associated traditional knowledge systems. The process is being carried forward through negotiations between the various stakeholders aimed at proactive change in order to overcome the barriers forest communities are presently facing in interacting with their natural environment. These stakeholders include local, district, regional and national government agencies, non-governmental organizations and private concerns such as entrepreneurs. While tackling this as a key theme, national and international agendas such as the Convention on Biological Diversity (CBD) and the much publicised Millennium Development Goals (MDGs), for example, are also being addressed.

In the spirit of the International Decade for Indigenous Peoples, developments for the establishment of the National Policy on Traditional Knowledge (NPTK) were set in motion in 2003. The NPTK and its associated strategies were finally declared on 9 August 2007, a day recognised internationally for the celebration of indigenous peoples. Pre-existing policies, such as the National Biodiversity Action Plan and National Forest Policy, have already highlighted the importance of preserving traditional knowledge practices and their associated communities. However, the NPTK exists as a government policy solely dedicated to the promotion and facilitation of traditional knowledge, and to the maintenance of the eco-cultural well-being of indigenous communities that have nurtured such wisdom for thousands of years.

Model programme on livelihood recovery

A model for the livelihood recovery of forest-dependent Vadda communities has been established through the IWGLRIP in Ratugala. Ratugala is included, along with six other traditionally forest-dependent and/or displaced forest-dwelling communities, in a five-year-long programme under Phase I. The seven areas included are: Ratugala: environs of Gal Oya National Park (Monaragala District), Pollebadda: environs of Nuvaragala Forest Reserve (Ampara District), Dambana: environs of Maduru Oya National Park (Badulla District), Henanigala: environs of Maduru Oya National Park (Ampara District), Gallinda, Rotavava and Minneriya: environs of Sigiriya Wildlife Sanctuary, Minneriya-Giritale Nature Reserve and Minneriya-Giritale National Park (Polonnaruva District), Dimbulagala and environs; environs of Flood Plains National Park and Vasgamuva National Park (Polonnaruva District), Panama: environs of Kumana Wildlife Sanctuary, Yala and Lahugala-Kitulana National Parks (Monaragala District)

This pilot programme in Ratugala serves as a model applied action research programme through which to establish guidelines for Phase I, selected on a priority needs basis, identified by the local community and jointly implemented by its representative local society. It endeavours to protect the rights of traditional forest-dwelling communities and promotes sustainable alternative economic practices while addressing Article 8j of the CBD for equitable sharing of the benefits of biodiversity. Furthermore, it endorses planned initiatives for socio-economic enhancement and cultural and environmental conservation through participatory community initiatives for direct, long-term benefits to the communities concerned. The pilot programme has so far come up with the following recommendations:

- To minimize conflicts of interest between stakeholders such as protected area managers and forest peoples
- To minimize the adverse effects of community dependency on protected areas
- To establish "eco-cultural" villages to provide alternative means of livelihood
- To set up documentation methods for traditional knowledge practices related to natural resource management .
- To establish a community interpretation programme on traditional cultures and scaling up of existing facilities
- To empower and enhance the skills of local forest-dwelling communities
- To set up a mechanism for equitable sharing of benefits from protected areas and bio-prospecting
- To establish a market for the sale of non-timber forest products
- To set up a financial assistance mechanism for re-acquiring community properties
- To raise awareness and address issues of social and community health concerns
- To address gender issues.

The programmes hitherto established through multi-stakeholder initiatives and proactive participation also involve the local communities that depend on protected forest resources. The multi-partite organisational network established nationally and regionally has paved the way for a constructive dialogue. Wider stakeholder participation in planning, implementing, monitoring and restructuring, in accordance with national interests and local benefits, is the key success achieved so far. Conflicts of interest between the stakeholders, involving government institutes and local forest-dwelling communities, are negotiated via the IWGLRIP in order to minimise them, with priority given to forest people's livelihood recovery through recognition of community rights, as custodians of the forest ecosystems in which they live.

The stakeholders of the pilot programme in Ratugala, comprising two Vadda representatives from Pollebadda and Dambana, representatives of the BS-MENR, DWLC, CES and UNDP/GEF-SGP, participated in the Regional Dialogue on Indigenous Peoples and Natural Resource Management, held in Chiang Mai, Thailand from 10 to 14 November 2007. This consultation was part of a process initiated in 2005 through the Regional Initiative on Indigenous Peoples. Its aim was to identify the gaps and opportunities existing at regional level in order to better address the urgent issue of natural resources, land and climate change. The involvement of the Sri Lankan participants in Chiang Mai has since opened up regional networks and a "way forward", with plans to set up a National Dialogue in Sri Lanka in early 2008, using the model in question.   ❏

Notes & References

1   Sources: **Geiger. W., (ed.), 1950:** *Mahavamsa:* pp.74-75; **Ievers, R.W., 1899:** *North Central Province, Ceylon.* Colombo: George J.A. Skeen. pp.89-90. **Knox, R., [1681] 1981:** *An Historical Account of Ceylon.* Colombo: Tisara Prakasakayo. p. 196

2   Sources: **Obeysekere, G., 2002:** *Colonial Histories and Vadda Primitivism: An Unorthodox Reading of Kandy Period Texts.* G.C. Mendis Memorial Lecture. P.2, p. 11; **Dart, J., 1990:** The Coast Veddas: Dimensions of Marginality. *The Vanishing Aborigines: Sri Lanka's Veddas in Transition.* Edited by Dharmadasa, K.N.O. and S.W.R. de A. Samarasinghe. P.68; **Brow, James, 1978:** *Vedda Villages of Anuradhapura: The Historical Anthropology of a Community in Sri Lanka.* Seattle: University of Washington Press. Pp. 40-41; **Ievers,** *Ibid.* p. 90

3   **Spittel, R.L., (1956) 2000:** *Savage Sanctuary.* Colombo: Sooriya Publishers. P. 13; **Spittel, R.L., (1950) 2001:** *Vanished Trails.* Colombo: Sooriya Publishers. pp. 23-26.

4   **Ranasinghe, A.G., 1950:** Census of Ceylon 1946. Vol. 1. Part I, *General Report by Department of Census and Statistics.* Colombo: Government Press. pp. 161-162.

5   **Stavenhagen, R., 1990:** The Plight of the Indigenous. *The Vanishing Aborigines: Sri Lanka's Veddas in Transition.* Edited by Dharmadasa, K.N.O. and S.W.R. de A. Samarasinghe. Colombo: International Centre for Ethnic Studies. pp.17-20, 22; **Dharmadasa, K.N.O., 1990:** The Veddas' Struggle for Survival: Problems, Policies and Responses. *The Vanishing Aborigines: Sri Lanka's Veddas in Transition.* Edited by Dharmadasa, K.N.O. and S.W.R. de A. Samarasinghe. pp.141, 165-166.

Sudarshani Fernando has been researching Vadda lifeways since 1991 and is representing IWGLRIP as the Coordinating Secretary of the Centre for Eco-cultural Studies (CES) with colleague *Sujeewa Jasinghe*, as the Project Director of CES. Other Working Group members are *Shireen Samarasuriya*, National Coordinator of the United Nations Development Programme/Global Environment Facility-Small Grant Programme (UNDP/GEF-SGP).

Gamini Gamage, Director, Biodiversity Secretariat of the Ministry of Environment & Natural Resources (BD-MENR).

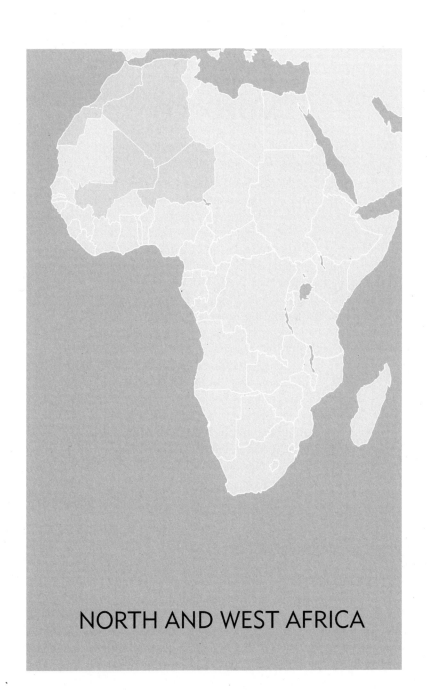

NORTH AND WEST AFRICA

MOROCCO

The Amazigh (Berber) peoples are considered to be the indigenous peoples of North Africa. The most recent census in Morocco (2004) estimated the number of Amazigh speakers at 28%
of the population. Amazigh associations strongly challenged
this result and instead put forward a rate of 65 to 70%. This
means that the Amazigh-speaking population of Morocco may
well number around twenty million, with around thirty million
throughout the whole of North Africa and the Sahel.

The administrative and legal system of Morocco has been
highly Arabised, and the Amazigh culture and way of life is
under constant pressure of assimilation. Recent years have,
however, seen positive changes, with the establishment of the
Royal Institute of Amazigh Culture, recognition of the Amazigh
alphabet, introduction of mother-tongue education in the
Amazigh language in state schools, and the gradual opening up
of the media to the Amazigh language. The Amazigh people
have organised, both within Tamazgha (Amazigh Land or
North Africa in the Amazigh language) and internationally, and
there may now be as many as 300 associations spread throughout the whole of Morocco.

At constitutional level

The foundation of the modern Moroccan state and of North Africa
as a whole was based on the idea of unitarism: a strong state needs
centralised power, one religion, one language, hence the systematic
marginalisation of all aspects of Amazighité (the Amazigh identity)
throughout North Africa. Arabic became the only official language,
and the language of education and administrative life. The Moroccan

Constitution recognises only the Arab/Muslim and not the Amazigh identity. For the law makers, Morocco is - quite simply - an Arab country. This has consequences for other aspects of the Moroccan state such as justice, education and administration. And the law can prohibit an Amazigh-speaking citizen from speaking his or her language, forcing them to speak Arabic, given that it is the only official language in the Constitution. Consequently, legally, the Amazigh of Morocco can claim no rights given that the Constitution does not recognise their existence. When challenged by civil society organisations on the subject of Amazigh rights, government members have often resorted to this argument. Aware of the importance of constitutional protection for the

Amazigh identity, the Amazigh cultural movement is focusing its struggle on recognition of the Amazigh identity and officialization of the Amazigh language in the Constitution.

Civil and political rights of the Amazigh

In September 2007, the Ministry of the Interior asked the Administrative Tribunal to dissolve the Moroccan Democratic Amazigh Party (Parti amazigh démocratique marocain - PDAM). This action was taken on the basis of article 4 of the law on parties, which criminalizes the establishment of parties that have a language, ethnic, religious or regional basis. The first hearing took place on 15 November 2007 without the PDAM being invited to attend, and the next hearing took place on 13 December 2007, this time with the presence of the PDAM. The case will be examined by the Administrative Tribunal on the 14 February 2008.

A number of Amazigh activists were detained for questioning during 2007. Abdelaziz Elwazani was prosecuted, as reported by the Amazigh World Congress:

Abdelaziz Elwazani, President of the Ouzgan Association for Development (Souss region) and member of the Amazigh League for Human Rights (Ligue Amazighe pour les Droits Humains) was prosecuted by the Moroccan state under the pretext that he had made remarks injurious to the sacred values of the kingdom during a conference on land rights held in Bouyzakarn in February 2007. In actual fact, Mr. Elwazani's comments, which were made in Tamazight, were misrepresented in their translation into Arabic in order to be able to accuse him and thus attempt to reduce him to silence. Legal proceedings are underway.[1]

In addition, 2007 saw the arrest and conviction of Amazigh activists, and 10 students from the Amazigh cultural movement were given harsh sentences on 22 May 2007.

Fifteen Amazigh activists in Boumallene Dades in the southern part of Morocco were arrested following demonstrations and protests at the situation of poverty and marginalisation, and the absence of infrastructure (roads, schools, hospitals) in the Warzazat Region. The case will be examined in February 2008.

Lack of equal opportunities

Equal opportunities are, in theory, guaranteed among Moroccan citizens but, in practice, only a few families close to the echelons of power have a chance to accede to senior posts of responsibility, and they use their power to sideline those Moroccans who call themselves Amazigh. The competitive examinations for entry to these posts have lost all credibility and students from Amazigh-speaking regions (e.g. the Souss) do not have the same opportunities as their colleagues from other regions. Most ministers in the new government come from Ma-khzan[2] families in the north of the country. Senior civil servants are appointed without considering those from the Amazigh cultural movement. This is why this movement is demanding that a federal system be established to guarantee a sharing of power, resources and values. For the Amazigh, only regional autonomy will guarantee democracy and equal opportunities.

From 2-4 August 2007, the Confederation of Amazigh Associations in the North organised a large conference on Federalism and Autonomy in Nador City with the participation of many professors and Amazigh personalities. Likewise in 2007, several Amazigh organisations in the three large regions of Morocco announced the importance of autonomy and federalism for a democratic society.

Following the adoption of the UN Declaration on the Rights of Indigenous Peoples on September 13, 2007, Amazigh organisations held celebrations and, in a meeting with the Minister of Justice, they requested that the rights of the Amazigh people should be respected on the basis of this Declaration.

Information and education

The situation changed little during 2007, and the government failed to keep its promise to establish an Amazigh TV channel, ostensibly through lack of budget, although six channels were set up in Arabic and French. As the Amazigh World Congress put it:

> *The state-run mass media speaks to Moroccans virtually only in Arabic. The audio-visual information and entertainment system is thus totally out of tune with Moroccan reality. For a number of years, the RTM and 2M TV channels have broadcast three 10-minute information programmes in Amazigh every day, although their terms and conditions anticipate 30% of their channel's time being devoted to Amazigh culture and language. Although 2/3 of Moroccans are Amazigh, the television devotes 18 hours per day (i.e. 75%) to programmes in Arabic, 5 ½ hours (i.e. 23%) to programmes in French and ½ an hour to programmes in Amazigh (i.e. 2%). The Amazigh language also experiences discrimination on the national radio, where restrictions are imposed on it, particularly in terms of reporting and reduced broadcasting hours. Amazigh-speaking journalists working for state radio and television (RTM) do not enjoy the same working conditions as their colleagues (no Amazigh department, significantly reduced resources…). Similarly, there is no structure specialising in Tamazight within the Institut Supérieur de Journalisme (Higher School of Journalism), which is a handicap to students choosing an Amazigh-speaking option.*[3]

In terms of Amazigh language teaching, despite a theoretical stated will, this teaching remains fragile and weak and is reliant on the goodwill of those running the local education authorities.

Towards a rights-based Morocco

By focusing on principles of peace and tolerance, the Amazigh movement will continue its peaceful struggle while recognizing the rights that have already been gained. Despite the suffering of the indigenous peoples in terms of their rights, Morocco is open to reconciliation with the Amazigh movement, working towards a constructive dialogue. 2008 will remain a year of hope for the Amazigh cultural movement with regard to recognition of its identity and officialization of the Amazigh language, as well as recognition of all legitimate rights such that the Amazigh can fully enjoy their citizenship, and can contribute to building a modern Morocco worthy of its history, a Morocco of equal opportunities. 2008 will remain a year of hope. ❑

Notes

1   Amazigh World Congress report. Note 1.
2   The makhzen is an old concept of Moroccan power (State of Morocco)
3   Ibid.

Mohamed Handaine *is a historian and writer and has published a number of works on Amazigh history and culture. He is president of the confederation of Amazigh associations of southern Morocco and founder member of the Amazigh World Congress.. He is currently president of the Coordination Autochtone Francophone (CAF).*

ALGERIA

The Amazigh (also known as Berbers) are the first inhabitants of the whole North African region, the Sahara and the Sahel. Rough figures suggest that the Amazigh-speaking population comprises between 20-30% of Algeria's total estimated population of 32.9 million (2006 estimate), spread over an area of 2,381,741 km². Amazigh speakers are found in four large linguistic areas, namely: Kabylia, the main Amazigh-speaking region situated in the north; Aurès (Chaoui region) situated in the east; Mzab in the centre-south; and the Tuareg Territory (nomadic Amazigh people known as the Blue Men) in the far south. There are also many other Amazigh-speaking groups dotted around in islets, not exceeding a few tens of thousands of people. Since independence in 1962, the rural exodus has meant that there are very large Amazigh-speaking communities in the main towns, where the dominant day-to-day language is a dialect of Arabic (as opposed to the classical Arabic learnt at school).

The Algerian Constitution recognizes the indigenous Amazigh language as a national language. However, the Amazigh identity remains marginalised by the state institutions.

Linguistic rights

During the "Black Spring" of Kabylia in 2001,[1] under pressure from the people, political parties and international NGOs, the UN Economic and Social Council (ECOSOC):[2] "recommended that the Algerian state take measures to recognise the Amazigh language as an of-

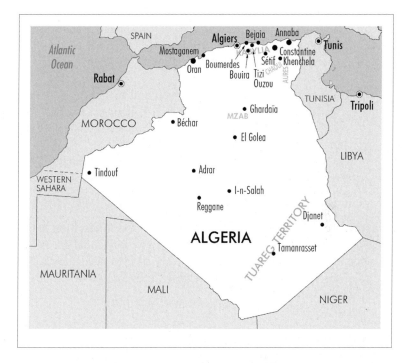

ficial language". Following this, on 8 April 2002, in the absence of deputies from the democratic opposition – the *Rassemblement pour la culture et la démocratie* (RCD) and the *Front des forces socialistes* (FFS) - who boycotted the session, the National Algerian Assembly unanimously approved a constitutional amendment to Article 3b, introduced by the President of the Republic, which stipulates: "Tamazight is also a national language. The State shall work for its promotion and development in all its linguistic variations in use in the national territory."[3]

Despite this official recognition within the country's first fundamental law, the indigenous Amazigh language has not benefited from the financial resources that would enable its promotion and development. It is mere rhetoric, since the situation is very different on the ground. The associations working for the development of the Amazigh culture receive no support; they are marginalised and frowned upon, unlike associations that are close to the government.

Recognition of Tamazight in the Algerian Constitution should have been followed up by practical action. The Government Council thus met on 19 June 2007, under the presidency of Mr. Abdelaziz Belkhadem, head of government, to consider and endorse two draft presidential decrees presented by the Minister for National Education, namely:

- On the creation, tasks, organisation and management of the Algerian Academy for the Amazigh Language (*Académie Algérienne de la Langue Amazighe*), which is a national scientific and cultural institution.
- On the creation, tasks, organisation and management of the Higher Council for the Amazigh Language (*Conseil Supérieur de la Langue Amazighe*), which is a national body.

These two institutions were to be placed under the supervision of the Presidency of the Republic. But, to date, the two presidential decrees in question have not been adopted by the Council of Ministers for publication in the Official Journal, which raises questions as to why their application is being delayed.

Teaching of the Amazigh language

The right to study one's mother tongue, the right to culture, etc. are enshrined in the International Covenant on Economic, Social and Cultural Rights, a text that Algeria has ratified, along with the Association Agreement signed with the European Union in 2001 and many other international texts ratified by Algeria.

However, teaching of the Amazigh language (from 4th year primary on), in force since 1995, is currently only provided in around seven departments (mainly Kabylia) instead of being available in all Amazigh-speaking regions. Without the necessary human and material resources, it is still floundering in a random and never-ending experimental stage.

According to figures provided by the Ministry of Education and the High Commission for Amazighness (*Haut Commissariat à l'Amazighité* - HCA) for 2006-2007, published in the press,[4] there are

655 teachers for 122,248 pupils in the 7 departments where the Amazigh language is taught. Of these, 631 work in the three main departments of Kabylia (Tizi Ouzou with 297 teachers for 60,155 pupils), Bejaia (222 teachers for 29,245 pupils) and Bouira (112 teachers for 27,447 pupils). Figures for the other regions outside of Kabylia are as follows: Algiers (the capital): 4 teachers for 1,643 pupils; Boumerdes (11 teachers for 2,541 pupils); Khenchela (Chaoui region): 5 teachers for 323 pupils); Tamanrasset (Tuareg region): 4 teachers for 894 pupils.

These figures are clearly an improvement on previous years but remain insignificant in relation to the teaching of Arabic in Algeria as a whole and in the Amazigh-speaking regions in particular. And yet there is no lack of Amazigh language teachers given that, in 2006, a number of Amazigh language graduates from the two Kabylia universities (two Amazigh language and culture departments have been running in Kabylia since 1990) could not find jobs due to lack of available funding.

Cultural production in the indigenous language

As of the end of 2007, Amazigh-speaking populations had a right to a mere few minutes of news a day and a weekly broadcast in the Amazigh language on national state television. All other programmes are broadcast in Arabic. The government refuses to open up the audiovisual sector to private investors, who are waiting for a green light from the government to set up private chains. This would certainly provide an opportunity for the Amazigh language to emerge on television.

Fortunately, there is a national state radio channel that broadcasts programmes in the Amazigh language (in its different regional variations), and local state channels that broadcast programmes in both Arabic and Amazigh languages. Here too, there are unfortunately currently no private radio networks and the public service is state-controlled.

The few Amazigh-language newspapers that saw the light of day in the early 1990s soon disappeared through lack of state support. Now, the only private fortnightly newspaper published in Kabylia and entitled "*Racines*" (bilingual French – Tamazight) has recently closed after 6 years in existence due to financial problems, through lack of state support or corporate advertising. Indigenous industrialists who support the cause are hesitant to advertise in such Amazigh-language newspapers for fear of finding sanctions imposed on them by the government in the form of taxes.

Literary publishing in the indigenous Amazigh language also finds itself up against problems given that there is no policy of supporting literature in Algeria. Books in the Amazigh language are thus doubly penalised.

Film production in the Amazigh language is beginning to emerge, although there are very few films made, through lack of funding.

Nevertheless, a national Amazigh film festival was established in March 2006. The 7th festival took place in January 2007 in Tlemcen, an Arabic-speaking region in the west of the country. A "Golden Olive Tree" worth 500,000 Algerian Dinars (approx. US$7,500) is awarded for the best feature film by an international panel sitting at each festival.

Within the context of the "Algiers, capital of Arab culture" event, which cost the state more than 4.5 billion Algerian Dinars, only six Amazigh-language films were funded. Even though this level of action is to be congratulated, there was also an ulterior motive insofar as the government was hoping, through this event, to merge the Amazigh culture into Arab culture via a policy of assimilation.

Marginalisation

In some regions, indigenous people are still prohibited from giving their children Amazigh names. The names of former Amazigh kings and princes are not recognised by the authorities as they do not appear on the official list held by the state since independence in 1962. Enforcement of this ban is left to the judgement of local authority staff. Although it is less of a problem in Kabylia, where the local authorities are run by indigenous Amazigh, many people outside Kabylia are unable to register their children's births. It is the same for road signs and other commercial and administrative signs in the Amazigh language. Although tolerated in Kabylia, this is not the case in other regions.

During the different local, parliamentary and presidential elections, keeping a tight grip on the administration and attempting to commit electoral fraud at every ballot, the central authority does all it can to restrict the parties with a strong Amazigh base (Kabylia) and prevent them from having a voice outside of Kabylia. Those Amazigh (politicians and others) that hold key posts in government do so because they support the government's policies. The others are systematically excluded and do not even have access to the state media, except during electoral campaigns in order to legitimise the ballot.

Only Kabylia's municipalities are largely run by two political parties of this region's democratic opposition, namely the Rally for Culture and Democracy (*Rassemblement pour la culture et la démocratie* - RCD) headed by Said Sadi and the Socialist Forces Front (*Front des forces socialistes* - FFS) under the leadership of Hocine Ait Ahmed.

These parties, with a strong foothold in the Amazigh regions and with active grassroots members, are beginning to win ground in Arabic-speaking regions. For example, the RCD, which currently has two senators and 19 deputies, snatched seats in various communes outside Kabylia during the November 2007 local elections, managing to take the lead in ten or so municipalities in Arabic-speaking areas.

There is also a Movement for Kabylia Autonomy (*Mouvement pour l'Autonomie de la Kabylie* - MAK), headed by Ferhat Mehenni, which held its founding congress on 14 August 2007 at Bejaia in Lower Kabylia. It should, however, be noted that only a very small minority of indigenous activists demand autonomy.

Economically, the Amazigh-speaking regions suffer from a lack of development projects. The state has only implemented a few projects in these regions, as mere "window dressing". In Kabylia, the region manages to finance a few projects itself through the support of Kabyl emigrants (around 800,000 Kabyls live in France).

Unemployment is rampant in this region, and social scourges are widespread through lack of state attention to the problems of young people. Suicides recorded in some areas over the last few years are worrying. Due to a lack of reliable statistics, precise figures cannot be given to quantify the extent of this phenomenon in relation to other regions of the country. By way of example, however, according to an evaluation published by the national police department, at least 30

people committed suicide in Kabylia out of the 128 cases noted in Algeria throughout 2007 (19 in Béjaïa and 11 more in Tizi Ouzou department)[5]. This puts the two main departments of Kabylia, where unemployment, misery and despair are rampant, at the top of the country's
regions in terms of suicides.   ❑

Notes

1   In April 2001, following the arrest then murder of a young Amazigh in Kabylia
    by police officers demonstrations broke out across Kabylia (three departments).
    The police fired live ammunition on the young demonstrators. After a year of
    events (from 2001 to 2002), the death toll stood at 126. This was Kabylia's Black
    Spring...
2   y means of its final resolution of 30 November 2001, which approved this Coun-
    cil's sittings for Algeria's hearings.
3   Official Journal dated 10-04-2002.
4   El Watan.
5   L'Expression dated 8 February 2008.

*Mohamed Si Belkacem is a chemist engineer and has taught chemistry at
the Mouloud Mammeri University in Tizi Ouzou. In 2000 he turned into
journalism and from 2000 to 2003, then from 2005 to 2007 he was editorial
director of a bimonthly newspaper* "Racines" *(bilingual French-Amazigh).
From 2003 to 2005 he worked as a journalist on the general daily newspaper*
"Liberté" *and since January 2008 he has been working on the daily paper* "Le
Soir d'Algérie" *as a freelance journalist. Mohamed Si Belkacem has been
President of the cultural association* Iles Umazigh *(an indigenous Amazigh
organisation) since 2000, and he is a member of the executive of CAF* (Coordination autochtone francophone/*French-speaking Indigenous Coordinating Body). From 1999 to 2005 he was vice-president of CMA (World Amazigh
Congress). He is the author of a book entitled* "Chroniques de la Kabylie
martyrisée" *("Chronicles of a martyred Kabylia") published by l'Harmattan
in 2004.*

NIGER

The indigenous groups in Niger include the Tuareg, Toubou and Peul (including the Bororo and Wodaabe), who are all mainly pastoralists. Out of a total Nigerien population of more than 12 million inhabitants,[1] the Tuareg who live in the northwest and north of the country are estimated to number a little over one million. Most Tuareg practise livestock rearing (camels, sheep, goats) while others work in the oases, or as craftsmen. The Toubou camel rearers represent less than half a million people and live in the regions of Agadez, Zinder and Diffa. The Peul people who live in all regions of the country are officially estimated to number 900,000 but the actual number is probably much higher. Some Peul have become settled agricultural and livestock farmers, but a significant minority, including the Bororo Peul and the so-called "red" Peul (Gorgabè and Tolébès Peul) remain nomadic pastoralists.

There is no general legislation in Niger that takes the specific nature of the pastoralist people into account. However, a Pastoralist Code aimed at organising the legal system for livestock production in Niger is currently being drafted.

In Niger, the year 2007 was marked by two major events: on the one hand, a rebellion broke out in the north of the country and, on the other, the 3rd annual meeting of pastoralists/livestock herders took place at EGGO, which is a Fulani encampment to the north of Dakaro department.

Rebellion in the north of Niger

A rebellion has been ongoing in the Agadez region of northern Niger since February 2007. Initially instigated by members of the Tuareg community, this rebellion now seems to be taking on a national air, insofar as members of other national communities are joining it. What are the causes of this rebellion? Who is organising it? And what are the risks of it becoming derailed in the near future? The sources of this rebellion (described by official channels as simply banditry or terrorism) are, in our opinion, two-fold: internal and external.

Internal sources

Internal causes can be inferred from three aspects of governance that leave much to be desired.

First of all, there is clear political mismanagement, which means that values such as justice, and equality between citizens in all its dimensions, are extremely rare. This is all underpinned by endemic corruption and nepotism and the whole unhealthy political environment breeds many frustrations.

Secondly, there is socio-economic mismanagement, the best expression of which can be found in Arlit (an industrial town in north-eastern Niger), the place where nearly all Niger's natural resources (uranium,[2] coal) are mined. In fact, anyone going to Arlit for the first time is soon possessed by a sense of unease, a bizarre feeling of being in a post-war ruin (dusty roads, the only asphalt road aimed at transporting the uranium is in complete disrepair, slums built with what looks like irradiated scrap materials etc). This state of affairs is at the heart of the rebellion's protest.

The response of the Niger authorities to these concerns is that the region of Agadez is in no way the poorest of all Niger's regions. The relevance of this argument is questionable given the region's specific nature (size, access, presence of wealth, etc.) and its populations (transhumant, nomadic, etc.). This being the case, one very quickly realises the specific nature of poverty in the north. It is a truism to say that most people in Niger are not well-endowed with riches. Tchirozérine, a department in the northern part of Niger is, in absolute terms, no poorer

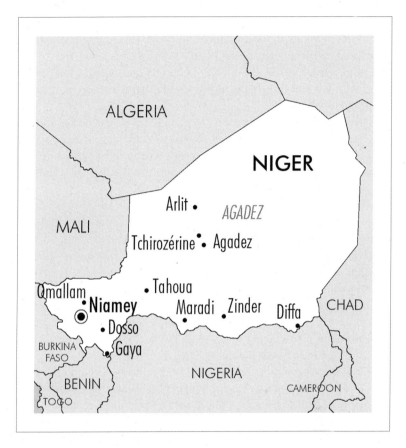

than Ouallam.[3] However, the difference is that someone living in Tchiro-zérine is poor but surrounded by wealth, and that makes all the difference. For this reason, his poverty is all the more unbearable for him.

Thirdly, the delay in implementing the recommended measures of the 1995 Peace Agreement has frustrated many.

External sources
The external sources are related to the geostrategic interest of the Sahara, on the one hand, and to a renewed recognition of the highly strategic nature of uranium, on the other.

The north of Niger forms part of the vast Sahara Desert linking Sudan in the east with Mauritania in the west. This immense and little populated territory right in the heart of Africa constitutes one of the last mining reserves in the world, hence its geostrategic interest to those regional and non-African powers that have the necessary technology to develop it.

Furthermore, the Sahara forms an ideal place in which to conduct a number of illegal activities, such as drugs trafficking, weapons trafficking, secret military training, dangerous weapons testing, etc. States, drugs/weapons traffickers and all manner of fundamentalists are interested in controlling the Sahara.

The uranium in which northern Niger abounds has always been a strategic resource for France, virtually Niger's sole partner in this regard. After a period during which uranium had become rather unfashionable on the world market, global energy needs have meant that the strategic nature of uranium has now been rediscovered for present and future years. Controlling the whole uranium cycle (exploration, exploitation, processing, etc.) has become vital to the world's economic powers, be they states or private companies. To control this resource and maintain a privileged position in Niger, the competition is stiff and willing to use destabilising strategies.

Without categorically stating that any particular foreign interest is involved, through the rebel Movement for Justice in Niger/*Mouvement des Nigériens pour la Justice* (MNJ), in weakening Niger in its ambition to make the most of this uranium-bearing context, it can be stated without risk of error that this is highly plausible.

The players: the MNJ and other frustrated people

The MNJ is the main instigator of this rebellion. It comprises essentially Tuareg people and some of its initiators apparently have links with large-scale trans-Saharan banditry. The main and official demand of the MNJ is the establishment of justice in Niger.

Other people, frustrated rightly or wrongly by the different areas of mismanagement mentioned earlier, have gradually joined the Tuareg of the MNJ. This includes soldiers thrown out during Niger's different mutinies of 2000-2001, along with other communities, particularly livestock herders, who are joining the rebel front, such as Toubou and Fulani herders.

Immediate possible derailments

This rebellion has been on-going for almost one year now. The way in which it is being handled by the Niger authorities is of concern, given the absence of any prospect of serious negotiations to bring it to an end. On the contrary, the government strives to present the rebels as a group of bandits, stateless people whom it will rapidly obliterate. Moreover, an inadequate communication strategy with regard to this rebellion tends to present the Tuareg community as collectively responsible for a situation that is aimed at impoverishing Niger and holding its independence to ransom. The persistence of such rhetoric may have terrible consequences in terms of human rights. The papers are already carrying stories of extrajudicial executions of Tuareg civilians in the conflict zone, to which the rebellion seems to respond by placing anti-tank mines in large towns such as Dosso, Tahoua, Maradi etc. A state of emergency has been declared in the Agadez area, and there is very limited reporting on the human rights situation in the area or the situation of the local population.

The 3rd annual meeting of EGGO pastoralists

The 3rd annual meeting of pastoralists/livestock herders took place at EGGO, which is a Fulani encampment to the north of Dakaro department. EGGO proved to be an excellent context in which to express and share knowledge about pastoralism – particularly on cultural and productive know-how. This annual meeting remains an important platform at which persistent prejudices about pastoralism are being overturned by what are now proven and unquestionable scientific arguments. For who could continue to objectively argue the primitiveness and backwardness of nomadic pastoralist cultures after these debates, or after the artistic and cultural displays put on by the participants?

The 3rd EGGO meeting was a place of demystification, of rich and deep debate, so much so that a modern technician would risk being completely "bowled over", "shaken" in his convictions and certainties when, for example, these pastoralist "engineers of the savannah" (for that is what they are) describe to him in great detail the indicators for choosing a good dairy cow on the market or a good sire bull, or when they explain the natural signs they use to predict droughts. After such discussions, one can but preach modesty and humility and adopt a new approach when talking to the pastoralists about all the issues affecting their environment.   ❑

Notes

1   C.f. general population census, 2001
2   Niger is the world's 5th largest producer of uranium.
3   Quallam, which is situated 100 kms to the north of Niamey, is known for its chronic food deficits.

Dr Gandou Zakara is the President of the ODLH (Organisation de Défense des Droits et Libertés Humains) and the Head of the Law Department at the University of Niamey, Niger.

MALI

The groups identifying as indigenous in Mali include the Tuareg and, to some extent, the Peul. This article focuses on the Tuareg. The Tuareg are a Berber people living in the central Sahara, spread across Mali, Niger, Burkina Faso, Algeria and Libya. In Mali, along with the Moors they probably represent around 10% of the total population of 13.5 million inhabitants. They live in the north, in the regions of Timbuktu, Gao and Kidal, which together cover 2/3 of the country's land mass of 1,241,021 km². They speak the Tamasheq language.

Traditionally, the Tuareg are nomadic pastoralists, rearing camels and small ruminants. They trade, bartering game and camel meat, along with rock salt, for dates, fabrics, tea, sugar and foodstuffs.

They can be distinguished from other Saharan peoples by their distinctive way of life and culture, in which camels play an important role.

The Constitution of Mali recognises cultural diversity and the National Pact[1] recognises the specific nature of the Tuareg regions. In addition, legislation on decentralisation (first commune-level elections took place in 1999) gives local councillors powers whilst failing, however, to transfer the resources necessary for their exercise.

Two important events marked 2007 for Mali as a whole and the Tuareg in particular: the elections and ongoing developments in the Tuareg uprising.

Local elections

On 18 March 2007 elections were held for the *Supreme Council of Local Government Authorities*, which advises the state on the running of local authorities and all local or regional developments.[2] The result was that Tuareg representation in numerical terms remained the same as previously. Its president, Oumarou Ag Mohamedou – a Tuareg - was re-elected. The heads of the Democratic Alliance of 23 May for Change (*Alliance démocratique du 23 mai pour le changement* - ADC)[3] became members: Iyad ag Ghali, head of the ADC was re-elected and Ibrahim ag Bahanga, who subsequently became head of the current rebel movement, was elected for the first time.

Presidential elections

During the Kidal region development forum held in March 2007,[4] the Head of State, President Amadou Toumani Touré, conducted an electoral campaign among the region's Tuareg. He entrusted responsibility for this campaign to ADC spokesperson, Ahmada ag Bibi, thus confirming his reconciliation with the former insurgents. The Tuareg voted for Amadou Toumani Touré *en masse*, hoping that once re-elected, having signed the Algiers Accords,[5] he would make an effort to implement them, as he had promised.

Legislative elections

The final results of the parliamentary elections, characterised by a low turnout of 32.29%, were declared by the Constitutional Court on 11 August 2007 (80% are new members). With 113 deputies out of a total of 147, the Democratic Alliance for Progress (*Alliance pour la démocratie et le progrès* - ADP) – which groups together the political parties of the presidential camp - won a resounding victory. Tuareg were elected in the same proportion as before (10 deputies out of 147). Assarid ag Imbarkawan was re-elected second vice-president of the National Assembly. The only difference was the election of Ahmada ag Bibi, ADC

spokesperson and Algiers Accords signatory. This has led many to hope that the Tuareg issue will now be a focus of discussion. In fact, for the first time in Mali's history, a deputy has dared to declare publicly – and in the capital Bamako! – that he is a rebel and proud of it and that the uprising is not a crime but a way of demanding one's rights. Speaking his mind in a manner rarely heard in the National Assembly, Ahmada ag Bibi called on the south to agree to share responsibility and resources with the inhabitants of the north![6]

The elections led to the formation of a government on 3/10/2007, with the appointment of one Tuareg as Minister for the Environment and one Moor as Minister for Culture.[7] By appointing a Tuareg as minister - Agatam ag Alhassan who is a former rebel of the Popular Front for Azawad Liberation (*Front populaire de Libération de l'Azawad*) - the President seems to be curtailing accusations of marginalisation of the Tuareg who, since the resignation on 3 May 2004 of Prime Minister Ag Hamani, have been absent from government. Despite this act of reconciliation, the Tuareg of Kidal region – the spearhead of all the uprisings - believe that the President has distanced them from government and that those Tuareg who have opted for peace will be the ones to have a say from now on.

The conclusion that can be drawn from this is that the President is attempting to encourage the emergence of a Tuareg leadership capable of competing with, if not supplanting, the Tuareg of Kidal, considered implacably rebellious. The Gao and Timbuktu Tuareg are represented at the highest level: Minister for the Environment and 2nd Vice-President of the National Assembly for the Gao region, and President of the Supreme Council of Local Government Authorities for the Timbuktu region.

The Ag Bahanga uprising

On 26 and 27 August 2007, a faction of the Democratic Alliance for Change (*Alliance Démocratique pour le Changement* - ADC), headed by Ibrahim Ag Bahanga, took 40 civilian and military hostages and demanded application of the Algiers Accords.[8] They took refuge in the mountains and laid mines on the roads. Internal mediations conducted first by Iyad ag Ghali, head of the ADC, and then by Alghabbas ag Intalla, Kidal deputy, ended in the release of some of the hostages. The Algerians and Libyans, acting as mediators, then obtained the release of a further sixteen on 29 December 2007.[9]

We will not go into the international context behind this uprising here (it has links with that of Niger and Chad) for lack of space.

As for the insurgents, they are calling for full application of the recent Algiers Accords, particularly the sections regarding withdrawal of the army from Kidal and Tinzawatan (a village through which the Algerian/Malian border passes) and development of the Kidal region. On these two points, it must be recognised that the authorities have not kept their word: army reinforcements continue to have a presence in the region; the development fund[10] established following the Kidal forum has thus far received only a few crumbs from Mali and Algeria[11] and the effect on the region is virtually nil. The moderate Tuareg argue that the country has just been through a long electoral period and that more time needs to be given to the government to apply the agreements. They uphold that whatever the grievances of the rebels are, they should have avoided using practices that are alien to their code of honour, to human and moral rights, namely, taking hostages and laying anti-personnel mines. Action should have been taken through the institutions, given that freedom of speech is effective in Mali.

The use of disproportionate means by the rebels has caused enormous damage to the image of the Tuareg. For the first time, hostage-taking, antipersonnel mines, drugs and religious extremism are affecting the Tuareg Sahara; an extremely worrying situation. Such actions are criminalized by international conventions and abhorred by the international community, and their association with the Tuareg risks causing serious damage to their image.

Planting antipersonnel mines amongst their own population - with innocent civilians as the victims – also harms the rebels' image among the Tuareg themselves, and the Kidal Tuareg risk losing their reputation among the other Tuareg of Mali. The Kidal Tuareg are now divided into those who clearly distance themselves from the uprising and those who only reluctantly do so.[12]

The ordinary Tuareg people are suffering and battling against enormous difficulties. They face the ostentatious presence of the security forces, and there is a climate of neither peace nor war, which means there are virtually no development actions taking place. Movement is being hindered by the anti-personnel mines and pastoralists live in fear of stumbling across these engines of death with their animals. More than a dozen have, in fact, already paid with their lives.[13] There has been a hike in prices and a lack of employment. Faced with this lack of jobs, young people are likely to be tempted by easy gains: the drugs and arms trade.

The greatest danger is that the infernal quartet of mines, drugs, fanaticism and arms – alien to the region until very recently – unfortunately risks taking root and distorting the Tuareg aims by casting a shadow over their legitimate demands for development and preservation of their specific cultural identity.

Future prospects

It cannot be said that the donors are exactly jostling at the doors of the development fund for the northern regions of Mali, although if this were to be organised and run by the Tuareg themselves it would create employment for the young people and dissuade them from turning to the drugs trade, smuggling or rebellion.

Although many acclaim the wisdom with which the Malian government is handling this crisis, there are worrying aspects. There is a tendency to divide the Tuareg into loyalists and rebels (the Malian army responsible for tracking down rebels is commanded by two senior officers themselves former Tuareg rebels).

The formation of a security union with the countries of the Sahel/Sahara is resonant of the abysmal security approach that prevailed in the handling of this issue under the former dictatorial regimes of Moussa Traoré, Ali Cheibou and Chadli ben Djedid. This approach seems to ignore the causes of the conflict and only address the symptoms and effects, and the Tuareg tend to be perceived as terrorists and drugs traffickers.

Finally it should be noted that Mali and Niger have just obtained funding for two large dams. In Mali, this will be at Taoussa and will enable the Tilemsi plain, between Gao and Kidal, to be irrigated over an area of more than 100 kms. Although vital for Mali, the consequences of this project will not necessarily be positive for the Tuareg since their pastureland will be reduced to the benefit of agriculture. Farmers will certainly come from other communities and the Tuareg will be invaded and, in the medium to long term, absorbed demographically.

❑

Notes

1   A pact agreed between the government of Mali and the Tuareg movement providing special status to the north of Mali. This pact allows for an interregional structure and regional assembly responsible for managing all development issues.

2   The *Supreme Council of Local Government Authorities* is one of the eight institutions mentioned in the Constitution of Mali. It is an advisory body to the government on local government issues.

3   "The Democratic Alliance of 23 May for Change" is a Tuareg rebel movement that instigated a rebellion on the 23 May 2006, and which signed the Algiers Accords with the Malian government on 4 July 2006.

4   This is a forum for the development of the northern regions of Mali. The establishment of this forum was part of the Algiers Accords signed between the government of Mali and the ADC and it is aimed at mobilizing Mali's development partners to contribute to the development of the Tuareg regions. The forum was held on 23-24 March 2007 in Kidal and adopted a ten-year programme for the development of the northern regions of Mali.

5   The Algiers Accords signed on 4/7/2006 between the Malian government and the ADC following the uprising of the Kidal Tuareg on 23 May of that same year stipulate, among other things, the organisation of a forum on development in the northern regions of Mali, the withdrawal of the army from urban areas of Kidal, the reintegration of deserted Tuareg and the creation of special security units made up primarily of Tuareg with a joint command, along with the creation of a regional council in Kidal to supervise the whole process. A development fund was also anticipated.

6   Statement by deputy Ahmada ag Bibi at the workshop on security, stability and development in the area of the Sahel/Sahara organised in Bamako on 30 November and 1 December 2007 by the Republican Democratic Front (*Front pour la démocratie et la République* - FDR); in "*Le Républicain*" newspaper dated 03/12/07, at http://www.maliweb.net/news.php?CID=179&act=cat

7   Press release from the Council of Ministers dated 21 November 2007; in the national daily "*l'ESSOR*" dated 22/11/2007, published by the Malian Press and Advertising Agency (*Agence malienne de presse et de publicité* - AMAP).

8   According to Hamma ag Sidahmed, spokesperson for the rebellion; in the Algerian daily newspaper "*Alwatan*" dated 9 September 2007

9   Reuters, 29/12/2007 at 22h 05 GMT

10 Point 7 of the Algiers Accord provides for the: "creation of a development and socio-economic rehabilitation fund for civilians, particularly young people affected by the events of 23 May 2006, without excluding all other young people from the Kidal region."

11 1.75 million US dollars, see the visit of the Malian President to Algiers 24/11/2007, at www.aljazeera.net

12 Press statement by Ahmada ag Bibi, in "*l'Indépendant*" dated 31/08/2007 at www.maliweb

13 Ten civilians killed by a mine in the north of Mali, see AFP dated 30 August 2007

Mohamed Khattali is a lawyer. He is Secretary General of the Association Synergie et Action in Mali and independent expert member of the Working Group on Indigenous Populations/Communities of the African Commission on Human and Peoples' Rights.

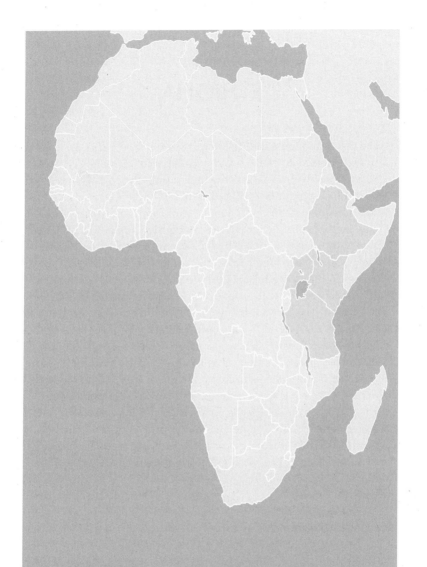

THE HORN OF AFRICA &
EAST AFRICA

ETHIOPIA

The pastoral population of Ethiopia makes up roughly 12-15% of the country's total estimated population of 80 million. These people inhabit almost the entire lowlands of the country, which constitutes around 61% of its landmass. The pastoral population is heterogeneous in its ethnic composition and social structure, having some larger ethnic groups such as the Afars, Oromos and Somalis with well over two million pastoral people each. The rest are Omotic pastoral groups such as the Hamer, Dassenech, Nygagaton and Erbore, and the Nuer and other groups in the western lowlands. Livestock production, trading and *take-a-chance crop farming* (subsistence rain-fed farming) constitute the pastoral livelihood systems. The pastoral communities have long been neglected and under pressure from successive governments, including the current one, to change their livelihood systems to crop cultivation. Large tracts of pastoralist areas have been converted to commercial farms and national parks from which the community has not benefited. Although the Federal Democratic Republic of Ethiopia Constitution (FDRE, 1994) recognizes pastoralism, there is no clear policy to protect the rights of pastoralists in Ethiopia.

Key pastoral events

The 9th Ethiopian Pastoralist Day (EPD[1]) was celebrated in the National Assembly Hall of the capital, Addis Ababa, on 25 January 2007. The key message of the day was *More Commitment for Good Governance and Sustainable Pastoralist Development in the New Ethiopian Millennium.* The EPD provided a forum for pastoralists to discuss and debate key issues and pass resolutions, and a forum for all pastoral groups to have face-

to-face discussions with the Prime Minister of the FDRE. This is the second time that the EPD has been organized since the government endorsed it as a national day in 2006. The government was persuaded to recognize the EPD after great advocacy and lobbying efforts.

The pastoralists have passed a number of resolutions at previous EPDs, some of which the government has addressed. Key issues such as the establishment of a federal-level pastoral institution such as a Ministry or Commission; the development and implementation of land use plans suitable for pastoralists; facilitation of the establishment of Pastoral Councils; and acceptance and promotion of livestock as collateral for bank loans have, however, received less attention.

Following the EPDs, the pastoralist advocacy organization, the *Pastoralist Forum Ethiopia,* has organized an annual national conference on pastoral development. The Fourth National Conference on Pastoral Development in Ethiopia was organized under the theme of Millennium Development Goals (MDGs) and Pastoral Development: *Opportunities and Challenges in the New Ethiopian Millennium.* The conference was attended by more than 160 people, of whom more than 40% were pastoral community representatives. These key representatives of Ethiopia's pastoral players discussed the status of pastoral development in relation to achieving the MDGs. It was stressed that, with the present level of development in pastoralist areas, fulfilment of the MDGs would be doubtful. For instance, aggregate health and water coverage figures in pastoral areas were reported at 40% and 25% respectively[2], whereas the national water coverage is above 50%. In this sense, there should be a mechanism that can bring the pastoralists' social development level to at least that experienced at national level. Between 28 November and 2 December 2007, pastoralists from the Horn of Africa and their partners gathered in the Somali region of Ethiopia to discuss the current situation and sustainable futures for pastoralists in Ethiopia and in the wider sub-region. The main point of discussion was the extent to which pastoralism is sustainable. The sustainability of pastoralism has been well documented in a research document.[3] The gathering was said to be the biggest in the Horn of Africa, accommodating 550 participants.

During 2007, civil society organizations continued to organize for the advancement of the pastoralist cause. The Afar Pastoral Development Forum (APDF) and the Somali Pastoral Development Forum (SPDF) were established, each with between 20 and 30 member NGOs. The two institutions have received funding from the EU and are now implementing capacity-building activities. The Eastern African Pastoralist Elder Council was also established in 2007, with the aim of lobbying decision makers to pay more attention to pastoralism and pastoral development issues. The Council has members from Ethiopia, Kenya, Uganda and Tanzania.

All these platforms have given the pastoralists and their partners increased possibilities for advancing the rights of pastoralists, and the media are increasingly covering events organized by pastoralists.

Socio-economic development

The country's biggest (US$ 750 million[4]) irrigation scheme for sugarcane plantations is underway in the pastoral area of Afar region. The

scheme will irrigate about 80,000 hectares and three new sugar factories will be established in the area. There are speculations that pastoralists are expected to benefit from the huge investment by developing
into sugarcane growers for the three sugar factories.

However, the sugar cane plantations and the sugar factories in
Wonji and Metahara, basically a pastoral area, have never benefited
pastoral communities, and the Kereyus and Afars have long complained about this. Unless the current government changes its approach to include the pastoralists' interests, there will be no difference
from the past regimes when it comes to development strategies. The
"development" strategy for pastoralists is still the same old policy of
the two former regimes, namely sedentarization. Due to a lack of continued consultation and participatory planning, it is therefore suspect-
ed that the new schemes will not benefit pastoral communities. Hence,
aggravation of poverty for pastoralists is likely.

The government is intent on settling pastoralists and is actively
working towards this. In the first phase of the sugarcane plantation
scheme in Afar, 700 pastoralist householders from the Somali pastoral
areas are reported to have been settled on 1,000 ha of irrigable land
(out of a total of 6,600 hectares planned for the purpose). As stated in
government policies/strategies, pastoral development is usually
geared towards the sedentarization of pastoralists. The following paragraph reflects this fact:

*Settlement in drought areas is solely a change of place of settlement. It is
taking a farmer from a place where he used to handle agriculture in a
sedentary base to a place where there is better rain and land and letting
him continue the same practice. However, settlement in pastoralist areas
is more than just a change of place; it is a change of life style (underlined
by the author). It is transferring a person who used to be engaged in nomadic livestock husbandry to a sedentary farmer. Since the pastoralist
does not have any tangible knowledge about sedentary farming, settling
a pastoralist is also a task requiring a difficult and complex task teaching
and training the pastoralist from the very beginning about sedentary
farming. It will require a major cultural change. Therefore, to make the
settlement program a success, it requires wide and basic training on sedentary farming on the one hand, and, on the other, by implementing the*

settlement step by step, developing a system in which the previous settler can introduce new settlers about sedentary farming (Ministry of Information Press and Audiovisual Department, 2001 pp79)5.

Over the last few years, the multilateral donors, the World Bank, IFAD and the European Union, have paid increasing attention to pastoral development. This is reflected in the fact that US\$ 50 million has been invested by the first two in livelihood, risk management and community investment fund programs, and EUR 5.3 million by the latter in pastoral capacity building and food security programs.   ❑

Notes

1   The EPD is a multi-faceted advocacy instrument for pastoralists and their partners to advance their right and a lively forum through which to lobby decision makers to pay more attention to the plight of pastoralists.
2   Performance report on Pastoral Areas presented on the 9th Ethiopian Pastoralist Day. Ministry of Federal Affairs. Jan. 2007, Addis Ababa.
3   **Stephen Devereux, 2006**: Vulnerable Livelihoods in Somali Region, Ethiopia. IDS Research Report 57. Institute of Development Studies 2006, UK.
4   Performance report on Pastoral Areas presented in the 9th Ethiopian Pastoralist Day. Ministry of Federal Affairs. Jan. 2007, Addis Ababa.
5   The Government of the Federal Democratic Republic of Ethiopia Rural Development Policies, Strategies and Instruments, 2003. Draft translation [From Amharic language]. Ministry of Information Press and Audiovisual Department. Addis Ababa.

Tezera Getahun Tiruneh is the Executive Director of the Pastoralist Forum Ethiopia (PFE), a local umbrella NGO with 27 members, working on pastoral advocacy, networking, coordination and capacity building. Since his graduation in 1998 from Alemaya University of Agriculture (now Haramaya University) with a MSc. in Agriculture and Animal Production, he has been engaged in various areas of development and advocacy work in different NGOs and government institutions. His areas of competency include advocacy and lobbying for the rights of marginalized social groups, project team building and management, and design and management of integrated rural/pastoral development.

KENYA

The communities who identify as indigenous peoples in Kenya are mainly pastoralists and hunter-gatherers as well as a number of small farming communities.[1] These include, among others, the Ogiek, Sengwer, Yaaku, Watta, Maasai, Samburu, Elmolo, Turkana, Rendille, Borana, Somali, Gabra, Pokot and Endorois. While pastoralists mainly occupy arid and semi-arid lands and make up approximately 25% of the population, hunter-gatherers occupy pockets of forested areas and have low population statistics. They all face land and resource tenure insecurity, poor service delivery and low political representation. Their situation seems to get worse each year, with increasing competition over resources in their areas. There is no specific legislation governing indigenous peoples in Kenya.

Frustration over elections

The year 2007 seemed like a long campaign period for Kenya and it witnessed a number of policies and programmes being passed mainly for the purpose of gaining political mileage. The land, forest and wildlife policies were rushed through as a way of showcasing the government's performance and wooing voters whose livelihoods are dependent on such natural resources.

Ethnic conflicts that often centre on competition for resources assumed political overtones, resulting in evictions and the arming and disarming of different communities. Certain communities were evicted from their ancestral lands for the purposes of reducing opposition elements in those areas. By the time the elections were held, most indigenous communities had made their stand and decided to support the opposition, citing failure by the present government to deliver on the promises of five years ago when it took office. Topping the list of such promises was the delivery of a new constitution which promised devolution and decentralization, two items that indigenous peoples believe will assure them rights to resources and some degree of self governance.

The voting process went off quite peacefully. Indigenous peoples received the initial results with excitement and merriment since all indications showed that the opposition party was leading in votes and in the number of parliamentary candidates. However, when it became apparent that the results of the presidential elections were being manipulated to suit the incumbent (the announcements were aired live on television), tension and frustration ensued. This reached a peak when the sitting president Kibaki was declared the winner and hastily sworn in during a closed ceremony at the State House. In a matter of minutes from the time of the swearing in of the president, people allied to the government side started celebrating the victory while others, afraid of reprisals, started retreating in haste. Others were attacked and their houses burnt. Ethnic conflicts, chaos and violence continue in some parts of the country to the present, the consequences of which are more than 500 deaths and more than half a million internally displaced persons.[2]

Policy issues

On a policy level, the government initiated adjustments in key areas such as land, forest, wildlife and environmental conservation, all of which have a bearing on indigenous peoples' livelihood systems. Changes to the forest policy are geared towards encouraging indigenous peoples' participation in forest management and utilization of forest resources, provided they form management associations. This pre-requisite may, however, hinder indigenous peoples' participation since they exist as communities and the concept of associations is strange to them. The wildlife policy is directly detrimental to indigenous peoples because it entails plans to further alienate indigenous peoples' land in order to create what are called wildlife migratory corridors. However, the year also recorded some positive developments for indigenous communities. K-Rep Bank, which is a micro-finance in-

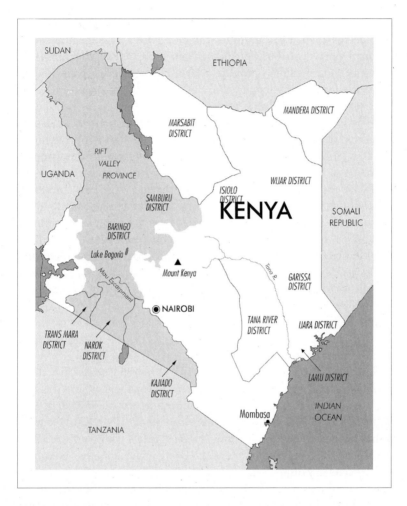

stitution, initiated a credit facility to help pastoralists while the government initiated a livestock vaccination programme following an outbreak of livestock disease.

Constitutional review process

At the beginning of the year a Multi-Sectoral Review Committee, which had spearheaded talks on the constitutional review process, met to work out strategies on how to reclaim control of the exercise, which had been stalled. The committee came up with a package of essential reforms that were to be implemented before the general election. These reforms were meant to provide a level playing field for all political players. However, by the time the elections came, the government had still not heeded the calls for reform.

The main subject that divided the competing political sides was the issue of devolution of power and resources (known in the local Swahili language as *majimbo*). Whereas the government was opposed to *majimbo*, the opposition used it as a platform to woo voters, especially among marginalized and impoverished indigenous communities.[3] Indigenous communities, who have not benefited from an over-centralized government, favored this system of equitable distribution of political power and wealth and voted overwhelmingly for the opposition party as a result. The leader of the opposition, Raila Odinga, included devolution in the manifesto of his party, the "Orange Democratic Movement" (ODM), under the slogan of "fairly we share, together we prosper".[4]

Land policy issues
Relatively early in 2007, the final draft of the national land policy document was finalized and serialized in the newspapers, where the various chapters were outlined, and a symposium was planned to present the draft to all stakeholders for their comments. The draft generated numerous reactions from various interest groups. Those who resented it claimed that it resembled the Wako Draft, which was rejected during the 2005 referendum.[5] Some Associations of Land Owners also had issues with the draft, including the reduction of lease periods from 999 years to 99; land productivity taxes; increasing squatters' rights; rescinding of bank rights over matrimonial properties; confiscation of idle land and maximum acreage limits. Indigenous peoples are positive about the draft policy as it touches on important aspects, such as providing for communal land ownership and addressing the thorny issue of historical injustices regarding land.

The government defended the draft policy on the grounds that it was not legislation but simply a framework of principles and values

that aims to provide guidelines as to how to review existing legislation, institutional structures and administrative mechanisms for better
land administration and management. The document was also said to
be a product of the best ever partnership in the country between the
public sector, civil society community-based organisations and the private sector in terms of developing a policy framework.

The Children's Act

The passing of the Children's Act is expected to provide some protection to indigenous girls, given that some retrogressive cultural practices still hamper their progress. Referring to this Act, the Speaker of
the National Assembly (himself a Laikipia Maasai) told chiefs from his
community to abandon retrogressive cultural practices that violate the
rights of the girl-child, including early marriage and female genital
mutilation.[6]

NEPAD report

During 2007, a report by the African Peer Review Mechanism (APRM)
of the New Partnership for Africa's Development (NEPAD) indicated
that increasing numbers of Kenyans cannot access proper housing, nu-
trition, clean water and services, all of which would stimulate economic growth. This is despite government efforts to improve the economy.
This situation is worse for indigenous peoples, who are mostly marginalized from national development circles. The negative effects are
most severe among the landless, subsistence farmers, unskilled workers, female-headed households and pastoralists in arid and semi-arid
areas. Pastoralists suffer more from the effects of clashes and they were
singled out as a socio-economic group that has not benefited whilst
other Kenyans were "enjoying an economic boom with great improve-
ments in health care, agriculture, education and infrastructure".[7] This
emerged in a UNDP report on the damning disparities between the
richest and poorest regions of Kenya, showing that pastoralists are
likely to remain marginalized if their development concerns are not
addressed.

UN Declaration on the Rights of Indigenous Peoples: Kenya abstains

Kenya became one of three countries in Africa to abstain from voting on the UN Declaration on the Rights of Indigenous Peoples in September 2007. While Kenya's position on the concept of indigenous peoples has always been negative,[8] many indigenous peoples felt that the fact that it did not vote against the Declaration demonstrates a softening of its position. Two reasons could have contributed to this change. Firstly, the amount of lobbying undertaken by indigenous peoples locally and internationally, facilitated by IWGIA. Secondly, the fact that Kenya received a grant of over Ksh 100 million (about US$1.48 million, ed.) from the World Bank at the end of 2006 with the condition that it implement a well-crafted *Indigenous Peoples' Planning Framework*, the focus of which was to ensure that "free, prior and informed consultation" was carried out for any project affecting indigenous peoples. By accepting the grant, it is possible that voting against the Declaration became untenable. It is important to note that neither the Ministry of Foreign Affairs nor the Kenya mission in New York were aware of the existence of the framework document prior to the lobbying even though the framework was implemented under the auspices of the Office of the President. This serves to underscore the significance and timeliness of the lobbying effort.

Implementation of ICERD

Kenya has also been discussing the implementation of ICERD (the International Convention on the Elimination of Racial Discrimination) this year, focussing purely on the discrimination faced by indigenous peoples in the country. One seminar was organized by the Ministry of Justice and Constitutional Affairs under the auspices of the United Nations Development Programme (UNDP) and required the involvement of government in collaboration with civil society organizations. The seminar was followed by a meeting to discuss preliminary findings. While the seminar went smoothly, the second meeting was dominated by government officials whose agenda seemed to derail the discussions, which ended rather acrimoniously. The process is still ongoing and positive results are expected in the end.

Ill Chamus win round one of another case against the state

The Ill Chamus Maasai, residing in Baringo district, have sued the government over the alleged introduction of a weed known as *Proposis juliflora*, which has negatively affected the health of their livestock[9]. The weed was nicknamed "Mathenge" after the officer who supervised the introduction of the weed. In 2006, the same community won a case in which it demanded a constituency to cater for its political representation in parliament. The Electoral Commission (ECK) was directed by the court to grant this but it has yet to be implemented.

Endorois evict mining company

The Endorois community, living on the shores of Lake Bogoria in Rift Valley province, has been battling it out with a mining company owned partly by the son of the former president and other investors. The mine produces precious rubies but is causing pollution to the environment, the livestock and people. The Endorois say that more than 1,000 animals have died from mysterious diseases and people are complaining of coughs and stomach upsets. The Endorois have complained to the authorities many a time but little is done. So, one day in April 2007, they went and stormed the mine and evicted the miners. In the mayhem that ensued, 34 people were arrested and charged with violent robbery, which is punishable by hanging. Of those arrested, 32 were later released with no charge and the cases of the remaining two are still in court. The company took the community to court claiming trespass and citing rights derived from the Mining Act. The case is still pending.

Ethnic clashes

The most serious violent conflicts this year were witnessed in the northern part of the country, involving the Pokot pastoralists and their neighbours the Samburu, Turkana, Ilchamus and Sengwer. According to Isaac Todokin, who is himself a Pokot, the Samburu and Pokot had "buried spears" in 1940s, which is an indication that they were not to raid or fight each other. But in 2007, following a shortage of water and grazing in their areas, and the availability of guns from their Ugandan cousins, the Karamojong, the Pokot decided to raid their neighbours.[10]

Mt. Elgon Clashes

The Mt. Elgon (an area on the border of Kenya and Uganda) clashes have continued throughout the past two years and are continuing still. The clashes have involved the agricultural Sabaot people and their neighbours, including the Ogiek, who have experienced the brunt of the fighting. The Sabaot have taken up arms against their neighbours as a way of defending their right to what they perceive as their land, which was initially taken away by the British and never returned to them. The renewed clashes in 2007 were sparked by the revocation of land allocations under Phase Three of the Cheppyuk Settlement Scheme, which was hived off from the Mt. Elgon forest in 1971 to resettle the Ogiek but ended up being settled by the Soi community. The revocation was meant to ensure that the Ogiek got more land than the Soi, as originally planned, but the Soi were opposed to this, sparking clashes between the two communities. In 2006, when the government directed that fresh allocations be undertaken, violence broke out. The Sabaot people, comprising the majority population in the area, opposed the allocation and took up arms under the banner of the Sabaot Land Defense Force (SLDF).

The violence has so far left many people dead, 5,000 displaced, 16 schools closed and property destroyed. According to Peter Cheruyiot, himself an Ogiek, the land that the Sabaot are laying claim to is part of the Mt. Elgon Forest "which had always been their (Ogiek) ancestral territory...there has been an attempt to re-write history to favour the new claimants". Since the beginning of the conflict, seven hundred members of the Ogiek community have been killed. Following the disputed election results, the General Service Unit (GSU- a Kenyan para-military unit) was reported to have attacked villagers and raped four Ogiek girls while other communities also attacked them and burnt their houses, as well as one of their public transport vehicles.[11] Now roads are blocked and people are going hungry for lack of food.

Clashes in Tana River District

Clashes in Tana River district have been ongoing for decades, pitting pastoralists against farming communities due to competition over land and land-based resources (water and grazing). Pastoralists are realizing that they are losing all their land and resources and are increasingly getting poorer. In most cases, the conflicts involve armed bandits from both sides. As in many other places, the year 2007 witnessed politically-instigated violence whereby politicians sought to create conflicts that would lead to the eviction or flight of groups or communities who were likely to be opposed to them.[12]

Arming and disarming of pastoralists for political gain

The Samburu, Turkana, Laikipia and Ilchamus pastoralists have all experienced harassment from Pokot raiders, allegedly with government support. According to Councillor Lengerded from Samburu district, the whole conflict centres around politics, insofar as the Pokot are supporting the government while the other pastoralist communities are supporting the opposition. This has earned the Pokot guns and ammunition with which to raid and subdue their neighbours. This was happening during a time when a disarmament exercise was apparently ongoing among other neighbouring communities. According to the same councillor, a total of 200 Samburu people were killed during 2007 and more than 20,000 head of livestock were raided. He adds that, "two days before elections, the Pokot were given guns and ammunition... and now one of their members has been given a Ministerial post".[13] While the government has been urged to find a solution to the problem, few people believe that it is capable of doing anything to end the conflict, which has contributed to the extreme impoverishment of pastoralists in the area.[14]

Rift Valley Fever

The outbreak of Rift Valley Fever continued from 2006 and devastated livestock all over the country. This is a contagious and fatal viral disease that can also be passed on to humans from livestock through mosquito bites or contact with the products or fluids of infected animals. Since the outbreak started in the northern parts of the country, the government has initiated a campaign to vaccinate 2 million livestock in the six districts of Garissa, Ijara, Wajir, Tana River, Lamu and Isiolo. The outbreak of the fever has affected trade in livestock as well as hides and skins.[15] Quarantine regulations were imposed on livestock movement and this brought livestock trading to a halt, making it difficult for pastoralists to access goods and services.

Kenya Meat Commission

The year also witnessed the re-opening of the Kenya Meat Commission,[16] which had been closed for nearly two decades. For the first six months, however, it was only government Agriculture Development Corporation farms that were permitted to sell their livestock to the Kenya Meat Commission. Its re-opening raises the possibility of exporting Kenyan livestock products to Mauritius and the Middle East,[17] which would offer better trading possibilities to indigenous pastoralists, and hence decreased poverty.   ❑

Notes

1   See the report of the Working Group on Indigenous Peoples/Communities of
     the African Commission on Human and Peoples' Rights.

2   This is an estimate of the BBC on 12 January 2008. Local estimates are more than 600,000. See also the Standard of 12 January 2008.

3   **Ng'etich, Peter, 2007:** Federal system to be adopted by June: Ruto. *Daily Nation,* 4 October 2007. **ODM advertisement, 2007:** It's time for the truth. *Daily Nation,* 2 November 2007. **Adan, Jibril, 2007:** ODM changes tune on majimbo system. *Standard,* 1 November.

4   **Odinga, Raila, 2007:** Fairly we share, together we prosper. I *Mabadiliko Times in the ODM manifesto.*

5   The people of Kenya had, through debate and discussion at a constitutional review conference whose sessions were held at the Bomas of Kenya, come up with the famous Bomas Draft Constitution. However, the government of Kenya mutilated it through the office of the Attorney General, resulting in the Wako Draft (the Attorney General is called Amos Wako hence the label Wako Draft).

6   **Ratemo, James, 2007:** Girls to undergo pain, misery in FGM season. *Daily Nation,* 10 December 2007. Also personal communication between the author and the Speaker of the National Assembly.

7   **Epat, L. Jordan, 2007:** Pastoralists have little to cheer about . *Daily Nation,* 29 March 2007. (Quoting from the UNDP report released in the same month).

8   Kenya's negative position vis-à-vis the concept of indigenous peoples is demonstrated by its refusal to allow the Working Group on Indigenous Populations of the African Commission on Human and Peoples' Rights to conduct a mission or an awareness-raising seminar in the country despite repeated requests. Its position has always been 'we are all indigenous' as stated during meetings with the Ministry of Justice and Constitutional Affairs and at the Kenya embassy in New York.

9   **Nation Correspondent, 2007:** State is to blame for weed, says Attorney General. *Daily Nation,* 17 July 2007.

10 Interview with Isaac Todokin 11 January 2008.

11 Interview with Peter Cheruyiot, 19 January 2008.

12 Standard 7 June 2007.

13 Interview with Councillor Lengerded 9 January 2008.

14 **Mkawale, Steve and Laboso, Solomon, 2007:** Samburu raid death toll now increases to 20. *Standard,* 9 July 2007.

15 **Bii, Barnaba, 2007:** Butcheries hit by fear of Meat: Outbreak of fever affected trade in livestock as well as hides and skins. *Daily Nation,* 28 February 2007.

16 The Kenya Meat Commission (KMC) is a government livestock-slaughter factory intended to provide a market to livestock herders, including pastoralists, as an outlet for surplus livestock. The management of KMC is charged with the purchase and slaughter of livestock and the marketing of livestock products.

17 Standard 29 March 2007, Op cit.

Naomi Kipuri is a Maasai from Kenya and an anthropologist by training. She is a human rights activist and director of the Arid Lands Institute.

UGANDA

Indigenous peoples in Uganda include the traditional hunter/ gatherer Batwa and Benet communities and pastoralist groups such as the Karamojong. They are not recognized as indigenous by the government.

The Karamojong are transhumant pastoralists who live in the neglected Karamoja region of north-eastern Uganda. They number around 955,245[1] people, out of a total population of approximately 26 million. The Benet, who number around 20,000 people, also live in the north-eastern part of the country. They are former hunter/gatherers. The 6,700 or so Batwa who live primarily in the south-western region of Uganda are also former hunter/gatherers.[2] They were dispossessed of their ancestral land when the Bwindi and Mgahinga forests were gazetted as national parks in 1991.[3]

The Constitution has no express protection for indigenous peoples but provides for affirmative action in favour of marginalized groups. The Land Act of 1998 and the National Environment Statute of 1995 protect customary interests in land and traditional uses of forests. However these laws also authorize the government to exclude human activities in any forest area by declaring it a protected forest, thus nullifying the customary land rights of indigenous peoples.[4]

Peace and security

The cessation of hostilities between the Lord's Resistance Army (LRA) and the Ugandan government in northern Uganda was largely respected throughout 2007 while peace negotiations continued. The truce entered into in August 2006 expired on 28 February 2007 but

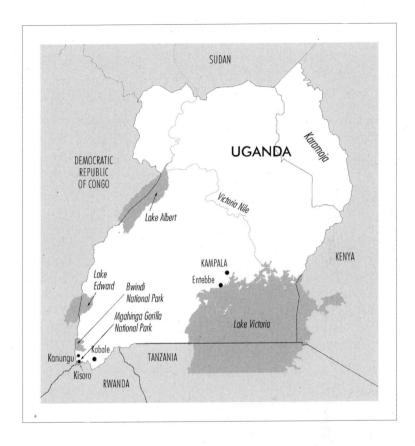

was renewed periodically over the course of 2007, with the current ceasefire due to expire at the end of February 2008. Agreements were reached on key outstanding matters including accountability – with both sides now seeking to achieve an internal solution rather than having the case proceed to the International Criminal Court where war crimes charges are still outstanding – and the need to find lasting solutions to the underlying causes of the conflict. The parties are now working to finalize a comprehensive deal to finally put to rest over two decades of fighting. While around 230,000 internally displaced Ugandans returned to their villages in northern Uganda in 2006, there were still an estimated 1.2 million living in camps in early 2007. The number of Internally Displaced Persons (IDPs) – 80 percent of whom are women and children – was reduced to approximately 900,000 by the end of June 2007.[5]

Uganda also continued to be susceptible to the instability in neighbouring DRC, with more than 10,000 Congolese fleeing eastern DRC into south-west Uganda in August and another 13,000 in October 2007.

Financial mismanagement

At least two international funding agencies cut funding to Uganda in 2007 over concerns of financial mismanagement, adding even more negative attention to the already marred reputation of the government, which has had a number of financial scandals involving senior government officials exposed in recent years. In early 2007, the Global Fund to Fight AIDS, Tuberculosis and Malaria declined to provide continued funding of US$16 million to Uganda because of concerns over financial mismanagement[6] and, in May, the World Bank's International Development Association (IDA) reduced its support to poverty alleviation programmes over similar concerns.[7]

Deforestation

Concerns were raised in 2007 over the rate of deforestation taking place in the country which, if not reversed, could lead to the loss of all forest cover within 50 years. Despite this, the government made plans to turn over 7,000 hectares of the 32,000 ha Mabira Forest Reserve near Kampala to sugar cane plantations.[8] After months of protest from environmental groups, the plans were dropped in October 2007.

Human Rights

Human rights advocates secured a victory in a case brought before Uganda's Constitutional Court in April 2007 to challenge the country's adultery laws, which discriminated against women by making the practice illegal for them while seemingly condoning it for men. A similar case was subsequently launched in 2007 to challenge the legality of female genital mutilation (FGM).[9]

Uganda commenced a process of review of its democracy and political governance, economic governance, corporate governance and socioeconomic development under the New Partnership for Africa's Development's (NEPAD's) African Peer Review Mechanism[10] in 2007, with a country self-assessment being launched in February and nationwide consultations subsequently being held with various sectors of society. The Batwa, through their community-based organisation, the United Organisation for Batwa Development in Uganda (UOBDU), made submissions on the human rights problems they face, including in respect of land, housing and education. They also participated in the subsequent validation meetings on the findings of the country self-assessment, which were held with stakeholders during late 2007. An important recommendation for indigenous populations, including the Batwa that came out of the country self-assessment was that Uganda should "compensate minority groups that had been deprived of their ancestral land".[11] This recommendation, if implemented, could have enormous impact for the Batwa who were deprived of all of their ancestral lands in Uganda when national parks were established on them without consultation or compensation. The recommendation does not, however, discuss restitution of those lands, which is a right and a remedy under international law. The APRM process will continue during 2008.

The African Commission on Human and Peoples' Rights issued its Concluding Observations on the November 2006 examination of Uganda's second periodic report, in which it stated that it was "concerned by the exploitation, the discrimination and the marginalization of indigenous populations" and recommended that Uganda "ensure that the rights of indigenous people and socially disadvantaged are respected".[12]

The Equal Opportunities Committee, a standing committee of Parliament in Uganda that was established in 2005, undertook a study of the Batwa in May 2007 and its report and recommendations are expected to be presented to Parliament and made public in 2008.

The United Organisation for Batwa Development in Uganda (UOBDU), the main community-based organisation representing the indigenous Batwa of south-west Uganda, continued its work supporting the

Batwa in the districts of Kisoro, Kabale and Kanungu. With a donation from UK-based Rainforest Concern and technical assistance from British NGO Forest Peoples Programme, UOBDU purchased 50 acres of private forested land adjacent to the Bwindi Impenetrable National Park, former homeland of the Batwa, which will be used by the Batwa according to a management plan currently being developed after consultations with the beneficiary communities. UOBDU continued to provide agricultural, education and housing support for the Batwa along with capacity building programmes in collaboration with a variety of local and international organisations. In an attempt to increase the voice of the Batwa in local affairs, two Batwa were selected to participate in local council meetings at the sub-county level.

Overall, the situation of the Batwa remains largely unchanged in Uganda. Although civil society efforts are underway, in collaboration with government agencies, to secure basic subsistence land for the landless Batwa, their rights to their ancestral lands remain unrecognised. Participation by the Batwa in local and national affairs remains virtually non-existent. Education and literacy rates among Batwa are among the lowest in the country, and housing and sanitation conditions remain appalling. Despite existing legal frameworks for the protection and promotion of human rights, including land and socio-economic rights, the government of Uganda took very few concrete steps in 2007 to meaningfully implement its legal and human rights obligations in respect of the Batwa people.

Commonwealth Meeting

From 23-25 November 2007, Uganda played host to the 20th Commonwealth Heads of Government Meeting (CHOGM), with 48 countries represented.[13] Among many other things, a *Commonwealth Climate Change Action Plan* was adopted during the meetings,[14] in the lead up to the December climate change meetings that subsequently took place in Bali, Indonesia. With the support of Minority Rights Group International, five Batwa men and five Batwa women attended the meetings, along with other indigenous and minority groups including the Benet and Basongora, and presentations were made primarily on land rights issues.   ❏

Notes

1   According to the final results of the September 2002 National Population and Housing Census, Kotido District has a population of 605,322 (302,206 males and 303,116 females). Moroto District has a population of 194,773 (98,145 males and 96,628 females). Nakapiripirit has a population of 155,150 (78,284 males and 76,866 females) (See http://www.ubos.org/preliminaryfullreport.pdf).

2   The Batwa are also known as Twa.

3   **United Organisation of Batwa Development in Uganda (UOBDU), 2004**: *Report about Batwa data.* August 2004, Uganda, p.3.

4   Land Act (1998), Articles 2 and 44; National Environment Statute (1995), Article 46.

5   Information on developments in the peace process was obtained from various news reports from the IRIN news service.

6   IRIN news service, 'Uganda: Global Fund declines grant as questions linger over financial mismanagement', 13 March 2007

7   IRIN news service, 'Uganda: Poverty funds cut over management concerns', 30 May 2007

8   IRIN news service, 'Uganda: Alarm over high rate of deforestation', 23 March 2007.

9   IRIN news service, 'Uganda: Women petition court to outlaw FGM', 30 April 2007.

10   See http://www.nepad.org/aprm/.

11   APRM National Commission (Uganda), *African Peer Review Mechanism (APRM) Country Self-Assessment Validation Process; Validation of the Uganda Country Self-Assessment Report (CSAR) and Plan of Action (POA)*, September 2007, section G.1.

12   African Commission on Human and Peoples' Rights, *Concluding Observations of the African Commission on the 2nd Periodic Report of the Republic of Uganda*, paras. 23 and 34.

13   For detailed information on CHOGM see http://www.thecommonwealth.org/subhomepage/33250/chogm/

14   See   http://www.thecommonwealth.org/document/34293/35144/173014/climateactionplan.htm.

Treva Braun holds a Bachelor of Laws (LL.B) degree from the University of British Columbia in Canada and a Masters in International Human Rights Law (LL.M) from University of Essex in the UK. Her principal areas of interest and expertise are indigenous issues and gender. She currently lives in London and works as Coordinator of the Africa Legal and Human Rights Programme at Forest Peoples Programme.

TANZANIA

Tanzania is estimated to have a total of 125 – 130 ethnic groups, falling mainly into the four racial categories of Bantu, Cushite, Nilo-Hamite and San. While there may be more ethnic groups that identify themselves as indigenous peoples, four groups have been organising themselves and their struggles around the concept and movement of indigenous peoples. The four groups are the hunter-gatherer Akie and Hadzabe, and the pastoralist Barabaig and Maasai. Population estimates[1] put the Maasai in Tanzania at 430,000, the Datoga group to which the Barabaig belongs at 87,978, the Hadzabe at 1,000[2] and the Akie (Ndorobo) at 5,268.

While the livelihoods of such groups are diverse, they all experience similar features in relation to their attachment to the land, distinct identities, vulnerability and non-dominance. They experience similar problems in relation to resource tenure insecurity, poverty and inadequate political representation. While there is no specific national policy or legislation on indigenous peoples *per se* in Tanzania, a number of policies, strategies and programmes are, however, continuously being developed that do not reflect the interests of the indigenous peoples in terms of access to land and natural resources, basic social services and justice, resulting in a deteriorating and increasingly hostile political environment for both pastoralists and hunter-gatherers.

Policy developments

The Environmental Management Act (EMA)[3] 2004, which was passed by Parliament in November 2004 and authorized by the President in February 2005, has become a framework overriding other

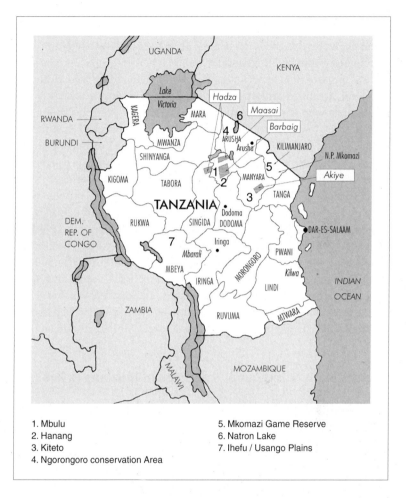

1. Mbulu
2. Hanang
3. Kiteto
4. Ngorongoro conservation Area

5. Mkomazi Game Reserve
6. Natron Lake
7. Ihefu / Usango Plains

pieces of legislation related to environment and natural resource management. Its application in certain areas constrains the use of resources, especially riverine resources,[4] which are critical for the survival of pastoralists and their herds during the dry season.

Over the course of 2007, implementation of the Strategy for Urgent Action to Mitigate Against Land Degradation and Water Catchments (SUALDWC-March 2006)[5] had far-reaching negative consequences for the indigenous peoples of Tanzania. This strategy was used in 2006 and 2007 to evict pastoralists from the Ihefu and Usangu plains in south-western Tanzania on the grounds that they would allegedly exhaust the water resources in the area. The SUALDWC strategy implies, among other things: *Evacuation (voluntary or forced) of all those who have invaded the plains and water basins in general.*[6] While there were different economic activities undertaken in the Usangu Plains, it was only the pastoralists who were evicted - a move that re-enforced the strong anti-pastoralist bias within policy and conservation circles. Rice irrigation schemes, which have been proved to use most of the water upstream of the Great Ruaha River in the Usangu Plains, were left untouched, thus evidencing a selective application of the strategy.

The revised Wildlife Policy (March 2007) transfers power over wildlife resources from local-level institutions to ministerial level, with excessive powers given to the Minister and the Director of the Wildlife Division. The policy incorporates the Ramsar Convention[7] but its application on the ground over-emphasizes conservation, and the protection approach poses inherent conflicts with the local communities. Indigenous peoples living in areas adjacent to Ramsar Sites such as Lake Natron feel that the concept of these sites, as interpreted and promoted by the Wildlife Division in Tanzania, is a threat to their resources.

The situation of indigenous peoples in Tanzania in 2007

The overall situation of indigenous peoples in Tanzania during 2007 continued to deteriorate. Access to natural resources, social services and enjoyment of other civil and political rights continued to be constrained by various policy and legal instruments. The year saw further losses of land among the Hadzabe, Barabaig, Maasai and Akiye (Ndorobo).

Hunter-Gatherers

Hadzabe
In 2006, some 6,500 sq. km of prime Hadzabe land in the greater Yaeda Valley in Mbulu district were given to the Eshkesh Safari Company, a United Arab Emirates (UAE) sports hunting company.[8]

The negotiations and the issuing of hunting rights to the foreign hunting company did not involve the Hadzabe peoples and, as such, there was no free, prior and informed consent. Agreements were negotiated between the foreign company and the Wildlife Division of the Ministry of Natural Resources and Tourism. The company promised that, in exchange for the land given to them, they would provide economic assistance and basic social services to the local communities in the area. The exercise hindered the Hadzabe people from accessing their traditional subsistence hunting resources and triggered serious food shortages and a near famine situation.[9]

On 20 May 2007, Tanzanian police arrested Richard Baalow, a Hadzabe spokesperson and activist who had been trying to help the community establish dialogue with the local government. Tanzanian human rights organisations saw this as a form of intimidation to ensure compliance with the decision to enter into a contract with the United Arab Emirates safari company.

The Hadzabe were not necessarily disputing the deal with the United Arab Emirates company but they argued that it should not put the Hadzabe at serious risk of displacement and cultural disintegration. Following intensive lobbying and negotiations involving the Hadzabe themselves and the District Council, the Eshkesh Safari Company decided to withdraw from the deal and surrender the rights it had secured in 2006 such that the land could be reverted back to the Hadzabe. This was a remarkable victory for the Hadzabe peoples.

The United Nations has embarked on two International Decades on the Rights of Indigenous Peoples to help make governments aware of the challenges faced by indigenous peoples and the importance of protecting their rights, languages, identities and knowledge systems. The Hadzabe are a classic example of a vulnerable indigenous people who need specific policy attention if they are to survive.

The Akie

The Akie in Kiteto district in Manyara Region continued to experience encroachment onto their land from neighbouring communities. Pastoralists and agriculturalists took further lands belonging to the Akie, with communities in the Napilukunya and Ngapapa sub-villages of the Kimana village reporting worsening environmental degradation, loss of habitat and a significant reduction in the flowers that are essential for honey production. The Akie honey collection, processing and packaging association, known as ISEKEMI and based in the sub-village of Napilukunya, reported a 50% reduction in the honey collected in 2007 in comparison with 2006. The community reported that health coping strategies were further eroded by depletion of some medicinal plants.

Pastoralists

In 2007, pastoralists in Tanzania experienced various resource-based conflicts, with some conflicts leading to serious displacement and evictions.

The evictions of pastoralists from the Usangu Plains in south-western Tanzania that started in 2006 continued into 2007. These mass evictions serve to illustrate the problems that pastoralists face in Tanzania due to the way in which the environmental conservation agenda is being used by the authorities. The migration of pastoralists to the Usangu Plains began in the 1950s. Large-scale irrigation schemes were developed in Mbarali and Kapunga districts before and after independence and the immigration of rice growers was encouraged. In 1979, the Mtera Dam was constructed downstream of the Great Ruaha River for hydropower generation. Competition for water resources in Usangu became a matter of national concern following the power cuts in the early 1990s and also in 2006 and early 2007. The drying-up of the Great Ruaha River that flows into the Mtera Dam caused the government to – wrongly[10] - blame the pastoralists and agro-pastoralists.

In March 2006, the government of Tanzania issued an eviction order to pastoral and agro-pastoral communities residing in Mbarali district in the Usangu/Ihefu Basin in the southern highlands of Tanzania. These communities include Sukuma agro-pastoralists and Ilparakuiyo, Taturu and Barabaig pastoralists (the latter two both belonging to the Datoga group). The state employed excessive use of force in executing the evictions, initially without even directing the pastoralists as to where to relocate their stocks to. Large numbers of pastoralists and agro-pastoralists were evicted during 2006 and 2007 from Usangu to other regions of Tanzania.[11]

The evictions of pastoralists from Usangu and other parts of Tanzania have always been executed violently without respect for the human and land rights of pastoralists. The evictions are most often based on inbuilt negative stereotypes of pastoralists, characterizing them as environmentally destructive, sources of animal diseases, enemies of wildlife and practitioners of economically unviable livelihood systems. Such stereotypes persist - even when they stand in sharp contrast to scientific proof[12] - so what happened in Usangu was unfortunately to be expected.

In March 2007, the Land Rights Research and Resources Institute teamed up with other civil society organizations, namely PINGOS Forum (Pastoralists Indigenous Non Governmental Organizations Forum) based in Arusha, the Legal and Human Rights Center based in Dar Es Salaam and HIMWA, a community-based organization, and conducted a fact-finding mission in Lindi district, where most pastoralists were evicted to. The team also comprised journalists from radio, television and local newspapers. The main objective of the mission was to conduct research into the whole process of evicting pastoralists from Usangu/Ihefu with a view to establishing the rationale behind the exercise and its implications for basic rights as provided for in the national Constitution and other legal documents. The findings of the report showed:

A dehumanization and oppression of pastoralists during the whole process of eviction from Mbarali-Mbeya to Lindi region, which threatened their future livelihoods as pastoralists. Some were brutally beaten, families were separated, people were forced to sell their livestock at very low prices, generally arranged by the district authorities, and large numbers of livestock died during the eviction process.

Government officials at central and local level had, in most cases, acted against the procedures laid down by the government on how to handle the eviction order thus causing deaths of livestock and financial losses.

The poor planning of the eviction exercise and the lack of necessary infrastructure for the smooth evacuation of animals and people forced many families to incur extra costs in transporting their livestock.

The unconstrained power of local authorities to tax pastoralists, sometimes with illegal charges, at different stations on their way to Lindi, was also noted. A shocking observation was made at the Benjamin Mkapa Bridge, where pastoralists were supposed to offload their livestock. Here, pastoralists were charged up to Tshs. 300,000 (approx. U$300) for each vehicle carrying livestock to obtain permission to move with their animals to Lindi region. This happened notwithstanding all the other charges they had already incurred on their way to the bridge.

Allegations of corruption in different forms were leveled against government officials both in Mbarali, Lindi and Kilwa districts. Leaders from different villages, in Kilwa district in particular, allegedly asked for money from pastoralists in order to allocate them relatively good grazing and settlement areas.

The report was presented to the Parliamentary Committee for Natural Resources and Environment on 15 April 2007. In May 2007, a special government-appointed commission was appointed to investigate the eviction process, and a report was presented to the President on 6 June 2007. The report has thus far not been made public.

The Barabaig

The Barabaig are holding on to their culture but are having a hard time holding on to their land. The main problems faced by the Barabaig include a lack of sufficient land for cultivation and grazing and a lack of access to education. In the Manayara region, where some of the Barabaig live, there are plans to expand a sulphur mine onto their grazing land and the Barabaig are currently trying to win a court case to prevent the government from selling their land to the mine.

In 2007, the Barabaig won back some of their land that had been taken by the National Agriculture and Food Corporation (NAFCO) in 1968. A total of 100,000 hectares of land were taken from the Barabaig. However, of the seven big estates that were allocated to the NAFCO, only two farms have been returned to the Barabaig residents of Hanang district. The remaining five have been sold to private buyers, including the Lutheran Church, and the rest given to agricultural communities and civil servants.

The Maasai

The Ngorongoro Conservation Area in the heart of Maasailand is one of the world's most important conservation heritage areas. Maasai communities living in the Ngorongoro Conservation Area are continuing to face a number of problems, for example, access to water and pastures throughout the dry and wet seasons. Their livestock herds have decreased and they have had to turn to cultivation to supplement the food derived from livestock. However, the management of the Ngorongoro Conservation Area considers cultivation to be incompatible with conservation and the Maasai of the Ngorongoro Conservation Area continue to live in very insecure conditions and under the shadow of eviction threats.

During 2007, the Maasai of Loliondo faced increasing land conflicts due to the immigration of people from Kenya, caused by the discovery of new gemstones in the Loliondo area.

The Maasai living near the Mkomazi Game Reserve in the northeastern part of Tanzania also faced a number of land conflicts during the year, in relation to officials from the game reserve and non-pastoral communities. Since their eviction in 1988, they have continued to lack access to pastures in the game reserve. ❑

Notes

1 Http:/www.answers.com/Maasai; www.answers.com/Datoga; www.answers.com/Hadza.
2 Other sources estimate the Hadzabe at between 1,000 – 1,500 people. See for instance **Madsen, Andrew, 2000:** *The Hadzabe of Tanzania. Land and Human Rights for a Hunter-Gatherer Community.* Copenhagen. IWGIA.
3 URT (2004) Environmental Management Act 2004 section 55 - 60
4 See section 55 of EMA, which stipulates that there are no activities to be undertaken within 50 meters of the river.
5 For further details about this policy see for instance **C.M. Shayo** (from the Vice President's Office), **2006:** *Adaptation Planning and Implementation: Agriculture and Food Security.* Workshop Paper 2006.
6 See action point number one of the SUALDWC.
7 **URT, 2007:** *Revised Wildlife Policy,* MNRT Dar es Salaam. The Ramsar Convention is an agreement on wetlands that came into force for the United Republic of Tanzania on 13 August 2000.

8   The alienation of Hadza lands infringes the rights of the Hadzabe peoples who legally own the said territory under the Village Land Act of 1999. as well as under the Local Government Act of 1982.

9   See Arusha Times, November 3-9, 2007).

10   **Walsh, Martin T., 2007**: *Pastoralism and Policy Processes in Tanzania. Case Study and Recommendations*. A Report to the Tanzania National Resource Forum, Arusha. **Walsh, Martin T., 2004:** *Pangolines, Science and Scape Goats. Environmental Narrative and Conflicts in the Great Ruaha Catchment, Tanzania*. Workshop paper, University of Oxford. SMUWC (Sustainable Management of the Usangu Wetland and its Catchment) reports and workshop papers 1999-2002. Available online at: http://www.usangu.org. RIPARWIN (Raising Irrigation Productivity and Releasing Water for Intersectoral Needs) reports 2001 – 2004. Available online at: http:/www.riparwin.org. **Franks, Tom, Lankford, Bruce A. and Mdemu, Makarius, 2004**: Managing Water Amongst Competing Uses: The Usangu Wetland in Tanzania. *Irrigation and Drainage* 53: 1-10. **Lankford, Bruce A., 2004:** Resource-Centred Thinking in River Basins: Should we Revoke the Crop Water Requirement Approach to Irrigation Planning? *Agricultural Water Management* 68: 33-46. Available online at: http:/www.Elsevier.com/locate/agwat

11   **Martin T. Walsh, 2007:** *Pastoralism and Policy Proceses in Tanzania. Case Study and Recommendations*. A Report to the Tanzania National Resource Forum, Arusha. *A Report on Eviction and Resettlement of Pastoralists from Ihefu and Usangu-Mbarali District to Kilwa and Lindi Districts*. By PINGOs Forum, Land Rights Research & Resources Institute (HAKIARDHI), Legal and Human Rights Centre (LHRC) and HIMWA. March 2006. **Mvula, Emmanuel (HAKIARDHI) and Kawawa, Chande (PINGOs Forum). Undated 2006-2007**. *Land/Resource Use Conflicts and Proposed Eviction of Livestock Keepers in Usangu Basin. A Report of Fact Finding Mission Submitted to PINGOs Forum*.

12   Scientific studies have concluded that the drying-up of the Great Ruaha River is not caused by the activities of pastoralists but rather by the expansion of irrigated cultivation, in particular the extension of rice and other crop growing into the dry season.

Benedict Ole Nangoro is a Maasai from Kiteto in Tanzania. He holds an M. Phil in Development Studies from the Institute of Development Studies of the University of Sussex, UK. He is currently working with the NGO CORDS (Community Research and Development Services).

Lilian Looloitai is a Maasai from Monduli in Tanzania. She holds a BA in Sociology from the Catholic University of Eastern Africa, Kenya and is currently working with CORDS as Projects Manager.

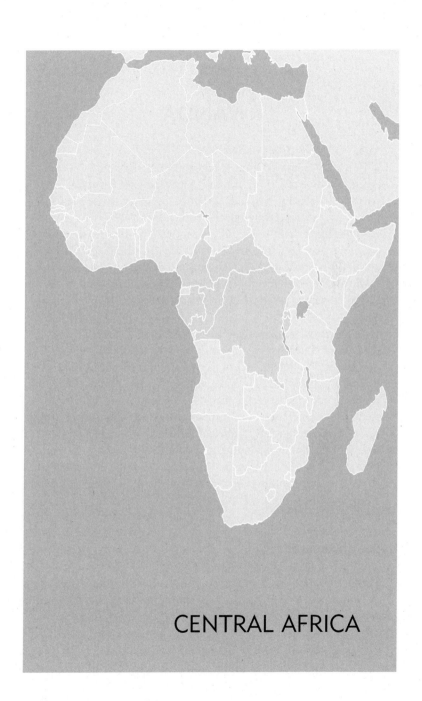

CENTRAL AFRICA

RWANDA

It is widely accepted that indigenous forest-dwelling Batwa (also known as Twa) are the first inhabitants of Rwanda. The Batwa self-identify, and are identified by other Rwandans, as Batwa and Abasangwabutaka ("original inhabitants"). The Batwa self-identify and are widely recognized within Africa as indigenous peoples, including by the African Commission.[1] There has never been a national disaggregated demographic census in Rwanda; however, the total number of Batwa is estimated to be 33,000, which represents approximately 0.4% of the population.[2]

The Batwa are amongst the poorest and most marginalised sectors of Rwandan society. They have been totally dispossessed of their traditional lands and territories, and forced to give up their traditional hunting and gathering lifestyle and cultural practices and subsist on the fringes of settled society. They experience increasing racial discrimination and stereotyping by the rest of Rwandan society as morally, physically and intellectually deficient, gradually becoming social outcasts despised for their ethnic origins. The Rwandan government fails to recognise them as an indigenous people, and has adopted a policy of (cultural) assimilation.[3]

Peace and security

While Rwanda itself remained stable, the Rwandan authorities continued to work with their counterparts in the Democratic Republic of Congo (DRC) during 2007 to address the Rwandan rebels that are maintaining strongholds in DRC. The rebel Democratic Forces for the Liberation of Rwanda comprises the remnants of the former Rwandan army and ethnic Hutu militias blamed for the 1994 geno-

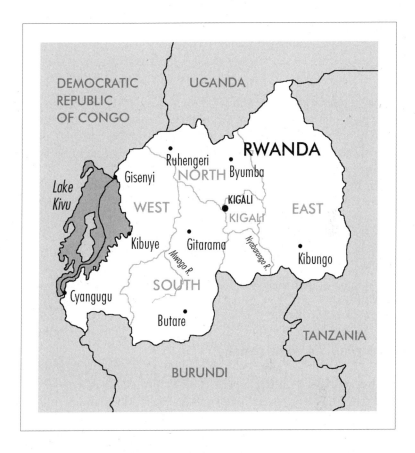

cide, who have remained active mostly in the North and South Kivu regions of DRC where indigenous peoples are among the local population.[4] Sporadic attacks on civilians and clashes between the rebels and DRC authorities continued throughout the year.

In November 2007, the two countries signed an agreement under which DRC agreed to prepare a detailed plan for the disarmament and repatriation of Rwandan Hutus by 1 December. DRC also agreed to transfer Rwandan genocide and war crimes suspects to either Rwanda or the International Criminal Tribunal for Rwanda. In return, Rwanda – which has been accused of backing Congolese rebel groups – agreed not to support any armed groups in eastern DRC and to prevent them from crossing its border in either direction.[5]

Land law

The land reform process continued throughout 2007, with a pilot phase moving nearer to completion, including demarcation and registration of plots and registration of disputes. Despite running smoothly overall, concerns were raised as to the impact of the pilot registration on women's land rights and the methodology for adjudication of disputes. Redistribution to "the poor" of land "grabbed" by army personnel and local administrators, particularly in the north-east of the country, has commenced although it remains unclear how the recipients are being selected. Issues also remain over the implementation of the agricultural policy, including in marshland areas. Marshlands have been rapidly converted to cash crops such as rice, maize and sugarcane, at the expense of their customary access and use, including by the indigenous Batwa.

Outlawing the death penalty

Rwanda outlawed the death penalty on 25 July 2007, a move that was hailed by human rights advocates and the international community. In addition to advancing human rights in Rwanda, this move spawned hopes that countries hosting genocide suspects would expedite their transfer to Kigali to face charges. Before the legal reforms, countries such as Belgium, Canada, Denmark, the Netherlands and Switzerland had refused to extradite suspects linked to the 1994 genocide for fear they would be executed after trial in Rwanda.[6]

CAURWA changes its name

Continuing its strict post-genocide stance against any references to ethnicity in Rwanda and its position that all Rwandans are indigenous, the Rwandan government finally forced the main Twa organisation, *Communauté des Autochtones Rwandais* or CAURWA (Community of Indigenous Peoples of Rwanda) to change its name and statutes to delete all references to the terms "indigenous" and "Batwa" and any related terms in order to obtain permanent registration as an NGO and continue its vital activities in support of the Twa community. After years of struggle to maintain its name and identity, the organisation found it had no choice but to change its name in order to obtain the much needed permanent registration from the Ministry of Justice that would permit it to obtain funding and carry out its work without continual disruption and uncertainty. Its members agreed to the new name *Communauté des Potiers Rwandais* or COPORWA (Community of Potters of Rwanda) and COPORWA was legally registered in October 2007. While not all Twa in Rwanda are potters and not all potters are Twa, more than 90% of the Twa are engaged in pottery and it is a craft widely associated with them. Nonetheless, the Twa are about much more than pottery and this incursion into their freedom of association and expression further entrenches their long-standing marginalisation in Rwanda. In a country dominated by Hutus and Tutsis, the Twa risk becoming even more invisible if their unique plight *as Twa* cannot be highlighted and special measures are not taken to remedy the particular historical and ongoing injustices they face by virtue of their ethnicity.

Efforts to improve the plight of the Twa

CAURWA/COPORWA continued its livelihoods, education and human rights work throughout 2007, and continued to receive some support from government in relation to social programmes for Twa communities, including education, health and housing. These programmes, initiated in 2005 partly in response to the findings that year of the NEPAD (New Partnership for Africa's Development) African Peer Review mechanism, have not been as robust as originally hoped. For instance, many Twa have encountered severe discrimination when trying to acquire their health insurance cards from local authorities, and as many as 60% of the Twa remained without cards during 2007. By September 2007, 15 houses had been built for Twa families and a further five were under construction. The district authorities only paid one term's school fees for Twa secondary school students in 2007.

With the support of IWGIA, the organisation broadcast weekly radio programmes with live debates involving both Twa people and representatives of the national, provincial and local authorities. The topics included presentation of CAURWA's/COPORWA's programmes and the situation and problems of the Batwa communities. The radio programmes were successful in terms of sensitization and creation of dialogue and CAURWA/COPORWA plans to continue with the radio programmes in 2008.

The "Dancing Pots" pottery project, an initiative of COPORWA and the Forest Peoples Project (FPP), continued to improve the livelihoods and reduce the social exclusion of Twa potters by helping them set up a Fair Trade craft enterprise. A substantial grant awarded by the UK's BIG Lottery Fund in 2007 enabled implementation of a new four-year business plan aimed at increasing the potters' production capacity and skills, along with their access to national and international markets.

African Commission

Rwanda's eighth periodic report to the African Commission on Human and Peoples' Rights was examined at the Commission's 42nd Ordinary Session in November 2007. In its report and during the examination, Rwanda expressly denied the characterisation of the Twa as an indigenous people, referring to them instead as a "marginalised" or "vulnerable" group but without addressing the specifics of their dire human rights situation in the country. COPORWA submitted a shadow report on the situation of the indigenous Twa in Rwanda and, with the support of British NGO the Forest Peoples Programme, attended the session and delivered an oral intervention to the Commission, as a result of which several questions on the Twa were posed by the Commission to the government delegation. The concluding observations of the Commission are awaited.

COPORWA's Director, Mr. Kalimba Zephyrin, continued in his role as a member of the African Commission on Human and Peoples' Rights' Working Group on Indigenous Populations/Communities, whose work is supported by IWGIA. Among other contributions, he participated in a research and information mission to Gabon in October 2007, investigating the human rights situation of indigenous peoples in Gabon and meeting with several ministers and other high-ranking officials as well as with international organizations, NGOs and indigenous communities.   ❑

Notes

1   African Commission on Human and Peoples' Rights (ACHPR) and International Work Group for Indigenous Affairs (IWGIA), 2005: *Report of the African Commission's Working Group of Experts on Indigenous Peoples/Communities, Submitted in accordance with the "Resolution on the Rights of Indigenous Populations/ Communities in Africa", adopted by the African Commission on Human and Peoples' Rights at its 28th ordinary session*. Gambia, Denmark, which states that "all the Batwa Pygmies of Central Africa recognise their common ancestors as being the first hunter/gatherer inhabitants of the tropical forests", p.16 and pp. 92-93

2   This estimated Batwa population comes from a national survey conducted in 2003 by the Forest Peoples Project, CAURWA (Community of Indigenous Peoples of Rwanda) and the Office of National Statistics of the Rwandan Ministry of Finance. The results were published in a report: **CAURWA ,2004**: *Enquête sur les conditions de vie socio-économique des ménages bénéficiaires de la Communauté des Autochtones Rwandais*. CAURWA, Kigali. Rwanda's population is now approximately 9 million, with an average population density of 366 people per square kilometre, making it the most densely populated country in Africa. See: **UNDP, 2005**: *Human Development Report 2005: International Cooperation at a Crossroads; Aid, Trade and Security in an Unequal World*. New York; **International Bank for Reconstruction and Development/World Bank, 2006**: *World Development Report 2007: Development and the Next Generation*. Washington, DC, p. 289.

3   Rwanda was one of the first countries to submit itself to NEPAD's (New Partnership for African Development) Peer Review mechanism. The NEPAD report notes with regard to the Twa that the authorities appeared to be adopting a policy of assimilation, and recommended the government begin intensive dialogue with the Twa. The government's official response states that it has never had a policy of assimilation but admitted that the "Batwa community continues to have a disproportionate number of vulnerable members, and seems not to benefit sufficiently from the national policy that supports socio-economic integration of all Rwandans." The authorities also noted that "it is clear that a targeted response to [the Twa's] specific problems is recommended and shall be reflected in the plan of action." **Government of Rwanda, 2005:** *Response to Issues Raised and Best Practices Suggested in the Country Review Team (CRT)'s Report*. Section on "Democracy and Good Political Governance", p. 4, June 2005.

4   IRIN news service, "Rwanda-DRC: Kagame seeks co-operation on rebels", 7 May 2007.
5   IRIN news service, "DRC-Rwanda: New pact on armed groups in the Kivus hailed", 14 November 2007.
6   IRIN news service, "Rwanda: New law brings hope for extradition of genocide suspects", 3 August 2007.

Treva Braun holds a Bachelor of Law (LL.B) degree from the University of British Columbia in Canada and a Masters in International Human Rights Law (LL.M) from the University of Essex in the UK. Her principal areas of interest and expertise are indigenous issues and gender. She currently lives in London and works as Coordinator of the Africa Legal and Human Rights Programme at Forest Peoples Programme.

BURUNDI

The indigenous Batwa (also known as Twa) of Burundi form part of the wider Batwa population in the Great Lakes region of Central Africa. With no official census, and information from different sources varying widely, it is currently estimated that between 80,000 – 100,000 Batwa live in Burundi,[1] representing approximately 1.25 percent of the total population. Having lost their ancestral forests decades ago due to clearing for agricultural use, the majority of the Batwa are now landless and their traditional hunter-gatherer lifestyle has long been eliminated. While the majority of Burundian Batwa work as labourers, potters and beggars, some are now practising agriculture and animal husbandry.

Despite constitutional protection against servitude, an estimated 8,000 Batwa live in subjugation under Hutu and Tutsi "masters".[2]

Unique to the region, the 2005 Constitution provides for three Batwa representatives in both the National Assembly and the Senate.[3] There are currently three Batwa representatives in each house. The Honourable Liberate Nicayenzi, a Batwa Member of Parliament, is also the President of *Unissons-nous pour la Promotion des Batwa* (UNIPROBA), one of the principal Batwa NGOs in Burundi, based in Bujumbura.

Humanitarian crisis

Burundi started 2007 in the grip of devastating floods that led to widespread displacement, hunger and disease. The World Food Programme estimated that affected households lost 50 to 60 percent of their income, and this led to an international call for food aid for two

million people. The government created a solidarity fund to which all
Burundians were compelled to contribute.[4]

Peace and security

During 2007, the national peace process suffered a setback, with a resumption of fighting between the National Defence Forces and the
rebel FNL (*Forces nationales de libération*).[5] Increased FNL activities
against civilians included looting, extortion, ambushes and kidnappings and, in September, 4,000 people were displaced following FNL
raids in the north.[6]

The UN Peacebuilding Commission (PBC)[7] adopted a Strategic
Framework for Peacebuilding in Burundi. Although there is no mention of the Batwa, there are references to meeting the socio-economic
and land needs of so-called "vulnerable" groups and prosecuting vio-
lators of their human rights.[8]

Political deadlock

The political situation in Burundi deteriorated due to the delayed implementation of the September 2006 ceasefire and internal divisions
within the ruling CNDD-FDD party (*Conseil National pour la défense de
la démocratie-forces pour la défense de la démocratie*). The opposition used
the conflict within CNDD-FDD to restate power-sharing and good
governance demands, and effectively boycotted the work of Parliament for most of the year.[9]

Justice and human rights

In January, the Supreme Court acquitted the former transitional President, Vice-President and two others of plotting a coup in 2006 through
lack of evidence, although two others were convicted. The acquittals
eased some of the tension between the government and the opposition
after the latter had accused the authorities of fabricating the coup in

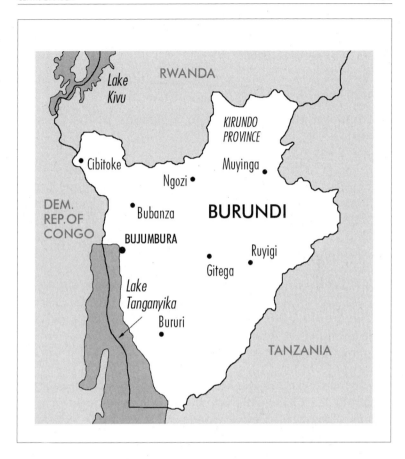

order to silence them. Human rights organisations condemned the case, indicating that it was only one example of the poor human rights situation in Burundi.[10]

During the year, there were widespread reports of arbitrary arrests and detentions. Sexual violence against women and children was prevalent in some areas, as was murder and theft (including armed and roadside robbery), including by the security forces.[11] A UN expert noted continuing ill-treatment and torture of suspects by the police and violations of legal procedure by police and judicial officials.[12] Human Rights Watch observed that children face torture and sexual abuse while in detention.[13] Another UN representative stated that more had to be done to protect children from armed conflict and to improve detention facilities for minors charged with membership of armed groups.[14]

International attention given to violations of the Batwa's rights

In January, a UN-appointed expert visited a Batwa community in Burundi whose members had complained of discrimination and its consequences for their food, housing and land rights, and access to potable water. The Batwa explained that their children were dropping out of school due to hunger, and that non-Batwa were taking their land. They submitted a petition to the expert, who noted that

> *The [Batwa] community remains marginalized and discriminated against in all areas of life in Burundi, and although they now enjoy a measure of political representation in the Parliament and Senate under the new Burundi Constitution, it has not translated into corresponding opportunities in the Government and its institutions.* [15]

The UN High Commissioner for Human Rights also expressed her concern at the situation of the Batwa and urged the government to end discrimination against them, including the practice of bonded labour.[16]

Land reform

Land remained a crucial issue for the Batwa. A draft land law was presented to the National Assembly but the political stalemate postponed its adoption to 2008. Unfortunately, the current draft fails to directly address Batwa land rights and landlessness. With support from the UN Development Fund (UNDP) and Dutch Embassy, amongst others, the National Land Commission (CNTB) began its substantive work in 2007. A staff member of UNIPROBA is the only Batwa representative on the CNTB. He was appointed President of the CNTB Land Inventory Sub-Commission, which has identified and reclaimed previously illegally acquired land throughout the country. The CNTB will redistribute this land to landless Burundians. The CNTB Vice-President indicated that it is treating landless Batwa as a priority, and pledged to find them all suitable plots.[17] However, he confirmed that the principle of *"mise en valeur"* would still apply.[18] With support from IWGIA, UN-IPROBA is identifying all the landless Batwa in Burundi and supplying the CNTB with this information.

With support from the Forest Peoples Project (FPP), UNIPROBA instigated a project to analyse and develop recommendations on the draft land law and land reform process and lobby for action to address the widespread discrimination and landlessness facing the Batwa, and violations of their land rights.[19]

Batwa advocacy

During 2007, UNIPROBA representatives carried out international advocacy, with support from FPP and IWGIA, at the African Commission on Human and Peoples' Rights. While participating in the UN Permanent Forum on Indigenous Issues, Batwa delegates extensively lobbied African governments to support the adoption of the UN Declaration on the Rights of Indigenous Peoples. In May, UNIPROBA and FPP organised a national workshop for representatives of the Batwa community, the CNTB and parliament on indigenous land rights and the national land law.   ❑

Notes

1   According to information obtained from UNIPROBA.
2   **African Commission on Human and Peoples' Rights Working Group of Experts on Indigenous Populations/Communities, 2005:** *Rapport de la Mission d'information au Burundi du 27 Mars au 9 Avril 2005*, p. 15.
3   Constitution of Burundi (2005), Articles 164 and 180.
4   Reuters, 'Thousands displaced by Burundi floods', 15/1/07, available at: http://www.alertnet.org/thenews/newsdesk/L15304648.htm.
5   UN Security Council: *Second Report of the Secretary-General on the United Nations Integrated Office in Burundi*, UN Doc. No. S/2007/682, 23/11/2007.

6   IRIN, *Burundi: Rebel activity displaces hundreds in Bubanza*, 10/9/2007, available at: http://www.irinnews.org/Report.aspx?ReportId=74202.

7   The United Nations Peacebuilding Commission was established in 2006 to help countries in post-conflict recovery avoid reverting to violence. Burundi and Sierra Leone are currently on its agenda.

8   A reference to "vulnerable" groups in Burundi could be interpreted as including the Batwa, in the same way that it does in Rwanda.

9   UN Security Council: *Second Report of the Secretary-General on the United Nations Integrated Office in Burundi*, op. cit. The deadlock was broken after a government of national unity was appointed in November.

10 IRIN, *Burundi: Court acquits ex-president over coup plot*, 16/1/2007, available at: http://www.irinnews.org/report.aspx?reportid=64326.

11 See, for example: Ligue ITEKA, *Point de presse de la Ligue ITEKA a l'occasion du 59ieme anniversaire de la Déclaration Universelle des Droits de l'Homme*, available at: http://www.ligue-iteka.africa-web.org/article.php3?id_article=2302.

12 UN General Assembly: *Situation of human rights in Burundi*, UN Doc. No. A/62/213, 8/8/2007.

13 Human Rights Watch, *Burundi: Paying the Price: Violations of the rights of children in detention in Burundi*, March 2007, Volume 19, No. 4(a).

14 UN Press Conference, *Press Conference by Special Representative for Children and Armed Conflict*, 16/2/2007, available at: http://www.un.org/News/briefings/docs/2007/070316_Coomaraswamy.doc.htm.

15 UN General Assembly, *Interim report of the independent expert on the situation of human rights in Burundi, Akich Okola*, UN Doc. No. A/HRC/4/5, 26/2/2007.

16 UN General Assembly Peacebuilding Commission High-Level Briefing, *Burundi Must Seize Present Opportunity For Peace, Justice, Development Human Rights Chief Tells Peacebuilding Commission: Strengthening Rule Of Law, Combating Impunity Main Challenges As Country Seeks To Make Fresh Start*, 30 May 2007, available at: http://www.un.org/News/Press/docs/2007/pbc13.doc.htm

17 Personal communication with the author, 7 December 2007.

18 This principle means that state-owned land must be used for officially sanctioned purposes, which is usually agriculture in the case of small family-owned plots. If not, it can be legally expropriated by the state for use by someone else. This principle is a *de jure* violation of the rights of indigenous peoples to own, occupy, use and enjoy their lands, territories and resources. Further, because of the Batwa's indigence and lack of agricultural know-how, it necessitates substantial support to help these communities make use of land once granted, unless it ceases to be state-owned and full title is transferred, in which case the principle of *mise en valeur* does not apply. Although the CNTB has offered to find land for the Batwa, it has not guaranteed either that full title will be granted or, if not, that assistance will be given to help communities use this state-owned land and thus avoid expropriation.

19 The African Commission has noted that landlessness is a root cause of the Batwa's severe poverty and marginalisation. **African Commission on Human and Peoples' Rights (ACHPR) and International Work Group for Indigenous Affairs (IWGIA), 2005:** *Report of the African Commission's Working Group of Experts on Indigenous Peoples/Communities, Submitted in accordance with the "Resolution on*

the Rights of Indigenous Populations/Communities in Africa", adopted by the African Commission on Human and Peoples' Rights at its 28th ordinary session, (Gambia, Denmark), p.18.

Lucy Mulvagh *holds a Masters in Human Rights from the UK's University of Essex and is Project Officer on the Africa Legal and Human Rights Programme of the Forest Peoples Project (lucy@forestpeoples.org).*

DEMOCRATIC REPUBLIC OF CONGO (DRC)

There are four main groups of indigenous peoples in the vast territory of the Democratic Republic of Congo (DRC): the Bambuti, Bacwa, Western Batwa and Eastern Batwa (also known as Twa). In the absence of a census, their total number is unknown; however, estimates of the indigenous population range from 270,000 to 4 million, approximately 0.4%-7% of the total population.[1]

As a direct result of historical and ongoing expropriation of indigenous lands for conservation and logging, many have been forced to abandon their traditional way of life and culture based on hunting and gathering and become landless squatters living on the fringes of settled society. Some have been forced into relationships of bonded labour with Bantu "masters". Indigenous peoples' overall situation is considerably worse than the national population: they experience inferior living conditions and access to services such as health and education.[2] Their participation in DRC's social and political affairs is low, and they encounter discrimination in various forms, including racial stereotyping, social exclusion and systematic violations of their rights.

Peace and security

While much of DRC remained peaceful during 2007, violent conflict continued in the east.[3] Indigenous peoples have been disproportionately affected by armed conflict, with different factions committing atrocities, including summary execution, abduction, pillaging and cannibalism.[4]

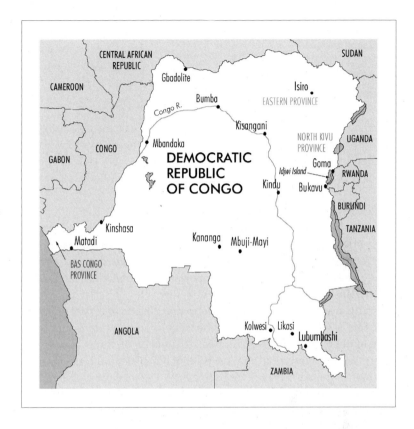

An historic conference of all parties seeking an end to the conflict was postponed to January 2008. It resulted in an agreement among the belligerents to disarm but failed to address the key issue flaming the violence: the commercial exploitation of DRC's natural resources.[5]

The humanitarian crisis and internal displacement

An NGO survey estimates that around 5.4 million people have died in DRC since 1998, and that 45,000 people continue to die every day.[6] During 2007, conflict in the east hampered humanitarian efforts, thus exacerbating the spread of diseases such as Ebola, typhoid and cholera.[7] By the end of 2007, there were an estimated 1.2 million internally displaced people.[8]

Human rights

Human rights violations continued on a daily basis throughout 2007, including murder, summary executions, torture, beatings and rape, including by the national security forces (FARDC). The lack of rule of law and culture of corruption means crime is committed with impunity.[9]

Sexual and gender-based violence are endemic. A UN expert has noted that "atrocities perpetrated [against women] are of an unimaginable brutality that goes far beyond rape", and that "sexual violence ... is rampant and committed by non-state armed groups, the Armed Forces of the DRC, the National Congolese Police and increasingly also by civilians."[10]

Indigenous women are subjected to horrific acts of sexual violence. They are targeted because their attackers operate in areas that form part of their traditional territories. A number of these attacks are grounded on negative cultural beliefs that having sexual relations with a "Pygmy" woman is a cure for back-ache.[11] The medical problems that result, including increased rates of HIV/AIDS, are difficult to treat because indigenous women lack resources and access to decent healthcare. Survivors also fear speaking about or reporting such crimes because they are often stigmatised by their communities.[12]

DRC's forestry reforms and the impact on indigenous people

DRC's forests play an essential role in ensuring the physical, cultural and spiritual well-being of indigenous people, and they suffer extreme levels of poverty and ill-health without them. However, DRC does not recognise or protect indigenous peoples' collective land rights and no efforts have been made to delimit or demarcate their lands. This disregard for indigenous peoples' rights is typified by the 2002

Forest Code and forestry reforms being implemented by the government with support from the World Bank.[13]

Although it includes provisions on forest zoning for conservation and commercial exploitation, the Forest Code fails to indicate what forest will be regularised as indigenous-owned. Amongst other things, the Forest Code determines forest zoning, with at least 40 percent allocated to commercial exploitation and 15 percent to conservation. Although referred to as "protected", the remaining forest – at least 45 percent – will also be subject to concessions.[14] Furthermore, it is difficult to determine what relationship, if any, exists between the zoning proposed in the Forest Code and the process currently underway to convert old forestry concession titles into new contracts.

In 2005, DRC ordered a review of all existing concession titles – with a view to "converting" them into new contracts – and the creation of an inter-ministerial commission (CIM) to oversee the process and approve new contracts. Of the 156 concessions submitted for consideration, 102 are on or in very close proximity to indigenous peoples' lands.[15]

The law states that one indigenous representative may participate in the CIM if there are indigenous communities living in proximity to the concession area under review.[16] This provision is welcome because it recognises that indigenous peoples live in DRC, but it falls short of recognising indigenous peoples' rights to own, use, control or otherwise enjoy their traditional lands, territories and resources, or of ensuring their security of tenure. It also fails to fulfil the criteria for full and effective indigenous participation in and consent to decisions that may affect them.

During 2007, indigenous support NGOs visited communities to inform them about the review and help them select representatives to sit on the CIM. During these consultations, the communities made several recommendations, including that the CIM take their observations into account – even if it means rejecting applications for concessions – in order to avoid the impression that the CIM's approval of new contracts has been predetermined without indigenous consent.[17]

World Bank Inspection Panel

In 2005, indigenous peoples filed a formal complaint with the World Bank Inspection Panel alleging, among other things, serious violations of the Bank's safeguard policies on indigenous peoples.[18]

The Inspection Panel's final report, made public in January 2008, upholds the complaint.[19] It notes that the Bank failed to adequately identify the existence of indigenous peoples and breached its policy by failing to develop an Indigenous Peoples' Development Plan. The report concludes that "it was only after this Request for Inspection that the Bank paid more attention to the plight of the Pygmy people and the many others dependent upon the forests".[20]

UN CERD

In 2007, the Forest Peoples Programme (FPP), the CAMV (*Centre d'Accompagnement des Autochtones Pygmées et Minoritaires Vulnérables*) and five other local organisations submitted a report on the situation of indigenous peoples to the UN Committee on the Elimination of Racial Discrimination (CERD) (see *The Indigenous World 2007*). As a result, CERD made several recommendations to the government, including that it take

> *urgent and adequate measures to protect the rights of the Pygmies to land and: (a) make provision for the forest rights of indigenous peoples in domestic legislation; (b) register the ancestral lands of the Pygmies in the land registry; (c) proclaim a new moratorium on forest lands; (d) take the interests of the Pygmies and environmental conservation needs into account in matters of land use; (e) provide domestic remedies in the event that the rights of indigenous peoples are violated.*[21]

International advocacy by indigenous peoples

Indigenous activists lobbied the World Bank and other members of the international community at a conference on the sustainable management of DRC's forests hosted by Belgium in February 2007. Activists also lobbied for indigenous rights at a side event to the International Monetary Fund (IMF)/World Bank Spring Meetings in Washington DC in April 2007.

With support from IWGIA, a CAMV representative participated in the UN Permanent Forum on Indigenous Issues, and with assistance from FPP, two CAMV representatives participated in the November 2007 session of the African Commission on Human and Peoples' Rights.   ❏

Notes

1   The estimate of 270,000 is found in: **African Commission on Human and Peoples' Rights (ACHPR) and International Work Group for Indigenous Affairs (IWGIA), 2005**: *Report of the African Commission's Working Group of Experts on Indigenous Peoples/Communities, Submitted in accordance with the "Resolution on the Rights of Indigenous Populations/Communities in Africa", adopted by the African Commission on Human and Peoples' Rights at its 28ᵗʰ ordinary session*. Gambia, Denmark. page 6. The estimate of 4,000,000 is found in: **ARD, Inc**: *Conflict Timber: Dimensions of the Problem in Asia and Africa, Volume III: African Cases – Final Report Submitted to the United States Agency for International Development*, Vermont, USA, page 17.

2   A September 2006 report published by the UN highlighted the increasing prevalence of HIV/AIDS amongst indigenous communities, spread by sexual violence and left untreated due to their poverty and social isolation. **United Nations' Integrated Regional Information Networks (IRIN), 13 September 2006:** *DRC: Sexual violence, lack of healthcare spreads HIV/AIDS among pygmies.* Available at: http://www.plusnews.org/aidsreport.asp?reportid=6371

3   Violent conflict was not confined to the east, however. In February, there were widespread reports of violence resulting in 134 deaths in the western Bas Congo Province following provincial elections. In March, intense fighting over a two-day period between the national security forces (FARDC) and personal security guards of Senator and former Vice-President Jean-Pierre Bemba resulted in around 300 deaths, including civilians, and significant property damage. Bemba sought refuge in the South African embassy, and was formally charged with high treason. However, he was allowed to leave the country for Portugal with his family in April, supposedly to seek medical treatment. See: UN Security Council, *Twenty-fourth report of the Secretary-General on the United Nations Organization Mission in the Democratic Republic of Congo*, UN Doc. No. S/2007/671, 14/11/2007. DRC's six-year war officially ended in 2003 with the creation of a Transitional Government that paved the way for the first national elections in 40 years, held in 2006. From 1998-2003, an estimated 4 million Congolese died as a result of violence, hunger and disease. It is considered the most lethal conflict since World War II.

4   **Jackson, D.:** *Twa women, Twa rights, in the Great Lakes region of Africa*, MRG, London, 2003; **Lattimer, M.:** *'Erasing the Board': Report of the International Research Mission into*

crimes under international law committed against the Bambuti Pygmies in the eastern Democratic Republic of Congo, MRG, London, 2004.

5   BBC, *Is this peace for eastern DR Congo?*, 24/1/2008, available at: http://news.bbc. co.uk/1/hi/world/africa/7206823.stm.

6   International Rescue Committee, *IRC study shows Congo's neglected crisis leaves 5.4 million dead*, 22/1/2008. Available at: http://www.theirc.org/news/irc-study-shows-congos0122.html. The IRC claims that the vast majority of deaths are caused by malaria, diarrhoea, pneumonia and malnutrition, i.e. non-violent and easily preventable and treatable conditions.

7   See, for example, IRIN, *DRC: Aid workers struggle to reach IDPs in South Kivu*, 25/7/2007, available at:
     http://www.irinnews.org/report.aspx?ReportID=73401, and IRIN, *DRC: Fighting restricting humanitarian access in North Kivu*, 7/9/2007, available at: http://www.ir-innews.org/report.aspx?ReportID=74176. UN Daily News from the United Nations News Service, *DR Congo: Teams on ground to allow quicker diagnosis of disease* – *UN* (20/9/2007); IRIN, *DRC: Typhoid confirmed in western Kasai Province*, 20/9/2007, available at:
     http://www.irinnews.org/report.aspx?ReportID=74403; UN Daily News from the United Nations News Service, *DR Congo: UN agency steps up efforts to curb spread of cholera in North Kivu*, (9/11/2007).

8   UN Security Council, *Twenty-fourth report of the Secretary-General on the United Nations Organization Mission in the Democratic Republic of Congo*, op. cit. This includes the estimated ½ million people who were displaced during 2007 alone. The Secretary-General also notes in his report that only 56 percent of the US$686 million requested through the 2007 Humanitarian Action Plan had been received. IDP estimates vary and are difficult to assess because of what is termed 'pendulum' displacement, whereby IDPs spend nights in areas they consider safe and return to their homes/farms etc. during the day. See, for example, IRIN, *DRC: 'Pendulum displacement' in the Kivus*, 1/8/2007, available at: http://www.irinnews.org/report. aspx?ReportID=73524

9   MONUC, *Monthly Human Rights Assessment: February 2007*, available at: http:// www.monuc.org/News.aspx?newsId=14119, and *Monthly Human Rights Assessment: March 2007*, available at:
     http://www.monuc.org/News.aspx?newsId=14383

10   UN Press Release, *UN Expert on violence against women expresses serious concerns following visit to the Democratic Republic of Congo*, 30/7/2007. Available at: http://www. unhchr.ch/huricane/huricane.nsf/NewsRoom?OpenFrameSet. The expert told the UN General Assembly that *"The scale and brutality of the sexual violence currently faced by women in the Democratic Republic of the Congo (DRC) amounts to war crimes and crimes against humanity."* See: UN Daily News from the UN News Service, *Sexual violence against women in DR Congo amounts to war crime: UN expert*, 26/10/07.

11   **Jackson, D.:** *Twa women, Twa rights*, op. cit.

12   A representative of the indigenous support organisation, CAMV (*Centre d'Accompagnement des Autochtones Pygmées et Minoritaires Vulnérables*), brought this situation to the attention of the African Commission on Human and Peoples' Rights during its November 2007 session.

13 For background information on the 2002 Forest Code and ongoing forestry reforms in DRC, see *The Indigenous World 2007*.

14 *Loi 011/2002 du 29 Août 2002 Portant Code Forestier* (Law 011/2002 of 29 August 2002, Forest Code). Any translations of the 2002 Forestry Code and implementing regulations are unofficial translations by the author. For an early analysis of the 2002 Forest Code and indigenous peoples, see: **Forest Peoples Programme and Réseau des Associations Autochtones Pygmées, 2004:** *Guide pour la compréhension du Code forestier à l'usage des populations locales et du peuple autochtone 'Pygmée'*, page 10.

15 Greenpeace, *Carving up the Congo*, 11 April 2007, available at: http://www.greenpeace.org.uk/media/reports/carving-up-the-congo.

16 *Décret No 06/141 du 10 novembre 2006 portant nomination des membres de la Commission Interministerielle de conversion des titres forestiers* (Decree No 06/141 of 10 November 2006 on the Nomination of Members of the Commission on Forestry Title Conversion).

17 See, for example, CAMV, *Le Forestier No.1*, July 2007.

18 Organisations Autochtones Pygmées et accompagnant les Autochtones Pygmées en République Démocratique du Congo, *Requête adressée au Panel d'Inspection de la Banque Mondiale*, 30 October 2005, Kinshasa, DRC. The Inspection Panel's 2006 preliminary report noted that the World Bank was not in full compliance with Operational Directive 4.20, its safeguard policy on indigenous peoples, and in response the Bank committed to preparing an Indigenous Peoples' Plan. See: The Inspection Panel, *Report and Recommendation on Request for Inspection, Democratic Republic of Congo: Transitional Support for Economic Recovery Credit Operation (TSERO) (IDA Grant No. H192-DRC) and Emergency Economic and Social Reunification Support Project (EESRSP) (IDA Credit No. 3824-DRC and IDA Grant No. H064-DRC)*, undated.

19 The Inspection Panel, *Investigation Report: Democratic Republic of Congo: Transitional Support for Economic Recovery Grant (TSERO) (IDA Grant No. H 1920-DRC) and Emergency Economic and Social Reunification Support Project (EESRSP) (Credit No. 3824-DRC and Grant No. H 064-DRC): Executive Summary*, Report No. 40746 – ZR, 31/8/2007. Available at: http://siteresources.worldbank.org/EXTINSPECTIONPANEL/Resources/EXECUTIVESUMMARYFINAL.pdf

20 *Ibid.* page 9.

21 UN, *Concluding Observations of the Committee on the Elimination of Racial Discrimination: Democratic Republic of Congo*, UN. Doc. No. CERD/C/COD/CO/15/CRP.1, 17 August 2007, para. 18.

Lucy Mulvagh holds a Masters in Human Rights from the UK's University of Essex and is Project Officer on the Africa Legal and Human Rights Programme of the Forest Peoples Project (lucy@forestpeoples.org).

REPUBLIC OF CONGO
(CONGO BRAZZAVILLE)

The total population of the Republic of Congo, also known as Congo Brazzaville, is estimated at almost 3,800,000 people, with a growth rate of 3.2% per year and an average population density of 11 inhabitants/km^2, unequally distributed throughout the national territory.[1] Its inhabitants can be divided into ten large groups: the Baya, Kongo, Kota, Mbere Nzabi, Mbochi, Makas, Punu, Sangha, Teke and the semi-nomadic Pygmies[2]. There is no official census of the number of Pygmies, who are considered to be the indigenous peoples of the Republic of Congo. However, it is estimated that they represent around 10% of the country's whole population, i.e. around 300,000 people.[3] They are divided into two broad groups: the Babongo and the Bambenga, and then sub-divided again into various smaller groups: the Batswa, Baaka, Babi, Babongo, Bagyeli, Bakola, Baluma, Bangombe, Mbendjele and Mikaya.[4] As elsewhere in Central Africa, the Pygmies live in forested areas, more specifically in the departments of Bouenza, Kouilou (in Mayombe, towards Kola), Lékoumou, Likouala, Niari, Plateaux and Sangha.[5]

The Pygmies share the same way of life based on hunting and gathering, with a deep affinity for the forest. The indigenous peoples of the Congo today live in a situation of extreme poverty, marginalisation and vulnerability.

In general, no Congolese constitutional or legislative text provides any specific protection measures for the indigenous peoples. However, a pioneering bill on indigenous peoples' rights is underway.

Testing ground for indigenous peoples' rights

The Republic of Congo is now emerging as a testing ground for the recognition and protection of the rights of the indigenous Pygmy population of Central Africa. This is for at least two reasons: the first is the emergence of an organisational dynamic among the Pygmies themselves, through the creation of a national network of several Pygmy associations. The second is due to the historic decision taken by the Congolese government to organise the First International Forum on

Indigenous Peoples in Central Africa (FIPAC) from 10 to 15 april 2007 in Impfondo, Likouala department, in the north of the country.

The process of recognising, promoting and protecting the rights of indigenous Pygmy populations involves developing a Pygmy leadership, and this is taking place within the National Network of Indigenous Peoples of Congo (*Réseau National des Peuples Autochtones du Congo* - RENAPAC).

The emergence of an indigenous civil society

Under the coordination of the Ministry of Health, Social Affairs and Family, and with the support of UNICEF, an assembly was organised from 8 to 10 August 2007 to establish the National Network of Indigenous Peoples of Congo (RENAPAC). This assembly was attended by some fifty participants. Its overall objective was to contribute to the emergence of an indigenous leadership by creating a network of NGOs and associations, and building the capacities of indigenous leaders. Two bodies were set up: an executive team and a Board of Directors. The executive team is made up of six members,[6] and the Board of Directors comprises seven.[7] The members of both structures have received training on participatory development approaches, the importance of information technology in network management, administrative correspondence, project formulation, network management, submission of funding requests and accounting procedures for funds received.

Taking advantage of the celebrations around the UN International Day of Solidarity with Indigenous People on 9 August, the participants watched the advocacy film *"Nous les Pygmées"* (**"We the Pygmies")**, produced by UNICEF Congo. Echoing the sentiments of the film, RENAPAC's national coordinator, Mr. Bernard Ngouonimba Toto, justified creating the network with the need to "call upon people's consciences to improve indigenous living conditions". He urged the government to bring the process for adopting the national law on promotion and protection of indigenous rights to its successful conclusion and to vote in favour of the UN Declaration on the Rights of Indigenous Peoples.

The creation of this network, which brings all the indigenous peoples' associations and their partners together, marks an important stage in the Pygmies' organisational process, aimed at ensuring their full participation in the country's development. It will enable the emergence of leaders who can become trusted contacts for the government and development partners when promoting the recognition and development of Pygmy populations. Much work remains to be done, however, in terms of building the network's institutional and technical capacities and establishing it in the different regions of the country - where indigenous peoples are fighting for their survival on a daily basis – and, above all, in terms of implementing development programmes with the indigenous peoples.

Innovative arena for dialogue

One event in the lives of Congo's indigenous peoples that will undoubtedly be remembered for a long time to come was the government's historic decision to organise the First International Forum on Indigenous Peoples of Central Africa (FIPAC) from 10 to 15 april 2007 in Impfondo, Likouala department, in the north of the country.

This was the first time in Central Africa that a state had taken the decision to organise a forum on indigenous peoples. The overall theme of the Forum was "Involving indigenous peoples in the sustainable management and conservation of Central Africa's forest ecosystems", and it took place with the technical, financial and material support of various development partners, namely the WWF-World Bank Alliance, WWF, the Central African Forest Commission (COMIFAC), German Technical Cooperation (GTZ), UNICEF, UNEP, WHO, WFP, IUCN and Congo's private forestry sector.

The deliberations were presided over by His Excellency Mr. Henri Djombo, Minister for the Forest Economy of the Republic of Congo, on behalf of the President of the Republic of Congo, His Excellency Mr. Denis Sassou Nguesso. The following also took part: Mr. Désiré Kolingba Nzanga, Minister for Youth, Sports, Arts and Culture of the Central African Republic; Ms Awa Outh Mam Djame, Minister for the Natural and Living Environment of the Republic of Chad; Mr. Gilbert

Djombo Bomondjo, Prefect of Likouala Department; Mr. Laurent Magloire Some, Regional Representative of the WWF for Central Africa;Mr. Kapupu Diwa Mutimanwa, General Coordinator of the Network of Indigenous and Local Populations of Central Africa on Sustainable Forest Management.

Members of the diplomatic corps posted to the Republic of Congo also attended (the ambassadors of the Republic of South Africa, Central African Republic, Democratic Republic of Congo and France), along with indigenous delegates from eight countries (Burundi, Cameroon, Uganda, Central African Republic, Republic of Congo, Democratic Republic of Congo, Gabon and Rwanda), representatives of international organisations (UNEP, World Bank, ILO, the Secretariat of the United Nations Convention to Combat Desertification), national and international NGOs (FPP, WCS, CED, CERAD, WWF, CARPE/USAID...) and forestry companies (CIB, etc.). Delegations from Cameroon and Gabon joined in the deliberations, led by Mr. Nana Aboubakar, Minister Delegate under the Minister for Environment and Protection of Nature, and Mr. Alphonse Owele, Advisor to the Minister for the Forest Economy, Water, Fishing and National Parks of Gabon respectively.

The main aim of the forum was to:

- Strengthen the capacity of Central Africa's indigenous peoples around the rights that are recognised to them in international conventions and national legislation on sustainable management and conservation of forest ecosystems;
- Encourage exchanges of experience and of cases where indigenous rights have been recognised and protected in the area of sustainable management and conservation of Central Africa's forest ecosystems;
- Identify ideas for a sub-regional action plan to ensure greater involvement of indigenous peoples in the sustainable management and conservation of Central Africa's forest ecosystems, in accordance with the provisions of international conventions and national legislation on biodiversity management and conservation.

At the end of the conference, the participants identified the main stages that needed to be established in order to strengthen the dialogue between Central African states and indigenous peoples. These related primarily to continuing and completing the process of producing a sub-regional strategic action plan on indigenous peoples in relation to the sustainable management of Central Africa's forests, in line with methods to be defined by COMIFAC. This plan aims to strengthen:

- The "Convergence Plan" ("*Plan de convergence*"), which is the sub-regional plan for the concerted management of Central Africa's forest ecosystems;
- FIPAC's institutionalisation, over a three-year period, and the establishment of a monitoring mechanism involving COMI-FAC's Executive Secretariat;
- The signing of a cooperation agreement between REPALEAC (Regional network of the local and indigenous people for the sustainable management of Central Africa's forests ecosystems) and COMIFAC;
- Consideration of the concerns and specific features of indigenous peoples within national poverty reduction strategies and sectoral policies;
- The establishment – within all the countries – of an impact assessment mechanism for projects and programmes affecting indigenous peoples;
- The implementation, on the part of Central Africa's states, of actions aimed at adopting the UN Declaration on the Rights of Indigenous Peoples.

As can be seen, these actions - without comprehensively covering all that needs to be done in the Congo to ensure the well-being of the indigenous Pygmy peoples - form a legal and dignified start that will necessarily need to be improved and, above all, used to build a future for these peoples, whose basic rights are still being ignored and threatened. This requires more than simple good intentions aimed at satisfying the international community, easing consciences or simply being fashionable. And it also requires that the indigenous peoples themselves invest in the spaces that have been created so that they can take their destiny into their own hands.

Law on the rights of indigenous peoples

A draft law protecting the rights of indigenous peoples has been submitted to the Government Secretariat and is under review and administrative analysis. Questions raised about its adoption relate to the advisability of such a development in a state that promotes national unity and the non-specific treatment of citizens. There is therefore a need to raise awareness among all government bodies as to the importance of supporting this innovative reform.   ❑

Notes

1   Human Development Report, UNDP, PNUD, 2005.
2   Whilst aware of the pejorative and derogatory nature of the word, this article uses the term "Pygmy" for lack of an alternative that can encompass the different groups that make up this community in the Republic of Congo.
3   **UNICEF, 2001:** *Aide-mémoire du Projet Pygmées*, UNICEF, Brazzaville, 2001, p. 1 and *Rapport final UNICEF au donateur du Projet d'amélioration des conditions d'accès aux services sociaux de base de la minorité Pygmée (Baka) en République du Congo*, August 2004, p. 4. Figures taken from a speech by Mr. Koenraad Vanormiligen, UNICEF representative to the Republic of Congo at the opening of a national consultation workshop on improving the quality of life of indigenous peoples in Congo, Brazzaville, 29 November 2007, p.1. See also, from an historical perspective, the *Rapport Général de l'Habitat et de la Population, République du Congo*, Ministère du Plan 1984, quoted by Mafoukila (Constance Mathurine); *La scolarisation des enfants Pygmées au Congo*, Yaoundé, Presses Universitaires d'Afrique, 2006, p. 42. For more general information on the indigenous Pygmy populations of the Republic of Congo see **Gambeg, Yvon-Norbert, Gami, Norbert and Bigombe Logo, Patrice, 2006:** L'insertion des Pygmées du Congo dans l'économie moderne, in: A Séverin Cécile and Bigombe Logo, Patrice (eds.): *La Marginalisation des Pygmées d'Afrique centrale*, Paris, Maisonneuve et Larose et Afrédit, pp. 125-139 ; **GambegYvon Norbert, 2006:** Les Politiques d'intégration des Pygmées dans la Société Congolaise, in Abega,Séverin Cécile and Bigombe Logo, Patrice (eds.); *La Marginalisation des Pygmées d'Afrique centrale*, op. cit., pp. 209-223.
4   **Observatoire Congolais Des Droits De L'Homme, 2006:** *Les droits des peuples autochtones en République du Congo: analyse du contexte national et recommandations sur l'avant-projet de « loi portant promotion et protection des Pygmées au Congo*, report produced for the General Directorate of Human Rights and Fundamental

Freedoms as civil society's contribution to the drafting of the "Law on the promotion and protection of the Congo's Pygmies", Brazzaville, OCDH, May 2006, p.6.

5 **Mankassa,Côme, 1970**: *Notes sur les Pygmées de la Likouala*, Brazzaville, p. 5; **Mafoukila, Constance Mathurine, 2006**: *La scolarisation des enfants Pygmées au Congo*. Yaoundé, Presses Universitaires d'Afrique, p. 43.

6 The executive team members are: The National Coordinator, Mr. Bernard Ngouonimba Toto, the General Secretary, Mr. Jean Nganga, the treasurer, Ms Schella Ngouebara Ngouenoni, the legal affairs and human rights secretary, Ms Carine Nzimba Zere, the education, training and communications secretary, Mr. Alain Nsende and the children and gender secretary, Ms Stéphanie Mayinguidi.

7 The Board of Directors comprises the president Mr. Louis Ngouele Ibara; vice-president Mr. Adrien Kombe Mabotawa, rapporteur Mr. Désire Iwouangou and members: Antoine Ngoma, Charles Koumba, Paul Ombi and Edmond Ekoumé.

Patrice Bigombé Logo is a political scientist, teacher/researcher in the Groupe de recherches administratives, politiques et sociales (GRAPS) of Yaoundé II University, a researcher with the Fondation Paul Ango Ela (FPAE) on geopolitics in Central Africa and director of the Centre de recherche et d'action pour le développement durable en Afrique Centrale (CERAD), e-mail: patricebigombe@hotmail.com. His research work focuses on the sociology and anthropology of the state, in particular, the recognition and survival of Pygmy populations and the analysis of national resource management policies in Central Africa.

GABON

Indigenous hunter-gatherer communities (often referred to as Pygmies) are located throughout Gabon and include numerous ethnic groups (Baka, Babongo, Bakoya, Baghame, Barimba, Akoula, Akwoa, etc.) separated by locality, language and culture. Pygmy communities are found in a range of socio-economic situations: urban and forest-based. Their livelihoods and cultures remain inextricably tied to the forest areas of the country (85% of Gabon is forested). It has recently been estimated that the number of Pygmies in Gabon is 20,000 out of a national population of 1,400,000.[1]

The last decade has seen the rise of the indigenous movement and four[2] officially recognised indigenous organizations..[3]Two of the leaders currently hold regional positions in IPACC.

Since 2002, due to increasing environmental threats posed by expanding extractive industries, the Country has received a large influx of foreign funding and human resources to support Congo Basin conservation initiatives, in particular the establishment of 13 National Parks. In 2005, Gabon agreed to its own Indigenous Peoples' Plan as part of a World Bank policy loan agreement for the Forest and Environment Sector Program (Schmidt-Soltau, 2005). This marked the government's first official recognition of the existence of and responsibility towards indigenous peoples.

Political and legislative developments

Forest-based hunter-gatherers have increasingly relocated to roadside locations, a process initiated by colonial resettlement programmes and sustained throughout post-independence and present-

day development policies. The majority of Gabonese hunter-gatherer communities based in roadside settlements experience problems of marginalisation, poverty through lack of access to basic resources, and social segregation.

Current threats and challenges for the Pygmy population in Gabon include severe environmental damage to ancestral lands and resources, infrastructural transformations (roads, dams and railways), large-scale commercial bush-meat hunting, insecurity of land tenure and encroachment through logging and extractive activities, conservation developments and regulations, resettlement and integration plans, insufficient representation in community land claims and lack of sufficient funding and support for indigenous organizations.

Recent developments in forest policy and national park legislation are of serious concern for the future welfare of indigenous populations. In September 2007, the new National Park Law was adopted, five years after the establishment of 13 national parks in 2002. According to the Law, access to and local subsistence activities within the parks are illegal except in certain approved fishing and ecotourism zones. In delineated "buffer zones" surrounding the parks, local activities will be monitored and limited to traditional hunting methods identified as having a low environmental impact, e.g. excluding firearms. Indigenous populations are located in the proximity of (and their ancestral lands and hunting territories may extend to) several of the national parks, including Minkebe, Waka, Lope and Ivindo.

It is not yet clear how this legislation will affect indigenous populations through the implementation of individual park management plans. Negotiations continue between the ministries, park managers, legal experts and indigenous representatives on how to produce Park specific regulations that take into account the importance of traditional cultural activities. Progress in this area has been delayed largely due to the restructuring of the government and ministries, notably the establishment of the National Park Agency (ANPN), created by the National Park Law to replace the National Park Council (CNPN). The ANPN will be under the new Ministry of Tourism and National Parks.

In July, following the official visit of the French President Nicolas Sarkozy, as a commitment to conservation, President Bongo agreed to redirect foreign debt repayment into the Forest-Environment sector and held an hour-long meeting with environmental NGOs and stakeholders. Reportedly, no indigenous representatives were present.

In the wake of the 2006 national elections, 2007 was dominated by negotiations concerning large-scale developments in the north-east of the country. The government's decision to sell iron-mining rights to Chinese firms in Belinga - involving the construction of a new railway line and a hydroelectric dam on the Kongou waterfalls within Ivindo National Park - has raised major concerns amongst national and international environmental agencies and NGOs. The work continues despite calls for greater transparency and environmental safeguards. The area to be affected by these developments is close to two other national parks and local indigenous Bakoya and Baka communities. The road construction has begun cutting through the Ivindo National Park to the site of the hydroelectric dam that will supply the mining operation with electricity.

Conflicting conservation and commercial interests surrounding matters such as Belinga and the resumption of oil prospecting operations in Loango National Park came to a head in December 2007 when the Minister of the Interior suspended (and later re-instated) the activities of twenty local non-governmental organizations that had been campaigning against the environmental impacts on the area.

The Indigenous Peoples' Plan (IPP) has been further delayed this year pending the signing over of the World Bank loan tied to the PSFE-GEF Project, which finally took place at the end of the year. The IPP is part of the Forest Environment Sector Plan and is a national programme designed to streamline and coordinate all stakeholders' and partners' involvement in the country's natural resource management. It is thus a key document in the framing of future policy and national legislation. Through a number of specific projects focusing on, for example, mapping the demography of indigenous populations, capacity building of indigenous representation, resettlement programmes etc., the IPP aims to ensure that the respect, dignity and culture of indigenous peoples are protected during these developments and due benefits and compensation received. Planned projects are now rescheduled to start in 2008.

Policies, programs and projects

The UNICEF nationwide outreach project, entitled "Integrated Development for Pygmy Communities", with its focus on improving basic health and access to birth certificates, continued throughout the year. This has been an extensive project involving indigenous leaders, local NGOs and government representatives and has encouraged a number of visits by officials to remote areas. The Baka organization Edzengui collaborated with the Ministry for Social Affairs and National Solidarity, resulting in a meeting in Esseng (Baka village near Minvoul) and an official visit from the *préfet* (local government administrator) to distribute birth certificates to children.

Regional programs for delineating community forests have continued, notably in the north-east of Gabon around the national park of Minkébé, where Nature Plus, a European NGO, is continuing its 5-year program to establish community forestry. The project "Developing Community Alternatives to Illegal Forest Exploitation" (DACEFI) is underway in this region, involving partners such as Nature Plus, FUSAGx (the Gembloux Faculty of Agronomic Science) and the Worldwide Fund for Nature (WWF). Through DACEFI, the Baka organization Edzengui, in partnership with WWF, is planning a venture to promote agriculture amongst Baka communities.

Several projects focusing on indigenous communities are still at the planning stage and have emerged out of a strengthening of international partnerships and indigenous organizations. For example, the Rainforest Foundation, in consultation with the Forest Peoples Programme (FPP) and the Indigenous Peoples of Africa Coordinating Committee (IPACC), has held meetings with indigenous organizations and conservation organizations to plan pilot participatory mapping projects in the vicinity of National Parks and areas threatened by logging concessions.

In November 2007, IPACC conducted a mission to Gabon. Meetings took place involving leaders of the Gabonese indigenous organizations, the Tropical Forest Trust and Conservation organizations WWF and Wildlife Conservation Society (WCS). Leonard Odambo, leader of the Pygmy organization MINAPYGA (*Mouvement des minorités autochtones, indigènes et pygmées du Gabon*), traveled with IPACC and WCS to visit the area of Waka National Park where the Babongo and Mitsogho communities have been seriously affected by large-scale destructive logging activities conducted by Sino-Malaysian companies. The situation is predicted to worsen due to a large contract to cut the rainforest between the Lopé and Waka National Parks, which are the traditional territories of the Babongo and Mitsogho. MINAPYGA has signed an agreement with IPACC, WCS and the Waka National Park Conservator to help support local representation through the formation of community associations in the area of the Waka National Park.

In October 2007, the African Commission's Working Group on Indigenous Populations/Communities visited Gabon. The delegation met with Gabonese indigenous representatives and government officials in Libreville and travelled to the interior to meet indigenous communities and organizations.

Indigenous representation

2007 saw a marked increase in the involvement of Gabonese indigenous representation in national and international human rights and conservation forums. Consequently, indigenous organizations have built important partnerships with external agencies that have assisted them in the planning of future projects.

Leonard Odambo (representing MINAPYGA) has emerged as a key spokesman to represent Gabonese indigenous issues on the international scene. Throughout the year, he traveled widely to national and international conferences and regional training programmes. On returning to Gabon from New York where the UN Declaration on the Rights of Indigenous Peoples was adopted, Odambo gained the support of the President's daughter who agreed to an official visit to his home region of Mekambo (a town in north-eastern Gabon, in the vicinity of which there are several Bakoya mixed villages) to promote the Declaration at national level. During 2007, Odambo travelled frequently within Gabon to reinforce grassroots networks and to provide information on the rights of indigenous peoples and the recently adopted UN Declaration in remote areas of Gabon.

After a very eventful 2006, the Baka organization Edzengui had a challenging year in 2007. Attempts to attend international forums had to be aborted due to logistical and financial problems. WWF Libreville continues to support the organization in planning future projects and enabling Baka attendance at several key meetings and workshops within Gabon.

The Babongo organization ADCPPG (*Association pour le Développement de la Culture des Peuples Pygmées du Gabon*), in consultation with the World Bank and government ministries, has continued plans for future projects linked to the Indigenous Peoples' Plan. Mr. Massandé, representing ADCPPG, participated in several key national and regional meetings and workshops, for example, the government hosted the *Forum International des Peuples Autochtones des Forêts d'Afrique Cen-*

trale held in Impfondo in the Republic of Congo and the First International Central African Indigenous Peoples' Meeting in April 2007 held in the Democratic Republic of Congo.

Recently NGOs have been established that prioritise work with indigenous representatives to ensure that development processes and ecotourism ventures promote indigenous knowledge and retain standards of dignity and fairness. In 2007, the NGO *Le Fleuron d'Afrique Equatoriale* was established with the purpose of creating ecotourism activities in Gabon that benefit local and indigenous communities. ❏

Notes

1   In 2005, based on existing research and the current national census, the Association for the Development of Pygmy Peoples' Culture in Gabon (ADCPPG) estimated the highest total to date for Gabonese Pygmy populations, at 20,005 out of a national population of approximately 1,400,000 (Massandé 2005).
2   Kutimuvara was established as an indigenous NGO in 2002 to represent southern Varama groups. Due to the challenge posed by Bavarama communities being so dispersed, and the organization being based outside of the capital, without any strong partnerships or external support, this organization is less developed and well-known than the other indigenous organizations and has consequently been overlooked in previous reports and publications.

References

Massandé, D., 2005: Organisation Territoriale du Gabon Demographie Chiffres Des Peuples Autochtones Pygmées de Gabon. *ADCPPG report*, 30 June 2005.
Schmidt-Soltau, K., 2005: *Programme Sectoriel Forêts et Environnement (PSFE) Plan de Développement des Peuples Autochtones. Rapport Final.* July 2005. World Bank, Washington.

Judy Knight, is a consultant anthropologist based in Gabon. She has been working on various projects with Central African indigenous forest communities since 1992, and has worked in consultation with indigenous NGOs and major conservation organisations on indigenous peoples' rights and the safeguarding of traditional forest-related knowledge, in and around protected areas. Contact: Judyknight@uuplus.com/jkanthro@yahoo.co.uk.

CAMEROON

Among Cameroon's more than 17 million inhabitants, some communities identify themselves as indigenous. These include the hunter/gatherer Pygmies, the nomadic Mbororo pastoralists and the Kirdi communities. The indigenous Pygmies can be further divided into three sub-groups, namely, around 4,000 Bagyeli or Bakola, more than 40,000 Baka and around 300 Bedzan.[1] These communities live along the forested borders with Gabon, the Republic of Congo and the Central African Republic. Together the Pygmies represent around 0.4% of the total population of Cameroon. The Mbororo living in Cameroon are estimated to number over 60,000, living primarily along the borders with Nigeria, Chad and the Central African Republic.[2] The Kirdi communities live high up in the Mandara Mountain range, in the north of Cameroon. Their precise number is not known.

The constitution of the Republic of Cameroon uses the word "indigenous".[3] The country has adopted a Plan for the Development of the "Pygmy" Peoples within the context of its Poverty Reduction Strategy Paper. A Plan for Indigenous and Vulnerable Peoples has also been developed in the context of the oil pipeline carrying Chadian oil to the Cameroonian port of Kribi.

Land and citizenship

Irrespective of their diversity, the Pygmies share a number of values around which their very specific culture is based. This relates primarily to a deep attachment to the forest and an attachment to social traditions as a way of maintaining and reproducing the social order, mobility and religion. The whole of Pygmy life is focused around its links with the forest and the forest alone represents everything for Pygmies. This is not conducive to helping Pygmies adapt to the way in which national citizenship is currently politically constructed.

The state and the dominant Bantu populations as a whole still do not completely recognise the Pygmies as full citizens of Cameroon. In practical terms, this denial of citizenship, consisting of a lack of recognition of the basic civil and political rights of the Pygmy community, is demonstrated in problems accessing land, difficulties in obtaining administrative recognition of their villages and limited access to basic social services (education and health). Now, unlike in the past, relations between Pygmy and Bantu populations are dominated by confrontation and conflict and the Bantu affirm their supremacy and superiority over the Pygmies. The most significant issue of concern between the Pygmies and the Bantu is generally conflict over land. This is more intense in regions where there is significant pressure on the land, for example, in the east of Cameroon, in Lolodorf district, where there are specific problems between Bantu from Ngoyang village and Bakola Pygmies from Nkuongio village.[4]

The issue of access to land, recognition of Pygmy chiefdoms and the recognition and implementation of Pygmy citizenship were key issues addressed in Cameroon during 2007.

The dynamics of creating Pygmy chiefdoms

Citizenship is both a status and a quality: that of being members of a political community.[5] The idea of status refers to a group of rights (civil, political and social) and duties (respect for laws) that have to be effectively enjoyed by an individual in the context of positive law, and that of quality or identity refers to a feeling of belonging or allegiance to the wider political community.[6] The creation of community or "3rd degree" chiefdoms in regions where Pygmies have long become settled forms a part of the recognition and affirmation of their citizenship. It is a prerequisite to the long-term security of their land rights.[7] As the chiefdom has a geographical basis, the creation of any chiefdom, and

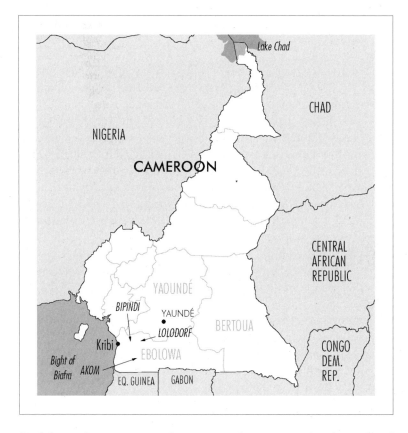

"3rd degree" ones in particular, requires demarcating the physical and spatial territory over which the chief will be called to exercise power.

In Cameroon public law, the creation of "3rd degree" chiefdoms is governed by Decree No. 77/245 dated 15 July 1977 on the organisation of traditional chiefdoms, amended and completed by Decree No. 82/241 dated 24 June 1982. This stipulates that traditional authorities are to be organised into chiefdoms, on a geographical basis. They are to be structured into three hierarchical levels: 1st, 2nd and 3rd degree. Our analysis refers to "3rd degree" chiefdoms, and these correspond to villages or rural/urban districts. "First degree" chiefdoms are created by prime ministerial decree, "2nd degree" chiefdoms by the Minister for Territorial Administration and "3rd degree" chiefdoms by the Regional Prefect. The chiefs are, in principle, chosen from among those families that have been customarily called on to exercise traditional command.[8]

In terms of ownership, the 1974 land reform established three categories of domain: lands belonging to the state and other public authorities; lands of national domain; and those of the private domain. Of these three categories, the national domain is an exceptional category, defined as being all lands forming neither part of the state nor the private domain. The following thus forms part of the national domain: lands of habitation, cultivation, plantation, pasture and passageway the occupation of which results in man's clear hold over the land and its proven development; (and) lands free from all effective occupation. National ownership, as indicated by its name, is administered by the state with a view to ensuring the lands' rational use and development.

In its role as administrator of these assets, the state therefore reserves the right to allocate to the local authorities, their members or any other person of Cameroon nationality "dependencies of the national domain, occupied or free from effective occupation, in the form of a temporary concession and on condition of their development. This is a condition of transfer to a permanent concession carrying full ownership and consequent registration of the plot. Once established, the land title is irrefutable, intangible and final, unless error or irregularity is noted by the relevant authorities".[9]

The main innovation in the 1974 reform was the abolition of the customary land system and the prevalence of written law, particularly registration, which has since then become the only legal method for appropriating land, with a land title being the only way of proving ownership. Apart from its unifying function, the 1974 reform aimed to free up lands that could have been managed customarily so that they could become tools of agricultural production, above all in the context of the national development strategy. To the detriment of local populations and their customs, this reform strengthened the state's monopoly over the land. It made dispossession of the indigenous peoples' land base a concrete reality.

As with the creation of "3rd degree" chiefdoms, the state does not discriminate with regard to the possibility of Pygmies accessing lands and forests of the national domain if they can fulfil the requirements of the regulations. The state law thus offers Pygmies the possibility of accessing lands and forests. It is instead Bantu customary land and forest law that forms an obstacle to the Pygmies effective accessing of land and forest ownership. The Bantu allow the Pygmies to use the land for agricultural purposes as long as they do not sow perennial crops.

In order to respond to this problem, civil society players, particularly local and national NGOs, under the leadership of the Centre for Environment and Development (*Centre pour l'Environnement et le Développement* - CED), have since 2004 been implementing a project to guarantee the land rights of the Baka and Bagyéli- Bakola with the technical and financial support of the Rainforest Foundation UK and the Forest Peoples Programme (FPP), among others. The actions are based on a participatory mapping of Pygmy traditional villages and land issue negotiations between the Bantu chiefs and the Pygmy communities under the supervision of the local administrative authorities, mainly the Sub-Prefect of the region. This has enabled, on the one hand, land agreements to be signed between some Bakola-Bagyéli communities and their Bantu neighbours in the districts of Bipindi and Kribi in the south of Cameroon. The process of negotiation and signing of the agreements was facilitated by national NGOs, CED and Planet Survey, with the technical and financial support of Forest Peoples Programme. Secondly, the creation of Bagyéli chiefdoms has been achieved, also in the south of the country, more specifically in Akom II district in the Océan division of Cameroon. Additional financial support has also been given to obtaining identification documents, such as birth certificates and ID cards, which has been of important success within the communities, and four Bagyéli villages in Akom II district had their community chiefs established in June and July 2007: Awomo, Mefane, Mingoh and Nko'omvomba.

The introduction of community chiefdoms must culminate, finally, in the creation of "3rd degree" chiefdoms if it is to have a decisive and lasting effect on Pygmy citizenship and access to land. It forms an important transitory stage and a considerable change in the relationship between the state and the Pygmy communities, and between these latter and their Bantu neighbours. An innovative change in Pygmy status within land negotiations between themselves and the Bantu can also be observed. To date, 19 Bagyéli communities in Bipindi district in the

South province of Cameroon have obtained legal recognition of the lands they occupy. Depending on the local pressure on the land, the areas granted vary between 0.4 hectares for Log Diga and 1,500 hectares for Bokwi, both in the Bipindi district.

Prospects for securing Pygmy land rights

The results achieved so far, both in relation to chiefdoms and land-use recognition, have been obtained through tripartite negotiations involving the local administrative and religious authorities, Bantu and Pygmy populations and NGOs.[10] These practical actions in relation to chiefdoms and land use rights have been followed by training seminars for NGO staff, organised by the Forest Peoples Project, on: a) securing land rights for indigenous peoples and b) the African human rights system. These were held in February and October of this year, respectively.[11] Despite the changes that have begun to take place through these different actions, for the most part pioneering and innovative, we shall clearly have to wait for implementation of these agreements and functioning of the chiefdoms, and their interaction with the Bantu communities as a whole, along with validation of what has been achieved at the local level by public authorities at the highest level before we can hope and conclude that they may be lasting.

With regard to issues of logging and indigenous peoples' rights in 2007, the main news is that some logging companies are using the Forest Stewardship Council (FSC) certification system, for example, R.PALLIS-CO, ALPICAM, and others have agreed to draft specific policies to address indigenous peoples' problems in terms of sustainable forest management. Some studies have been carried out to understand the links between indigenous people and forest resources. Operational programmes will be set up to deal with critical issues arising out of the studies.

The Mbororo

Mbororo communities have continued to face marginalization and human rights abuses, lack of social infrastructure and education facilities.

Within Mboscuda, their national association and network, some activities have been established to handle these issues. Among these are the para-legal extension activities, mainly in the north-west province of Cameroon, the gender and women's promotion programmes (micro-credit with 18 women's groups) and capacity building in group dynamics and small business management. ❑

Notes

1 **Barume, A.K., 2005** : Etude sur le cadre légal pour la protection des droits des peuples indigènes et tribunaux au Cameroun. International Labour Organisation, ILO, Geneva, p.24.

2 Ibid, p.25.

3 The preamble to the Cameroon Constitution stipulates: "the State shall ensure the protection of minorities and preserve the rights of indigenous populations, in accordance with the law".

4 A land conflict that has emerged between the Bantu community of Ngoyang and the Bakola Pygmies of Nkuongio since the creation of the Bakola community chiefdom degenerated into clashes between members of the two communities in September 2006. Read the complaint from Mr Ngally Sadrack, dignitary from the Bakola chiefdom, submitted on 04 September 2006 to the Brigade Commander of the Lolodorf National Gendarmerie against Owona Amougou Rémy, Tami Andegue Roland, Amougou Andegue Martial, Tsoungui Andegue Etienne and Alima Sophie, for violation of domicile, interference with the right to enjoyment, bodily harm and ill-treatment.

5 **Constant Fred, 2000**: La Citoyenneté, 2nd edition, Paris, Montchrestien, p. 27.

6 **Castillo, Monique, 2002**: La Citoyenneté en question, Paris, Ellipses, p. 8

7 See on this subject **Bigombe Logo, Patrice, Nkoumbele, Francis-Nazaire and Ngima Mawoung, Godefroy, 2006:** La création des chefferies de troisième degré pygmées au Cameroun: faisabilité politique et juridique et contraintes sociologiques. In: Abega, Séverin Cécile and Bigombe Logo, Patrice; *La Marginalisation des Pygmées d'Afrique centrale, Paris, Maisonneuve et Larose et Afrédit*, pp. 225-233 and BIT-PRO 169; Rapport de l'atelier national sur les questions des peuples indigenes et tribaux au Cameroun, Yaoundé, 15-17 June 2007, 102 pages.

8 Article 8 of Decree 1977.

9 Article 1 of Decree 76-165 dated 27 April 1976 establishing the conditions for obtaining land title

10 For an exhaustive analysis of the results of this countrywide project, see **Handja, Georges Thierry, 2007**: *La reconnaissance des droits des communautés Pygmées du Sud Cameroun sur les resources naturelles, communication à l'atelier RRI*, Douala, Cameroon, December 2007; **Kim Noëlle Brice, 2007**:*Avant nous avions les yeux clos, maintenant nos yeux sont ouverts. Maintenant je m'exprime. Ce n'était pas le cas*

avant. Une évaluation du programme de sécurisation des droits des Bakas, des Bagyélis et des Bakola (2004-2007), Yaoundé, July 2007, 56 pages; **Mefoude Sandra, 2007**: *Des Bagyéli propriétaires terriens, in Bubinga, n° 117*, July 2007, pp. 6-7 and **Nelson, John, 2007**: *Securing indigenous land rights in the Cameroon oil pipeline zone*, London, Forest Peoples Programme, July 2007, 24 pages.

11   See **Forest Peoples Project, 2007**: *Les droits fonciers des peuples autochtones: normes et mécanismes internationaux dans une perspective africaine*, London, February 2007, 77 pages and **Braun, Tréva and Mulvagh, Lucy, 2007**: *Le système africain des droits humains: un guide pour les peuples autochtones*, London, October 2007, 180 pages.

Patrice Bigombé Logo is a political scientist, teacher/researcher in the Groupe de recherches administratives, politiques et sociales (GRAPS) of Yaoundé II University, a researcher with the Fondation Paul Ango Ela (FPAE) on geopolitics in Central Africa and director of the Centre de recherche et d'action pour le développement durable en Afrique Centrale (CERAD), e-mail: patricebigombe@hotmail.com. His research work focuses on the sociology and anthropology of the state, in particular, the recognition and survival of Pygmy populations and the analysis of national resource management policies in Central Africa.

CENTRAL AFRICAN REPUBLIC

The indigenous population of the Central African Republic is made up of the Mbororo and Pygmy (known as Aka or BaAka). The former are pastoralists while the latter are hunter-gatherers, although both pursue a nomadic lifestyle. The Mbororo population is estimated at around 40,000 or more or less 1% of the total population, and is spread throughout the country, while the Pygmies, estimated at several tens of thousands, are found only in the forested area of the country.[1] A census conducted by the Italian NGO COOPI in 2004 suggested that there could be as many as 15,880 Aka living in Lobaye prefecture alone.[2] The preamble to the Central African Constitution proclaims the country's ethnic, cultural and religious diversity, and calls for the construction of a state based on the protection of minorities, which includes indigenous peoples. The cultural heritage of indigenous peoples is, moreover, protected by a decree dated 1 August 2003 issued by the Ministry of Youth, Sports, Art and Culture. A process to ratify ILO Convention 169 is underway.

The Central African Republic (CAR) is currently undergoing a period of political instability, marked by recurrent internal conflicts that continue to affect the life of the whole population, including the indigenous Mbororo and Aka peoples. The following provides an overview of some of the initiatives and events of 2007 that affected the lives of the CAR's indigenous population.

Armed conflicts

On a political level, armed conflicts in the north-west of the country caused more than 40,000[3] indigenous Mbororo to flee to Cameroon with their cattle, leading to a consequent hike in beef prices throughout the country. This has led to increased pressure on the south-western forests of the Aka Pygmies, where the availability of wild game is in rapid decline due to poaching.

Ratification of ILO Convention 169

After delays caused by internal disagreements among numerous government offices, the process of ratifying ILO Convention 169 is now back under the responsibility of the Ministry of Youth, Sports, Art and Culture, which is deemed to have a better mastery of the procedure. There is thus renewed hope that this text will be ratified during 2008.

Granting of substitute birth certificates

A major problem for Pygmies is that they are not registered and this has serious implications for citizenship rights. From 19 May to 22 June 2007, the *Conseil Inter ONG en CentrAfrique* (CIONGCA) identified 3,258 Pygmy children in Bimbo, Pissa and M'baïki districts[4] and issued 1,688 certificates of apparent age, which were sent to the M'baïki County Court with a view to producing substitute birth certificates.[5] These documents confirm the legal identity of the children in question and also offer them the possibility of enrolling at primary school.

Projects affecting indigenous peoples

The Ministry of Water, Forests, Hunting, Fishing and the Environment, along with its international partners, the World Wildlife Fund (WWF)

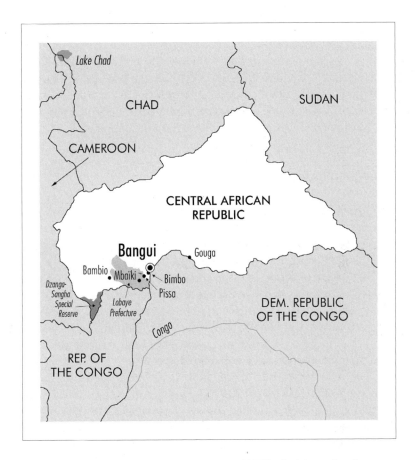

and the German Technical Cooperation (GTZ) , has been implementing the following projects:

A project entitled *"A sustainable lifestyle for the people of the Dzanga-Sangha Special Reserve in the Central African Republic"* is being commenced in partnership with WWF and with funding from the European Union. With an expected project start date of April 2008, its overall objective is to reduce poverty among the inhabitants of the Dzanga-Sangha Special Reserve (in the south-western CAR on the border with Cameroon and the Republic of Congo), and among the Aka Pygmies in particular. Its specific objective is to obtain formal rights for these latter in terms of the sustainable use of natural resources and adequate health and education services.[6]

GTZ has funded the drilling of two wells: one in Monasao[7] on 7 December 2007 to relieve the conflict between the Bilo[8] and the BaAka, created by a local Catholic church. A second at Mossapoula[9] on 9 December 2007, next to the health post, where a planned maternity unit and nutritional centre are to be built for the Aka Pygmies.[10]

Education programmes

The *Jesus-Christ aux Pygmées d'Afrique Centrale (JAPAC)* mission this year opened a primary school in Gouga,[11] the last Central African village before the border with the Republic of Congo. This is currently providing schooling for 185 Pygmy pupils from both countries.[12]

The Soobaajo Initiative, an association founded by a group of Central African Christians, opened a primary school in the Zacko 2 district on the northern fringes of Bangui in January 2007, and it now has 264 Mbororo children enrolled. Out of these, 138 children (57 girls and 81 boys) have just passed from the first level of basic education (Cours d'Initiation) to the second (Cours Préparatoire).[13]

The NGO *Maison de l'Enfant et de la Femme Pygmées* (M.E.F.P), founded in 2000, has taught 334 Aka Pygmies to read and write over the period 2006-2007, including 203 out of a total of 250 (81.2%) in Londo[14] village and 131 out of a total of 211 (62.09%) in Moloukou village – a village shared by the Bilo and Bantu, 178 kms from Bangui, in the sub-prefecture of M'baiki.

Self-organisation

Following a series of meetings facilitated by the Forest Peoples' Programme (FPP), an NGO based in the UK, during 2006 and 2007, on 11 December 2007 indigenous Aka from the Dzanga-Sangha Special Reserve, meeting in Yondo village, decided to set up an association known as the *"Association des BaAka de Sangha-YOBE"*. This association is credited with being the first authentic indigenous association in the

Central African Republic, as the idea came spontaneously from the indigenous peoples themselves.[15]

Important meetings

From 10 to 15 April 2007, Amadou Yamsa Abdoulaye, an indigenous Mbororo, Benard Malala, Antoine Zoko, Jérôme Ngama, Benjamin Mokondou and Pauline Koti, all indigenous Aka, attended the first International Forum of Indigenous Peoples of Central Africa held in Impfondo, Republic of Congo, entitled "Involving Indigenous Peoples in the sustainable management and preservation of Central Africa's forest ecosystems". Benoît Dimalet and Souma Marie Thérèse, both indigenous Aka, underwent training on the African human rights system in Yaoundé, Cameroon from 5 to 8 November 2007, where they learnt how to prepare and present an oral intervention and a supplementary report to the African Commission on Human and Peoples' Rights.

International Fair for the Sale of Pygmy Handicrafts

From 26 to 28 March 2007, the UNESCO National Commission for the CAR, in association with the Ministry of Youth, Sports, Art and Culture, organised the first International Fair for the Sale of Pygmy Handicrafts[16] in Bangui, including a number of objects exhibited and sold at the International Forum of Indigenous Peoples of Central Africa, held at Impfondo in the Republic of Congo in April 2007. This fair attracted large numbers of visitors and offered an opportunity for many to learn about the culture of indigenous Pygmy peoples.

Ill-treatment of indigenous peoples

During the Independence Day celebrations on 1 December 2007, indigenous Aka invited to Bangui for this purpose went on Radio Ndeke-Luka[17] to denounce the ill-treatment they were receiving at the hands of a number of civil servants who were supposed to be dealing with their issues. Their complaints focused on bad housing, bad food aid and a failure to receive all the money granted them by government. This situation demonstrates how indigenous rights continue to be flouted in the CAR.   ❑

Notes

1   La RCA en Chiffres, Résultats du Recensement Général de la population et de l'Habitation, December 2003
2   **Giolitto, Anna, 2006**: *Etude des cas de discrimination, abus et violations des droits de l'homme envers les pygmées Aka de la Lobaye République Centrafricaine.* Etude faite pour COOPI, Caritas et OCDH, Bangui, p.17
3   45,000: figure given by the head of Cameroon HCR on Radio France Internationale in December 2007
4   Bimbo: Administrative centre of the prefecture of Ombella-MPOKO, a town located to the south of Bangui and adjoining it.
     Pissa: A district within Lobaye prefecture, approximately 70 kms from Bangui, the capital of the CAR.
     M'baïki: Administrative centre of Lobaye prefecture located 107 kms to the south of Bangui.
5   **Siriibi, Rodonne, 2007**: Rapport d'activites de la phase b d'octroi d'acte de naissance aux enfants pygmées de 0 à 14 ans, a Bimbo, Pissa et M'baiki, Période du 19 mai au 22 juin 2007 (5 p.) CIONGCA (Bangui).
6   **WWF-RCA, 2007**: Une mode vie durable pour les populations de la Réserve Spéciale Dzanga-Sangha, Formulaire de demande de subvention soumis à l'Union Européenne.
7   Monassao: Pygmy village set up by Catholic priests on the outskirts of the Dzanga-Sangha Special Reserve.
8   Bilo: name given by the Aka Pygmies to the non-Pygmy populations of the CAR.
9   Mossapoula: Aka village in the Dzanga-Sangha Special Reserve, approximately 5 kms from the town of Bayanga.
10   Information taken from a page of information requested from Sylvain DANGOLO, who works for GTZ in BAYANGA.
11   Gouga: Village shared by the indigenous Aka and the Bantu, on the border with the Republic of Congo, 20 kms from the sub-prefecture of Mongoumba.
12   Source: meeting with the Founding President of the JAPAC Mission, 21 December 2007
13   The primary education system in the DRC consists of 6 levels.
14   Londo: Pygmy village 249 kms to the south-west of Bangui, in the sub-prefecture of Bambio.
15   Source: Meeting with John Nelson, Forest Peoples' Programme facilitator, on 12 December 2007.

16 **UNESCO National Commission for the CAR (CNCU), 2007:** Rapport de la foire exposition vente de l'artisanat pygmée (27p) CNCU (Bangui)

17 Radio Ndeke-Luka: Independent radio station run by the United Nations and based in Bangui in the Central African Republic.

Saint-Jérôme SITAMON holds a first degree in Linguistics and a post-graduate degree in French literature from Bangui University in the CAR. He taught French at the Lycée des Martyrs in Bangui for 8 years but now lives with his wife and six children among the Aka Pygmies of Londo, in Bambio sub-prefecture. Until 2000, he ran a literacy programme in the Akaka/yaka language in association with the Eglise Cooperation Evangelique en Centrafrique (E.C.E.C) and the Association Centrafricaine pour la traduction de la Bible et l'Alphabétisation (ACATBA). Presently he works for ACATBA in the area of awareness raising among the churches and coordinates the activities of the NGO Maison de l'Enfant et de la Femme Pygmées (M.E.F.P,). As a literacy consultant Saint-Jérôme SITAMON designs educational materials, translates documents into the Pygmy yaka/AKA languages and supports the indigenous communities of Central Africa by accompanying their leaders to international and regional fora.

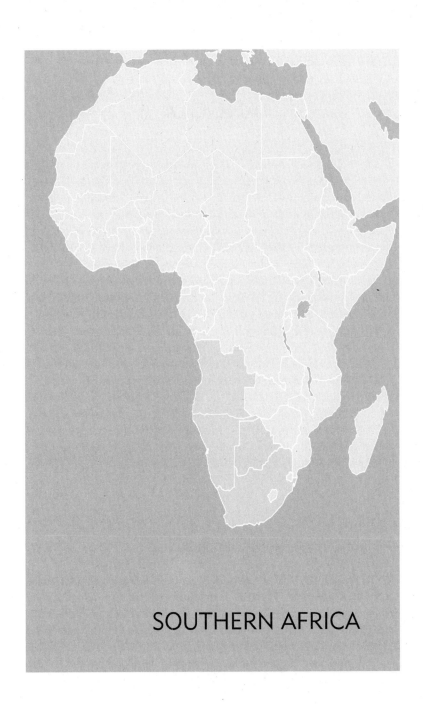

SOUTHERN AFRICA

ANGOLA

The indigenous San peoples of southern Angola, also known as Bushmen, are the oldest inhabitants of Angola and southern Africa and are mainly located in remote and inaccessible areas. Many (mainly in Kuando and Kubango provinces) still live as hunter-gatherers, staying in rudimentary shelters and moving within their ancestral territories, while others have settled in homesteads where they practise agriculture, surrounded by Bantu neighbours, or live in urban communities.

The population of Angola numbers around 15.5 million people and the San are estimated to account for approximately 0.04 percent of that figure. The majority of the San reside in Huíla, Kunene and Kuando Kubango provinces in southern Angola and probably also in Moxico Province in south-western Angola. The exact numbers and location of all San communities is not, however, known.

Angola has ratified ILO Convention 107, Concerning the Protection and Integration of Indigenous and other Tribal and Semi-Tribal Populations in Independent Countries. However, there are no specific laws on indigenous peoples' rights in Angola.

The first San conference in Angola

The NGO OCADEC (Christian Organisation Supporting Community Development) has, in partnership with international organisations such as Trócaire, Terre des Hommes, Christian Aid, Norwegian Refugee Council, FAO (UN Food and Agriculture Organization) and WIMSA (Working Group of Indigenous Minorities in Southern Africa), worked on developing broad and long-term developmental interven-

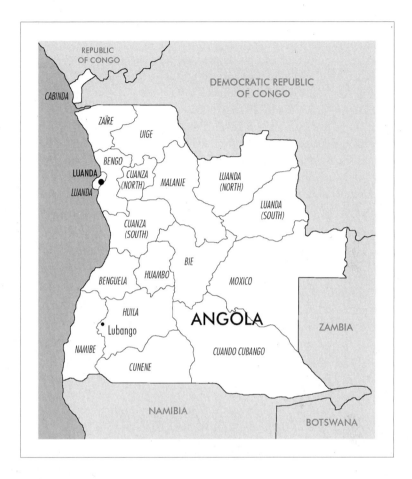

tions for the San in Angola. So far, OCADEC has been working with 5,000 San people.

The interventions focus on securing the ancient lands of the San by working with the Angolan government to get these areas registered; supporting the San in their efforts to rebuild and regain their identity and pride in their culture; improving agricultural methods and management of livestock; promoting greater education for children; developing mechanisms for resolving conflicts between the San and their Bantu neighbours (frequently over access to water), as well as promoting income-generating opportunities. The San have also benefited from Trócaire's Global Gift campaign as goats have been provided to some communities.

A very important and innovative activity was the first ever Angolan San Conference that was hosted in Lubango, capital of Huíla Province, in April 2007 and funded by the Office of the High Commissioner for Human Rights (OHCHR) in Angola, OXFAM, NOVIB, IWGIA, Trócaire, Terre des Hommes, FAO and the European Union. This conference brought together a considerable number of San community representatives, members of the provincial governments of Huíla, Kunene and Kuando Kubango, representatives from the embassies of the USA, the Netherlands and South Africa, San representatives from Namibia, Botswana and South Africa, officials of national and international NGOs, UN agencies, and civil society activists. The conference was preceded by a 2 day pre-conference during which Angolan San representatives and San from Namibia, Botswana and South Africa shared experiences, hopes and visions for improving their living conditions. The conference produced resolutions and recommendations to the government, to the community itself, to the international community and to the donor organisations.

As a direct result of this conference, in October 2007, the MINARS (Ministry of Assistance and Social Reinsertion) in Huíla Province and OCADEC conducted a survey, which visited all the San communities living in Huíla Province. The aim of the visit was to find out how the San in this province are living and what the government could offer to overcome some of their major problems. The survey concluded that the San were living under very bad conditions and that they needed more attention from the government on the basis of a more concrete and practical joint action plan and strategy aimed at fighting poverty among the San people.

Following this survey, the Provincial Directorate for water and electricity installed two hand water pumps in the villages of San living in Chibia district.

Unfortunately, the provincial government has not yet been able to build schools near the San villages. Providing education for the San would be a means of paving their way out of discrimination and building their self-esteem and self reliance.   ❑

Gaspar Daniel is Angolan and works as administrator for OCADEC – the Christian Organisation Supporting Community Development. OCADEC works for the development and protection of the human rights of Angolan San communities.

NAMIBIA

The San (Bushmen), who number some 38,000 in Namibia, are widely believed to be indigenous to the country. San were, in the past, hunter-gatherers but today many of them raise crops and livestock, produce crafts, engage in rural and urban labor and work on commercial farms. San are found scattered throughout many parts of Namibia, especially in the central and northern parts of the country. They are divided into a number of different groups, each speaking their own language and having distinct cultural identities, traditions and histories. The two largest groups are the Hai|om, who number some 11,000 and reside near the Etosha National Park in the center north of the country, and the Ju|'hoansi, who number some 7,000 and live mainly in the Otjozondjupa Region in the eastern part of the country. The San are some of the poorest and most marginalized peoples in Namibia. Over 80% of the San have been dispossessed of their ancestral lands and territories.

Another group usually recognized as indigenous to Namibia is the Himba, who number some 25,000 and reside mainly in the semi-arid north-west (Kunene Region). The Himba are pastoral (herding) peoples who have close ties to the Herero, also pastoralists who reside in central and eastern Namibia. Two other groups that see themselves as indigenous to Namibia are the Nama, a Khoesan-speaking group who number some 70,000 and the Basters, a group of Afrikaans-speaking people who number 35,000. Both groups reside in the south of Namibia. Together, the indigenous peoples of Namibia represent some 8% of the total population of the country.

Namibia does not have any national legislation that deals directly with indigenous peoples but, in 2005, the Office of the

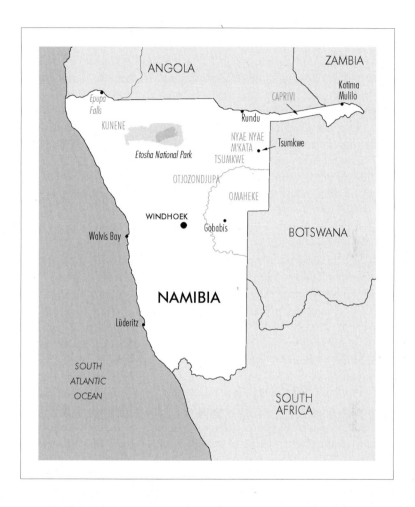

Prime Minister initiated a San Development Program aimed at helping San citizens, as a poverty-stricken minority. Namibia is also a signatory to the Declaration on the Rights of Indigenous Peoples, which was passed in the United Nations General Assembly in New York on September 13, 2007.

Land issues

Many indigenous people in Namibia are landless, and unemployment and under-employment are common.[1] Indigenous people often depend on other groups, the state or non-government organizations for support. A sizeable percentage, some estimate as high as 75%, are thus dependent on food provided by the government of Namibia, and a relatively high number of people live on less than US$2.00 per day - in some cases, even less than US$1.00 per day.

Approximately half of all San in the country live in communal areas, meaning that they do not have de jure (legal) land tenure rights. Today, only 15% of San in Namibia retain de facto (customary) rights to land.[2] The history of land allocation in Namibia largely accounts for the vulnerable land tenure situation of its indigenous minorities: the land that was granted to Africans under the colonial government became communal land (formerly, native areas), and amounts today to only 26.5% of the country. Over half of Namibia's land (57 %) is under private commercial freehold tenure (i.e. privately owned). Nearly 13.9% of the land area is made up of national parks, game reserves and monuments, and the diamond areas, some 2.5% of the country, belong to the state but are leased out to private companies.

The government of Namibia holds that, even though the communal areas are occupied by local people, the land belongs to the state. This means that indigenous communities hold a "use right" but have no "ownership right", either privately or collectively. This also means that they can legally be moved against their will without compensation.[3]

The only places in Namibia's communal areas where local people are granted customary rights, and where they have some control over natural resources, are in those areas designated as conservancies under Namibian government legislation.[4] There are at least 15 conservancies in Kunene Region in northern Namibia, where the Himba people live. Five of these have majority Himba membership. In the Otjozondjupa region, there are currently two San majority conservancies: one is the N‡a Jaqna Conservancy in Tsumkwe District West; the other is the Nyae Nyae Conservancy in Tsumkwe District East, which has majority Ju/'hoan membership. One other conservancy, Otjituo, gazetted in September 2005, has both Herero and Ju/'hoansi members. It was estimated in 2007 that the economic returns to the Nyae Nyae Conservancy and its membership totaled some N$350,000[5] or approximately US$ 48,000.

Two new conservancies for San were designated in 2007 as part of an agreement between the Hai‖‖om people and the Namibian government. The Hai‖‖om, who were forcefully evicted in 1953 from their ancestral land in the Etosha National Park in the center north of the country, have for years claimed alternative land for resettlement and, in 1997, they blockaded the two main entrances to the Park, carrying bows and arrows. This was an unprecedented protest action. The recent agreement, which includes the purchase by the government of two farms adjacent to the Park where the San can settle and develop their conservancies, should be seen in the light of the centenary celebrations of the Etosha National Park (it was created in 1907).[6] But as Willem Odendaal[7] points out: "On the one hand, this is a positive step, but on the other, this can only be regarded as a start considering that there are 9 000 Hai//om living in the area, most of whom are dispossessed, poverty stricken and landless."

Land reform plans

In 2007, the Namibian government focused strongly on trying to achieve a more equitable land ownership structure through a land distribution and resettlement scheme that would give the historically disadvantaged majority (Africans) access to some of the commercial (freehold) land largely owned by whites. In some communal land areas, however, this scheme attracted people from other places with the prospect of being given arable and grazing land. Tsumkwe District West, already gazetted as the N‡a Jaqna Conservancy, has been designated as a potential area for land distribution. These plans could well affect the situation of the !Kung, Khwe and !Xun San residents, since only a few of them would be able to meet the necessary economic requirements to benefit from the land scheme (e.g., making boreholes, putting up fences, etc.). There is also concern that the existing work of the N‡a Jaqna Conservancy Council could be affected. The government has not yet approved the conservation management plan submitted by the San when the conservancy was established in July 2003. The San have therefore been left powerless and unable to oppose the hundreds of cattle herders from other ethnic groups who have brought thousands of cattle illegally into the conservancy.[8] Now, they face government plans to divide part of the land belonging to the conservancy into plots and put fences up. This would not only result in losses of land but also negatively affect the wildlife, and thus indirectly impact on the income that can be made from tourism and safari hunting companies.

Human rights violations

Nearly half of all San in Namibia are farm workers, either on the cattle posts of livestock owners or on commercial ranches.[9] San farm workers are often mistreated, and there were reports in the Namibian media in 2007 of beatings, torture and sexual assaults. There were also stories about suspicious deaths of people in the custody of Namibian security forces and the Namibian National Police. Local people also complained of long periods in pre-trial detention and situations where they were not informed of the charges against them. Some of these reports were investigated by Namibian human rights organizations such as the Legal Assistance Center and the Namibian Center for Human Rights, who wrote to the government to protest at the treatment.

The Epupa Dam

In early 2007, it was announced that consideration was being given once more to the construction of the Epupa Dam on the Kunene River, which forms the border between Namibia and Angola. This has raised grave concerns among the Himba living in the region, as it would affect their gravesites and grazing along the Kunene River and would also have an impact on the Epupa Falls, a place sacred to the Himba and a scenic area favored by tourists. The possible construction of a hydropower station in the Baines Mountains area of Kunene was also announced. This is not the first time the Himba have faced such a challenge; in the 1990s they, along with a number of non-governmental organizations including the Legal Assistance Center (LAC) in Windhoek, had sought to stop the proposed Epupa Dam.[10] This time too, the proposal to build a dam and power station at Epupa Falls has generated a storm of protest. In October, it was finally announced that the Epupa Falls site would not be touched and that the governments of Namibia and Angola had instead agreed to start building a hydropower station in the Baines Mountains which, according to the protesters, was "a better option than Epupa Falls because it will be a smaller project with a lesser environmental and social impact".[11]

San Development Program

In 2005, the government of Namibia announced the establishment of a San Development Program in the Office of the Prime Minister; this program has included training in income-generating projects, provision of draught animals, tools and seed, as well as scholarships for San children. In 2007, a training course for coffin makers was offered as part of this development program. Deputy Prime Minister Libertina Amathila provided the reasoning behind this:

It really hurts me to see that still today in our independent Namibia some San people are being buried in plastic bags or left in mortuaries for a long time, until their families collect money to afford a funeral for them. One cannot blame these families, as they are not in a position to afford even a meal for themselves, let alone a burial for a family member.

The San Coffin Manufacturing Project was launched in the Otjozond-jupa Region as a pilot project to train the first group of five San trainees in coffin manufacturing for a period of two months. During the

San graduation ceremony in Windhoek in May 2007, Libertina Amathila said that something positive had come out of the training in
terms of the San Development Programme, and she called "upon regional councillors to make sure that we empower the San people".
She went on to say, "This programme is specifically meant for San
people, as government felt that they need a special programme which
will fast track their integration into the economic mainstream." Support will be provided to the graduates so they can start their own
coffin-making projects in their communities.[12] The Namibian government has pointed out that this program is not ethnically based but
rather aimed at empowering the San who "are a very poor community".[13]

Climate change and HIV/AIDS

Two other major challenges faced the indigenous peoples of Namibia
in 2007: climate change and the spread of HIV/AIDS. Namibia, as a
water-scarce country, is especially vulnerable to the impacts of global
climate change and could witness significant declines in water availability, agricultural yields and livestock productivity.[14] People in the
Caprivi Region who had to cope with floods in 2007 and those in
northern and central Namibia dealing with drought conditions were
concerned that the pace of environmental change was quickening in
Namibia as a result of human-induced climatic shifts. Local communities were concerned that climate change was causing an expansion
of livestock diseases and leading to more unpredictability in wild
food and medicinal plant availability and crop losses.

HIV/AIDS was on the increase amongst virtually all of the indigenous populations in Namibia in 2007. It was estimated that the AIDS
prevalence rate for San living around Tsumkwe was 10% and rising.[15]
At the national level, efforts were being made by the government of
Namibia and various non-governmental organizations and international agencies to cope with the AIDS crisis. AIDS education and prevention programs were being implemented, and efforts were being
made by the government and NGOs to expand the distribution of
antiretroviral drugs, condoms and supplemental food for people in

rural and urban areas of the country. Particular attention was being paid to the connection between HIV/AIDS and tuberculosis, another disease that is expanding rapidly in some parts of Namibia. ❑

Notes

1   **Suzman, James L., 2001**: *An Assessment of the Status of San in Namibia*. Windhoek, Namibia: Legal Assistance Center, 2001.
2   **Harring, Sidney L. and Odendaal, Willem, 2006**: *"Our Land They Took": San Land Rights under Threat in Namibia*. Windhoek: Land, Environment and Development [LEAD] Project, Legal Assistance Center.
3   See **Harring, Sidney L.,2004**: "Indigenous Land Rights and Land Reform in Namibia." In R. Hitchcock and D. Vinding, (eds.): *Indigenous Peoples Rights in Southern Africa*. Copenhagen, Denmark: International Work Group for Indigenous Affairs, p.71.
4   Conservancies in Namibia are locally planned and managed multipurpose areas on communal land in which land users have pooled their resources for wildlife conservation, tourism and wildlife utilization. Conservancy members are granted wildlife resource rights under an amendment to Namibia's *Nature Conservation Amendment Act of 1996*.
5   Estimate obtained from the Nyae Nyae Development Foundation of Namibia, Windhoek, Namibia, January, 2008.
6   See *The Namibian Economist*, March 30, 2007.
7   See **Odendaal, Willem, 2005**: "100 Years of Etosha: Not everyone is celebrating." *The Namibian*, 5 October 2007. Can be accessed at http://www.lac.org.na/news/news05102007.htm
8   **Harring, Sidney L. and Odendaal, Willem, 2006**: *"Our Land They Took": San Land Rights under Threat in Namibia*. Windhoek: Land, Environment and Development [LEAD] Project, Legal Assistance Center.
9   See **Harring, Sidney L. and Odendaal, Willem** *"Our Land They Took": San Land Rights under Threat in Namibia*..
10 For a discussion of this issue, see **Harring, Sidney L., 1991**: "'God Gave Us This Land': The OvaHimba, the Proposed Epupa Dam, the Independent Namibian State, and Development in Africa." *The Georgetown International Environmental Law Review*, vol. 14, no. 1 (1991), 35-106.
11 "Angola and Namibia Plan Huge Dam". BBC News, 25 October 2007. http://news.bbc.co.uk/2/hi/africa/7062544.stm (accessed February 4,2008).
12 **Gaomas, Surihe, 2007**: "The price after death", *The New Era*, May 31, 2007.
13 **Bause, Tanja, 2008**: "First San Coffin Makers to Graduate," *The Namibian*, May 24, 2007.
14 **Kamupingene, Alfred, 2008**: "Climate Change: Can We Live on a Prayer?" *New Era (Windhoek)*, January 11, 2008.
15 Estimate from Health Unlimited, 2007.

Robert K. Hitchcock is Professor and Chair of the Department of Anthropology at Michigan State University in East Lansing, Michigan, USA and a member of the Board of the International Work Group for Indigenous Affairs. His work focuses on human rights, development and the environment, with particular reference to indigenous peoples, refugees and small-scale farmers and herders in Africa, the Middle East and the Americas.

Adrianne M. Daggett is an archaeologist and graduate student in anthropology from Michigan State University. She is currently helping to edit a book on the Ju/'hoansi San of Namibia and is working on ethno-archaeological and archaeological data drawn from San communities in Botswana.

BOTSWANA

The Botswana government does not recognize any specific groups as indigenous to the country, maintaining instead that all citizens of the country are indigenous. However, some groups in Botswana define themselves as indigenous. These groups include the San, who were traditionally hunter-gatherers. Today the vast majority of them are small-scale agropastoralists and people with mixed economies who reside both in urban and rural areas, as for instance in the Kalahari Desert and in the eastern region of the country. The San are sub-divided into a large number of named groups, most of whom speak their own mother-tongue San languages. The San are some of the poorest and most underprivileged people in Botswana, with a high percentage of them living below the poverty line.

Other groups that identify themselves as indigenous include the Balala,[1] who number some 1,500 and live in Southern (Ngwaketse) and Kgalagadi Districts, and the Nama, who number 2,000 and who are found especially along the Namibia-Botswana border and in Tsabong. Most of the Balala live and work on the Molopo Farms in Southern District as herders and domestic laborers. The Nama are small-scale agropastoralists and farm workers and speak a Khoekhoe language, and Setswana. The percentage of the total population in Botswana who consider themselves indigenous to the country stands at 3 per cent of the total population of 1.8 million (2007).

In spite of constitutional protections against discrimination under the Botswana Constitution, indigenous and minority peoples have found it difficult to get their land and resource rights and other human rights recognized.[2] There are no specific laws on indigenous peoples' rights in Botswana. The country has not ratified ILO Convention No. 169 but was a signatory to the UN Declaration on the Rights of Indigenous Peoples.

DITSHWANELO, the Botswana Center for Human Rights, has sought to promote the rights of San and other people seeking to retain their land and resource rights.

The Central Kalahari Game Reserve legal case

A major challenge for the San in 2007 has been the government's failure to implement the decisions reached in the Central Kalahari Game Reserve legal case, which was decided in favor of the San and Bakgalagadi in December 2006, after the longest and most expensive case in Botswana history. This case revolved around the claim made by 243 San and Bakgalagadi, on behalf of some 2,000 people who had been evicted from the Central Kalahari Game Reserve (CKGR), to have the right to return to their home areas.[3]

As of the end of 2007, the Botswana government had yet to live up to the legal agreements made as a result of the High Court case and the former residents were still waiting to get permission to return to the CKGR. As for the dozens of former residents who had either refused to leave the reserve in 2002 or had later chosen to return without permission – according to estimates a total of 50 to 100 adults - they continued to face difficulties through lack of water. A request to have the only borehole with potable water reopened after having been sealed in 2002 was turned down by the Botswana government. They are also at risk of being arrested if they engage in hunting since the government has not made Special Game Licenses available for subsistence hunting, although this was a stipulation made by the Botswana High Court.

The diamond conundrum

The debate relating to the Central Kalahari Game Reserve issue has largely centered on why the government of Botswana chose to relocate

people outside of the reserve. Survival International (London) and First People of the Kalahari (a local San non-government organization) have argued that the relocation was undertaken because of the government's desire to exploit diamonds in the reserve.[4] The Botswana government's official website addresses the issue of "relocation of Basarwa" and explicitly rejects the charge that people were relocated outside of the reserve because of mining. It maintains instead that the relocation was undertaken (a) because of land use conflicts, (b) for environmental conservation, (c) in order to facilitate development and poverty alleviation, (d) to ensure adequate provision of social services, and (e) to promote empowerment of local people. Botswana also claims that the cost of providing physical infrastructure and social services in such remote and sparsely populated areas as the CKGR is prohibitive.[5]

The government does freely admit, however, that mineral explorations are on-going in the Central Kalahari. "Retention Licenses" had already been granted in 2000 to Gope Exploration, a joint venture between Falconbridge and DeBeers. But although kimberlite deposits indicating the presence of diamonds were found, reports from the company to the government showed that there was no economic justification for exploiting the diamonds in Gope.

In June 2007, it was announced that a mining company, Gem Diamonds, had purchased the mining licenses for sites around Gope in the Central Kalahari Game Reserve. As of mid-2007, a total of 745 sq km had been set aside around Gope, where a kimberlite pipe that shows promise has been found.

If and when mining operations start, the issue for former CKGR residents will of course be what rights they will have to benefit from these operations on their ancestral lands, which they have fought so hard to retain. Gem Diamonds spokespersons maintain that the company has policies in place and that it was planning to consult with the people from the Central Kalahari. In September 2007, Gem Diamonds contracted a firm from Johannesburg to carry out the consultation and assessment of the situation in the Central Kalahari Game Reserve. According to people from settlements in the vicinity of the Central Kalahari, this consultation and assessment had not started by the end of the year.

Conservation-related resettlement

Another challenge has been rumors concerning the potential resettlement of communities for conservation purposes in the Western Kgalagadi Conservation Corridor (WKCC). WKCC lies between two major protected areas in the south-western part of the country, the Kgalagadi Transfrontier Park and the Central Kalahari Game Reserve.

Indigenous and other peoples have a long history of being removed from conservation areas, the most recent example being the Central Kalahari Game Reserve. The plans for development of the WKCC[6] therefore caused concern. The area is home to some of the poorest people in Botswana, a number of whom reside in remote area dweller (RAD) settlements (for example, East and West Hanahai, Bere, and Ka/gae). Some of these settlements have well over a thousand inhabitants, and moving will be painful, difficult and expensive. Some of the residents have already said that they do not want to move, and they are seeking to get the Ghanzi and Kgalagadi District Councils and the government of Botswana to state publicly that there will be no new removals as a result of the newly planned conservation corridor.

The Botswana government has promised the people of the corridor region that community trusts will be formed and that people will be able to benefit from income generated from safari hunting and subsistence hunting in the community-controlled hunting areas that form part of Botswana's Wildlife Management Areas.[7] Thus far, however, Special Game Licenses have not been made available to people in the wildlife management areas and, as a consequence, people are being arrested for engaging in activities that they had been told they could engage in.

HIV/AIDS

Indigenous peoples and others in Botswana face serious disease problems and other health hazards, including nutritional stress and exposure to sexually transmitted diseases such as HIV/AIDS. While HIV/AIDS rates are currently lower among San, Nama and Balalala than among other groups in Botswana, the HIV/AIDS prevalence rate is on the rise, and it is likely that it will increase substantially in the next few years.[8] It also appears that San women in Botswana communities are becoming infected by HIV/AIDS at a faster rate than men. This may be explained by the fact that indigenous women in Botswana are collectively and individually highly vulnerable, in part because of their social and economic status, and are therefore often exposed to a relatively high degree of gender-based violence, such as rape and other abuses. A corollary to HIV/AIDS is TB, which is also prevalent in many San communities, where the most elementary form of primary health care is lacking. The Community Health Programme being im-

plemented by Letloa[9] in some of the remote San and non-San communities in the Okavango area and Ghanzi District is currently trying to
address these issues through awareness raising and training task forces in each community. The overall objective is to build local capacity so
that health programmes can be localized and managed by the people
themselves.

San celebrations

From August to December 2007, a local San NGO, the Kuru Family of
Organisations (KFO), celebrated its 21 years of formal existence by
promoting more awareness in Botswana of the status of the San as well
as of the positive contribution they make to society as a whole. In August, the annual San Dance Festival in D'Kar was especially magnifi-
cent, gathering some 450 dancers and 1,000 visitors and being attended
by a number of Botswana VIPs, including the Vice President of Botswana, Lt. Gen. I.S.I Khama. The Dance Festival also created an opportunity for San dancers from across the 14 San language groups to meet
each other and celebrate and reinforce their age-old culture.

In November, the Festival moved to Gaborone so that the larger
public could be informed about the variety of positive activities the
San are involved in: their achievements as well as the factors that still
hinder their full integration into Botswana society. This was done by
means of a historical and contemporary photographic exhibition and a
contemporary art and craft exhibition. A side programme to the exhi-
bitions was developed, with a series of public discussions on relevant
topics organised by the University of Botswana/University of Tromsø
Collaborative San Research Programme and the Botswana Society. ❑

Notes

1 The Balala is a group considered by some analysts and themselves to be indigenous but who speak Sekgalagadi and Setswana, having lost their mother-
   tongue language over time.
2 **Working Group on Indigenous Populations/Communities in Africa,2005**:
   Draft Report of the Working Group on Indigenous Populations/Communities in Africa

Mission to the Republic of Botswana, 15-23 June, 2005. Banjul, The Gambia: African Commission on Human and Peoples' Rights, African Union.

3   See Central Kalahari *Legal Case No. MISCA 52/2002 in the Matter Between Roy Sesana, First Applicant, Keiwa Setlhobogwa and 241 others, Second and Further Applicants, and the Attorney General (in his capacity as the recognized agent of the Government of the Republic of Botswana);* for a discussion of the results of the case, see **Julie J. Taylor, 2007**: *Celebrating Victory too Soon? Reflections on the Outcome of the Central Kalahari Game Reserve Case.* Anthropology Today 23(5):3-5.

4   See the discussions on the Survival International website (www.survival.org) and on the website www.iwant2gohome.

5   www.gov.bw

6   The development of the WKCC is being managed by Conservation International (a South African NGO), in partnership with the government of Botswana, the European Union and *Fonds Français pour l'Environnement Mondial* (FFEM).

7   Wildlife Management Areas are multiple-use areas zoned for communities to engage in conservation and development-related activities, including tourism and community-based natural resource management. WMAs make up over 25% of the total surface area of Botswana.

8   Information from the Kuru Family of Organizations presented at a national conference on HIV/AIDS and other issues facing San and other peoples, Gaborone, Botswana, November, 2007

9   Letloa is part of the Kuru Family of Organisations (KFO), a local San NGO.

Robert K. Hitchcock *is Professor and Chair of the Department of Anthropology at Michigan State University in East Lansing, Michigan, USA and a member of the Board of the International Work Group for Indigenous Affairs. His work focuses on human rights, development and the environment, with particular reference to indigenous peoples, refugees and small-scale farmers and herders in Africa, the Middle East and the Americas.*

Adrianne M. Daggett *is an archaeologist and graduate student in anthropology from Michigan State University. She is currently helping to edit a book on the Ju/'hoansi San of Namibia and is working on ethno-archaeological and archaeological data drawn from San communities in Botswana.*

SOUTH AFRICA

The various indigenous groups in South Africa are collectively known as Khoi-San. They comprise three main San peoples, various Nama communities, Griqua associations, Koranna and "revivalist Khoisan" people reclaiming their historical heritage. In addition, there are small pockets of family groups and small communities, such as the so-called "hidden San" in the KwaZulu-Natal and Mpumalanga provinces.

South Africa's total population is 47 million, with the indigenous groups comprising less than 1%. The South African Census does not record indigenous groups separately, and they are probably subsumed under the "coloured" population total (4.2 million), comprising 8.9% of the total South African population.[1]

In South Africa today, the Khoi-San communities exhibit a range of socio-economic and cultural lifestyles and cultural practices. Among the San communities, members of the older generation have maintained strong links to some traditional cultural practices, although representations of the traditional hunter-gatherer lifestyle are largely practised in the context of cultural tourism and cultural revival.[2] The youth continue to grapple with the issues of identity and loss of cultural knowledge.[3]

Indigenous Peoples are not recognised in the 1996 Constitution but it does promise redress for past racial discrimination and affirmative action.

South African indigenous peoples are expanding their areas of policy dialogue with the state and forms of civil society organisation. They are moving from creating bodies that represent their identity (cultural associations) to bodies that represent their interests in development and policy issues (e.g. intellectual property rights, traditional

knowledge, environment and education). However, the official channels for negotiating their formal recognition by the government still
appear to be cumbersome and unproductive. A major challenge for
indigenous peoples is to strengthen their civil society and hold the
government and other agencies accountable for implementing the 1996
Constitution.

In 2005, the UN Special Rapporteur on the Fundamental Freedoms
and Human Rights of Indigenous People visited South Africa. His report highlighted the strong commitment to human rights and the important constitutional protection of human rights and freedoms in
South Africa. However, the report also noted the weak communication
between different levels of government and the *de facto* vulnerability
and marginalisation of indigenous peoples on the ground. In 2007, indigenous peoples asked the Department of Provincial and Local Gov-

ernment (DPLG) to explain how the state intended to follow up on the UN Special Rapporteur's report but were told that the civil servants did not know as this would require political decisions.

At international level, South Africa played a leading role in promoting the adoption of the UN Declaration on the Rights of Indigenous Peoples at the Human Rights Council in June 2006. However, when Namibia submitted its anti-Declaration *'aide memoire'* in November 2006, South Africa remained silent in the face of the Africa Group's opposition to the Declaration within the General Assembly. South Africa took on a UN Security Council position in January 2007 but did not play an active role in encouraging African states to support the Declaration. South Africa held to its usual position of solidarity with the Africa Group rather than adhering to its own democratic policy priorities.

Despite its foreign policy ambiguities, South African diplomats continually express support for the indigenous issue, and the passage of the Declaration in September 2007 will likely make it easier for them to follow up in other areas of the UN system.

Inter-Departmental Working Group

At home, the Inter-departmental Working Group on Khoe and San Issues[4] proceeded with its mandate and the Department of Provincial and Local Government (DPLG) organised a fresh election for the stale National Khoe-San Council (NKC), the official body which is in dialogue with the state over the recognition of rights.

Indigenous activists have expressed concern that the NKC process is not substantially advancing the rights of indigenous peoples or resolving the impasse over recognition of traditional authorities. To date, a policy document developed during consultations between the NKC and the Inter-departmental Working Group has been submitted to the Minister of the DPLG, Sydney Mufamadi. Adoption of the policy document is now awaited, which will then go out for consultation with the broader Khoekhoe and San communities.

By the end of 2007, the DPLG was ready to release a "criteria" document on traditional authorities. This has involved a nine-year process of consultation. It is likely that most of the "revivalist" Khoe-San groups will fail to convince the state that they have traditional authorities. However, the results will likely benefit the older organisations,[5] such as the Griqua National Conference, which does have a clear line of traditional authorities. Khoe and San leaders are still concerned that the state is putting too much emphasis on traditional authority issues and failing to recognise that most surviving indigenous peoples did not have or no longer have chieftancies. The state is focussing on this complex issue rather than developing a clear policy on recognition of the social, cultural and economic rights of the first peoples.

Civil society

The civil society efforts to create a nationwide umbrella organisation, the National Khoe-San Consultative Conference (NKCC), have also not materialised into an effective and united voice for the first peoples. A major cause in the breakdown of the NKCC was a lack of adequate funding and administrative capacity amongst the affiliated organisations and member representatives. Another factor which has hampered civil society efforts is the ongoing challenge created by individuals competing for traditional leadership positions. Opportunists allegedly penetrated the traditional authority review process, greatly complicating the work of the DPLG.

Three civil society initiatives showed promise during 2007. The South African San Council (SASC), in cooperation with the Working Group of Indigenous Minorities of Southern Africa (WIMSA), was active in setting up the Hoodia Trust. An important intellectual property rights agreement will see the San of southern Africa benefit from the profits arising from the sale of *hoodia gordonii,* a Kalahari plant which can be used for safe dieting. *Hoodia* products are not yet officially licensed but hundreds of legitimate and fraudulent versions are being marketed all over the Western world and in South Africa.

A Hoodia Trust has been created with San members from different ethnic groups. The Hoodia Trust, as part of the WIMSA network, has negotiated benefit-sharing with Nama indigenous people on the Orange River and with the mostly white Hoodia Growers Association. The multi-million rand agreement offers great potential for the San to fight poverty and redress current marginalisation. The agreement will see profits from the growers going to indigenous development projects, and a joint effort by all parties to force the private sector to comply with the intellectual property rights protocol. The agreement and new structures also create models of how indigenous peoples in Africa can benefit from their traditional knowledge of genetic resources.

Richtersveld update

In 2003, the Nama people of the Richtersveld, a diamond-rich territory on the border with Namibia, won a major court victory protecting their land and resource rights. The South African Supreme Court of Appeal dismissed Alexkor mining company's controversial attempt to use colonial-era laws that claimed that the indigenous Nama were too uncivilised to own land. The Land Claims Court initially backed the mining company, but its decision was overturned by the Supreme Court. Yet the Supreme Court still preferred to leave the final decision of whether Nama's had a pre-existing title to the Constitutional Court. The Constitutional Court made a landmark decision recognising the principle of "Aboriginal title" in the case of the Nama people. The Court used Canadian and Australian precedence to rule that the present government still had to acknowledge that the Nama people had a legal system that pre-existed the colonial one, and that this aboriginal right had not been extinguished.

The South African government agreed, in a memorandum of 2006, that the Namas could exercise mining rights either through Alexkor or a partner of their choice. As part of the memorandum agreement, the Richtservelders would drop their claim for damages in return for the transfer of mining rights and the payment of R200 million (US$28 million) in compensation for the loss of land. However, in 2007, the Minister of Trade and Industry withdrew the memorandum offer, on the basis that the Nama community was unwilling to cut a deal with

Alexkor. The government decision is taking place in the ongoing vacuum of a policy on the rights of indigenous peoples.

At the same time, the South African government submitted the Richtersveld National Park, which is leased from the Nama community, as a UNESCO World Heritage Site. The UNESCO committee accepted the "natural" World Heritage site but turned down the government's management plan and application for a "cultural" World Heritage Site.

Khoe-San Studies Unit

The University of the Free State (UFS) has created a Unit for Khoekhoe and San Studies which promises to provide an anchor for the indigenous movement in South Africa as well as to upgrade the academic and research skills of Khoe and San people. The Unit is currently running a grant programme in cooperation with the University of Tromsø (Norway) to fund the KhoeSan Culture and Memory project, which focuses on identifying Khoekhoe language speakers in South Africa. The project is also funded by the National SA Heritage Resource Agency.

Another UFS project is the KhoeSan Early Learning Centre Pilot Project. This project is a practical attempt to re-establish the Khoekhoegowab language, culture and heritage in an urban community by establishing an Early Childhood Development Centre. As Khoekhoe and San research develops, one area of concern for KhoeSan activists is the lack of policy regarding the relationship between academic institutions and researchers on the one hand, and indigenous peoples, on the other. KhoeSan activists are of the opinion, for example, that synergies that are of benefit to both parties (in financial terms as well as skills acquisition) have to be formed between the researcher and indigenous peoples during the process of data collection as well as during the analysis and final documentation phase.

In June, the Indigenous Peoples of Africa Coordinating Committee (IPACC) worked with the KhoeSan Unit at UFS to host a three-day training course on human rights instruments for indigenous southern African activists.

Environmental policy

In April 2007, Griqua and San activists from South Africa participated in the Indigenous Peoples of Africa Co-ordinating Committee (IPACC) strategic planning workshop on the environment and natural resources. The South African delegation highlighted the threats to their survival due to temperature and rainfall changes in the Kalahari and Karoo deserts. They identified dialogue with Pretoria on the three Rio Conventions as a high priority, as well as a stronger alliance between indigenous peoples.

IPACC supported the revival of the South African Indigenous Peoples and Protected Areas Working Group (SAIPPAWG). Members of the working group met in Port Nolloth to review the strategic action plan and learn more about climate change instruments and issues. Indigenous activists then attended the CBD (Convention on Biological Diversity) meeting in Cape Town and hosted a national workshop in the Kgalagadi Transfrontier Park to hammer out a constitution for the Khoekhoe and San members of the network.

The workshop also reviewed the results of the 2006 Tsumkwe workshop on the certification of trackers in southern Africa. Trackers, elders and medicine men attended the workshop to promote the importance of an intergenerational transfer of knowledge of biodiversity. The ‡Khomani San are the first indigenous people to set up their own training and accreditation programme linked to national standards.

The SAIPPAWG workshop agreed to intensify discussions with the Department of Environmental Affairs and Tourism (DEAT), and indigenous leaders met with the focal point for the Rio Conventions, Mrs. Maria Mbengashe.   ❑

Notes

1   **Rodolfo Stavenhagen, 2005**: *Report of the Special Rapporteur on the situation of human rights and fundamental freedoms of indigenous people, Mission to South Africa;* www.southafrica.info; www.san.org.za.
    The total number of indigenous groups and their location:

Indigenous group	Number	Location
‡Khomani San	1.000	Kalahari, Northern Cape Province
Khwe San	1.100	Kimberley, Northern Cape
!Xun San	4.500	Kimberley, Northern Cape
Nama	10.000	Richtersveld, Riemvasmaak & Namaqualand, Northern Cape
Griqua associations	300.000	Northern Cape, Western Cape, Eastern Cape, Free State y KwaZulu-Natal
Koranna	Unspecified	Free State, Northern Cape
'Hidden San'	Unspecified	Chrissies Meer, Mpumalanga; Drakensberg, KwaZulu-Natal
Revivalist Khoisan	Unspecified	Western and Eastern Cape Provinces
Total	316.600	

2 **Nigel Crawhall, 2001**: *Written in the Sand: Auditing and Managing Cultural Resources with Displaced Indigenous Peoples. A South African Case Study.* SASI (in co-operation with UNESCO).

3 Many San youth have, however, begun to grasp opportunities to work with their elders to record their stories, learning about their culture and using cultural reclamation to build livelihoods for themselves.

4 In 2005, Cabinet agreed to the NKC recommendations, cited in the ILO report of 1996, that an inter-departmental working group be set up to review how indigenous peoples relate to different parts of the national government. The Working Group is chaired by the DPLG.

5 As a result of Apartheid negating the presence of indigenous peoples, and the weakening of their traditional decision-making, negotiations have been conducted with formally registered organisations of indigenous peoples, the oldest being the Griqua National Conference, which dates from the 19th century.

Priscilla de Wet is a Khoe-San activist working with the Khoe San Studies Unit at the University of the Free State, South Africa. She has a Masters in Indigenous Studies from the University of Tromsø. Her interest is in the bridge between academic institutions and communities working on indigenous language and cultural revitalisation, including oral history.

Nigel Crawhall is the Director of the Secretariat of the Indigenous Peoples of Africa Coordinating Committee (IPACC). He is currently a visiting scholar on the Erasmus Mundus programme at the University of Tromsø, Norway. His PhD is from the University of Cape Town, dealing with the decline in southern San languages.

PART II

INTERNATIONAL PROCESSES

THE UN DECLARATION ON
THE RIGHTS OF INDIGENOUS PEOPLES

In 2007, the UN Declaration on the Rights of Indigenous Peoples was formally adopted by the United Nations as a comprehensive international standard on human rights. The Declaration emphasises the collective rights of indigenous peoples. It elaborates upon existing international human rights, norms and principles as they apply to indigenous peoples. It catalogues the kinds of violations that have historically plagued and, sadly, continue to plague indigenous peoples such as attacks upon their culture, their land, their identity and their own voice. In short, the Declaration lays out minimum standards for the survival, dignity and well-being of indigenous peoples.

The Declaration on the Rights of Indigenous Peoples was formally adopted by the United Nations General Assembly on 13 September 2007. This historic event signalled the end of centuries of exploitation of indigenous populations around the world and heralded an era of partnership and cooperation between states and indigenous peoples.

2007 started out with great doubts as to how the concerns of certain states, particularly the Africa Group of States, would be resolved. It had emerged in late 2006, during the discussions in the UN Third Committee, that some African states had serious difficulties with the text of the Declaration. Many participants considered that the resistance of the Africa Group of States was being encouraged by the CAN-ZUS group (Canada, Australia, New Zealand and USA), which was politically opposed to the Declaration.

The Africa Group was not prepared to accept the recommendation made by the Human Rights Council to adopt the Declaration. Namibia and Botswana made statements in the Third Committee that revealed a number of concerns. Botswana, in particular, emphasised that the Declaration on the Rights of Indigenous Peoples would cause insurrection and division in Africa, where the majority of the population were "indigenous". The Declaration was considered by Botswana to be a threat because it did not define the term "indigenous peoples" and because "self-determination" was seen as a right to secession. Botswana also argued that "free, prior and informed consent" was a veto over governments and that tribal groups in Africa would use the "land and resources" provisions to control mining and other resource developments, against the interest of the state.

The indigenous peoples' delegations present during discussions in the Third Committee found it difficult to correct these views as there was very restricted access to the states' delegations, and the Africa Group declined to discuss these issues with "non-state representatives".

Consequently, when the General Assembly convened its final meeting for 2006, on 21 December, it resolved "to defer consideration and action on the United Nations Declaration on the Rights of Indigenous Peoples to allow time for further consultations thereon". Fortunately, the resolution carried the proviso that the General Assembly "conclude its consideration of the Declaration ... before the end of its sixty-first session". (This resolution was adopted by a vote of 83 in favour and 91 abstentions.) The 62nd session of the General Assembly commenced on 18 September 2007, so the delay was potentially a lengthy one, plus there existed the risk that a further delay to the next session could be engineered by opposing states.

The indigenous peoples' delegations and the supporting states agreed that a delay beyond the 61st session was unwanted because it would be too difficult to maintain momentum for the Declaration, and some states' support for the Declaration might be vulnerable to political changes in their countries.

The position of the states

Within the Africa Group, there were some states supporting the Declaration. These states opposed the views of Botswana and other dissenting states. However, the Africa Group agreed to consider the Declaration in unity and to delay any voting on it until they had had an opportunity to resolve the issues. It was clear that many of the 54 African
states were not well-informed about the Declaration and were becoming increasingly concerned about the negative interpretations of the
Declaration that they were receiving in various communications.

The action by the Africa Group to delay the adoption of the Declaration created a tense division within the UN member states over the
future of the Declaration. The states that supported the Declaration
consisted of the European Union members and the Latin American
countries. They were committed to the adoption of the Declaration
without any changes to the text. They were well aware that the Declaration was a compromise that had the most support from all sectors.
These supporting states were convinced that any organized revision of
the Declaration's text would lead to disintegration of the support giv-
en to the Declaration either by the indigenous peoples' delegations, on
the one hand, or by many states, on the other.

The group of supportive states agreed that they would not accept
any amendments to the Declaration without the support of the indigenous peoples' delegations. They took the position that the Declaration had to be passed intact, accepting only reasonable amendments or
revisions to the text of the resolution to adopt the Declaration. They
would not participate in any working groups or procedures that might
jeopardise the integrity of the Declaration.

The support for the Declaration was delicately balanced between
the geo-political divisions of the five regions of the United Nations.
The Africa Group's dissatisfaction with the Declaration had sympathetic political support from the Eastern European and Middle Eastern
countries, and from many of the Small Island Developing States (SIDS)
of the Caribbean. Some Asian states were also reticent to commit to the
Declaration but there was tacit support from powerful Asian countries
who were more familiar with it due to their involvement over the pre-

vious years and who wanted to conclude the process to adopt the Declaration.

The indigenous peoples' delegations were adamant that changes to the Declaration could not occur at this late stage of adoption, and they specified that no working groups should be established by the General Assembly to review the text of the Declaration. The creation of a working group was seen as a renewed effort to draft the Declaration without indigenous representation.

At first, at the beginning of 2007, it was not clear how states' concerns would be resolved or how support for the Declaration could be widened. The President of the General Assembly was responsible for seeing that the requirements of the General Assembly resolution on the Declaration were met, that is, that the Declaration was dealt with before the end of the 61st session. Additionally, it was the role of the President to try and broker a consensus or otherwise endeavour to resolve the differences between the opposing states.

Initially it was mooted that a "neutral" government might bring together key states from both sides of the controversy. This did not eventuate, mainly because the Africa Group was not progressing towards developing a unified position that could be addressed.

Eventually, anticipating a submission from the Africa Group, the supporting states presented a proposal to the President of the General Assembly on 10 May 2007, to placate the main concerns of the Africa Group. This proposal contained carefully-crafted text for the adopting resolution.

On 17 May 2007, the Africa Group sent the President of the General Assembly a revised text for the Declaration. This text contained over thirty amendments to the Declaration adopted by the Human Rights Council. The amendments were too numerous, unacceptable to indigenous peoples and flawed in human rights law.

The role of the President of the UN General Assembly and the UN Permanent Forum on Indigenous Issues

The Permanent Forum on Indigenous Issues held its sixth session in New York from 14-25 May 2007. The Permanent Forum heard statements from indigenous delegations regarding the Declaration on the Rights of Indigenous Peoples, and representatives from the Permanent Forum and indigenous delegations met with the President of the General Assembly to urge positive outcomes for the Declaration.

In particular, the Permanent Forum and indigenous delegations expressed concern about the role of the Canadian government in trying to manipulate the processes in the General Assembly to establish a working group and redraft the provisions of the Declaration. The President of the General Assembly indicated that she would now take a more prominent hand in the process to ensure that the Declaration would be concluded during the 61st session of the General Assembly, as required by the resolution.

On 6 June 2007, the President of the General Assembly announced the appointment of Ambassador Davide, Permanent Representative of the Philippines to the United Nations, as a "Facilitator" to undertake consultations with the parties to try and achieve a consensus on the Declaration. Although indigenous delegations were prevented from participating in Ambassador Davide's meetings with the states, Ambassador Davide did meet with the indigenous delegates in a private meeting to hear concerns. The Ambassador was responsive to the major concerns of the indigenous delegations and understood that the indigenous delegations were stakeholders in the outcome of the Declaration.

Although he had only limited time to undertake his consultations – his report was due on 15 July – Ambassador Davide was able to meet with all parties and urge them to commit to a common position. He did not find a common position during his brief appointment but he did set out some guidelines in his "Facilitator Report" to the President of the General Assembly, as follows:

The Facilitator is of the view that an effective middle-ground approach should, as much as possible, meet the following test:

- *Does it represent a genuine effort to address the various concerns?*
- *Does it build on, and not undermine, the efforts and achievements of the process at the Commission on Human Rights and Human Rights Council?*

- *Does it preserve the purpose of the Declaration on the Rights of Indigenous Peoples?*
- *Is it tangible and specific enough to enable the General Assembly to determine the particular adjustments to be made to the current text within the remaining period before the end of the 61st session?*
- *Will it ensure that the Declaration does not fall below existing human rights standards?*

The President of the General Assembly then wrote to all the states and pointed out that the report outlined a proposed way forward, and asked states to consider this proposed way forward in a "flexible and constructive manner". The President encouraged progress so that a decision could be taken on the Declaration by the General Assembly during the first week of September 2007.

The Government of Mexico undertook to open private discussions with the governments of Namibia and Botswana to see if an agreement could be negotiated. These discussions continued without commitment from the other states. There was no certainty that an agreement reached between these three governments would receive wider support.

Indigenous lobbying strategies

In December 2006, when the General Assembly decided to defer consideration and action on the Declaration, indigenous peoples' delegations had decided to create greater awareness amongst the African and other states in order to counter the misinformation they might have received. It was also a priority to inform and raise awareness of the state representatives in New York who had not been privy to the long and detailed negotiations in Geneva. To be most effective in the UN environment, the indigenous delegations rallied into regional groups and appointed regional coordinators to develop and promote the global campaigns. A steering group consisting of the regional coordinators undertook to monitor progress and address problem areas as needed.

During the summer of 2007, although indigenous delegations were aware that Mexico was undertaking negotiations with some African states, they were adamant that no changes to the text of the Declaration would be accepted in negotiations.

Indigenous delegations, discouraged by the lack of progress in states' negotiations, began to undertake systematic lobbying of governments. A number of strategies were launched to solicit more support for the Declaration.

Of most prominence was the lobbying undertaken with the African states. A key instrument used by the lobbyists working with the African states was the African Charter on Human and Peoples' Rights. Relevant reports and statements from the African Commission on Human and Peoples' Rights were also used as much as possible to reveal inconsistencies in opposing the Declaration on the Rights of Indigenous Peoples.

The first of these strategic areas of lobbying was launched by the Indigenous Peoples of Africa Coordinating Committee (IPACC) in January 2007 but, by September 2007, the African missions to the UN had been visited by a number of lobbying groups, including the Africa Experts on Human Rights, the African Caucus of indigenous peoples, human rights NGOs and others. There was a consistent message that the Africa Group of States was acting inconsistently with the pan-African Charter and other applicable standards.[1]

The last efforts towards the adoption of the Declaration

As September 2007 drew closer, there was no sign of a change in the Africa Group's position on the Declaration and it seemed that a close vote would again occur in the General Assembly meeting held to adopt the Declaration. By this time, concerns were mostly focussed upon the rush of amendments to the Declaration on the floor of the General Assembly. If the Africa Group remained opposed to the Declaration, it would be possible for any state to propose amendments to the Declaration and the outcome of each proposal would be unpredictable.

Despite the likelihood that a majority of states would vote in favour of the Declaration, it was also quite possible that many of the same states would see an opportunity if certain amendments were proposed. In this environment, dissenting states such as Canada could succeed in making significant amendments or otherwise causing such chaos as to delay the adoption of the Declaration for another session.

Then, a week before the session closed, Mexico advised supporting states and indigenous peoples' delegations that the Africa Group of States had agreed on a text that might be acceptable to the supporters of the Declaration. The negotiated text involved nine changes to the Declaration. The indigenous peoples' delegations, notably the regional coordinators for the Indigenous Peoples Regional Caucuses, met to examine the proposals and then speedily consult with their contacts in each of the regions. The time available was only a few days, including a weekend. When the regional coordinators met again it was clear that the overwhelming majority of indigenous delegations were able to accept the negotiated text and support the adoption of the Declaration with these amendments. This message was relayed to the supporting states who then prepared for the vote in the General Assembly.

On 13 September 2007, a large number of indigenous peoples' delegations had arrived in New York to witness the vote on the Declaration in the General Assembly. The atmosphere was still tense as there was no certainty as to the outcome. There had been little time for networking to establish the positions of all the state members of the United Nations. Many indigenous delegations were seated in the VIP area on the floor of the General Assembly and the public gallery was packed. Outside the General Assembly room, the media had gathered in a "media scrum" to interview states and indigenous peoples alike after the historic vote on the Declaration.

Time at first seemed to go so slowly on that morning, as some minor agenda items were dispatched, but then the Declaration became the topic on the floor and the room focussed upon the various speakers under this item. The giant voting screen soon blazed into action as green lights lit up everywhere to state emphatically that the Declaration on the Rights of Indigenous Peoples was now adopted by the General Assembly and was unequivocally a universal human rights standard. There was a long pause in proceedings as the room erupted with the clapping of hands and people scurried to congratulate and hug each other. Smiles and tears were seen all around the venue. The room finally settled and the General Assembly continued its work. Now it was time for the explanations of votes.

In an unprecedented move, the General Assembly meeting moved to informal mode to allow Vicky Tauli-Corpuz, Chairperson of the Permanent Forum on Indigenous Issues,[2] and Les Malezer, Chairperson of the Global Indigenous Peoples Caucus, to address the members of the General Assembly.[3] Their presentations emphasised the future, highlighting that ultimately the adoption of the Declaration was achieved through partnership between states and indigenous peoples and that the new challenge was now to see that the Declaration was implemented in order to improve the lives of indigenous peoples around the world.

The Declaration on the Rights of Indigenous Peoples[4] was at last adopted by the United Nations, with 144 votes in favour and 4 votes against, plus 11 abstentions.   ❏

Notes

1   The film released by film producer, Rebecca Sommer, on the progress of the Declaration in the General Assembly, proved to be very influential in mustering support for adoption of the Declaration.
2   Read the statement of the Chair of the UN Permanent Forum on Indigenous Issues at:
    http://www.iwgia.org/graphics/Synkron-Library/Documents/ InternationalProcesses/DraftDeclaration/07-09-13StatementChairofUNPFIIDe clarationAdoption.pdf
3   Read the International Indigenous Caucus' statement at:
    http://www.iwgia.org/graphics/Synkron-Library/Documents/ InternationalProcesses/DraftDeclaration/07-09-13IPCaucusStatementAdoptio nDeclaration%20.pdf
4   Read the General Assembly resolution, including the full text of the Declaration at:
    http://www.iwgia.org/graphics/Synkron-Library/Documents/ InternationalProcesses/DraftDeclaration/07-09-13ResolutiontextDeclaration. pdf

Les Malezer is the Chairperson of the Foundation for Aboriginal and Islander Research Action (FAIRA), an Aboriginal and Torres Strait Islander organisation based in Australia. He is currently the chairperson of the International Indigenous peoples' caucus during United Nations sessions and plays a coordinating role in the Pacific region on other matters including CBD issues.

THE UN PERMANENT FORUM
ON INDIGENOUS ISSUES

The UN Permanent Forum on Indigenous Issues (Permanent Forum) is a subsidiary body of the United Nations Economic and Social Council (ECOSOC). It is mandated to discuss indigenous issues related to economic and social development, culture, the environment, education, health and human rights.

The Permanent Forum is made up of 16 independent experts. Governments nominate eight of the members, and the other eight members are indigenous experts to be appointed by the President of ECOSOC. The Permanent Forum meets every year in a regular session in May for two weeks in New York.

Over the past six years, the Permanent Forum has become one of the largest conferences held at the United Nations. Participation of indigenous representatives has grown by 50% since its first session in 2002, with approximately 1,500 participants attending the sixth session. With 30 United Nations agencies, 70 member states, 30 Indigenous Parliamentarians and over 60 side events, the Forum has gained global recognition.

In April 2007, prior to the sixth session of the Permanent Forum on Indigenous Issues, the President of the Economic and Social Council (ECOSOC) appointed the eight indigenous experts to the Permanent Forum. Also in April, the ECOSOC members elected the eight governmental experts. The term of office for all 16 members is three years, beginning on 1 January 2008.[1]

The sixth session of the Permanent Forum on Indigenous Issues

The sixth session of the Permanent Forum met from 14 to 25 May 2007 at the UN headquarters in New York. The special theme of this year's session was "Territories, lands and natural resources".

The Permanent Forum had chosen this theme in response to the growing need to directly address the interconnectedness between indigenous peoples' rights to land and natural resources and environmental issues, cultural heritage, legal rights, spiritual attainment and indigenous knowledge. Due to indigenous peoples' deep connection and dependence on the land, they are often the most vulnerable to the effects of climate change, natural disasters and the environment's response to overuse of the earth's fragile resources.

The agenda for the sixth session also placed special emphasis on implementing previous recommendations and included a half-day discussion on Asia, a half-day discussion on urban indigenous peoples and migration and a discussion on data collection and disaggregation.[2]

Highlights of the discussions with agencies, governments and indigenous peoples

Territories, lands and natural resources

On the special theme, many agencies recognized the importance of the connection between indigenous peoples and their land. In particular, UNESCO emphasized the importance of land rights in identity and cultural preservation. Both WIPO and UNDP stressed the importance of protecting IPs' valuable intellectual property rights. There was also support from the UN agencies for empowering indigenous peoples by developing negotiation skills, smaller meetings outside of the Permanent Forum, as well as a need for codifying existing indigenous customary law.

Indigenous statements presented under this agenda item stated the serious and continuing violation of territorial rights and resources that are being suffered by the world's indigenous peoples. They referred, in large part, to the need for the General Assembly to adopt the UN Declaration on the Rights of Indigenous Peoples and to apply the articles relating to lands, territories and resources. Violations of rights were denounced in various countries of the world. The special and sacred relationship the indigenous peoples have with their land was mentioned, along with the impact of development projects (plantations, extraction industries, tourism, agro-industry) and evictions. Indigenous representatives also mentioned the situation of contamination, pollution, the impact of climate change and of the measures aimed at combating it.

The Permanent Forum urged states to take measures to halt land alienation in indigenous territories through, for example, a moratorium on the sale and registration of land - including the granting of land and other concessions - in areas occupied by indigenous peoples. The Permanent Forum also reaffirmed indigenous peoples' central role in decision-making with regard to their lands and resources, referring to the UN Declaration on the Rights of Indigenous Peoples. The Permanent Forum further stated that land and resource-related projects "shall not be implemented without the free, prior and informed consent of indigenous peoples".

Human rights

The agenda item on Human Rights is usually devoted to a dialogue with the Special Rapporteur on the situation of human rights and fundamental freedoms of indigenous people. This year, the Special Rapporteur on violence against women, its causes and consequences and the Special Rapporteur on human trafficking in persons, especially women and children, were also present and all three Rapporteurs presented their reports.

In his general report on the situation of indigenous rights, the *Special Rapporteur on the situation of human rights and fundamental freedoms of indigenous people*, Dr. Rodolfo Stavenhagen, referred to the fact that indigenous peoples are continuing to lose their lands, territories and resources, a process that is being aggravated by economic globalisation, particularly energy and water resource exploitation. The irrational exploitation of resources has various impacts, such as contamination and destruction, which lead to mass displacements of indigenous people, causing poverty and serious health and nutritional problems. The growing indigenous migration is also a reflection of globalisation and poverty, and the inequalities this creates. The results of policies that attempt to improve the indigenous situation have thus far been scant.

The Special Rapporteur on violence against women, its causes and consequences, Dr. Yakin Ertürk, referred to two issues on which there has been insufficient progress: the equal participation of indigenous peoples in the social, cultural, economic and political life of countries, and recognition of the specific gender discrimination suffered by indigenous women both inside and outside their communities, including violence against women, insufficient protection from the state justice system, marginalization and a high level of impunity in the case of violations by the armed forces in conflict zones.

The Special Rapporteur on trafficking in persons, especially women and children, Ms Sigma Huda, described the causes of human trafficking, noting among other things the marginalization and exclusion that make indigenous women particularly vulnerable. She noted added problems, such as the lack of identity documents and the high number of indigenous peoples affected by armed conflicts, in addition to the prejudices of non-indigenous society. With extreme poverty and dispossession forcing migration, the situation is worsening, especially for indigenous women, who are the most common victims of the trafficking of women in migratory processes. Violence against women and culturally determined practices (such as forced marriages) can also push indigenous women out of their communities and expose them to human trafficking. In addition to the seriousness of the situation, the Rapporteur noted the scarce information available on the trafficking of indigenous women, which makes it particularly urgent and necessary for all human rights bodies and the Permanent Forum to join forces to tackle this problem and take it up the international agenda.

Indigenous peoples in Asia, urban indigenous people and migration
In relation to indigenous peoples in Asia, attention was drawn to the continuing challenges facing indigenous peoples in the region, including non-recognition of their cultural identity, exclusion and marginalization, displacement from their traditional territories and dispossession of lands and resources as a result of logging activity, large-scale plantations, mega hydro-electric dams, extractive industries and also the designation of protected areas. In response to the priority discussion on the issue of urban indigenous people and migration, Permanent Forum members urged states to work with indigenous peoples to provide employment and economic development opportunities within their own territories and to provide centers in urban areas to meet the medical, legal and other needs of indigenous peoples.

UN Declaration on the Rights of Indigenous Peoples
Throughout the session, participants and Forum members reiterated their strong recommendation to Member States to adopt the UN Declaration on the Rights of Indigenous Peoples as adopted by the Human Rights Council in 2006 – in its entirety and without amendments - during the current session of the General Assembly.

Moving forward: recommendations and decisions

The Permanent Forum closed its session with the adoption of a number of recommendations regarding economic and social development, health, education, culture, environment and human rights, and discussed ways of implementing the recommendations within the framework of the Second International Decade of the World's Indigenous People in order to achieve the Millennium Development Goals. Recommendations were made to continue conducting studies on data collection and disaggregation, as well as to increase the participation of young people in the PFII, as well as in national political issues. While recognizing the accomplishments and successes of the

Forum, Forum members voiced the need to respond to violations of indigenous rights with active, local participation.

The Permanent Forum also approved the following decisions: The main theme for the seventh session will be "Climate change, bio-cultural diversity and livelihood: Stewardship Role of Indigenous People and New Challenges."

The Forum will also devote discussion to the issue of Indigenous languages, given that 2008 has been declared the International Year of Languages by the General Assembly and more than 4,000 of the world's remaining 6,000 languages are spoken by indigenous peoples, many of which are under threat of extinction.

The Forum also recommended devoting more time and attention to the Pacific region.

Next year's Forum is scheduled to be held in New York from 21 April- 2 May.

Brief overview of the Permanent Forum's intersessional work

Besides the annual session of the UN Permanent Forum on Indigenous Issues, the Permanent Forum members, the Secretariat for the Permanent Forum as well as the Inter-Agency Support Group on Indigenous Issues (IASG)[3] arrange and participate in various workshops and expert group meetings based on recommendations of the Permanent Forum, bringing together experts on issues related to indigenous peoples. The reports from these meetings are made available to all participants in the sessions of the annual session of the Permanent Forum and are posted on the Permanent Forum's website in advance of the session.

International Expert Group Meeting on the Convention on Biological Diversity's International Regime on Access and Benefit-Sharing and Indigenous Peoples' Rights (17-19 January 2007, New York)
Following a recommendation at the Permanent Forum's fifth session, the Secretariat of the Permanent Forum, in cooperation with the Sec-

retariat of the Convention on Biological Diversity (CBD), organised an International Expert Group Meeting on the Convention on Biological Diversity's international regime on access and benefit-sharing and indigenous peoples' rights in New York in January. The expert group meeting was attended by 61 people, including representatives from the UN system, five members of the Permanent Forum, other interested intergovernmental organizations, experts from indigenous organizations and interested Member States.

Presentations and discussions centered on human rights treaties and how they affirm indigenous peoples' rights to lands, waters, territories and natural resources, including rights to genetic resources and traditional knowledge; human rights treaties and other existing or emerging instruments that are applicable to Access and Benefit-Sharing (ABS) processes. The participants also discussed customary laws that are vested in traditional knowledge protection and transmission; indigenous participation in the ABS processes; the role of customary law in the protection of traditional knowledge; and development of regimes on access to genetic resources and benefit-sharing. The meeting resulted in 37 recommendations, including urging Parties to the CBD to recognize, respect and protect the rights of indigenous peoples in the development of an ABS regime as well as encouraging indigenous peoples' organizations to establish an informal, open-ended indigenous expert group on ABS and CBD's Article 8(j) in order to analyse, review and provide input directly to the CBD's Working Group on 8(j) and Working Group on ABS processes as well as to analyse the developments in the negotiation of an international regime on ABS.[4]

The International Expert Group Meeting on Urban Indigenous Issues, 27-29 March 2007, Santiago, Chile

The Expert Group Meeting was convened by UN-HABITAT and OHCHR, jointly with the Secretariat of the UNPFII.

At the meeting, the experts concluded that greater attention is required by the relevant authorities in order to address the issues and rights of indigenous peoples living in urban areas. In so doing, public authorities need to understand the multiple identities of indigenous peoples within urban areas and their continuing relationship to their traditional lands, natural resources and environments in rural areas. In this sense, indigenous peoples should not be seen as divided between urban and rural but rather as peoples with rights and a common cultural identity, adapting to changing circumstances and environments. The complexity and diversity of the situations of indigenous peoples whose members live in urban areas requires states to adopt culturally sensitive policies and models to respond to these needs.

It was recognized that the impacts of urban areas on indigenous peoples could vary greatly. Some are able to adapt and improve their situations considerably without loss of cultural identity; in other cases, indigenous peoples are subject to discrimination, exclusion, violence, etc. Urbanization is a phenomenon that requires immediate attention and states have obligations to ensure that indigenous peoples are not forcibly removed or driven from their homelands, nor subject to discrimination once in urban areas.

Briefing on Indigenous Peoples' Lands, Territories, Natural Resources: Livelihoods and Emerging Issues, 19 April 2007, New York

The briefing took place in New York in April and was organized by Department of Public Information/Non-Governmental Organizations (DPI/NGO) in cooperation with the Secretariat of the Permanent Forum and the NGO Committee on the UN International Decade of the World's Indigenous Peoples.

The briefing looked at the traditional lifestyles, practices and struggles of indigenous peoples around the world. There are over 370 million indigenous peoples living in some 70 countries. While they view themselves as the caregivers of the land, the needs, human rights and challenges of indigenous communities have remained largely neglected by national governments. Discussions included the current struggle to maintain indigenous peoples' traditional cultures; environmentally sound relationship with the land; and sustainable use of natural resources.

Round Table with African experts on the UN Declaration on the Rights of Indigenous Peoples

The Round Table took place in New York in May and was organized by IWGIA and the Secretariat of the Permanent Forum. The main objective of the Round Table was to encourage and facilitate a constructive dialogue between African states and other stakeholders on the key issues of concern expressed by the African Group of States in relation to the UN Declaration on the Rights of Indigenous Peoples. The presentations and discussions centred around the UN Declaration's consistency with all African constitutions, the African Charter and African states' practice, which guarantee equal enjoyment of all rights by all citizens, including disadvantaged groups. The Round Table provided an opportunity for on-going dialogue between African experts and the African group of countries regarding the UN Declaration.

International Expert Group Meeting on Indigenous Peoples and Protection of the Environment, 27 - 29 August 2007, Khabarovsk, Russian Federation

The Expert Group Meeting on Indigenous Peoples and Protection of the Environment was held in the Russian Federation in August and was organized by the Government of Khabarovsk, the Association of Indigenous Peoples of the Russian North, Siberia and the Far East (RAIPON), the Public Chamber of the Russian Federation and the Secretariat of the Permanent Forum. The objective of the meeting was to promote an opportunity to exchange information on the adverse effects of wide-ranging toxic, dangerous products and waste that impact on the well-being of indigenous peoples' spiritual, cultural and physical well-being, their food sources and lands. The meeting identified types of environmental discrimination and the forms that it takes and considered how indigenous peoples might seek administrative or legal remedies with regard to the effects of toxic, dangerous products and waste as well as natural and man-made disasters under existing international standards. The participants also highlighted good practice models and identified gaps and challenges.[5]

Other intersessional activities

In July, an international workshop was held in Salekhard, Russian Federation. The workshop focused on the prospects for relationships between indigenous peoples and industrial companies and was co-organized by Yamal-Nenets Autonomous Okrug, the Russian Association of Indigenous Peoples of the North, Siberia and the Far East (RAIPON) and the Secretariat of the Permanent Forum.[6] In October, the members of the Permanent Forum were invited to participate in an international meeting in Bolivia "For the Historic Victory of Indigenous Peoples of the World", in celebration of the adoption of the UN Declaration on the Rights of Indigenous Peoples. Likewise in October, members of the Permanent Forum participated in the fifth meeting of the Ad Hoc Open-ended Working Group on Access and Benefit-sharing of the Convention on Biological Diversity in Canada. The historic adoption by the UN General Assembly of the UN Declaration on the Rights of Indigenous Peoples in September has given a major boost to the demands of indigenous people in the ABS discussions and was often quoted by various states as the basis for an ABS regime. Finally, the Permanent Forum participated in the Working Group session regarding the Draft American Declaration on the Rights of Indigenous Peoples. In the meeting, the participants reflected on the Draft Declaration and how to achieve the necessary consensus for concluding negotiations in this regard as soon as possible. ❑

Notes

1 The eight indigenous experts appointed were: Hassan Id Balkassm (Morocco), Margaret Lokawua (Uganda), Victoria Tauli-Corpuz (Philippines), Lars-Anders Baer (Sweden), Elisa Canqui Mollo (Bolivia), Pavel Sulyandziga (Russian Federation), Tonya Gonnella Frichner (United States) and Michael Dodson (Australia). The eight governmental experts elected were: Xiaomei Qin (China), Paimaneh Hasteh (Iran), Carlos Mamani Condori (Bolivia), Bartolomé Clavero Salvador (Spain), Carsten Smith (Norway), Liliane Muzangi Mbella (Democratic Republic of the Congo), Simeon Adewale Adekanye (Nigeria) and A. A. Nikiforov (Russian Federation).
2 The official report of the Permanent Forum's sixth session can be found at: http://daccessdds.un.org/doc/UNDOC/GEN/N07/376/75/PDF/N0737675.pdf?OpenElement

3   The IASG was established to support and promote the mandate of the Permanent Forum within the United Nations system. Its mandate was later expanded to include support to indigenous-related mandates throughout the intergovernmental system. The IASG comprises 27 UN agencies.

4   The report of the Expert Group Meeting can be found at: http://www.un.org/esa/socdev/unpfii/documents/workshop_CBDABS_finalreport_en.doc

5   The report of the Expert Group meeting, along with the presentations, can be found at: http://www.un.org/esa/socdev/unpfii/en/workshopIPPE.html

6   The presentations can be found at: http://www.un.org/esa/socdev/unpfii/en/workshopPRIPIC.html

This article has been edited by **Lola García-Alix** *on the base of the information about the Permanent Forum's activities in 2007 published in the Forum's electronic newsletter "the Message Stick" and IWGIA's report on the 6th session of the UN Permanent Forum. The Message Stick can be found at: http://www.un.org/esa/socdev/unpfii/en/newsletter.html*

THE UN HUMAN RIGHTS COUNCIL

THE EXPERT MECHANISM ON INDIGENOUS PEOPLES' RIGHTS

The UN Human Rights Council was created by the UN General Assembly in March 2006 to replace the Commission on Human Rights. Its mandate is to be "responsible for promoting universal respect for the protection of all human rights and fundamental freedoms for all", to "address situations of violations of human rights" and to "promote the effective coordination and mainstreaming of human rights within the United Nations system".

Since its establishment and the subsequent dismantling of the Commission and its subsidiary bodies, indigenous peoples' organisations and IWGIA have campaigned vigorously to ensure that the promotion and protection of indigenous peoples are given appropriate consideration by the UN Human Rights Council.

On 14 December 2007, the UN Human Rights Council took a landmark decision regarding the promotion and protection of indigenous peoples' rights when the resolution to establish an "Expert Mechanism on the Rights of Indigenous Peoples" was adopted by consensus.

Brief description of the Expert Mechanism on the Rights of Indigenous Peoples

The new expert mechanism on the rights of indigenous peoples will report directly to the Human Rights Council. It will assist the Human Rights Council in the implementation of its mandate by providing thematic expertise and making proposals to the Council pertaining to the rights of indigenous peoples and will consist of five independent experts. Their selection will be carried out in accordance with the Council's formal procedures for nominating, short-listing and appointing independent experts to any of its mechanisms. Through this formal process, indigenous peoples' organizations will have the possibility of nominating indigenous experts. Furthermore, the resolution clearly recommends that, in the selection and appointment process, the Council should give due regard to experts of indigenous origin. The independent experts shall be appointed for a three-year period and may be re-elected for one additional period.

The new body will meet for five working days each year. The annual meeting of the Expert Mechanism will be open to the participation, as observers, of states, United Nations mechanisms, bodies and specialized agencies. The meeting shall also be open to indigenous peoples' organizations, non-governmental organizations, national human rights institutions, academics, etc. In order for the Expert Mechanism to enhance cooperation and avoid duplicating the work of the Special Rapporteur and the Permanent Forum, it shall invite the Special Rapporteur and a member of the Permanent Forum on Indigenous Issues to attend and contribute to its annual meetings.

The process that led to the establishment of the expert mechanism

The conversations and deliberations among states on the most appropriate mechanisms to continue the work of the Working Group on Indigenous Populations formally began during the negotiations on the institution-building of the Human Rights Council.

After one year of government negotiations, in June 2007 the Human Rights Council adopted an institution-building package[1] that set out the basic structure for the Council's new institutional machinery. In this document, the Council expressed its commitment to finding appropriate mechanisms to deal with issues formally addressed by the former Working Group on Indigenous Populations.

In September 2007, after some preliminary discussions on this issue, the Council adopted a resolution[2] requesting the Office of the High Commissioner for Human Rights to convene an informal meeting in Geneva, for a day and a half, open to states, indigenous peoples and other stakeholders, and preceding the resumed sixth session of the Council in December, in order to exchange views on the most appropriate mechanisms with which to carry forward the work of the Working Group on Indigenous Populations.

Following this decision, the Office of the High Commissioner for Human Rights (OHCHR) organized a meeting that took place in Geneva on 6 December and the morning of 7 December 2007.

The indigenous preparatory meeting

On 4 and 5 December, the international indigenous caucus held a preparatory meeting in which a proposal containing the basic elements and characteristics of a possible new expert body to replace the extinct Working Group on Indigenous Populations was agreed.[3] The proposal prepared by the indigenous caucus was later presented at the informal seminar organized by the OHCHR and was used as a basis for discussions during the informal seminar.

The informal seminar, Geneva 6-7 December 2007

Under Bolivia's presidency, the informal seminar gathered together a considerable number of state delegations, indigenous representatives and NGOs. As previously mentioned, the objective of the meeting was to exchange views and ideas on the establishment of a UN body responsible for protecting and promoting indigenous rights within the framework of the Human Rights Council. Most of the countries that attended the meeting welcomed the proposal presented by the indigenous caucus.

During the seminar, issues such as the placement of the expert body within the Council's structure, its scope and mandate, and its composition were discussed.

Although, all governmental delegations that participated in the seminar expressed their support for the idea of establishing a new expert body, different opinions and views were expressed regarding its mandate and composition.

The discussions that took place during the informal meeting were, however, very important as they first served to identify whether or not there was enough government support for the establishment of a new expert body to deal with indigenous peoples' rights and, second, they helped supportive governments to develop the text of a resolution that served as a basis for the negotiations that took place some days later, during the Human Rights Council's session that started on Monday 10 December.

The 6th session of the Human Rights Council, Geneva 10-14 December 2007

After the informal seminar, the indigenous caucus continued to exchange opinions with governmental delegations from Bolivia, Guatemala, Mexico and Denmark in order to prepare a proposal that could achieve the necessary consensus and be adopted by the Council before the end of its December session.

On Monday 10 December, negotiations began among states based on a proposal presented by Bolivia, which included the main suggestions made in the indigenous proposals.

Bolivia took the lead in developing and presenting the first draft of the resolution but, in subsequent negotiations, it became evident that this proposal did not have a government consensus. With the firm support of Guatemala, Mexico and Denmark, Bolivia continued negotiations on the text of the resolution throughout the whole week. These governments, in close cooperation with the indigenous caucus, worked hard to ensure that the resolution could be adopted by a consensus of the Council's 47 member states while at the same time maintaining a broad enough mandate to ensure its effectiveness.

On Friday 14 December, the Human Rights Council session considered the revised resolution (L.42/Rev.1) presented by Bolivia. In its presentation to the Council, Bolivia pointed out the most substantial changes in this version in relation to the one previously tabled. Other governments also took the floor and congratulated Bolivia for promoting the creation of this new mechanism and thanked the indigenous caucus for its work and its constructive approach during the negotiation process. The Human Rights Council then adopted the resolution by consensus.[4]

In the explanation of the vote after the adoption of the resolution, Bolivia asked to speak in order to point out that it wished to be withdrawn as the country that had sponsored the resolution, as it did not represent the principles and policies of its government. It pointed out that it did not oppose it, as the delegation had instructions to support the indigenous caucus' position, but found the text was not good enough because it did not mention the implementation of the UN Declaration on the Rights of Indigenous Peoples, the idea that it should cut across the work of the Council was not accepted and full indigenous participation was not guaranteed. Despite everything, Bolivia did not oppose the resolution because it was supported by the indigenous caucus and stated its willingness to continue supporting the indigenous caucus and the mechanism's work. Bolivia also highlighted the novelty involved in the elaboration and negotiation of the resolution, in which Bolivia and other governments had worked closely together with the indigenous caucus.

Cuba, in turn, also expressed its disappointment because the mandate of the previous Working Group on Indigenous Populations was not taken into account in the resolution and, particularly, because emphasis was given to studies and investigations. Finally, on behalf of the International Indigenous Caucus, the International Indian Treaty Council (an international indigenous organization of the Americas) presented a statement in which it expressed its satisfaction at the Council's decision to establish an expert body on the rights of indigenous peoples and expressed its commitment to making this new mechanism useful for the promotion and protection of indigenous peoples' human rights.

It is expected that the Human Rights Council will appoint the members of the expert group before the summer 2008 and that the expert group will be able to hold its first session in the autumn of that year.

Final remarks

The Expert Mechanism on the Rights of Indigenous Peoples was the final piece of the Council's institution-building package to be put in place. Its adoption was delayed until December 2007 due, in part, to the previous reluctance expressed by some member states to support the creation of a new body focused on indigenous peoples' human rights. IWGIA sees its adoption as a major step forward in the promotion and protection of indigenous peoples' human rights. ❏

Notes

1 A/HRC/5/21 of 7 August 2007
2 Human Rights Council Resolution 6/16 http://ap.ohchr.org/documents/E/HRC/resolutions/A_HRC_RES_6_16.pdf
3 Draft resolution submitted by the Indigenous Caucus http://www2.ohchr.org/english/issues/indigenous/docs/informal/crp-12-e.doc
4 HRC Resolution 6/36 http://www2.ohchr.org/english/bodies/hrcouncil/docs/ExpertMechanism/RES6.36_en.pdf

Lola García-Alix *is director of IWGIA.*

UNITED NATIONS SPECIAL RAPPORTEUR ON THE SITUATION OF HUMAN RIGHTS AND FUNDAMENTAL FREEDOMS OF INDIGENOUS PEOPLE

2007 was the sixth and final year of Rodolfo Stavenhagen's mandate as Special Rapporteur on the situation of human rights and fundamental freedoms of indigenous people and, in it, the Rapporteur continued to focus on three main areas of activity. First, thematic research into issues of particular importance to indigenous rights. Second, communications sent to governments and other stakeholders in relation to allegations of indigenous rights violations. And, third, official and private visits to different countries.

2007 was characterised by two events of great importance to the future activities of the Special Rapporteur. First, the adoption of the UN Declaration on the Rights of Indigenous Peoples by the General Assembly, which sets out a clear legal framework for the Rapporteur and provides this human rights mechanism with strong political backing. This backing was consolidated when the Human Rights Council renewed the Special Rapporteur's mandate as part of the special procedure mechanisms addressing thematic issues inherited from the former Commission on Human Rights.

The thematic report: A human rights-based approach to development and indigenous peoples

In his final report to the Human Rights Council, presented in December 2007, Rodolfo Stavenhagen wanted to consider an issue that has been of great interest to him throughout both his long academic career and his role as Special Rapporteur: development. In order to consider this issue and its implications for indigenous peoples, he took as his basis the adoption of the UN Declaration on the Rights of Indigenous Peoples, being the normative framework that must guide develop-ment activities amongst indigenous peoples.

His report starts by noting a failure: "Although over the past 50 years extensive efforts and resources have been devoted to overcom-ing the poverty and marginalization from which most indigenous communities suffer, the economic, social and human development lev-els of these communities generally remain very low".[1] He goes on to give an account of the previous strategies that have served as a frame-work for indigenous peoples' development – modernization, econom-ic growth and not forgetting the so-called ethnodevelopment - and then lists the reasons for their limited impact in terms of improving the living conditions of indigenous peoples:

> *Key to understanding the limited impact of development policies is that they have not attacked the structural causes underlying the marginaliza-tion of indigenous peoples, causes that are directly linked to the failure to recognize, protect and guarantee observance of their individual and col-lective human rights.*

On the basis of this observation, the Special Rapporteur's report looks at the human rights-based approach being promoted by different UN agencies. In the specific context of indigenous peoples, the UN Decla-ration, Convention 169 of the International Labor Organisation and other relevant instruments offer a series of practical principles with which to apply a human rights-based approach at all stages of the de-velopment process. These principles can be summarised as follows:

- *Indigenous peoples are subjects of rights*. A human rights-based approach demands that indigenous peoples are identified as subjects of collective rights, in addition to the rights of their individual members.
- *Duty bearers*. A logical corollary to the rights-based approach to indigenous development is that the state has an obligation

to implement a minimum set of public policies aimed at respecting, protecting, guaranteeing and promoting the rights of indigenous peoples, beginning with steps to improve their living conditions.

- *Free prior and informed consent.* Application of this principle (Article 19 of the UN Declaration on the Rights of Indigenous Peoples) in development programmes and projects on behalf of indigenous communities and peoples is a basic prerequisite for ensuring respect for the right of indigenous peoples to self-determination.
- *Participation and empowerment.* Participation and empowerment, two basic and interrelated principles of the human rights-based approach to development, are particularly important for indigenous peoples, who have been systematically excluded and marginalized from decision-making on matters affecting them.
- *Autonomy and self-management.* Of particular importance to the development of indigenous peoples is their right "to autonomy or self-government in matters relating to their internal and local affairs, as well as ways and means for financing their autonomous functions" (Article 4 of the United Nations Declaration on the Rights of Indigenous Peoples). This right builds on the principle of the participation of indigenous peoples in development projects and programmes managed by non-indigenous entities, affirming the additional principle that indigenous peoples themselves must play a role in their own development.
- *Territorial control.* One of the basic principles of a human rights-based approach to development is the indivisibility and interdependence of human rights. Respect for the rights of indigenous peoples to ownership of, control over and access to their traditional lands and natural resources is a precondition for the enjoyment of other rights.
- *Non discrimination.* The human rights-based approach to development highlights the importance of the principle of equality and non-discrimination, and the need to give priority attention to marginalized and socially excluded groups. The

United Nations Declaration also emphasizes the need for states to take "effective measures and, where appropriate, special measures to ensure continuing improvement of their economic and social conditions. Particular attention shall be paid to the rights and special needs of indigenous elders, women, youth, children and persons with disabilities" (Art. 21, para. 2).

The Special Rapporteur's final report identifies a whole series of projects and programmes involving indigenous peoples around the world that can be held up as best practice in terms of applying these different principles. These best practices are empowerment processes which are predicated on the assumption by indigenous peoples of ownership of their rights and on strengthening the ability of these peoples to organize and demand the observance and exercise of their rights, and also their political participation.

Official mission to Bolivia

The Special Rapporteur undertook an official visit to Bolivia from 26 November to 4 December 2007. The visit, for which only a preliminary note was presented to the sixth session of the Council in December 2007, was the last that Rodolfo Stavenhagen will undertake in his position as Special Rapporteur.

During his mission, Mr. Stavenhagen visited the departments of La Paz, Potosí, Oruro, Chuquisaca, Cochabamba, Santa Cruz and Beni, where he held information meetings with indigenous and human rights organizations to gain an understanding of the specific situation of different communities. Among others, he met with representatives of the Aymara and Quechua nations and the Ayoreo, Chiquitano, Guaraní, Guarayo, Mojeño, Movima, Tacana, Trinitario, Uru, Yuki and Yuracare peoples. The Special Rapporteur also met with several ministers and other officials of the national government, with prefectural and municipal authorities, members of the Constituent Assembly and the legislature, and the Ombudsman. He also met twice with President Evo Morales Ayma.

In the preliminary note on his visit, the Special Rapporteur highlighted the fact that, in 2005, an indigenous president was elected for the first time, announcing his intention to introduce sweeping changes in the country's social and economic policy aimed at benefiting the indigenous peoples and remedying the historic injustices perpetrated against them. The Special Rapporteur also noted the incorporation into domestic law of the United Nations Declaration on the Rights of Indigenous Peoples, adopted by the General Assembly in September this year.

One of the main issues that attracted the Special Rapporteur's attention during his visit was the serious persistence of racism and discrimination against indigenous people, and especially against indigenous women. This is still manifested in the behaviour of public officials at the national and subnational levels and in the attitudes of political parties and pressure groups, which sometimes incite violence against persons based on their indigenous status. Expressions of anti-indigenous racism frequently occur in some media, which often sacrifice principles of objectivity and impartiality for the sake of political interests.

The Special Rapporteur noted that a denial of access to land and territory, was the main focus of concern for indigenous communities in Bolivia. While the Special Rapporteur noted some progress in land reform and the granting of title, there are still many obstacles in the way of this process, which is a source of frustration for the communities. A matter of special concern was the bondage in which Guaraní communities are still living in three departments of Bolivia as a result of historical dispossession of their territories. The mobilization of indigenous peoples in recent years has led to substantial progress in recognition of their rights and their role in the national political process. The many documented instances of assault and attacks on indigenous leaders and human rights defenders, with the support of economic actors and local authorities, are a matter of concern, and reflect the difficulties in the way of building a pluralistic democratic society in the country.

The case of La Parota (Mexico)

In September 2007, the Special Rapporteur undertook a joint visit with the Special Rapporteur on adequate housing, Mr. Miloon Kothari, to the communities directly affected by the construction of the La Parota hydroelectric project in the State of Guerrero (Mexico). The project intends to build a dam in order to create electricity. In forming the reservoir, 19 agricultural population centres will be flooded, including indigenous communities, covering a total of 14,000 hectares of land. The project envisages the relocation of 15 settlements due to the flooding of the land, which will affect an estimated 3,039 inhabitants. According to its opponents, however, it will affect 30,000 people directly and 70,000 people indirectly.

During the course of their visit, the Rapporteurs met with the different relevant authorities, visited some of the communities that will be affected and spoke to people both in favour and opposed to the hydroelectric project. They were able to note that the planning and implementation of the La Parota Project has thus far not complied fully with the human rights standards laid out in international instruments signed by Mexico, including ILO Convention 169. The Special Rapporteurs have sent a communication to the government in this regard, setting out some of their preliminary conclusions on the La Parota situation on the basis of information gathered during their visit.

The situation of indigenous peoples in Asia

Alongside his visits to Bolivia and La Parota, the Special Rapporteur participated in a series of activities related to the situation of indigenous peoples in Asia. Amongst these were his attendance at the National Consultation with indigenous organisations in the Philippines in January 2007, as a follow-up to his official visit to this country in 2003; the holding of a regional consultation - the first of its kind - with indigenous organisations from Asia, in Phnom Penh, Cambodia, in February 2007; and his participation on a technical assistance mission to Nepal, organised by the Office of the High Commissioner for Human Rights in that country, along with the Special Rapporteur on Racism, Dodou Diène.

As a result of these activities, the Special Rapporteur presented a report to a special session on Asia of the 6th session of the Permanent Forum on Indigenous Issues that contains a series of general considerations on the situation of this region's indigenous peoples, which was also included as an annexe to his report to the Human Rights Council.

Renewal of the Special Rapporteur's mandate

2007 was also a crucial year for the future of the Special Rapporteur's mandate, this being renewed by the Human Rights Council as part of the new special procedures architecture inherited from the former Commission. The resolution to renew the mandate for an initial three-year period was proposed, by Mexico and Guatemala (as was the resolution for its establishment in 2001), and was approved unanimously by the Human Rights Council during its September 2007 session, following a discussion that included the Special Rapporteur himself.

In line with the Commission's previous resolutions, the new resolution grants the Special Rapporteur a wide mandate to fulfil his or her tasks, including visits to and communications with countries, along with the production of annual reports and recommendations for countries. The new resolution again includes a request that the Special Rapporteur pay particular attention to the situation of indigenous women and children, and identify "best practices" with which to overcome the obstacles existing to the protection of indigenous rights.

One new issue in the resolution gives the Special Rapporteur the task of "promoting the UN Declaration on the Rights of Indigenous Peoples and international instruments relevant to the advancement of the rights of indigenous peoples", thus establishing a clear normative framework for the Special Rapporteur's different activities. In addition, the collaboration between the Special Rapporteur and the UN Permanent Forum on Indigenous Issues is also expressly emphasised, thus formalising the Special Rapporteur's attendance at the Forum's annual sessions. This participation now replaces the interim report to the Third Committee of the UN General Assembly, a report that the Special Rapporteur presented annually from 2004 to 2007. ❑

Notes

1   *Promotion and protection of all human rights, civil, political, economic, social and cultural rights, including the right to development:* Report of the Special Rapporteur on the situation of human rights and fundamental freedoms of indigenous people, Mr. Rodolfo Stavenhagen, A/HRC/6/15, para. 62.

Luis Rodríguez-Piñero is Human Rights Officer, Special Procedures Division, at the Office of the High Commissioner for Human Rights (OHCHR), assisting the mandate of the Special Rapporteur on the situation of human rights and fundamental freedoms of indigenous peoples. He holds a PhD in Law from the European University Institute, in Florence. Before joining OHCHR he was part of the Indigenous Peoples Law and Policy Program, at the University of Arizona, in Tucson. His academic works include Indigenous Peoples, Postcolonialism and International Law (Oxford University Press, 2005).

THE CONVENTION
ON BIOLOGICAL DIVERSITY

The Convention on Biological Diversity (CBD) is an international agreement established by the United Nations. Its aim is to preserve biological diversity around the world. The CBD has three main objectives: to conserve biodiversity, to enhance its sustainable use and to ensure an equitable sharing of benefits linked to the exploitation of genetic resources.

Article 8(j) of the CBD recognizes the role of indigenous peoples in the conservation and management of biodiversity through the application of indigenous knowledge. The debate on indigenous knowledge and biodiversity is crucial as the CBD has commenced discussions on a proposed International Regime on Access and Benefit-Sharing. Issues on biological/genetic resources and associated indigenous/traditional knowledge have expanded from the deliberations of the Working Group on Article 8(j) and related provisions to discussions within the Working Group on Access and Benefit-Sharing, the Working Group on Protected Areas and within various other thematic and cross-cutting issues.

2007 was an inter-sessional year between the eighth Conference of the Parties (COP), held in Curitiba (Brazil) in May 2006 and COP9, which will take place in Bonn (Germany) in May 2008. The activities of the Convention on Biological Diversity (CBD) were this year framed by the decision adopted by the Parties to elaborate and negotiate an International Regime on Access to Genetic Resources and Benefit-Sharing by 2010. The countdown to the process to produce an international instrument has been unprecedentedly rapid for the UN.

Although a number of meetings were held during 2007 on the issue of the Convention,[1] this short summary will refer only to those directly related to the negotiations for the International Regime on Access to Genetic Resources and Benefit-Sharing, which is of great interest to indigenous peoples and their organisations given the significant impact that a legal instrument of this kind could have on the genetic resources found on their territories and on their associated traditional knowledge.

Events during 2007

Progress towards producing an International Regime on Access to Genetic Resources and Benefit-Sharing was very closely monitored by the indigenous organisations over the year, given the impact this instrument will have on their resources and knowledge. At its fifth session, the UN Permanent Forum on Indigenous Issues (UNPFII) received information on developments that had taken place at COP8 and the concerns of the indigenous organisations monitoring the CBD process through the International Indigenous Forum on Biodiversity (IIFB). These organisations emphasised that the negotiations needed to ensure the full and effective participation of the indigenous organisations, which was being resisted by a number of Parties, and that any possible instrument had to take account of the international framework recognising indigenous rights. The UNPFII recommended holding an expert seminar on the CBD's international regime and indigenous rights. In the report of the seminar,[2] which was held in New York in January 2007, specific recommendations were made regarding participation and the need to respect indigenous rights when elaborating and negotiating the International Regime (IR).

In that same month, a meeting of the group of technical experts took place in Lima (Peru) with regard to establishing an internationally-recognised certificate of origin/source/legal provenance.[3] In addition to the state-designated participants, expert observers were also invited, including an expert representing indigenous and local communities.[4] The group of experts examined different options for voluntary and compulsory certification to be transmitted back to the Working Group. It is interesting to note that, although the group identified protection of traditional knowledge as one of the aims of the possible certification, more specific proposals as to how this could be achieved were not made, the discussions being limited to indicating the complexity of the issue.

Over the course of the technical meeting, the co-chairs, Timothy Hodges and Fernando Casas, also held informal meetings with different countries and groups of countries in order to identify positions, concerns, agreements and differences between them. Although no specific meeting of this kind was held with indigenous representatives, the CBD Secretariat convened an international seminar with indigenous and local communities on developing the international regime in order to prepare for the meetings of the Ad Hoc Open-ended Working Group on Access and Benefit-Sharing (WGABS), which were to commence the concrete negotiations. This meeting, a report of which was sent to the WGABS and the Working Group on Article 8(j) (WG8J),[5] took place in Montreal in September with the involvement of UN agencies, the PFII and representatives from indigenous organisations from all regions, at the invitation of the Secretariat. It is important to note that the meeting was held after the adoption of the UN Declaration on the Rights of Indigenous Peoples. The participants stated that the Declaration contained articles of direct relevance to the issues under discussion with regard to the International Regime and that the Declaration should thus be considered an integral part of this, in the sense that any component or provision of the International Regime had to be consistent with the Declaration. The report of the consultation compiled the opinions of the indigenous organisations with regard to specific aspects of the regime and has been used by indigenous organisations as a reference document in subsequent meetings of the Parties.

Meetings of the Working Group

Two important and complex meetings were held in October: the fifth meeting of the Ad Hoc Open-ended Working Group on Access and Benefit-Sharing (WGABS) and the fifth meeting of the Working Group on Article 8(j) and related provisions (WG8J).[6] The COP had decided that two meetings of the WGABS and one of the WG8J were to be held between COP8 and COP9. The meeting of the WG8J was to be held immediately after the first meeting of the WGABS in order to be able to inform the second meeting of this group. It should be noted that the issue of traditional knowledge is directly related to negotiations on the International Regime, as this will affect traditional knowledge related to genetic resources.

One important aspect from an indigenous rights point of view was that the WGABS5 was the first multilateral negotiation meeting to be held since the adoption of the Declaration. A majority of the Parties welcomed the adoption and stated that its articles should be taken into account when elaborating the International Regime, necessarily resulting in full indigenous participation (Article 18) and full respect for their rights as recognised in the Declaration in relation to their resources and knowledge (articles 26 and 34). Canada repeatedly stated its opposition to such consideration of the Declaration.

In terms of progress in the negotiations, many of the Parties found the Montreal meeting frustrating. In order to avoid any confrontation that could block future progress, the co-chairs decided that the meeting should consist of a round of opinions of the Parties and observers on the different aspects of the IR. On the basis of these opinions, they would produce a document identifying areas of agreement and disagreement and compiling opinions.[7] The co-chairs' methodology and documents were not accepted by a number of the Parties and the meeting ended without any tangible results having been achieved in terms of a negotiable text. The open dialogue on controversial issues such as: whether the regime should be binding (supported by the African Group, the Like-minded Megadiverse Countries, GRULAC and others) or not (Japan, Australia, Canada, New Zealand); whether genetic resource derivatives and products should be included (Megadiverse, African Group) or only those genetic resources established in the CBD; whether internationally-recognised certificates of origin and compliance should be developed (Megadiverse, African Group) or whether such elements would merely increase the transaction costs and obstruct access (Japan, Canada, New Zealand) had a certain positive influence, however, as it clearly demonstrated the isolation of the more radical parties against the IR and the general agreement that existed around the need for the Regime. With regard to indigenous rights, the compilation texts of the co-chairs included some of the interventions of the regional caucuses of the International Indigenous Forum on Biodiversity (IIFB) on: the need for traditional knowledge to be included in the IR in order to guarantee its protection; full respect for indigenous rights over their resources and knowledge as recognised in the Declaration; compliance with the prior and informed consent of indigenous peoples in case of access to their genetic resources and traditional knowledge; the inclusion of place of origin and people owning the resource or knowledge in any possible certificate; and that the Declaration should be considered as one of the instruments on which the International Regime is based.

The difficult WGABS meeting had a very negative effect on the WG8J meeting, held the following week. Issues of potential interest to indigenous peoples were on the meeting's agenda, such as possible codes of ethical conduct in relation to accessing traditional knowledge; elements of *sui generis* systems for the protection of traditional knowledge and indicators.[8] The issue of how the WG8J was going to coordinate with the WGABS in order to advise on the issue of traditional knowledge paralysed the meeting, however. On the one hand, the group of Parties most against the IR and against indigenous participation blocked all outcomes because they did not want to adopt anything that might influence the discussions on the International Regime. In their opinion, any decision with regard to traditional knowledge had to be reached outside the discussions on the IR and through mechanisms such as completely voluntary guidelines or codes of conduct. Nor did they want the WG8J to play an important role in advising on traditional knowledge during the elaboration and negotiation of the IR. By the end of the meeting, on Friday 19 October, and despite various contact groups having been established, the WG8J had agreed nothing that could be transmitted to the WGABS regarding the IR and traditional knowledge. Nor was there any substantial or satisfactory progress for the indigenous organisations with regard to decisions on other agenda items. The WG8J had been neutralized, a clear signal that the Parties did not want to lose control over anything that could be decisive in the IR negotiations.

Although outside the timeframe of this Yeabook, we should refer to the sixth meeting of the WGABS, held in Geneva in January 2008, as this was considered as the second part of the Montreal meeting. After the scant results in October, many Parties had told the co-chairs in their bilateral meetings and in documentation provided to the Secretariat that they wanted to see palpable progress in terms of negotiation of the text. The Geneva meeting represented a change in spirit and in speed: its results have put a new framework on the table for the possible IR, containing specific text, although this is virtually all in parentheses and with different options with regard to the objective, scope, nature and principal components of the future IR.[9] At this meeting, the most recalcitrant Parties finally appeared resigned to accepting that the IR had to be produced. They are, however, maintaining their position that there should be a minimum of international regulation instead of national laws, on the one hand, and model contracts and other non-binding flexible instruments, on the other. The outline of a possible IR will be transmitted to the COP9, where negotiations will continue and an inter-sessional process will be established to ensure that the IR is finalised before COP10. Another issue that became clear at the Geneva meeting in terms of the traditional knowledge associated with genetic resources was that protection of this knowledge will be included within the scope of the IR, ruling out mere discretional protection through voluntarily applied instruments.

From the indigenous organisations' point of view, the start of real negotiations on the IR represents an immense challenge. Although the widespread recognition of the Declaration as a new framework to be taken into account means that there is greater openness towards indigenous participation in the different mechanisms (such as contact groups), such participation continues to be challenged whenever tangible results are required. It has thus been requested that at least one Party should have to explicitly support the indigenous proposals before they can be included as text for consideration. In addition, the recognition of indigenous rights in general declarations now has to take on specific forms within the instruments under discussion. Among these forms, there is a need to analyse how indigenous rights to ownership and control of their traditional knowledge and their genetic resources are reflected clearly in, for example, possible certificates; what specific training plans are being supported for indigenous peoples; how, in the possible definition of undue appropriation, human rights violations can be included as one of the causes; and what it means for the Declaration to be a component of the possible IR. The indigenous organisations will need to come up with concrete responses to these questions that will be able to help ensure that the new IR respects and supports the exercise of their rights and sovereignty over their resources and knowledge.

The International Indigenous Forum on Biodiversity's Working Group on Indicators

We should very briefly refer to an interesting initiative being implemented by the indigenous organisations within the context of the International Indigenous Forum on Biodiversity (IIFB). This relates to a Working Group on Indicators, the aim of which is to produce indicators related to traditional knowledge that can be included in the Convention's Multi-Annual Work Plan and into its objectives and goals within the context of the 2010 Target.

The need for indicators produced by the indigenous peoples themselves, in line with their interests, has been repeatedly noted by the IIFB but no response has been forthcoming within the planning of the Convention's work. Various indigenous organisations therefore proposed that the only way of achieving the desired result was to do the work themselves. During COP8, they managed to get their initiative supported by the Parties. Various preparatory regional workshops were held on the issue of indicators, the work was conducted in coordination with other initiatives underway around this issue within the context of the PFII and, in February 2007, an International Seminar of Experts was held in Banaue (Philippines) on indicators relevant to indigenous peoples, the CBD and the Millennium Development Goals. The next steps are already being taken to continue this work, testing some of the indicators in the field.[10]   ❑

Notes

1   The complete timetable for meetings can be found at: http://www.cbd.int/
    meetings/
2   E/C.19/2007/8. The UNFPII Secretariat presented the results of the seminar at
    the WGABS5.
3   UNEP/CBD/WG-ABS/5/7
4   Joji Cariño, from the Tebtebba Foundation, Philippines.
5   UNEP/CBD/WG8J/INF/13. Despite being an informational document, it was
    also distributed in Spanish and French.
6   More detailed reports on the meetings can be found at www.almaciga.org, as
    well as in the IISD's Earth Negotiations Bulletin at: http://www.iisd.ca/proc-
    ess/biodiv_wildlife.htm
7   The documents of the co-chairs were included as annexes to the final report of
    the Montreal meeting, UNEP/CBD/WGABS/5/8
8   All documents and the final report of the WG8J meeting can be found at: www.
    cbd.int
9   Annexe to the report of the meeting, in UNEP/CBD/COP/6
10 The initiative is being coordinated by the Tebtebba Foundation, Philippines.

Patricia Borraz is a consultant working for Almáciga. This work involves supporting the participation of indigenous organizations and representatives in multilateral negotiations, particularly around issues of environment and sustainable development, through capacity building, communications and information exchange and funding support for their attendance at meetings.

THE AFRICAN COMMISSION
ON HUMAN AND PEOPLES' RIGHTS

The African Commission on Human and Peoples' Rights (ACH-PR or African Commission) was officially inaugurated on November 2, 1987 as a sub-body of the then Organisation of African Unity. The OAU was disbanded in July 2002, and has since been replaced by the African Union. In 2000, the African Commission established its Working Group on Indigenous Populations/Communities in Africa, which was a remarkable step forward in the promotion and protection of the human rights of indigenous peoples in Africa. The Working Group has produced a thorough report on the rights of indigenous peoples in Africa, and this document has been adopted by the ACHPR as its official conceptualization of the rights of indigenous peoples.

The human rights situation of indigenous peoples has, since 2000, been on the agenda of the African Commission and henceforth has become a topic of debate between the ACHPR, states, national human rights institutions, NGOs and other interested parties. Indigenous representatives' participation in the sessions and the Working Group's continued activities – sensitisation seminars, country visits, information activities and research – all play a crucial role in ensuring this vital dialogue.

The African Commission on Human and Peoples' Rights (ACHPR or African Commission) continued its work to protect and promote the human rights of indigenous peoples in Africa during 2007.

The Working Group's activities during 2007

The Working Group met twice during 2007 and, at these two meetings, the Working Group planned its activities for the time ahead and evaluated those activities already undertaken.

The key activities carried out this year were:

Summary version in Portuguese of the Working Group's expert report
The Working Group has already published a summary version in English and French of its expert report on indigenous peoples' situation in Africa and, in 2007, this summary version became available in Portuguese.[1] The summary version debates the criteria for identifying indigenous peoples in Africa, documents violations of indigenous peoples' human rights, analyses the extent to which the African Charter on Human and Peoples' Rights protects indigenous peoples' human rights and makes recommendations to the African Commission. The summary version is more accessible than the original report, and it is therefore expected to be useful to a wider audience.

Research & information visits
During the autumn of 2007, the Working Group undertook a research & information visit to Gabon. During this visit, the Working Group held meetings with the government officials, civil society organisations, indigenous communities and other relevant stakeholders with a view to gathering information about indigenous peoples' human rights situation in the country. During the visit, the Working Group also sought to raise awareness among all the stakeholders of the African Commission's work on indigenous issues and sought to engage in a debate on how indigenous peoples' rights can be strengthened. The report from the visit to Gabon should be adopted by the African Commission during 2008.

The two reports from the research & information visits to Burundi[2] and the Republic of Congo[3], visits which were carried out in 2005, were published in a book format during 2007.

Media sensitisation seminars
During 2007, the Working Group organised three media sensitisation seminars: one for Tanzanian journalists, one for East African journalists and one for Central African journalists. The media seminars sought to engage journalists in discussions on indigenous peoples' rights and the African Commission's work in this respect. The seminars dealt with general issues such as the concept of "indigenous peoples" in Africa, indigenous peoples' human rights situation, and the Working Group's activities but also included issues such as the constraints journalists experience in reporting on indigenous issues and how journalists can establish contacts with indigenous communities. The seminars provided an excellent opportunity for interaction between journalists and experts on indigenous peoples' human rights, and created a forum for discussion and dialogue. The seminars have also raised the journalists' interest in indigenous issues, and have assisted journalists and indigenous peoples to gain access to each other, which in turn will allow all parties to advocate indigenous peoples' rights to a broader audience.

Research on African constitutions and legislation
The Working Group, in cooperation with the International Labour Organisation (ILO), has continued the joint research project on the extent to which African constitutions and legislation protect the rights of indigenous populations. Some 25 African countries have been selected as the focus for the research, and ten of these have been selected for in-depth case studies. During 2007, research was undertaken on Burundi, Egypt, Eritrea, Ethiopia, Kenya, Namibia, Nigeria and South Africa.

UN-related activities
During 2007, the Working Group focused particularly on promoting the adoption of the UN Declaration on the Rights of Indigenous Peoples (UN Declaration) and, in this respect, produced an advisory opinion on the UN Declaration. The Working Group has thereby sought to raise awareness among African states and the African Union of the fact

that the UN Declaration is in line with the African Commission's own position as well as with the African Charter on Human and Peoples' Rights. This effort seems to have contributed to the adoption of the UN Declaration in September 2007, as no African states voted against the Declaration. After the UN Declaration's adoption, the African Commission issued a communiqué which stressed that the UN Declaration would be a valuable tool for the African Commission's continued efforts to promote and protect indigenous peoples' rights in Africa.

The Working Group was also involved in a seminar on the implementation of the UN's Second Decade on Indigenous Peoples. This seminar, held in November 2007 in the Republic of Congo, was hosted by the African Commission and the UN's Office of the High Commissioner for Human Rights (OHCHR). The seminar was attended by state representatives, African Union representatives, UN agencies, ACHPR commissioners, NGOs and indigenous peoples' representatives from a range of countries. The recommendations from the seminar, which focus on how to implement the five key objectives of the Second Decade, are intended to feed into the OHCHR's work in the future.

The 2007 sessions of the African Commission

Indigenous peoples' participation in the ACHPR sessions is crucial as it allows indigenous peoples to engage directly with the African Commission and to give voice to the human rights violations from which they suffer. During the sessions, the indigenous representatives lobby commissioners, government delegates, national human rights institutions and NGOs, and this is central to raising awareness about indigenous peoples' critical situation. In 2007, it was particularly important that there were indigenous representatives present at the sessions in order to participate in the debate on the UN Declaration and to urge the African Union and its member states to support it.

During the 2007 sessions, Kenya and Rwanda were among the countries that underwent state examination. Some indigenous organisations had produced shadow reports on these two countries and circulated these to relevant commissioners and stakeholders. This, in turn, contributed to providing a stronger focus on indigenous peoples' rights during the state examination.

Indigenous peoples' human rights continue to be one of the African Commission's key areas of work, and the issue is discussed at each of the ACHPR's sessions. The Working Group's many activities, as well as indigenous representatives' participation in the sessions, is central to encouraging and assisting the ACHPR to uphold its focus on indigenous peoples' rights. The Working Group's and indigenous representatives' different activities have already contributed to much awareness raising, and hopefully these sensitisations efforts will be further strengthened in the future.   ❏

Notes

1   **Comissão Africana dos Direitos Humanos e dos Povos (CADHP) & Grupo de Trabalho Internacional sobre Assuntos Indígenas (IWGIA), 2007**: *Povos Indígenas Em África: Povos Esquecidos? Trabalho da Comissão Africana sobre os Povos Indígenas Em África* (Denmark).

2   **African Commission on Human and Peoples' Rights (ACHPR) & International Work Group for Indigenous Affairs (IWGIA), 2007**: *Report of the African Commission's Working Group on Indigenous Populations/Communities: Research and Information Visit to the Republic of Burundi, March-April 2005* (Denmark).

3   **African Commission on Human and Peoples' Rights (ACHPR) & International Work Group for Indigenous Affairs (IWGIA), 2007**: *Report of the African Commission's Working Group on Indigenous Populations/Communities: Research and Information Visit to the Republic of Congo, September 2005* (Denmark).

Dina Berenstein is Project Coordinator of IWGIA's African Commission Programme.

PART III

GENERAL INFORMATION

ABOUT IWGIA

IWGIA is an independent international membership organization that supports indigenous peoples' right to self-determination. Since its foundation in 1968, IWGIA's secretariat has been based in Copenhagen, Denmark.

IWGIA holds consultative status with the United Nations Economic and Social Council (ECOSOC) and has observer status with the Arctic Council and with the African Commission on Human and Peoples Rights.

Aims and activities

IWGIA supports indigenous peoples' struggles for human rights, self-determination, the right to territory, control of land and resources, cultural integrity, and the right to development on their own terms. In order to fulfil this mission, IWGIA works in a wide range of areas: documentation and publication, human rights advocacy and lobbying, plus direct support to indigenous organisations' programmes of work.

IWGIA works worldwide at local, regional and international level, in close cooperation with indigenous partner organizations.

BECOMING A MEMBER

IWGIA welcomes new members. If you wish to apply for membership and become part of our dedicated network of concerned individuals, please consult our homepage at www.iwgia.org for details and to download a membership form.

Membership fees for 2008 are:

EUR 50 (EUR 30 for students and senior citizens)
for Europe, North America, Australia, New Zealand and Japan.
EUR 20 for the rest of the world.

For IWGIA, membership provides an essential element of support to our work, both politically and economically.

All members receive IWGIA's journal *Indigenous Affairs* four times a year, IWGIA's Annual Report, and the yearbook *The Indigenous World*. In addition, members benefit from a 33% reduction on other IWGIA publications. If you want a support membership only and not receive our publications, the annual fee is EUR 8.

SUBSCRIPTION RATES 2008

INDIGENOUS AFFAIRS / *ASUNTOS INDÍGENAS*

Individuals: EUR 27
Institutions: EUR 36

THE INDIGENOUS WORLD / *EL MUNDO INDIGENA*

Individuals: EUR 24
Institutions: EUR 32

BOOKS / LIBROS

Individuals: EUR 47
Institutions: EUR 63

INDIGENOUS AFFAIRS & THE INDIGENOUS WORLD / *ASUNTOS INDÍGENAS & EL MUNDO INDÍGENA*

Individuals: EUR 51
Institutions: EUR 68

INDIGENOUS AFFAIRS, THE INDIGENOUS WORLD & BOOKS / *ASUNTOS INDÍGENAS, EL MUNDO INDÍGENA & LIBROS*

Individuals: EUR 98
Institutions: EUR 130

IWGIA's publications are published on a not-for-profit basis. All subscriptions to our publications form a direct contribution enabling IWGIA to continue its analysis and documentation work on the situation of the world's indigenous peoples.

IWGIA's publications can be purchased through:

Our website: www.iwgia.org
By email: iwgia@iwgia.org
or give us a call: +45 35 27 05 00